Gothic Art NOW

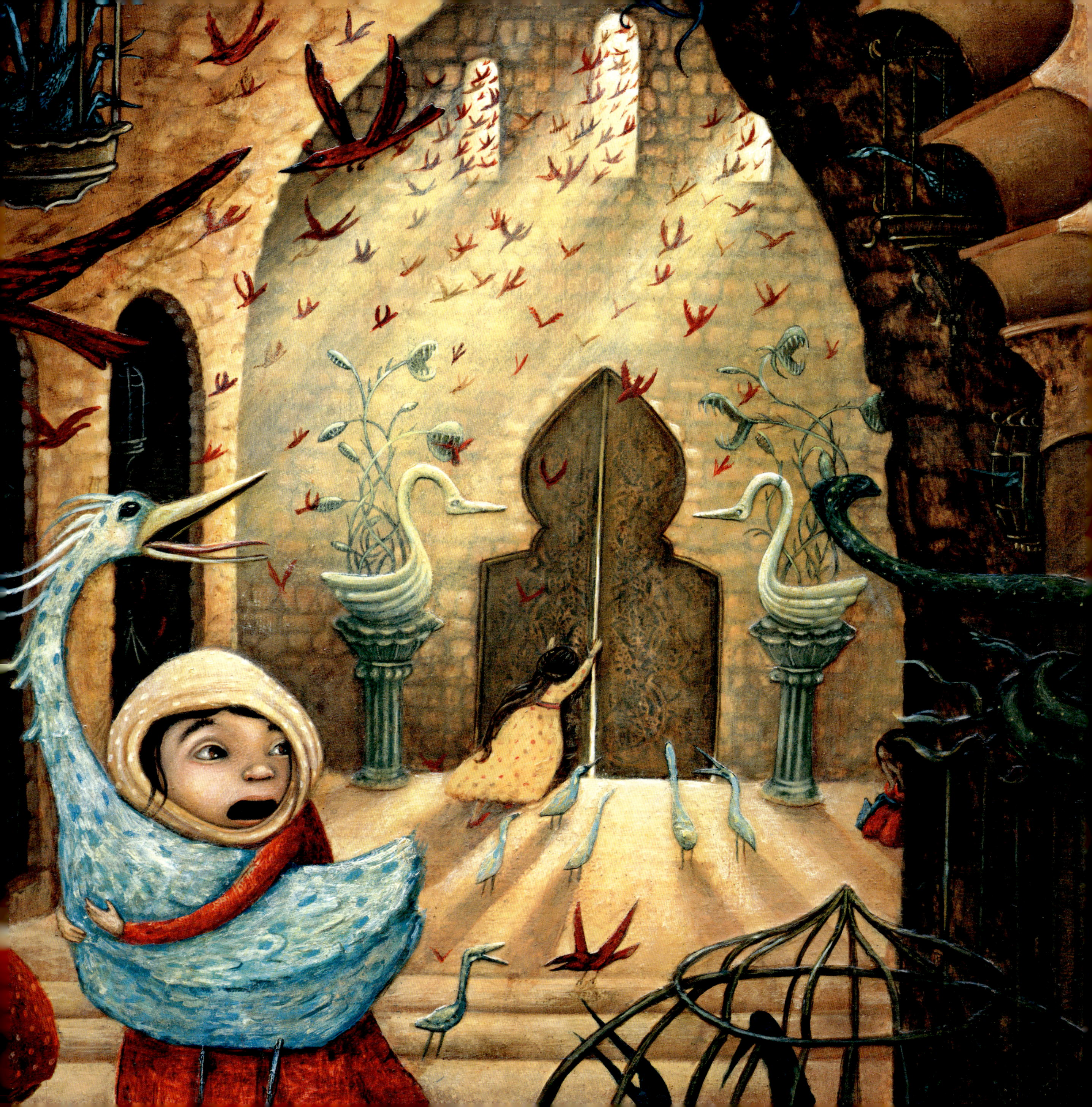

Gothic Art NOW

Jasmine Becket-Griffith

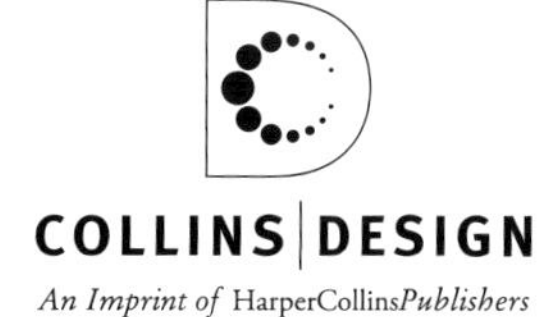
COLLINS | DESIGN
An Imprint of HarperCollins*Publishers*

GOTHIC ART NOW

First published in North America in 2008 by:
Collins Design
An Imprint of HarperCollins*Publishers*
10 East 53rd Street
New York, NY 10022
Tel: (212) 207-7000
Fax: (212) 207-7654
collinsdesign@harpercollins.com
www.harpercollins.com

Distributed throughout the United States and Canada by:
HarperCollins*Publishers*
10 East 53rd Street
New York, NY 10022
Fax: (212) 207-7654

This book was conceived, designed, and produced by ILEX, Cambridge, England

Library of Congress Control Number: 2008927268

ISBN: 978-0-06-162699-9

Printed in China
First Printing, 2008

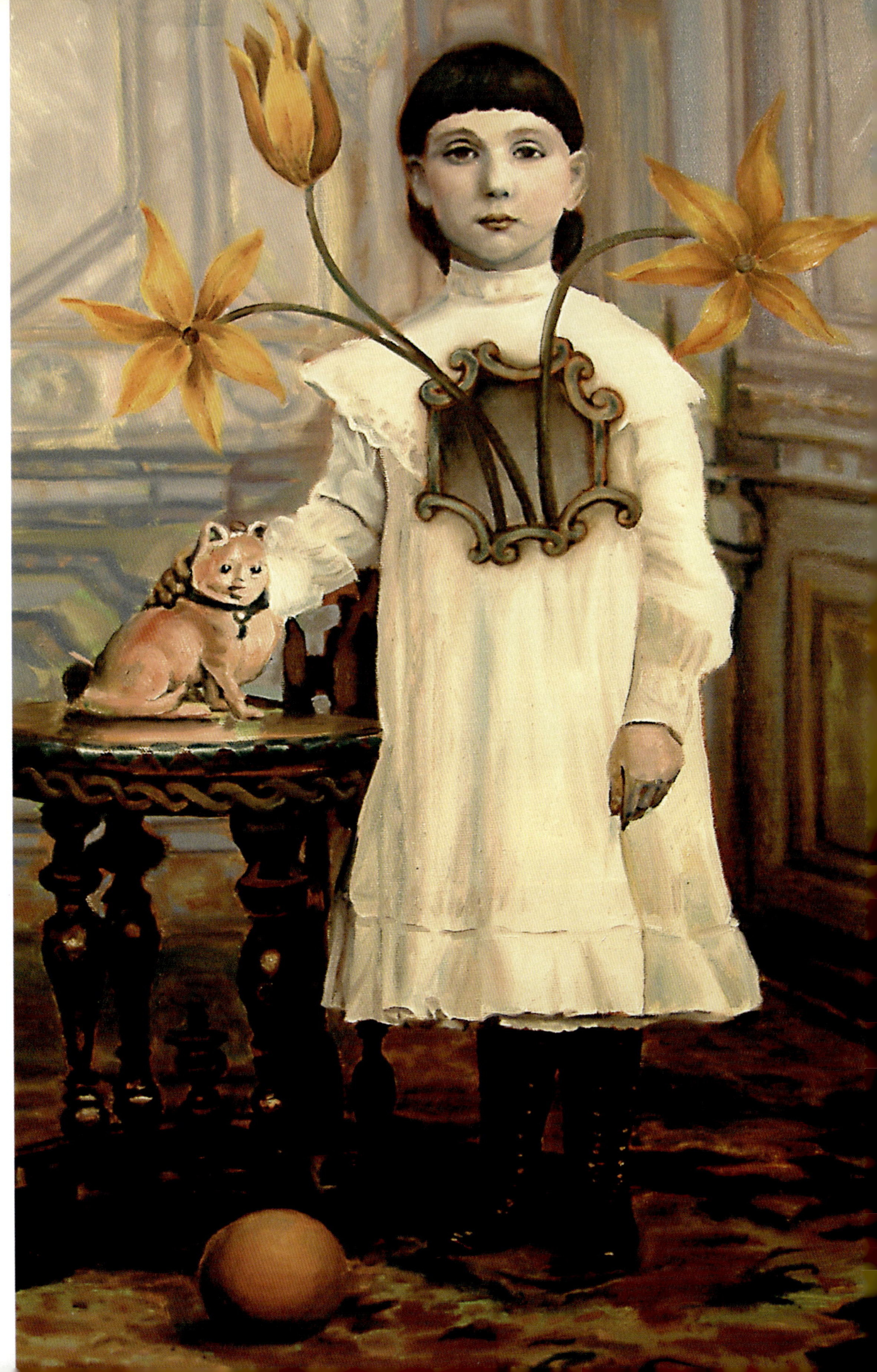

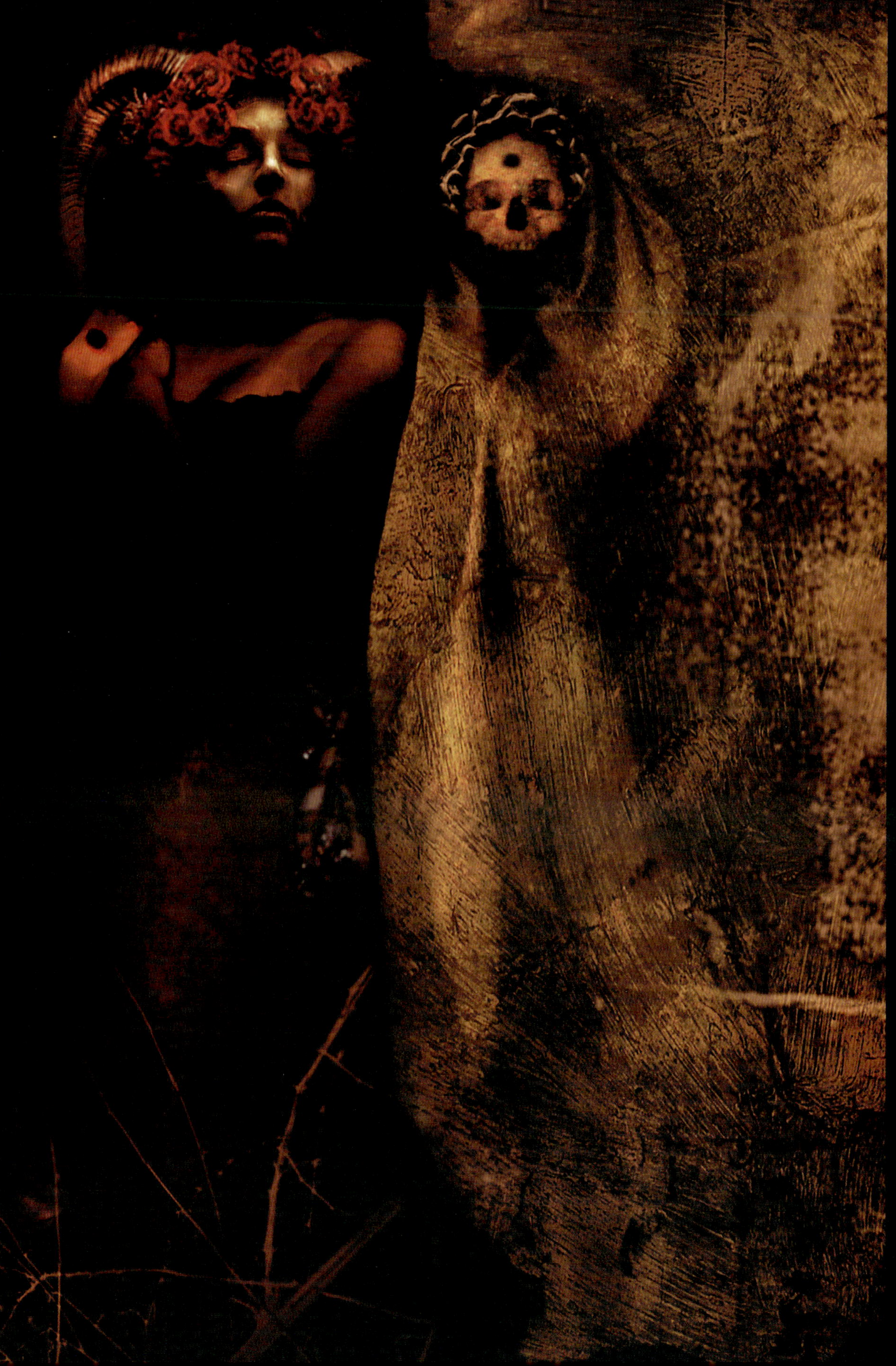

Contents

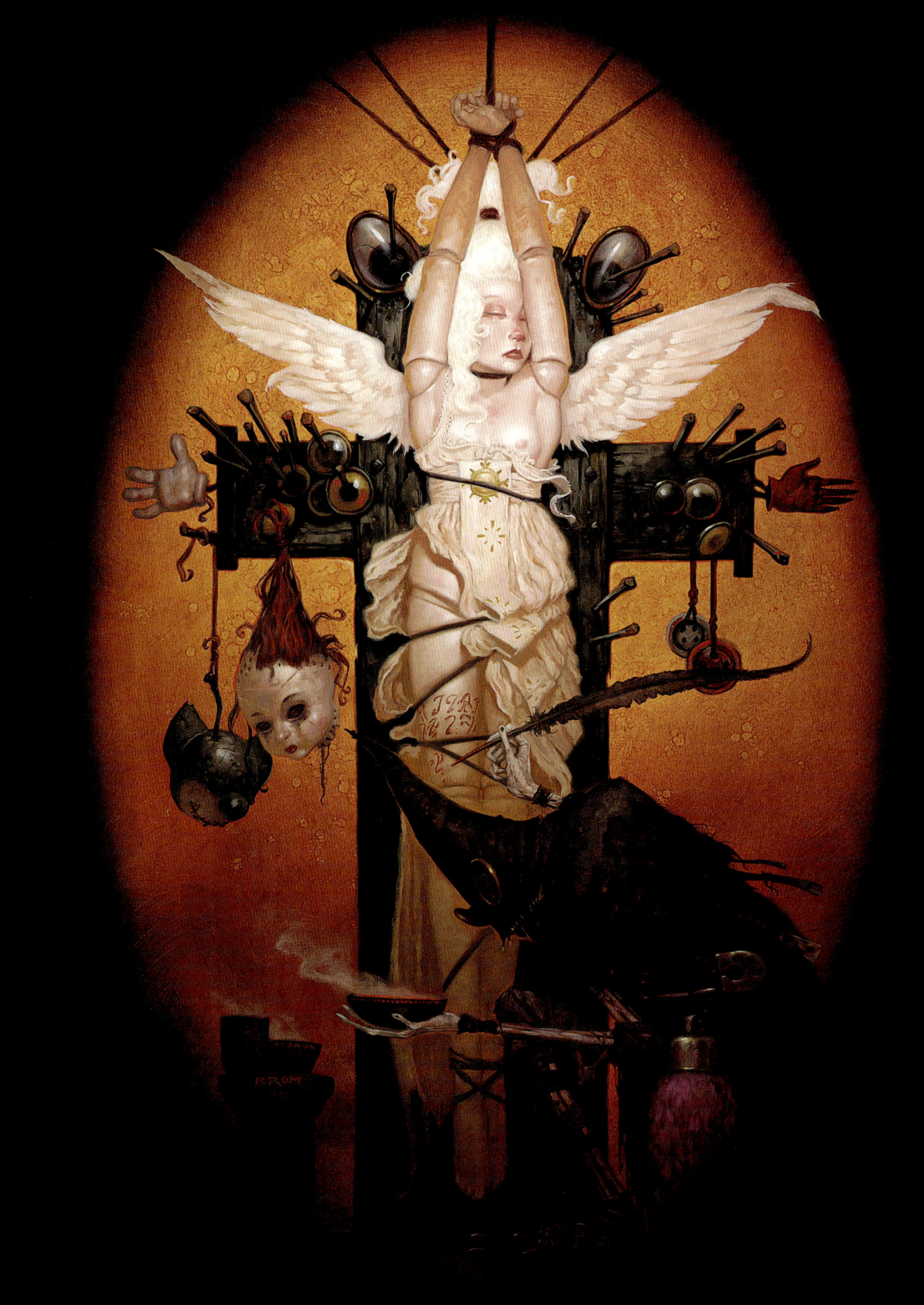
BROM

Foreword

I should start with the treacherous task of defining Gothic art. I'm, of course, not referring to the religious Medieval art movement of the late 12th century, though that certainly plays its part in modern Gothic art. I'm instead referring to the haunting aesthetic that began in earnest with the Pre-Raphaelites and their love of the romantic and tragic, and perfected by such genius as John William Waterhouse and Edward Burne-Jones—an aesthetic that has of late enjoyed a stunning cultural renaissance.

So then, what is Gothic art? To me it's the tragic and the resplendent, the monstrous and the angelic, the ominous and the romantic. It's this contrast of the horrible and the beautiful, whether in content or execution, that makes a work Gothic. A theme so well illustrated by John William Waterhouse's *Lady Shalott*, drifting down the river to her death in search of her love Lancelot, or John Everett Millais's depiction of Ophelia, floating there amongst the reeds, so dreamy, so beautiful, and...*oh, so dead*. And don't those images just make you want to slap on some Gregorian chants, light a few rose scented candles, and start painting? But, as much fun as painting beautiful dead women can be, Gothic art is in no way confined to such. The ghastly and the macabre all have their place, but sometimes it is simply the way such subjects are handled—imagine the Frankenstein monster standing amongst a rose garden if you will.

Probably the question I'm asked more than any other is: "Why? Why with all the beauty in the world do I insist on painting the dark and the dreary?" The short answer is: It's not a conscious effort, it's simply who I am, and what I'm drawn to (pardon the pun). Fellow brooding souls everywhere will understand this well, but for the uninitiated (y'know, those folks that live in a world of Laura Ashley wallpaper and miniature Zen rock gardens) I often use this example: If commissioned to paint a toaster I'd most likely respond by clutching my throat, but, if instead I was asked to paint a *wicked* toaster, I'd be happier than a ghoul in a graveyard. And if this same question were posed to a dozen elementary school children, why you'd get the same enthusiastic response. Why is this? Because conflict equals drama, and there is inherent conflict in the dark, the sinister, and the tragic. A painting of yet another blushing maiden sitting in her garden is nice, but toss in a few skulls about her feet and, oh my, what is going on here? The image suddenly becomes interesting—interesting to paint and interesting to look at.

I could pontificate about beautiful dead women forever, but art either speaks to you or it doesn't. For me, the works in this book sing. I hope they will sing for you as well.

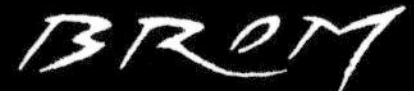

Brom is an accomplished artist, author, and all round creepy guy. He has worked as an illustrator since the age of twenty, and his award-winning novel, *The Plucker*, was the first in his series of illustrated novels. He has made his mark in all realms of the Gothic Fantasy genre: in games such as *Doom*, *World of Warcraft*, and *Dungeons and Dragons*; in comics by DC and Dark Horse; in novels by authors such as Michael Moorcock, Terry Brooks, R. A. Salvatore, and E. R. Burroughs; and in film, working on Tim Burton's *Sleepy Hollow*, *Ghosts of Mars*, and *Van Helsing*.

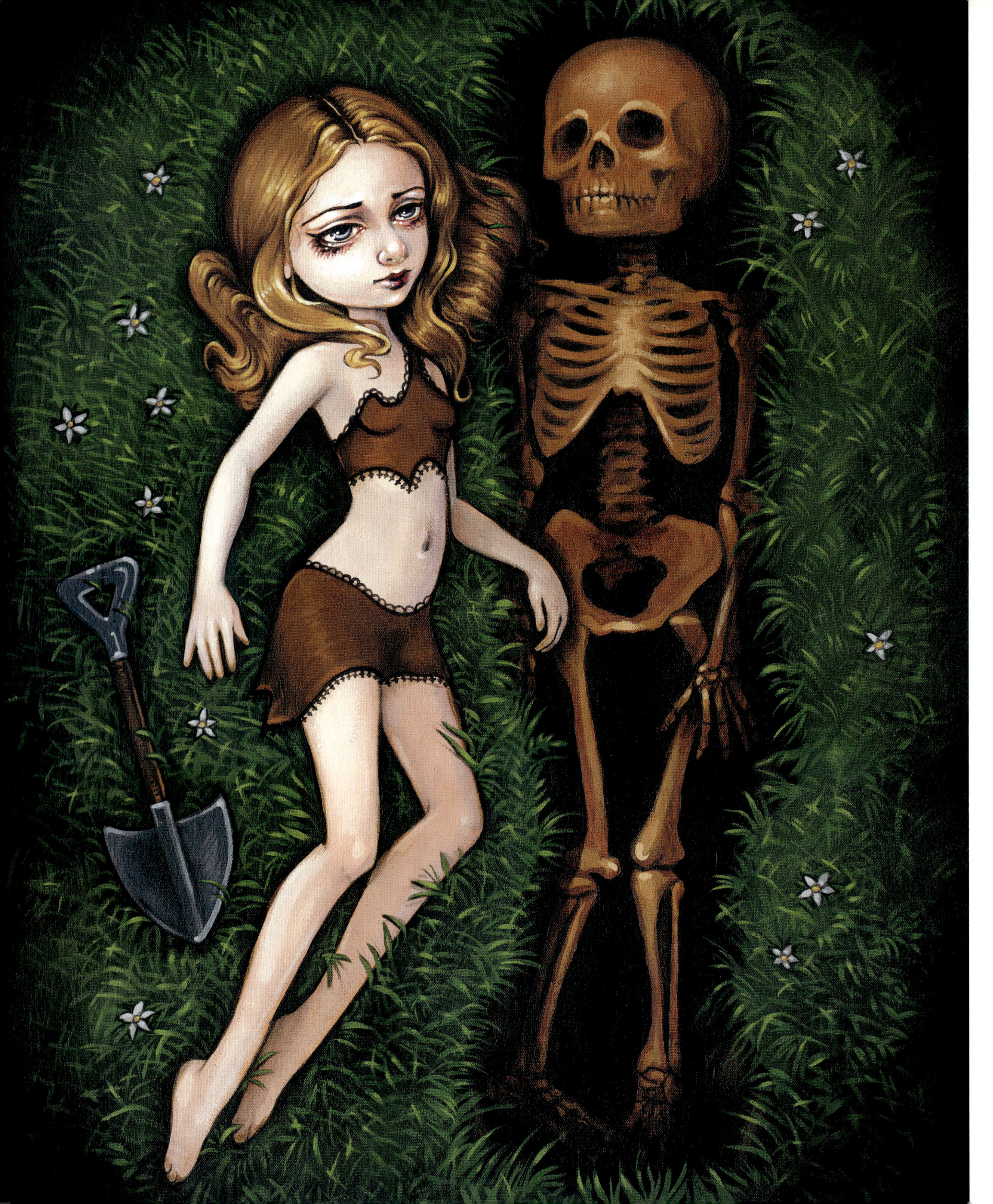

Introduction

What is Gothic Art? What is it exactly that makes a piece of artwork "Gothic?" Who decides such things?

Of course, there are no real answers; there is no litmus test for "goth;" no Mohs scale for melancholia. As with any art or cultural movement, labels can bring confusion and controversy. It is an ambiguous term and is, in the end, completely subjective. Some of the artists featured in this book may never have thought of their art as "Gothic," but their work often fits snugly within this genre. As the goth scene is constantly inventing and reinventing itself, incorporating more global and cultural inspiration, so does the Gothic art scene.

Gothic Art Now incorporates many varied elements that make up the Gothic aesthetic, with nods to different facets of the Gothic subculture: from artwork with distant roots in medieval and Renaissance classicism to pieces influenced by the post-punk revival and the contemporary "Gothic Renaissance" sensibilities of the internet age.

Over the long and storied decades, "goth" has been repeatedly decreed as having infiltrated the mainstream. It has been declared that "goth" is dead. Yet, it has crawled up through the root cellar and is now sitting in the parlor for the world to see.

Popular culture is showing its dark side—everything from mainstream books and comics to video games and movies are now occasionally brandishing a Gothic edge. While the state of the "scene" is up for constant debate in forums and message boards, the fact is that it has grown and developed into a very strong subgenre.

In the fine art scene, however, most gothic works are delegated to the "lowbrow" end of the fine art spectrum, and may be dismissed by some ivory tower critics as mere "illustration." Despite this, the Gothic genre has defiantly grown to include some of the most beautiful, relevant, and technically proficient works of contemporary art today—as you will see in the following pages.

Gothic Art Now exposes the beauty of Gothic art that truly transcends medium, culture, gender, and geography. Nearly every artistic medium is showcased: traditional oil painting; pencil and paper; digital creations; found objects and collage; dimensional sculpture; mixed media compositions; and even stained glass. Nearly every continent is represented, with artists from a myriad of countries and cultures, all who possess a unique vision of the Gothic aesthetic. The artworks in this book are sublime in their elegance and their dark appeal. Some are humorous, while some are iconic. There are epic masterpieces and spiritually poignant works, as well as seductive vampire chicks and gore-splattered horrors. There are also some pieces in this book that may be disturbing to some, but art should occasionally force the viewer to push their boundaries a little, provoke a bit of thought, and maybe even help redefine the socially accepted notions of what makes a pretty picture.

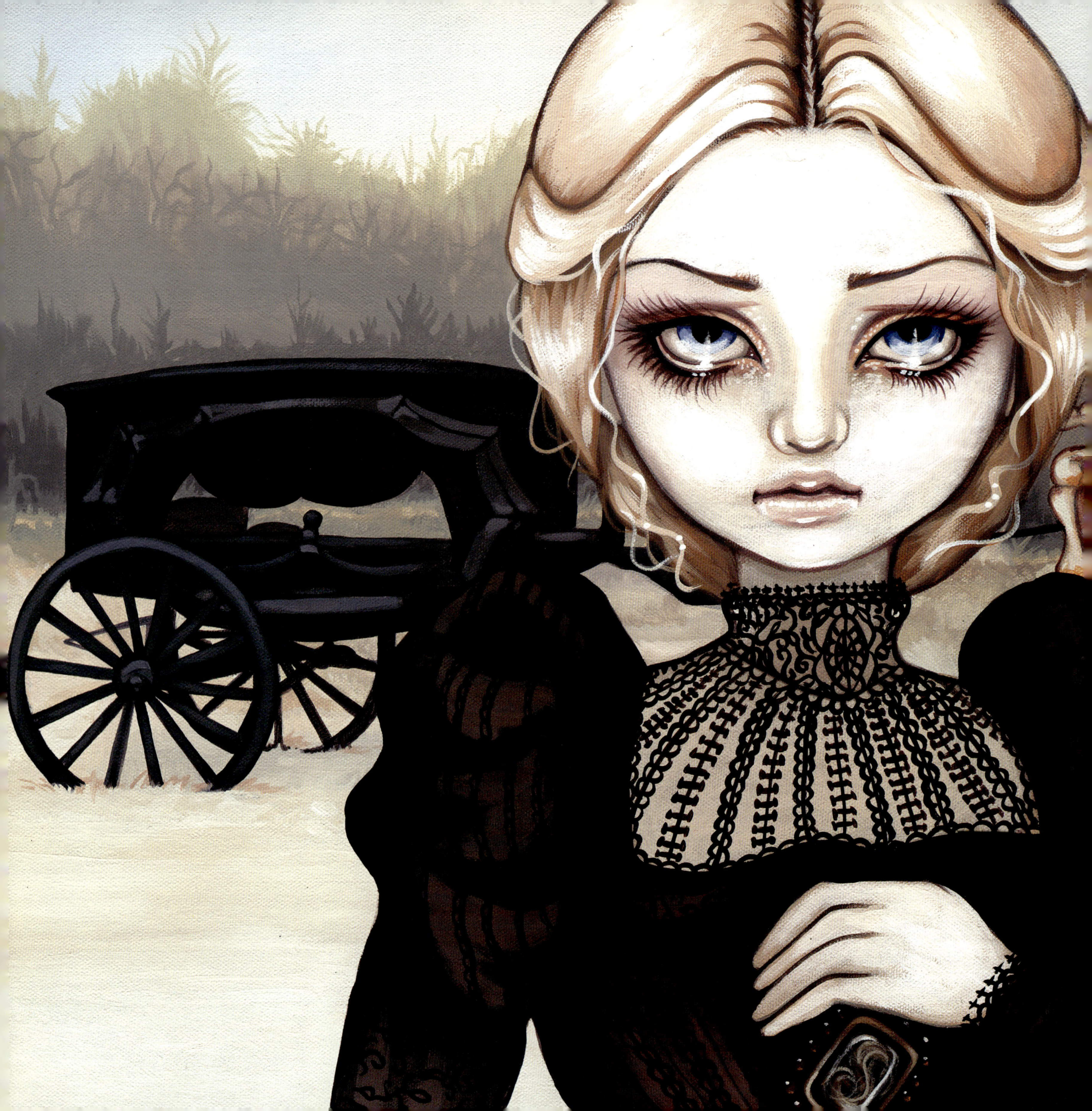

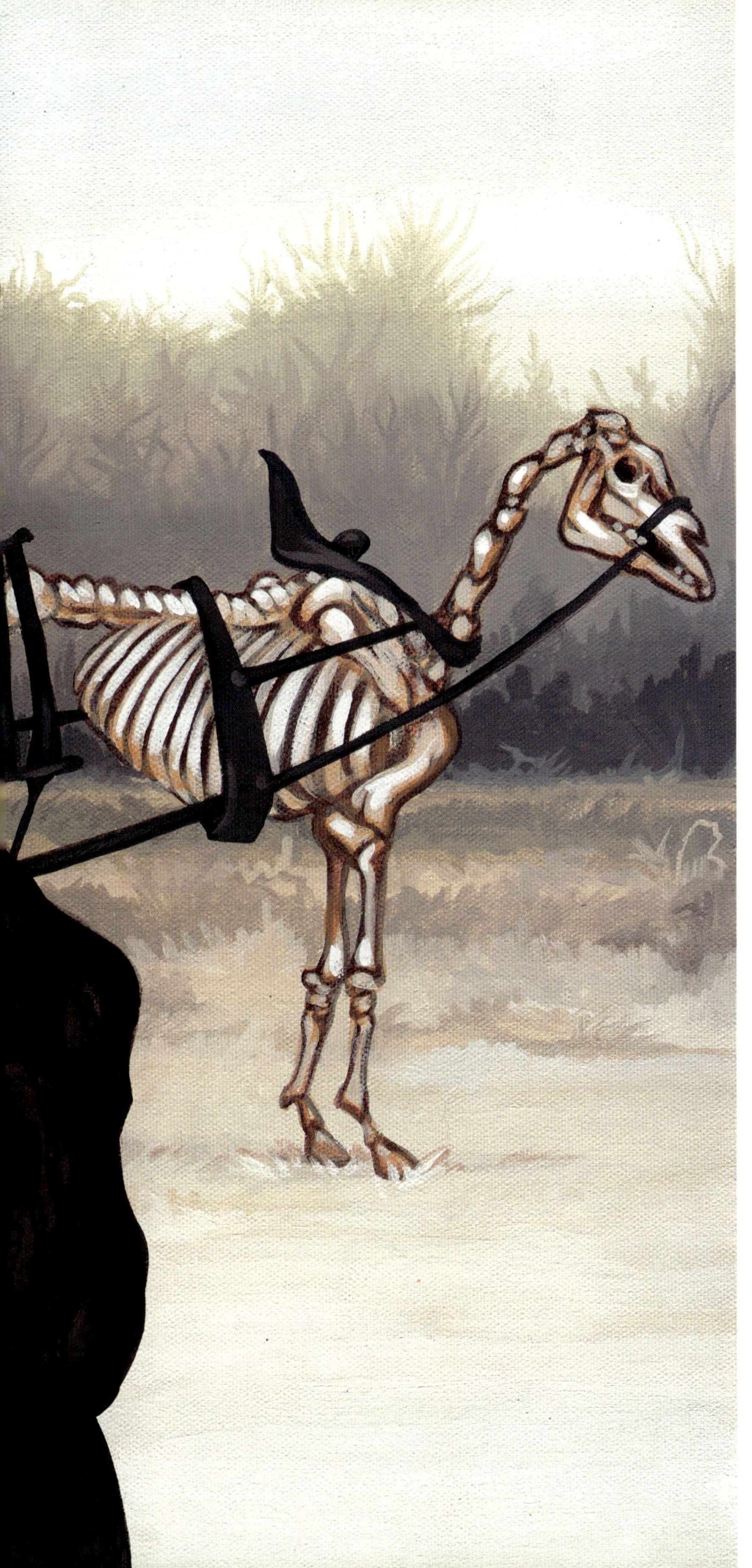

Gothic art aims to inspire and to intrigue: transporting you to alternate realities, to elegant pasts, and to nihilistic futures. Not to be seen always as simply eye candy, a common undercurrent in most Gothic art relies on deeper meanings, symbolism, social commentary, alternative ideas, mortal reckonings, and cultural explorations. That said, sometimes a hot vampire chick is just a hot vampire chick, and should be no less enjoyable!

So sit back and enjoy as the following pages unfold to reveal some of the very best in contemporary Gothic art. This is *Gothic Art Now.*

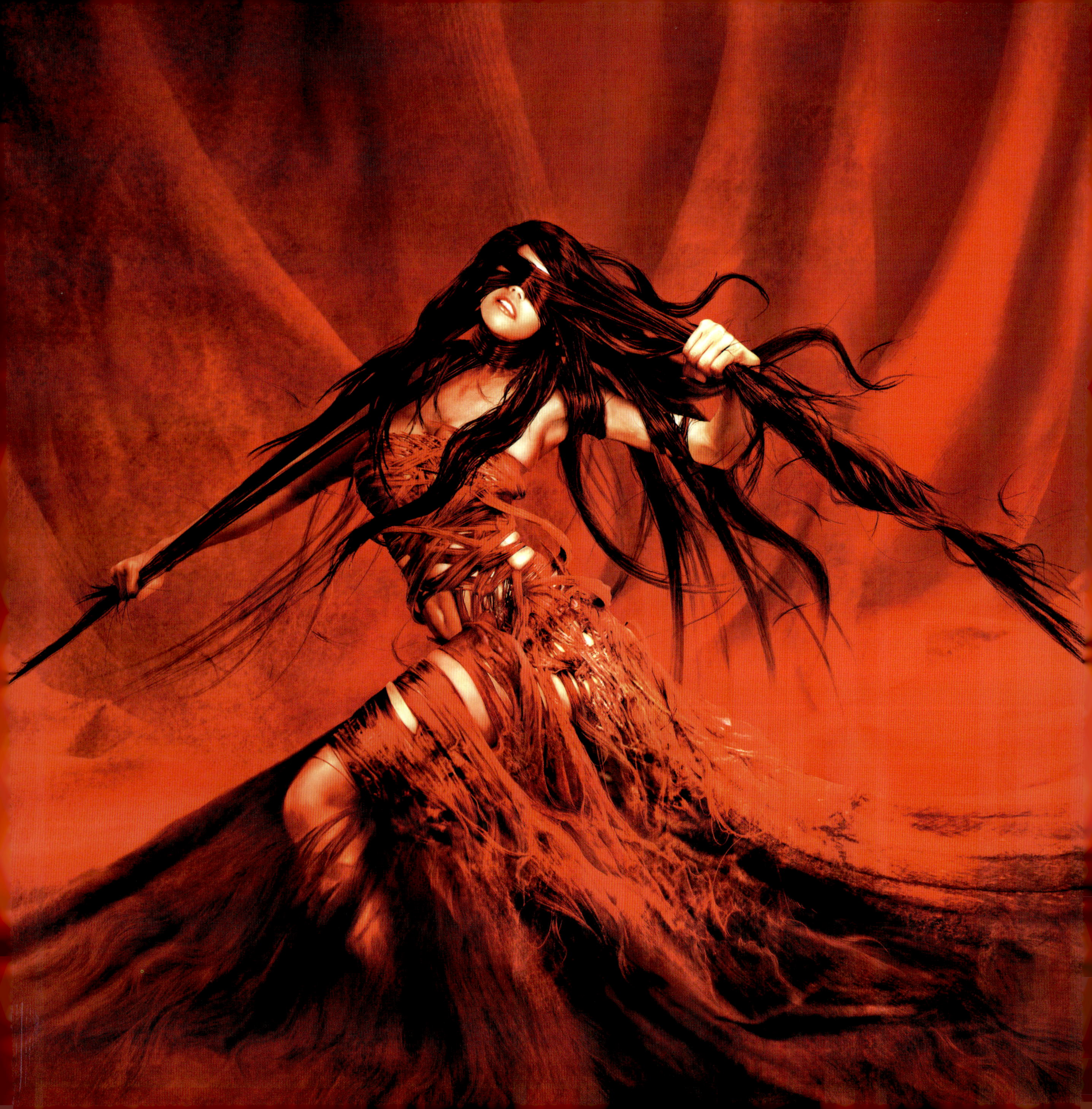

CHAPTER 1

FEMMES FATALES

◀ **Not Knowing Why She Can't See and Can't Breathe**
Ryohei Hase
Digital painting
www.ryoheihase.com

Hase's stunning digital painting features a dark-haired beauty, draped with an almost infinite amount of red fabric. The painting's wide format diminish the figure and evokes a feeling of insignificance. "The woman in th red dress is suffering and wants be relieved, but she doesn't notice she is the one who afflicts herself.

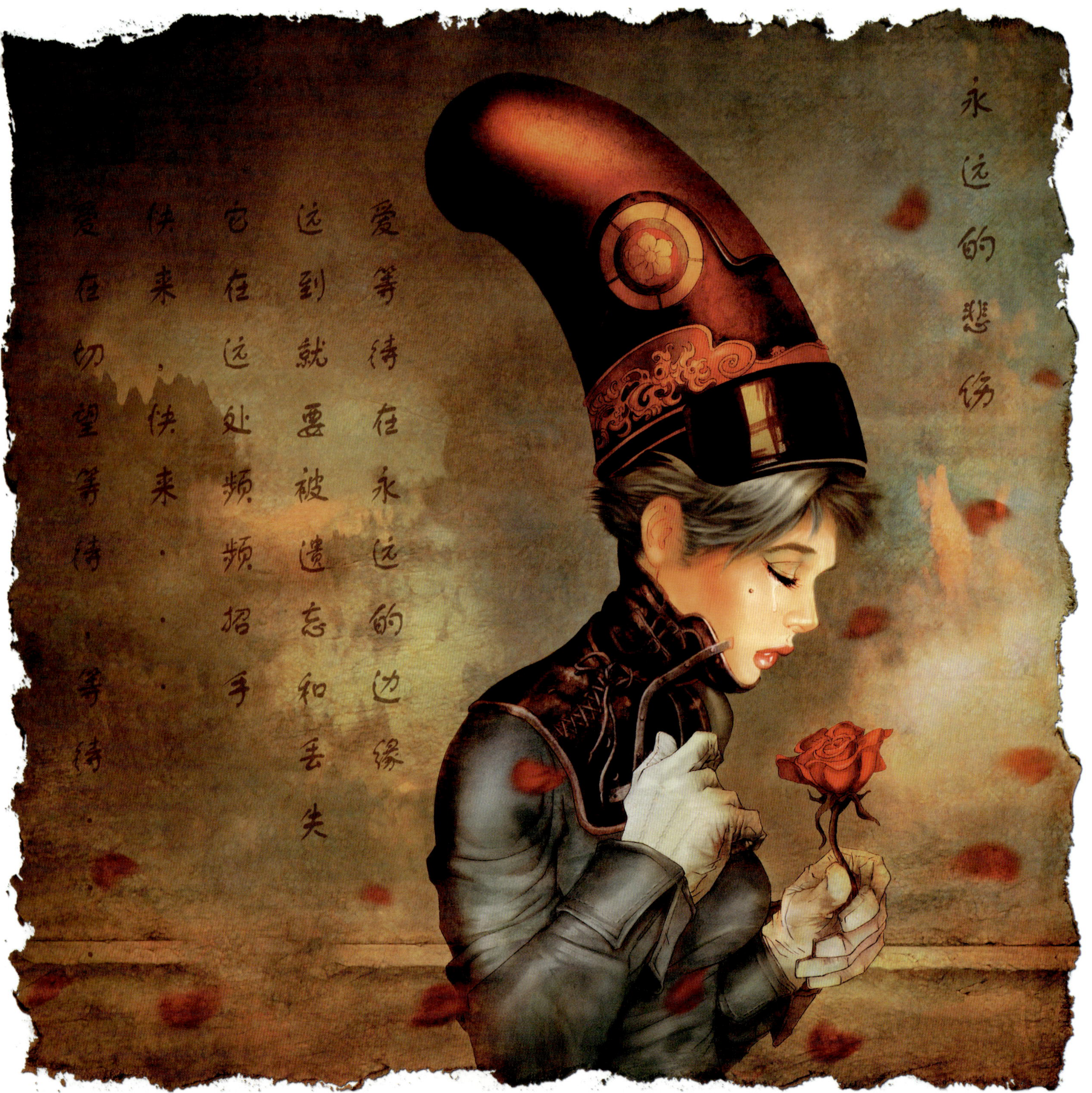
永远的悲伤
爱等待在永远的边缘
远到就要被遗忘和丢失
它在远处频频招手
快来，快来．．．
爱在切望等待．等待．．

◀ **Eternal Sorrow**
Hoang Nguyen
Digital painting
www.liquidbrush.com

"I started out using Tria markers, then transferred the drawing into Adobe Photoshop and proceeded to paint over it. The piece is about lost love and what could have been, or love that was never meant to be. It is based on a poem I wrote in Kanji. Translated it reads:

'Love awaits on the edge of eternity
Reaching far, forgotten, and long lost.
In the distance, beckoning
Come away, away...
For there love awaits,
yearning, yearning...'"

▶ **Memories**
Hoang Nguyen
Digital painting
www.liquidbrush.com

"I wanted to portray a girl caught in a moment, lost in time. I wanted to capture her essence, pain, sadness, elegance, and beauty. I decided to incorporate imagery from the World War II era and tattoos. Using Adobe Photoshop I was going to draw a serpent or dragon for the tattoo, but I decided to create something nondistinctive, hoping to represent various past memories in an interesting way."

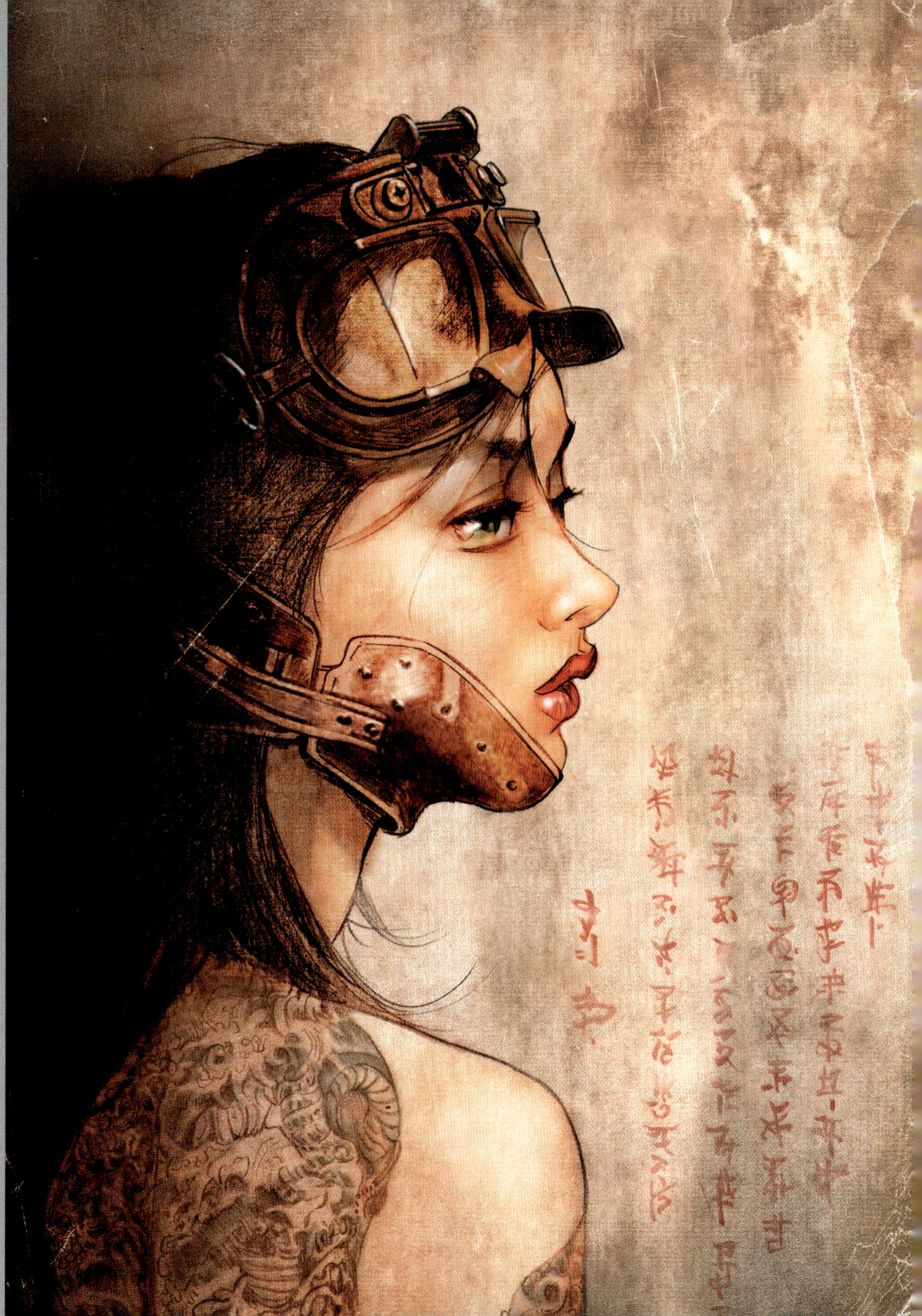

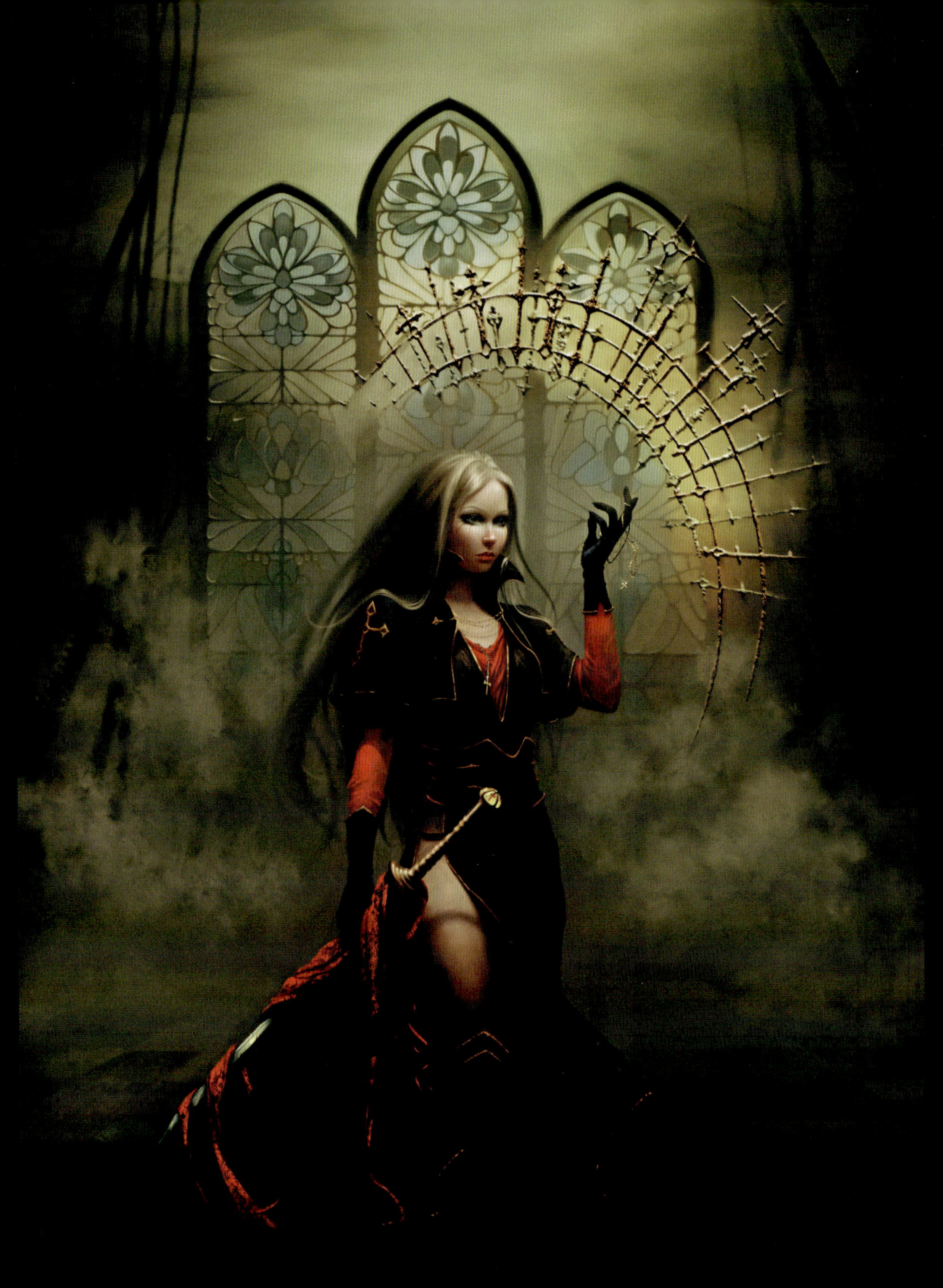

▶ **Lucrezia Navarre**
Benita Winckler
Digital painting
www.eeanee.com

*Winckler's powerful **Lucrezia** stands in front of an intricate Gothic background, surrounded by a haze of mysterious mist. Using Adobe Photoshop and Corel Painter, Winckler has created an atmospheric piece with a strong central figure. "Lucrezia Navarre is one of the main characters in German author Joe Mander's novel. He asked me to visualize Lucrezia for him. In keeping with the story the picture has elements of science fiction. Her clothes have a bit of a military look, but also priestly — black, golden, and dark red. She is a powerful but virtuous leader."*

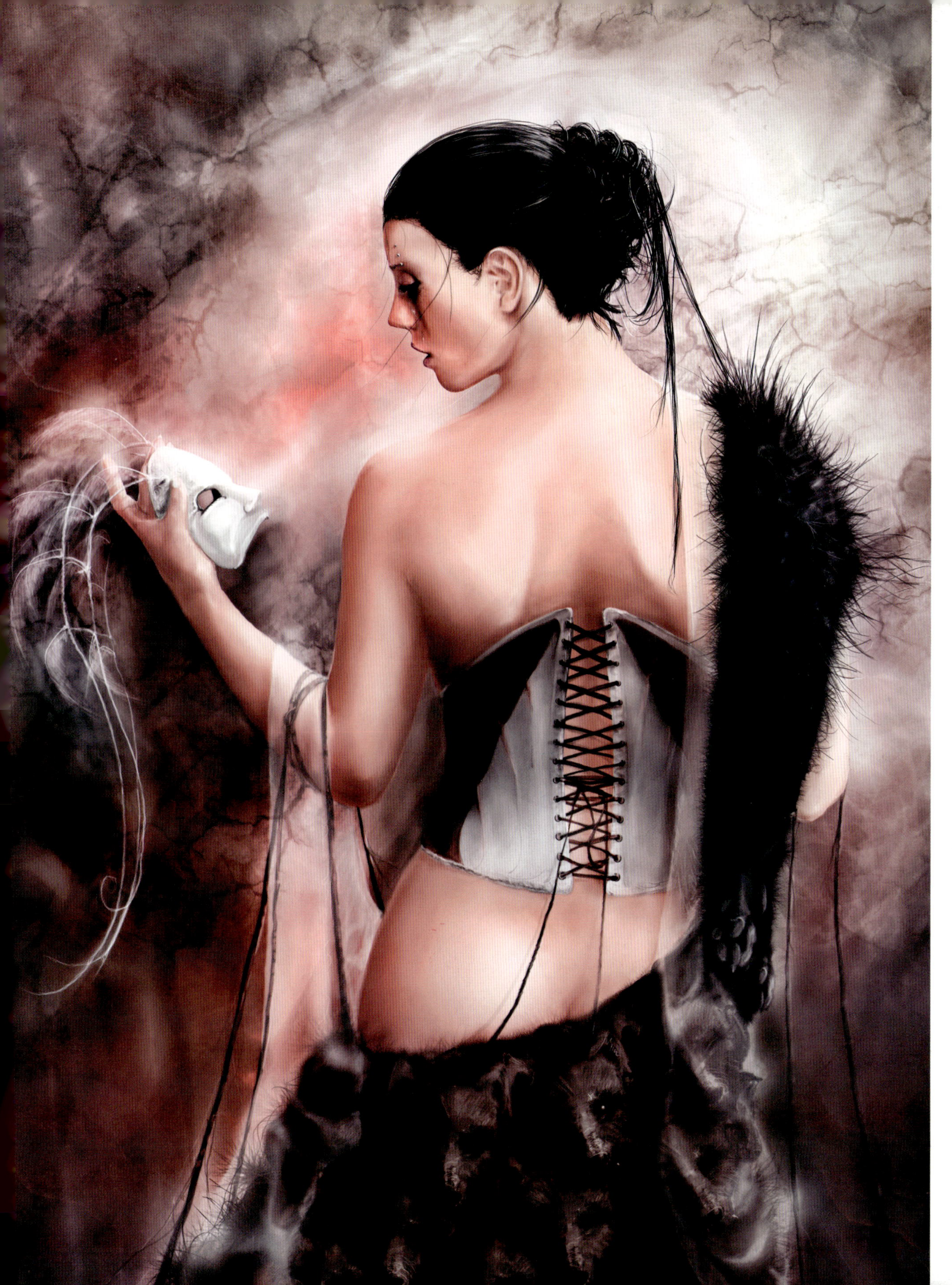

◀ **Masquerade**
Egil Paulsen
Digital painting
www.egilpaulsen.com

A romantic digital piece painted in Adobe Photoshop. Paulsen explains: "The idea behind this piece is that our social environment makes us put on masks to fit into different situations and roles. I think this image illustrates the point when we realize that we are becoming something we are not. We are living a great masquerade, hiding our feelings and pain behind a decorated and unconcerned mask."

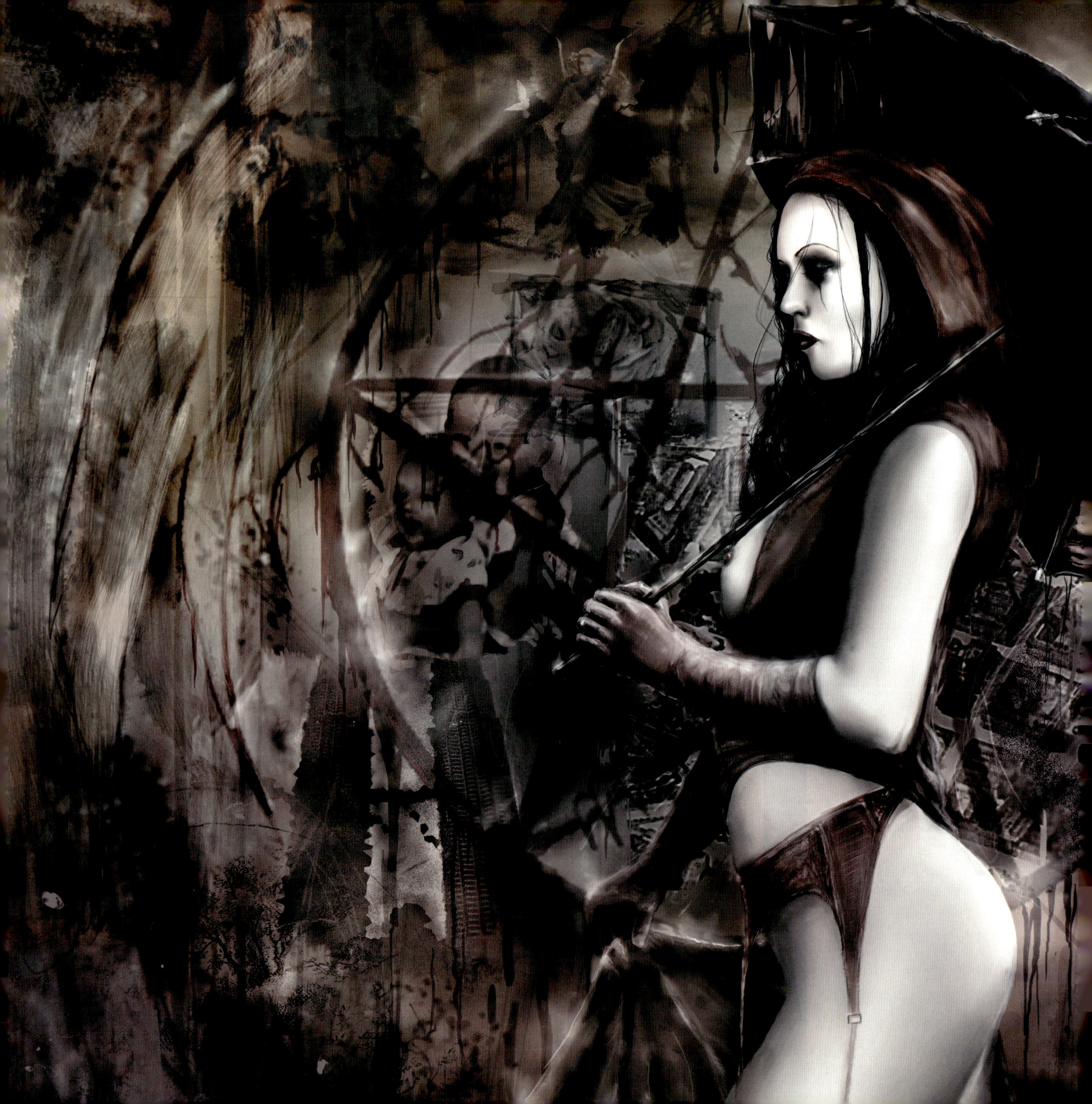

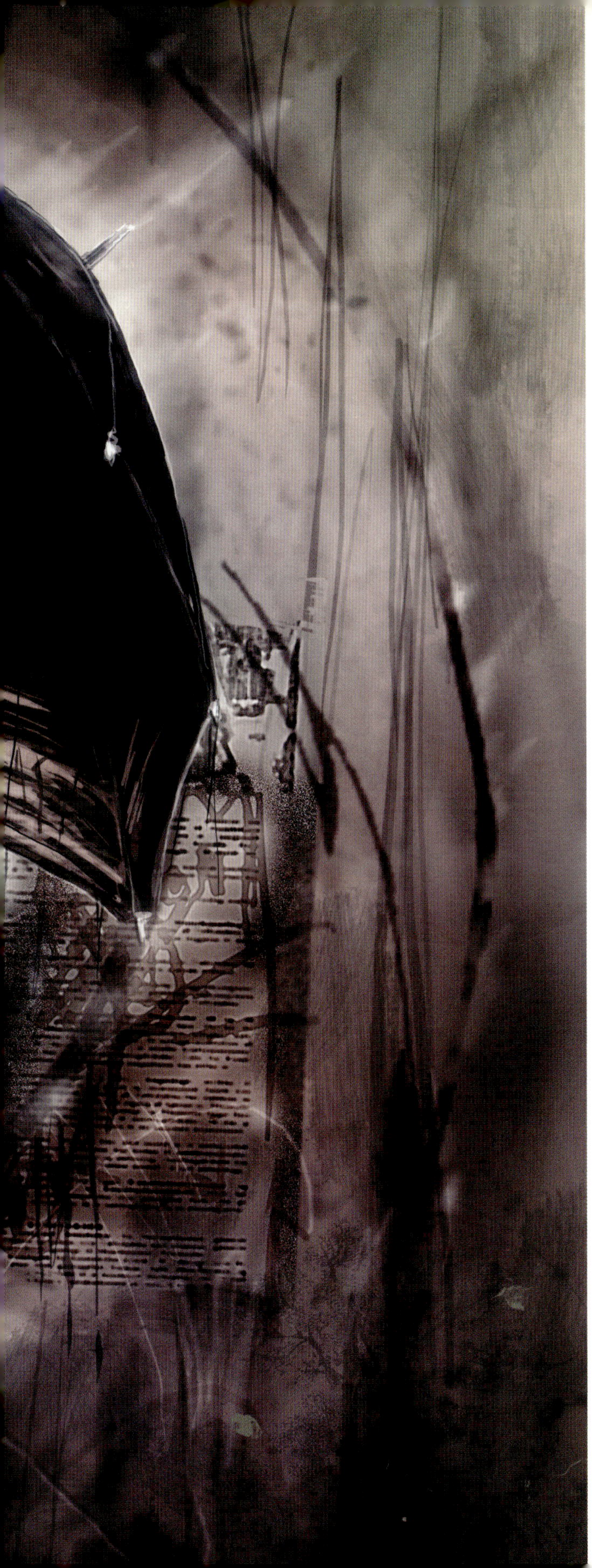

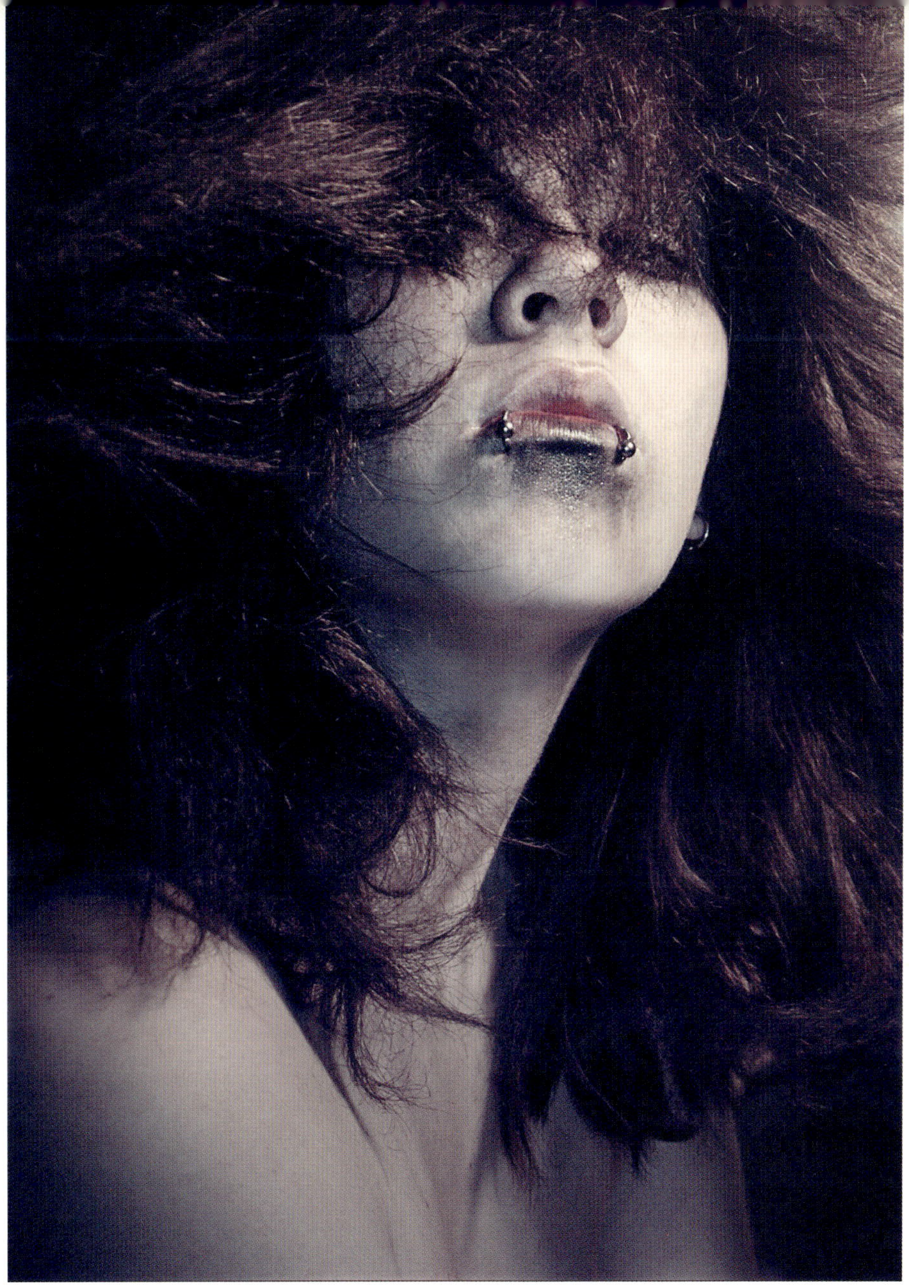

◀ **Lost Circle**
Egil Paulsen
Digital painting
www.egilpaulsen.com

"I wanted to create a dark Gothic scene, which expressed feelings about things once had, loved, dreamt, and believed in. The picture is painted digitally using a Wacom Graphics Tablet. The background was a collage of paint and photography. I played with light and color settings until I found a satisfying mood."

▲ **Evol**
Leslie Ann O'Dell
Photography and digital manipulation
www.shyble.com

Sometimes all it takes to capture the Gothic aesthetic of natural beauty is a camera. O'Dell used filtered natural lighting for the background and a lamp for the foreground. She explains: "This is a self-portrait that represents the messy, dark, and proud part of myself.

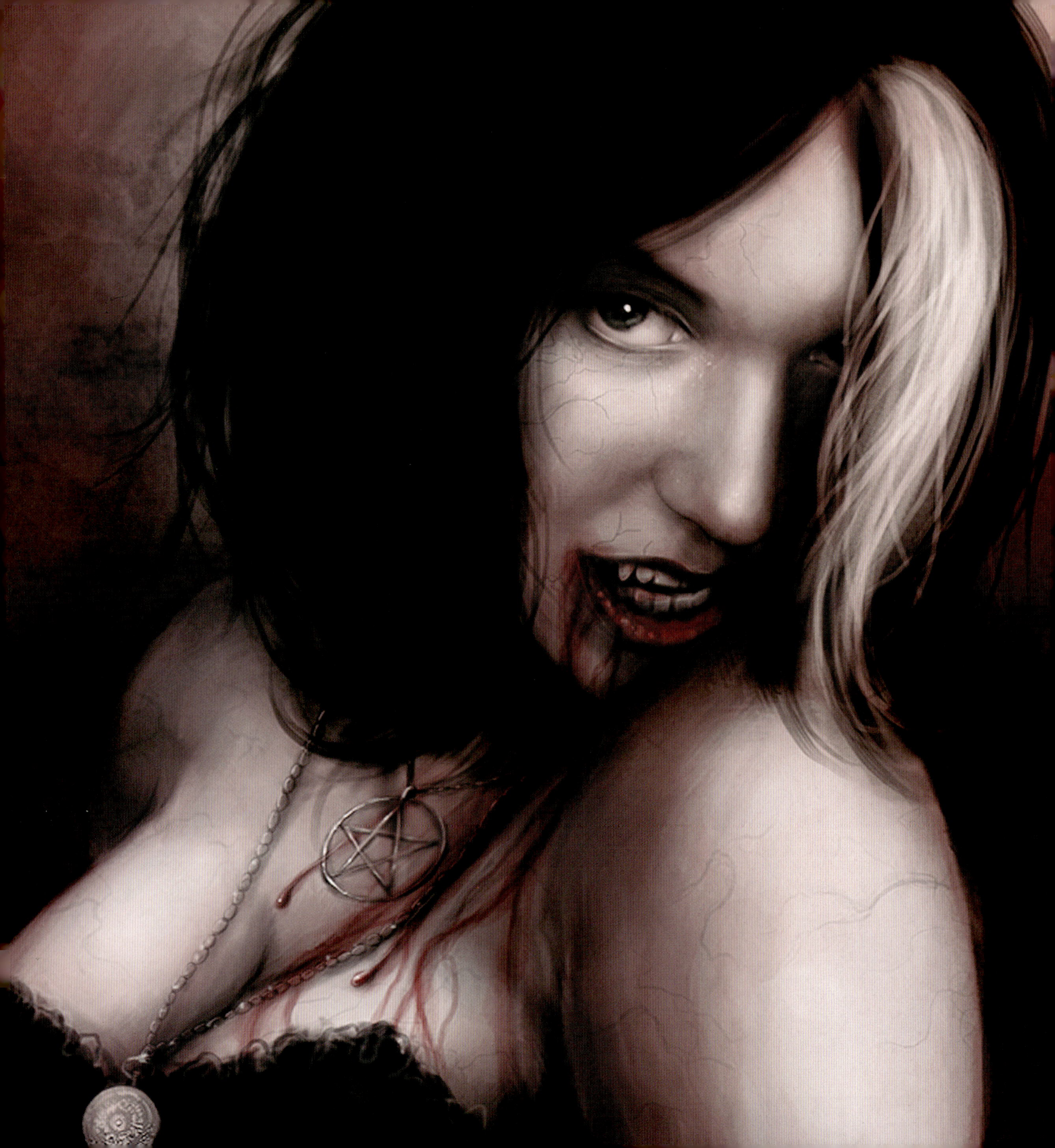

◀ **Unholy Feast**
Kimberly Myatt
Digital painting
www.beetlebones.net

Myatt's painting portrays a lurid femme fatale. She explains: "This is an illustration of a character in my novels. I took a photograph of myself in high definition to use as a reference, because I wanted to capture the texture and details in the skin and eyes. My technique was to paint a detailed, black-and-white foundation before painting the color layer beneath it. I also painted onto the flattened image afterwards to really get the feel of the texture."

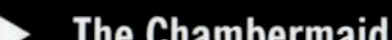

▶ **The Chambermaid**
Dorian Cleavenger
Acrylic on illustration board
www.dorianart.com

A stunning pin-up with decidedly Gothic and fetish overtones from Cleavenger. The beautiful Dita Von Teese modeled for this painting, which is painted using acrylic on illustration board. Fetish themes involving corsets, black vinyl, and S&M are common in artwork of the Gothic subgenre, especially with pretty pin-up portraits like this one.

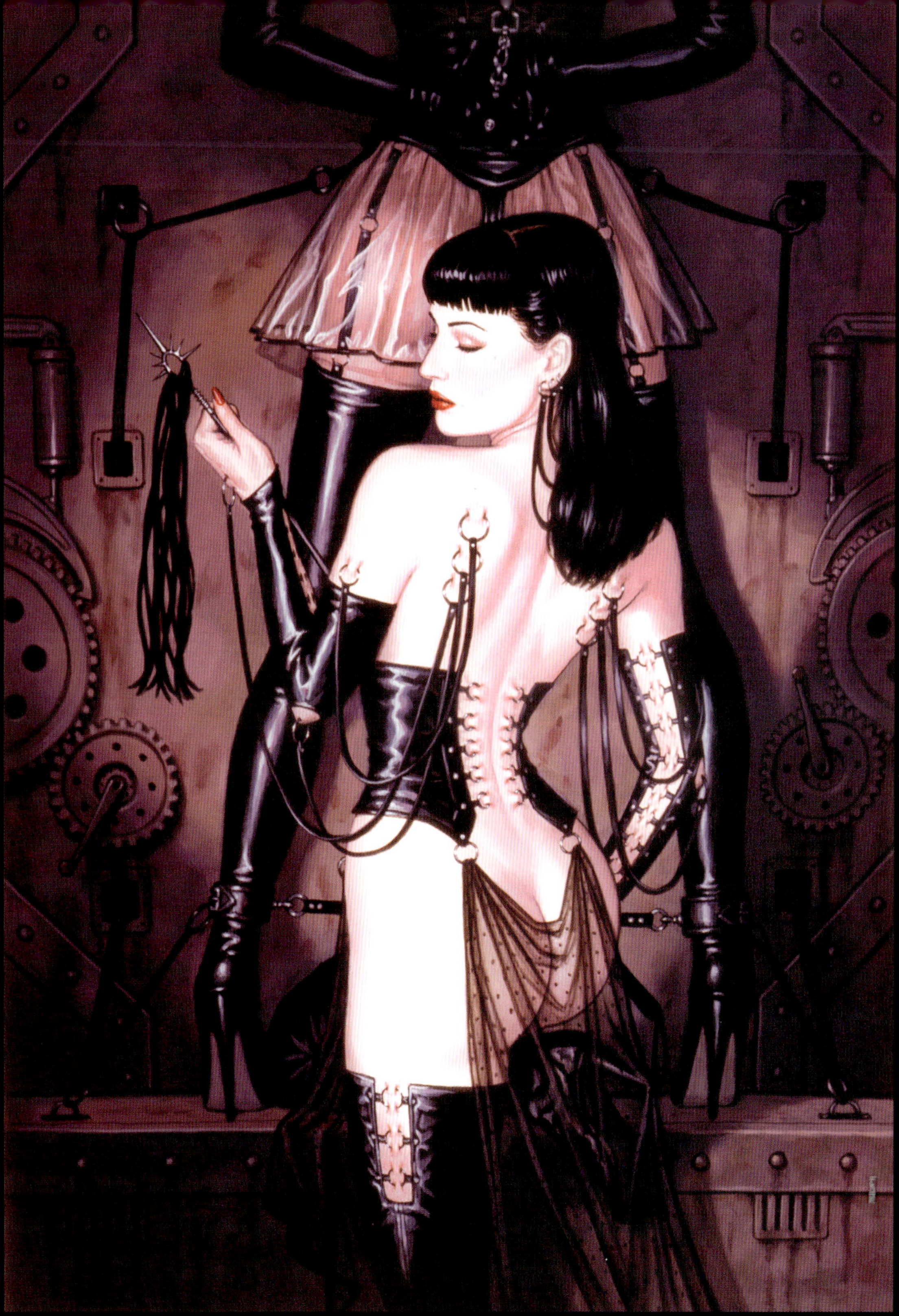

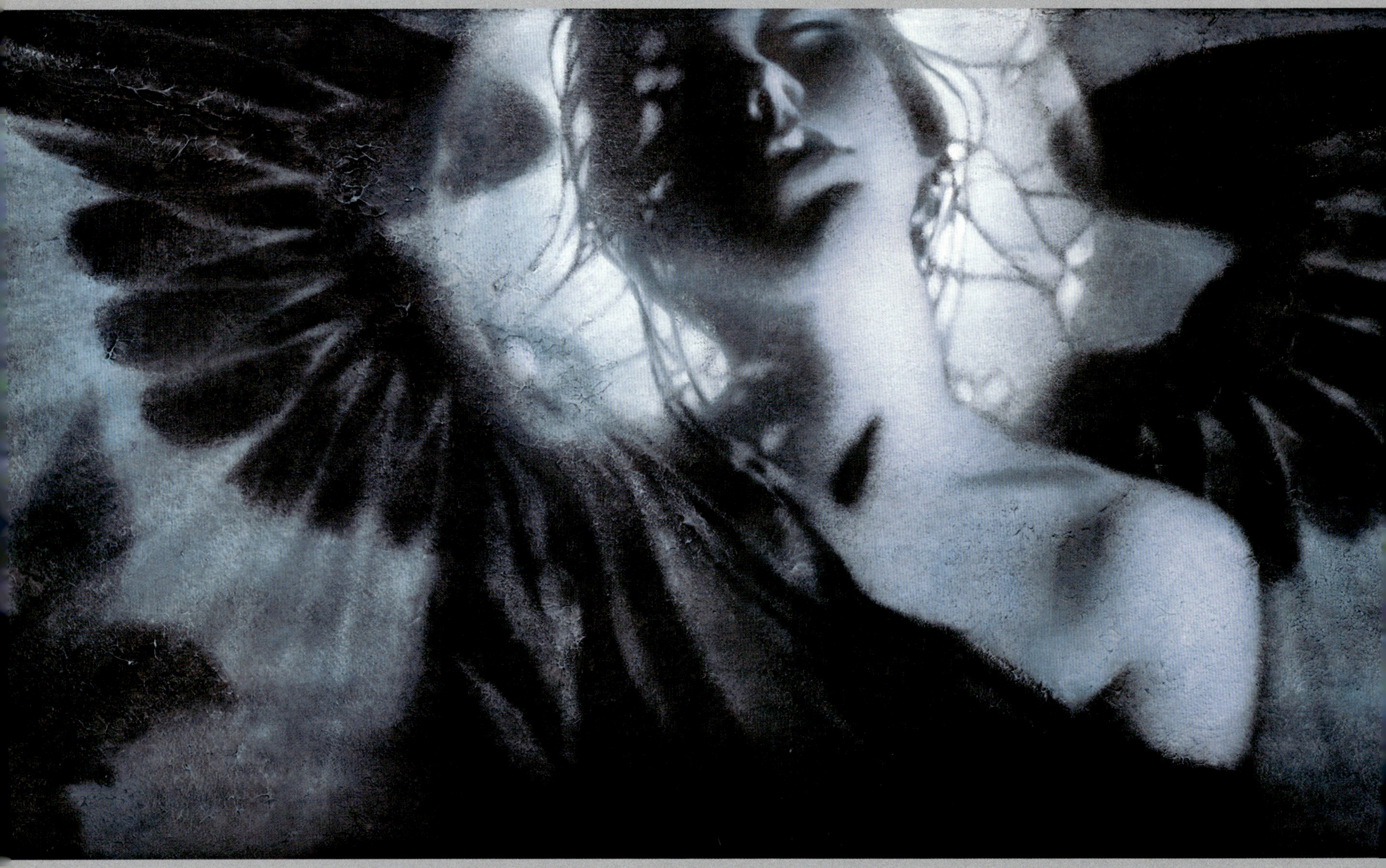

▲ **Angelique**
Linda Joyce Franks
Oil on paper
www.nimbvs.com

An angel with raven wings—Franks' oil painting ***Angelique*** *features a beautiful depiction of a holy being, with a look of ecstasy, or possibly agony, giving the creature a more human quality. Hints of fleur-de-lys designs on either side reinforce the overall Gothic impression of the painting.*

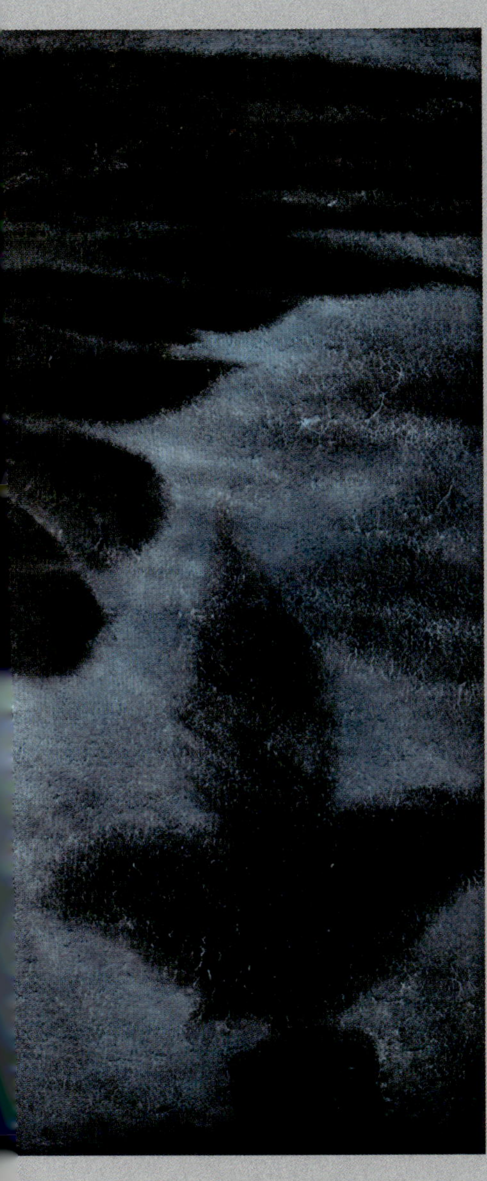

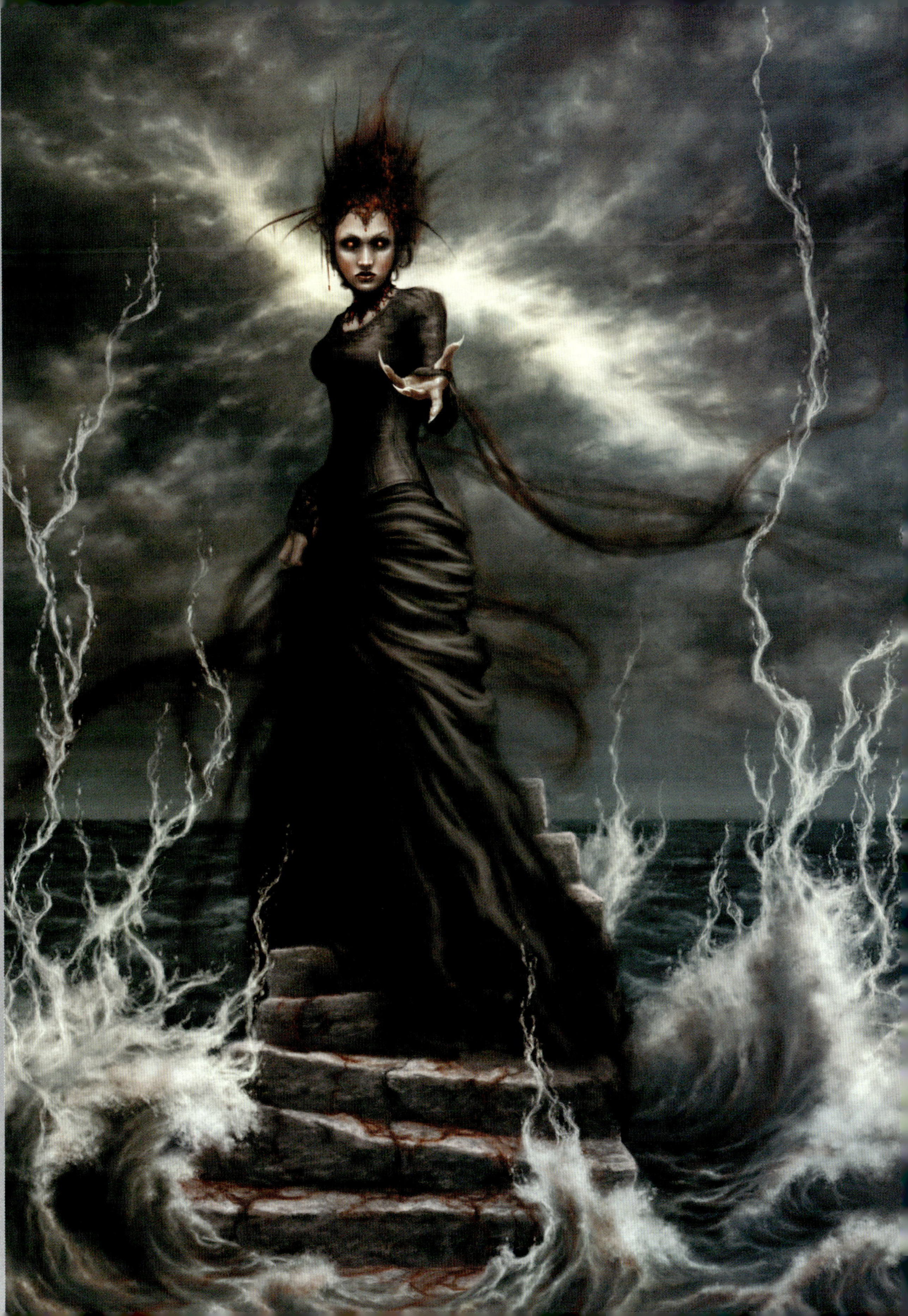

▶ **The Gate of Slaughter**
Lauren K. Cannon
Digital painting
www.navate.com

Cannon's adept use of Adobe Photoshop is evident in this image. "This is an illustration of a myth where I wanted to convey a sense of power. I used muted colors to emphasize the contrast in lighting, and composition to draw attention to the figure. The water floats upwards and adds a surreal feeling to the image."

▶ **Sometimes They Leave Fingerprints**
Gracjana Zielinska
Digital painting
www.vinegaria.com

A haunting, and slightly malevolent-looking maiden stands in front of bloody handprints smeared on lush wallpaper, which begs the question: whose blood is on the wall? Zielinska explains: "Done in Corel Painter and Adobe Photoshop, this piece is illustrating one of many stories I have in my mind. I like to depict an atmosphere which is a bit uncertain, where you're unsure of what has really happened."

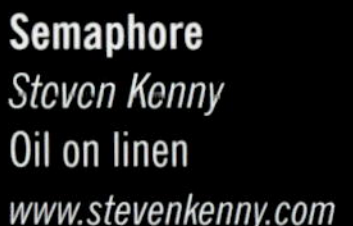

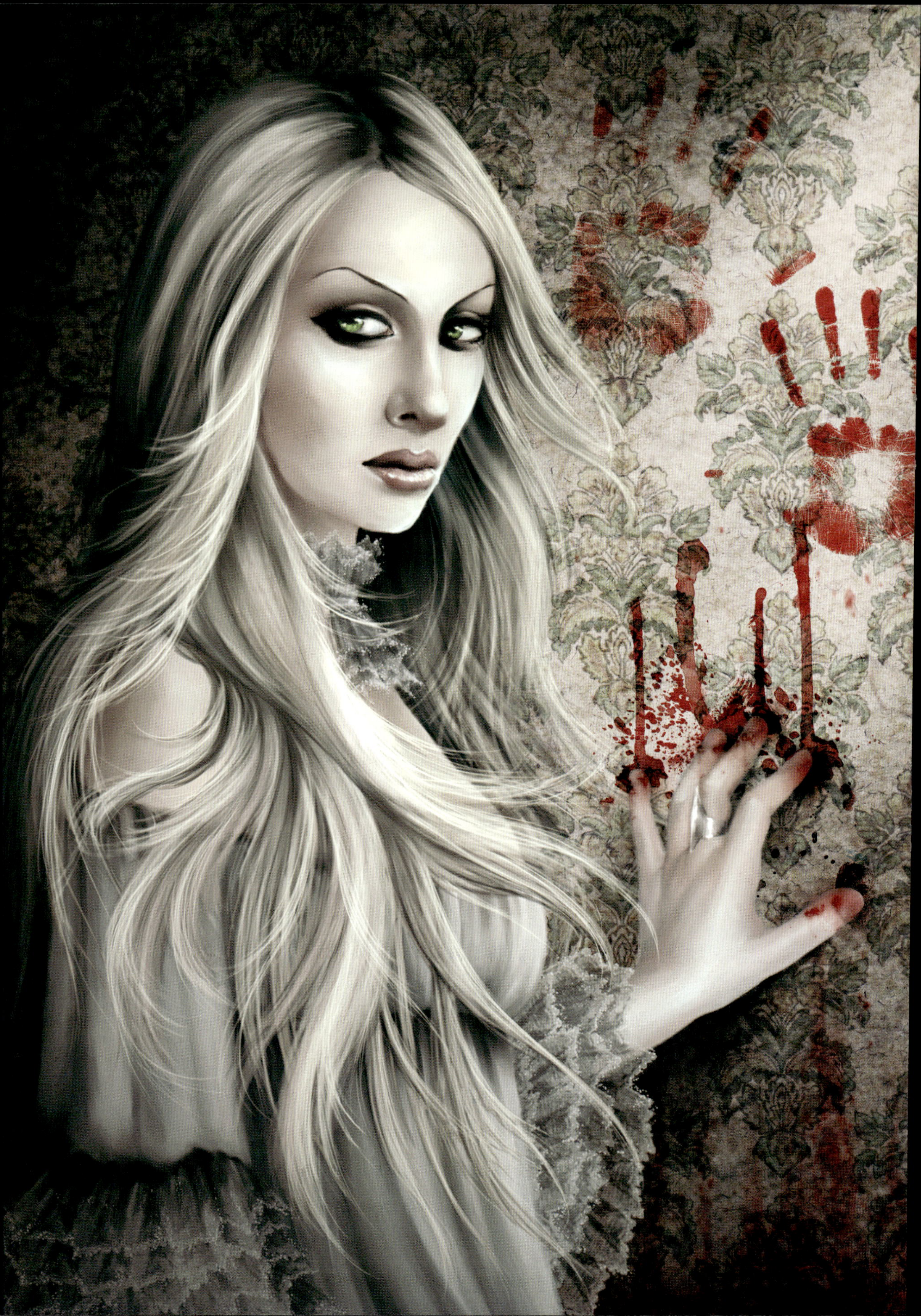

▶▶ **Semaphore**
Steven Kenny
Oil on linen
www.stevenkenny.com

A stunning oil painting from Kenny, ***Semaphore*** *features a symbolic and slightly surreal scene. He explains: "Often in my work I use birds to symbolize our hopes, dreams, and desires. They flutter by, circle, and sometimes come home to roost. But if not careful, they can become impaled on our self-imposed thorny crowns and die."*

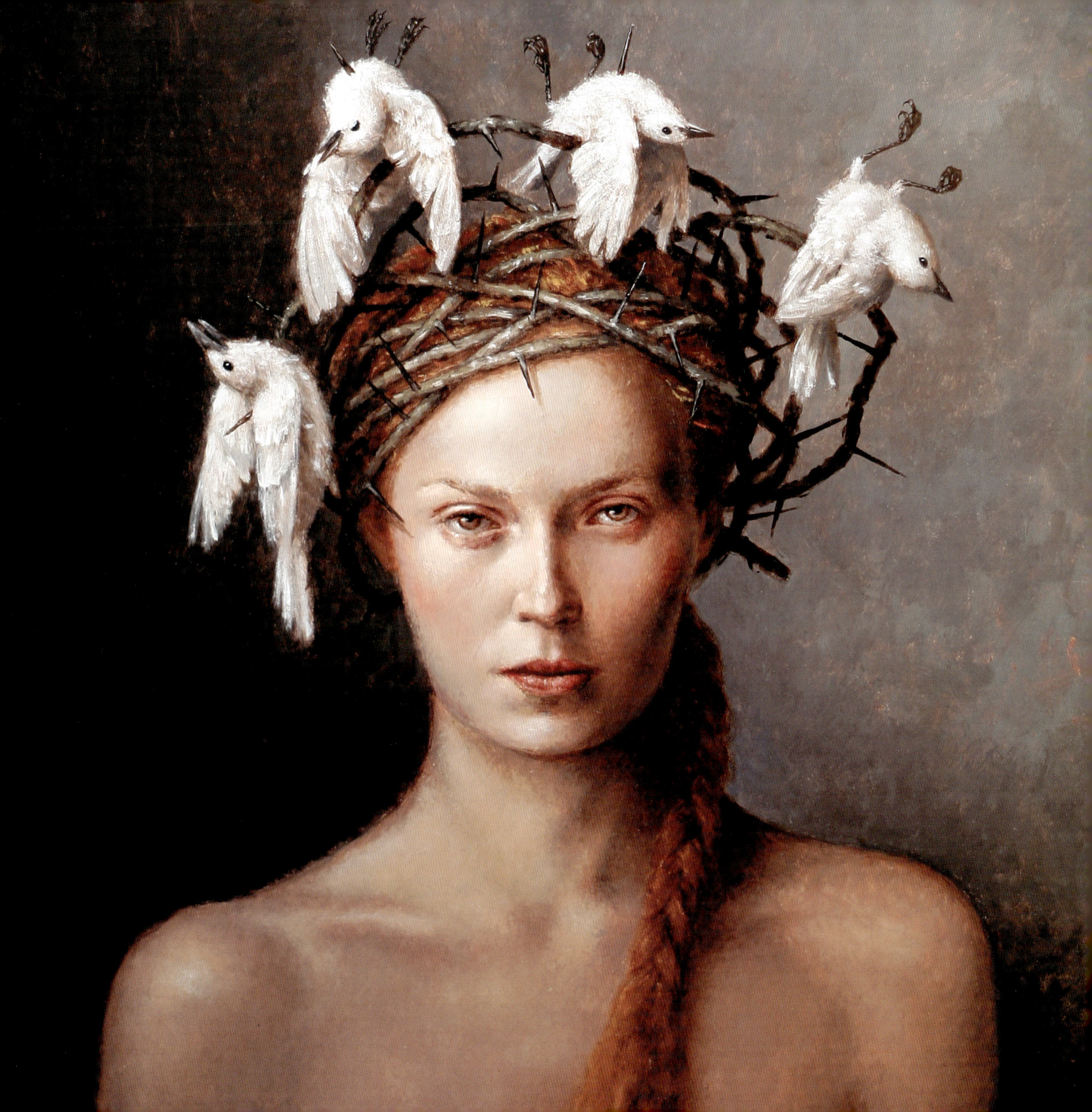

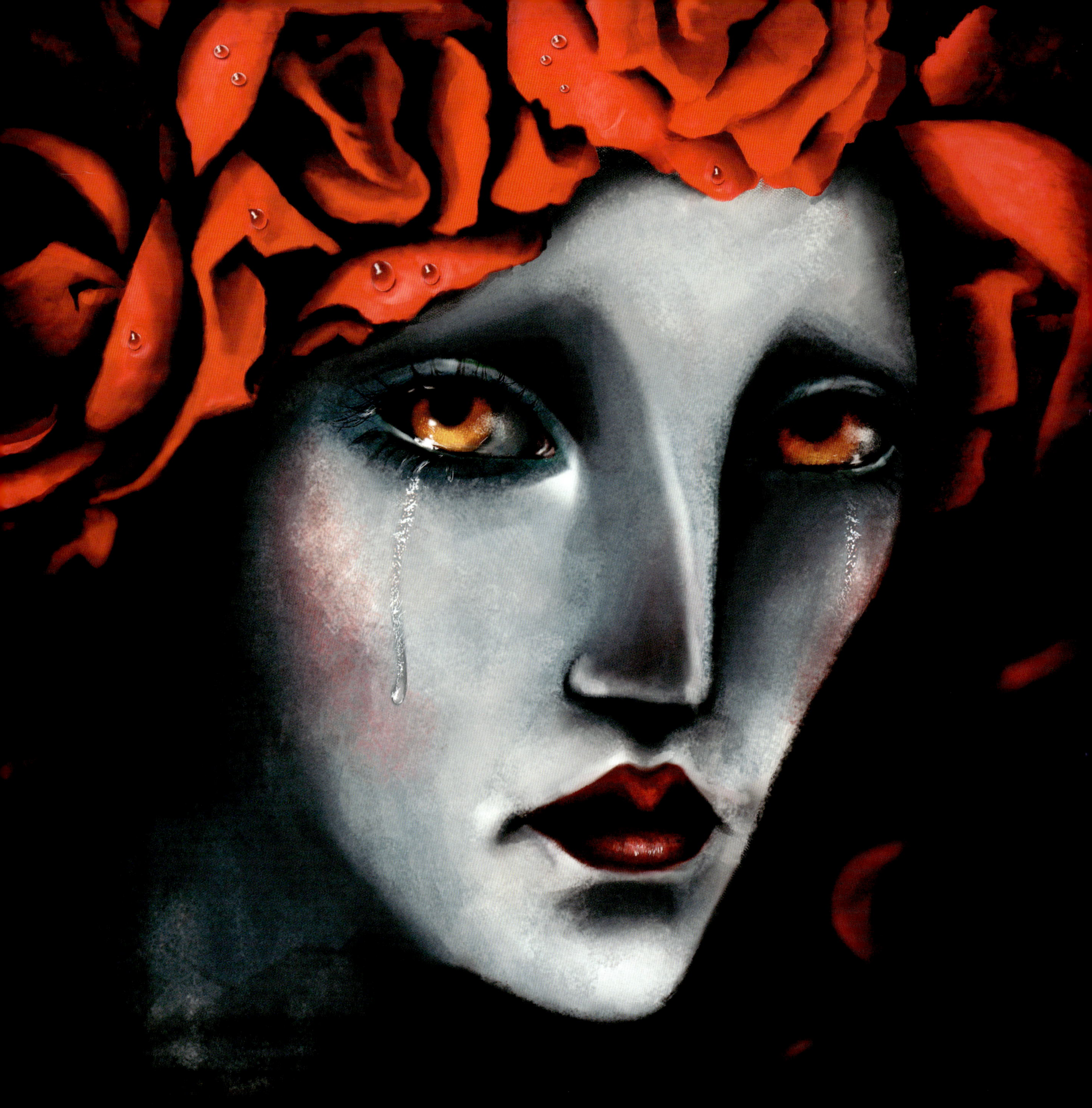

◀ **The Misery of Proserpine**
Lisa Falzon
Digital painting
www.lisafalzon.com

Classical mythology provides a wealth of inspiration for Gothic artwork. Falzon explains: "Mythology has always fascinated me. I chose to depict the fabled Proserpine, who was stolen by the god of the underworld to be his wife. A pact was struck between the god and Proserpine's mother, where each could keep her for six months per year. I see Proserpine as the ultimate helpless victim, caught up in the eddies and currents of godly politics, while her own life, and will, dwindle."

▶ **Mhiet'e**
Lauren K. Cannon
Digital painting
www.navate.com

*Lauren created this scarred beauty in Adobe Photoshop. "**Mhiet'e** is one of my most interesting characters so I chose to play up the details and create a mysterious atmosphere. The background is a combination of custom texture brushes and a lot of hand painting, kept simple so as to keep the focus on the figure. Loose references were used for her pose and the bird wing."*

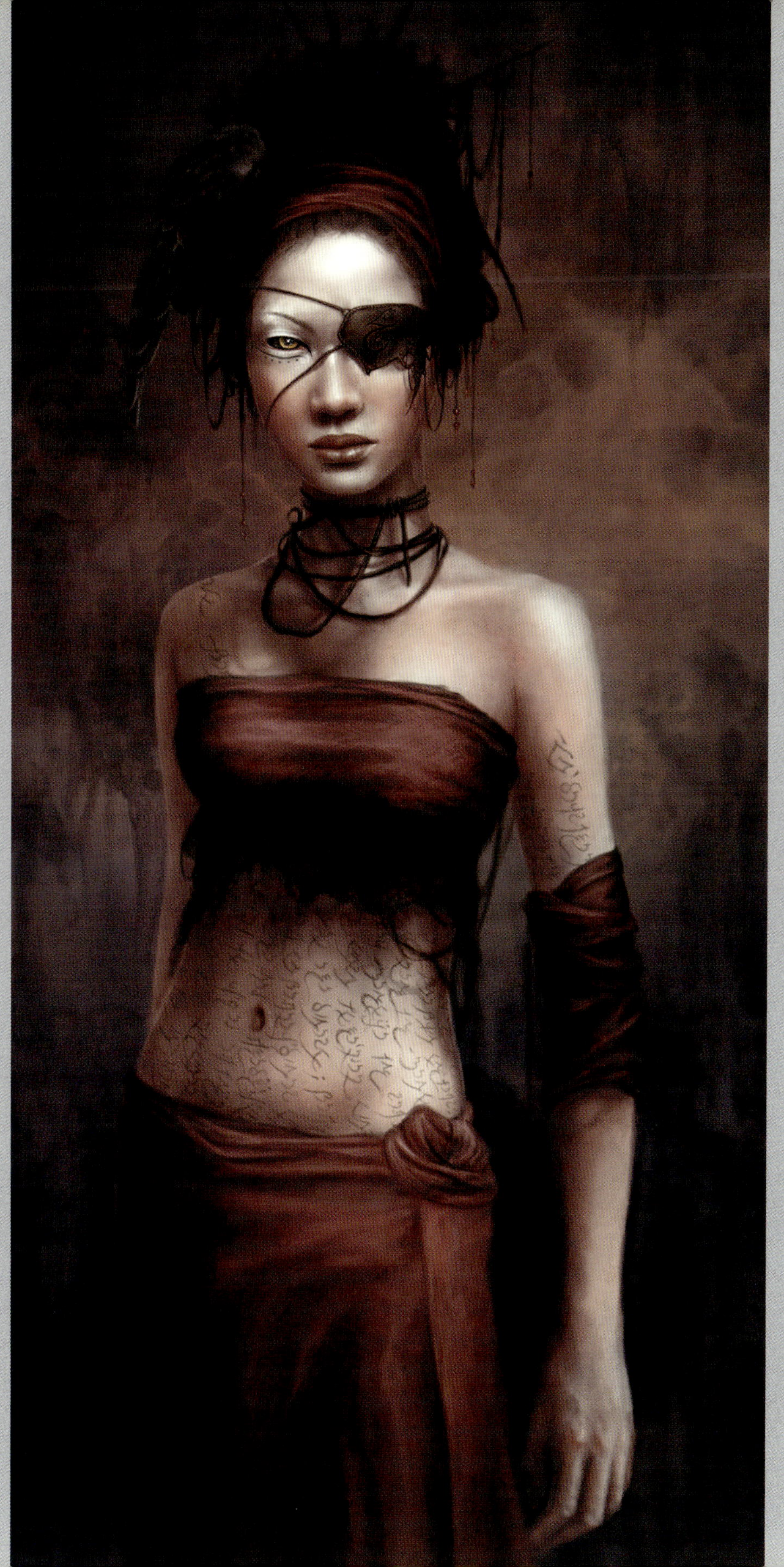

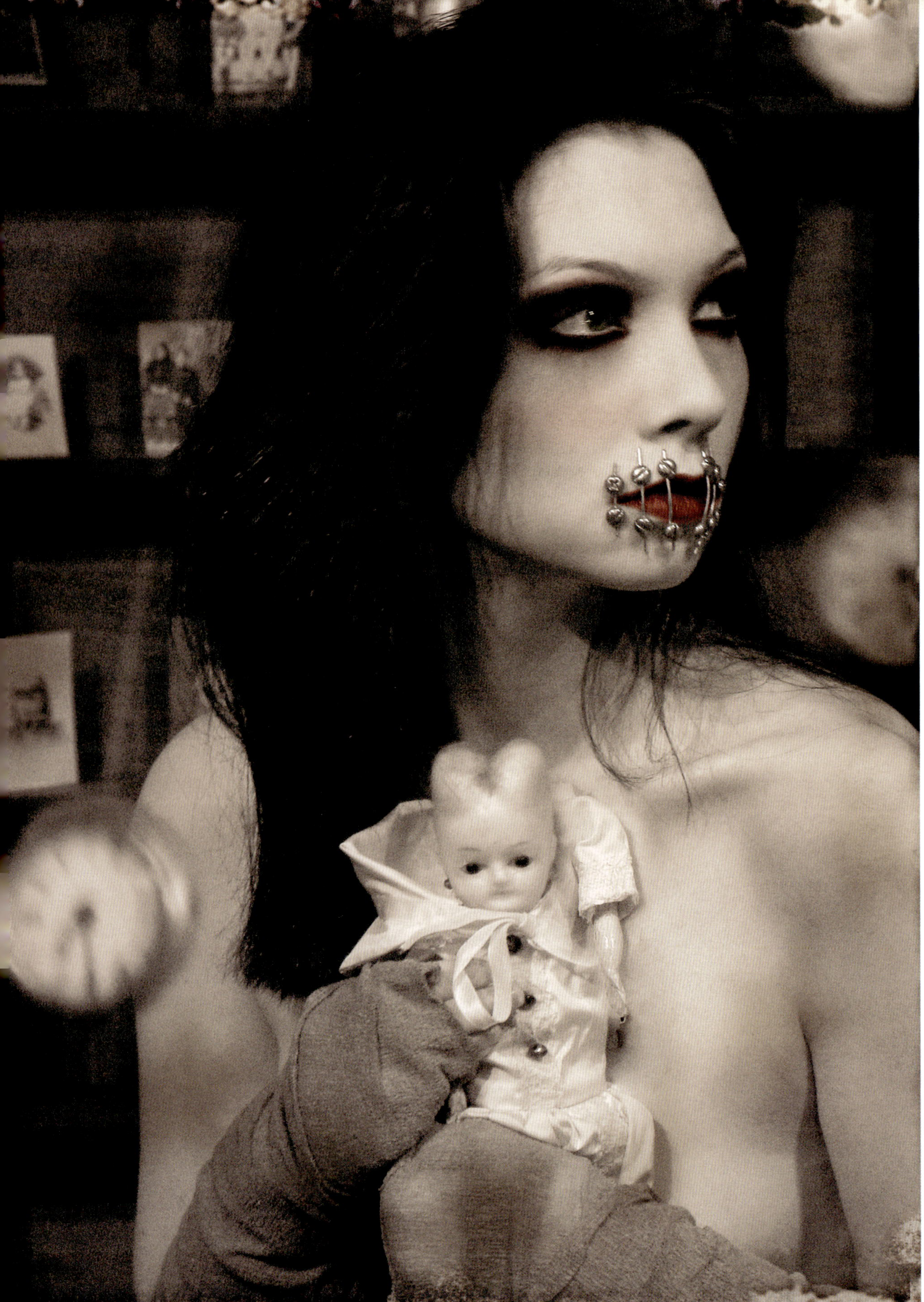

◀ **Beauty of Silence**
John Santerineross
Photography
www.santerineross.com

Contrary to popular belief, Santerineross's work is not digitally manipulated. Ninety-eight percent of what you see is what was on set the day of the shoot. All the blur and motion is created by an elaborate mechanized system of mobiles, or the model moving on Santerineross's command. All body modifications are either real or prosthetic in nature.

▶ **Porcelain Child**
John Santerineross
Photography
www.santerineross.com

John Santerineross's avant-garde photographic images are beautiful and intriguing. The foundation for each image is an elaborate set that he constructs entirely by hand. He can spend weeks building and finding the right props, clothing, and models for a particular photograph.

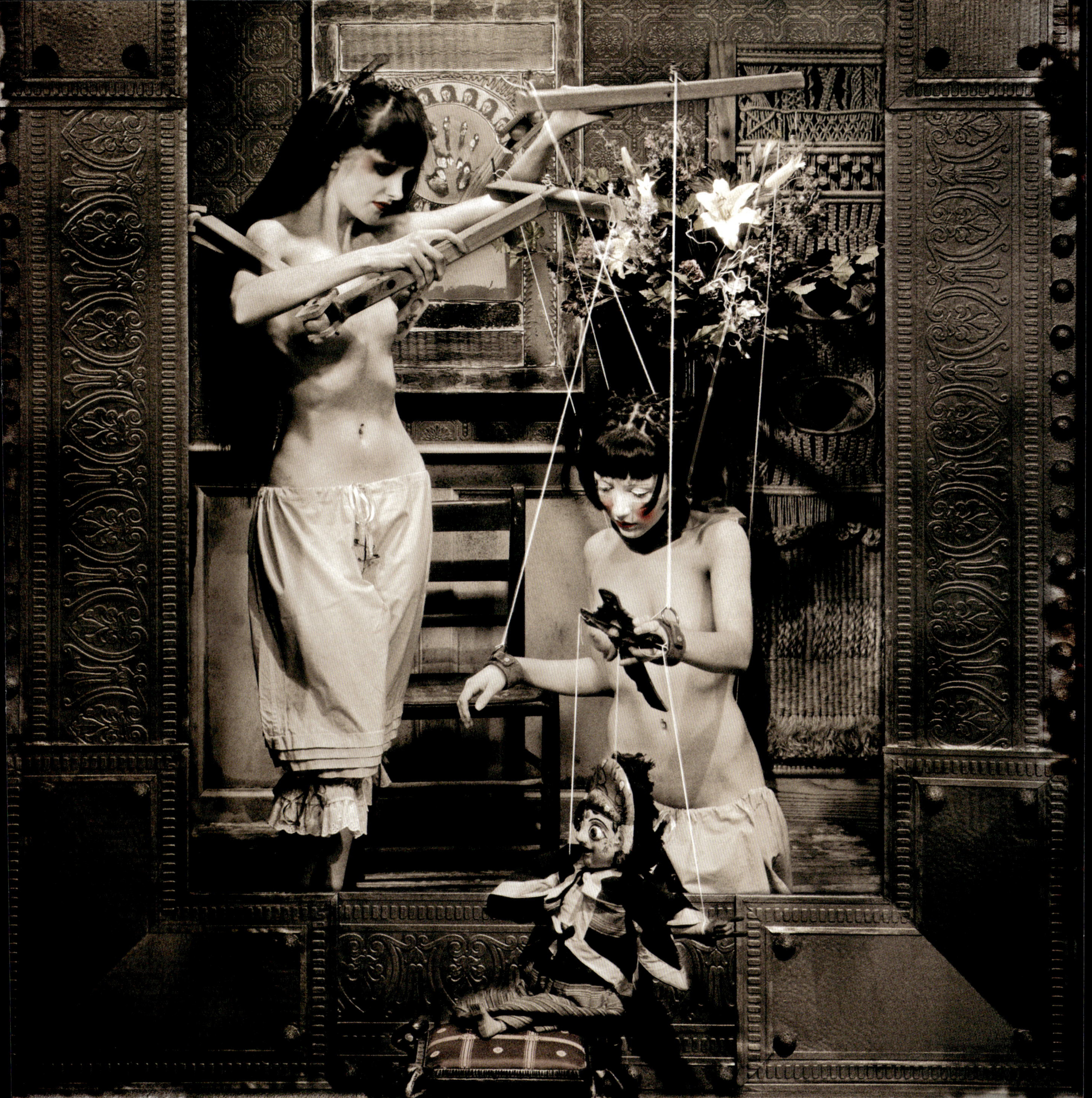

▶ **3**
Leslie Ann O'Dell
Photography and
digital manipulation
www.shyble.com

O'Dell has created a very striking image using a combination of her own photography and scanned, pressed Baby's Breath flowers for the mouth. She explains: "With this piece I wanted to create a portrait that symbolizes a darkness growing in the heart and spreading within, before finally finding its way out. I was inspired by my newly pressed flowers (a hobby I've had since I was a little girl) and how they retained so much life, even while they were slowly decaying."

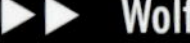 **Wolf**
Shannon Hourigan
Photography and
digital manipulation
www.shannonhourigan.com

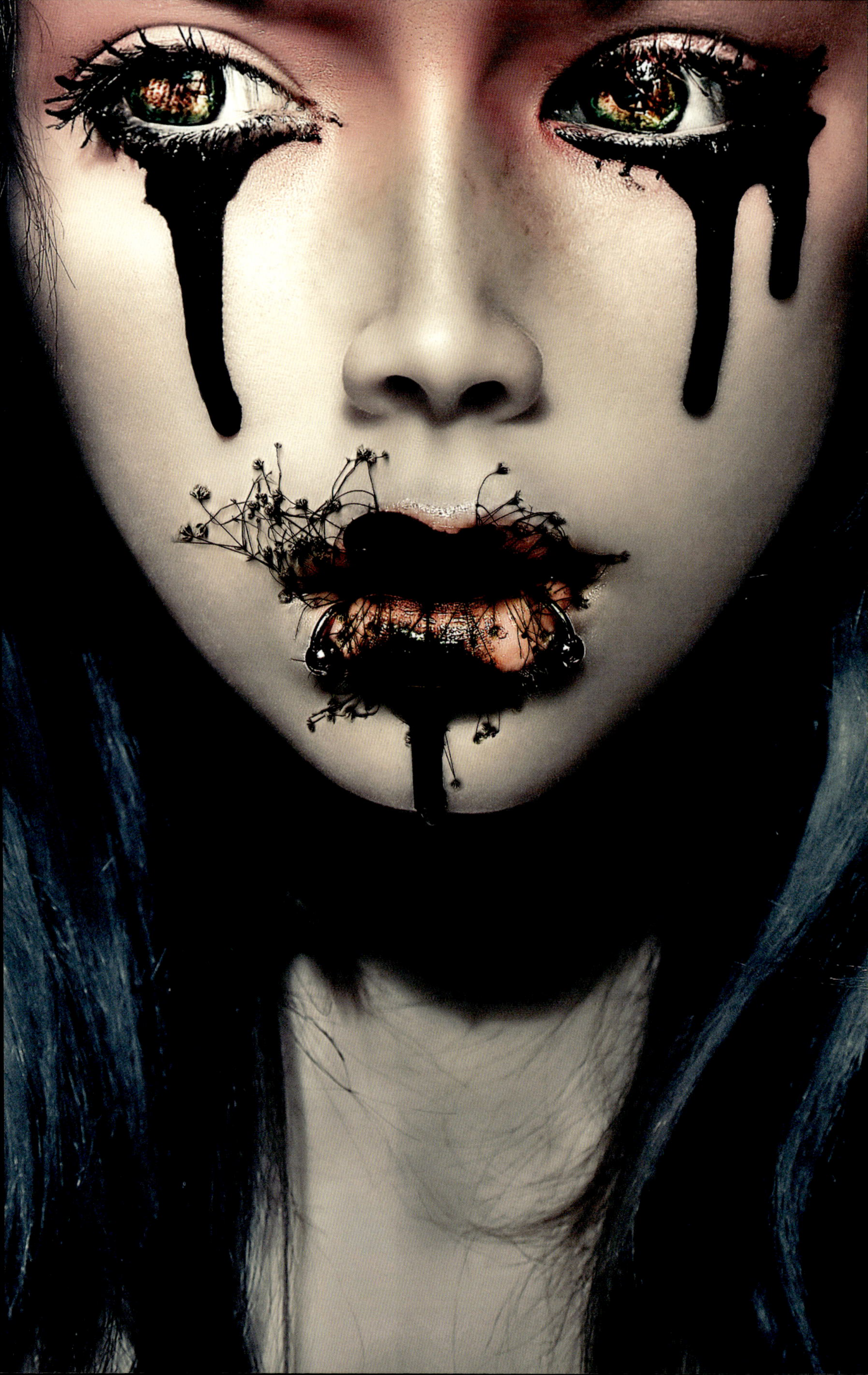

Werewolves and lycanthropes are a familiar theme in Gothic artwork and literature. Hourigan has put a slant on the classical depiction of a standard "Wolf-Man" by using Adobe Photoshop to create a beautiful "Wolf-Girl." Hourigan describes the piece as a "self-portrait as a wolf."

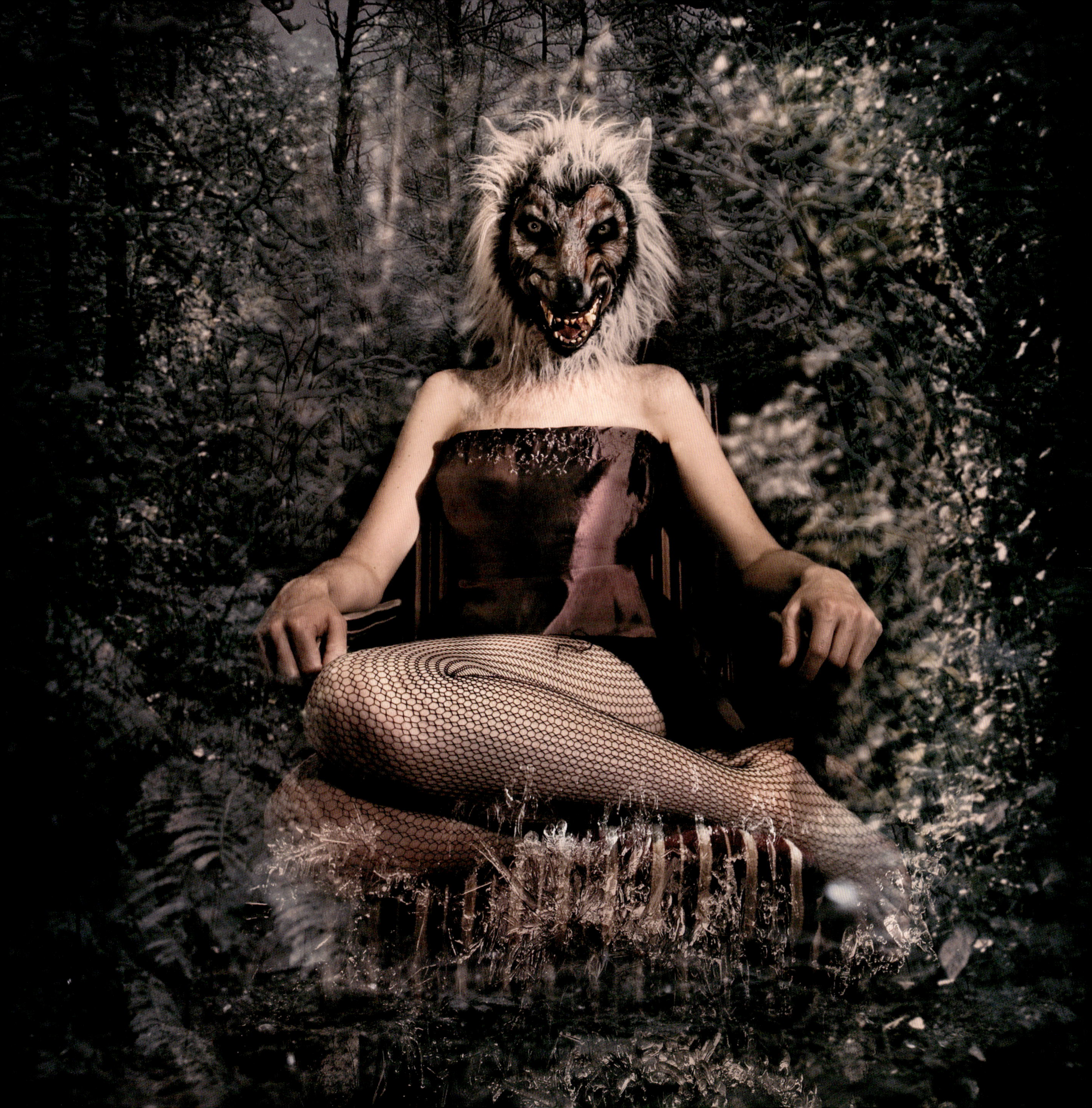

▶ **Black Widow**
Jason Juta
Photography and digital manipulation
www.jasonjuta.com

This is a classic Gothic image. Juta explains: "For this piece I collaborated with a Gothic model, Lady Amaranth, on a set for **Femmes Fatales** *— where a Gothic bride kills her mate, like a preying mantis. I chose the snowy setting to contrast with her black outfit. The blood-dripping flowers and red-marked spiders add a sharp splash of vivid color. Using Adobe Photoshop to compose the final piece, I shot the model with studio lighting, and used my photographs of the local Highgate wood and cemetery, with liberal amounts of digital paint and processing."*

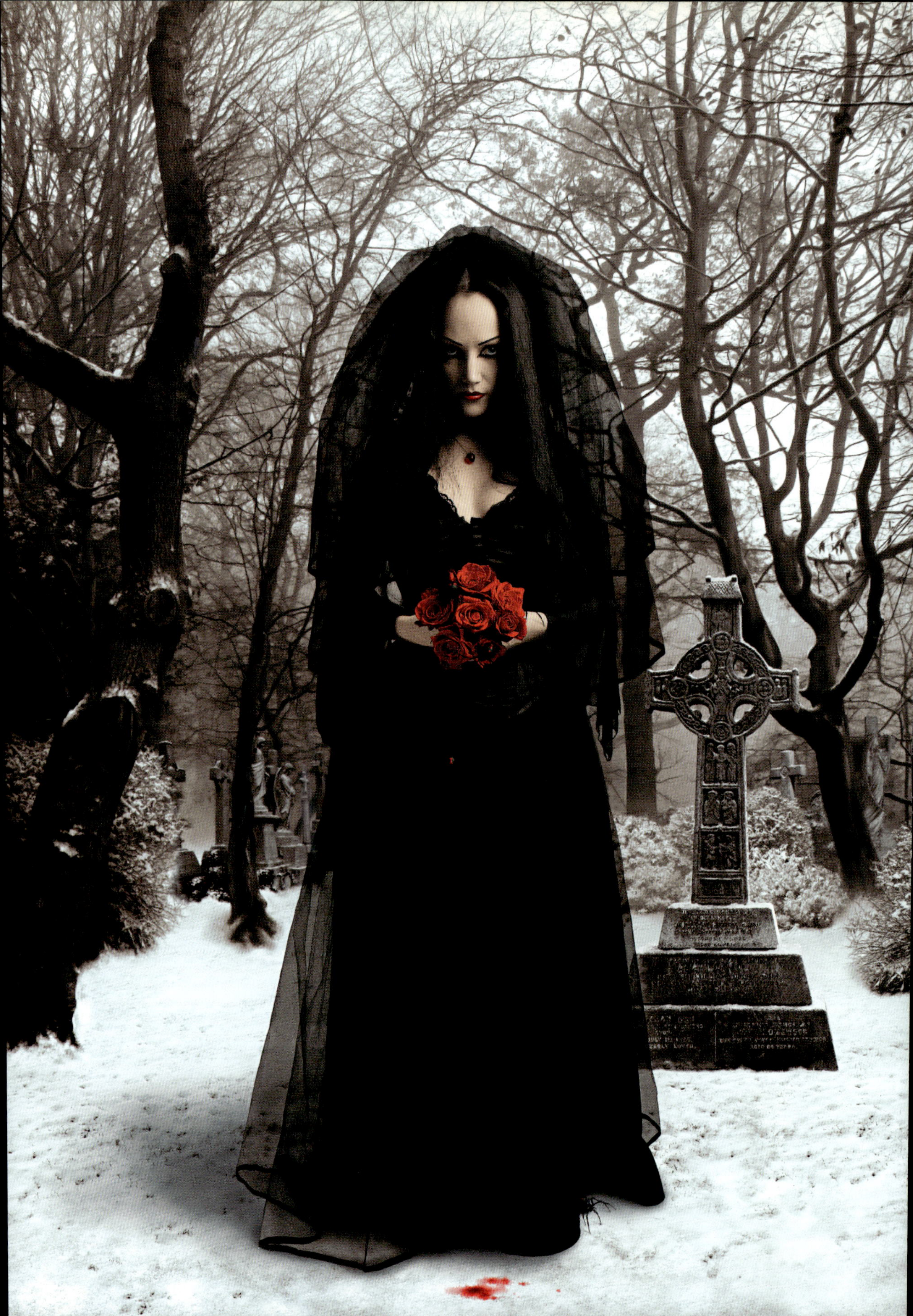

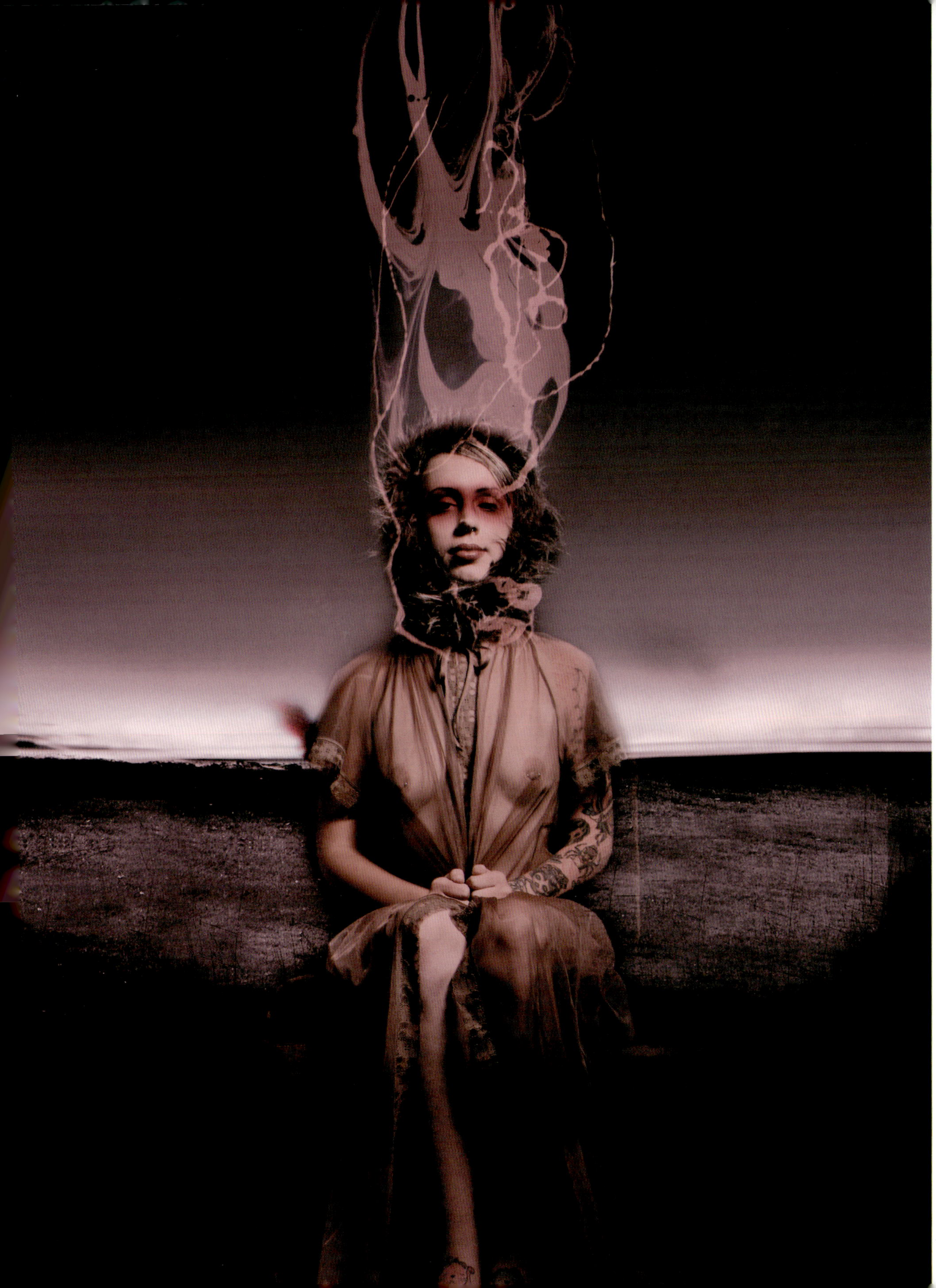

◀ **Cry**
Shannon Hourigan
Photography and
digital manipulation
www.shannonhourigan.com

***Cry** features a melancholic, but intriguing image of a lone female figure in a barren landscape. Hourigan created this beautiful image using her own photography and Adobe Photoshop.*

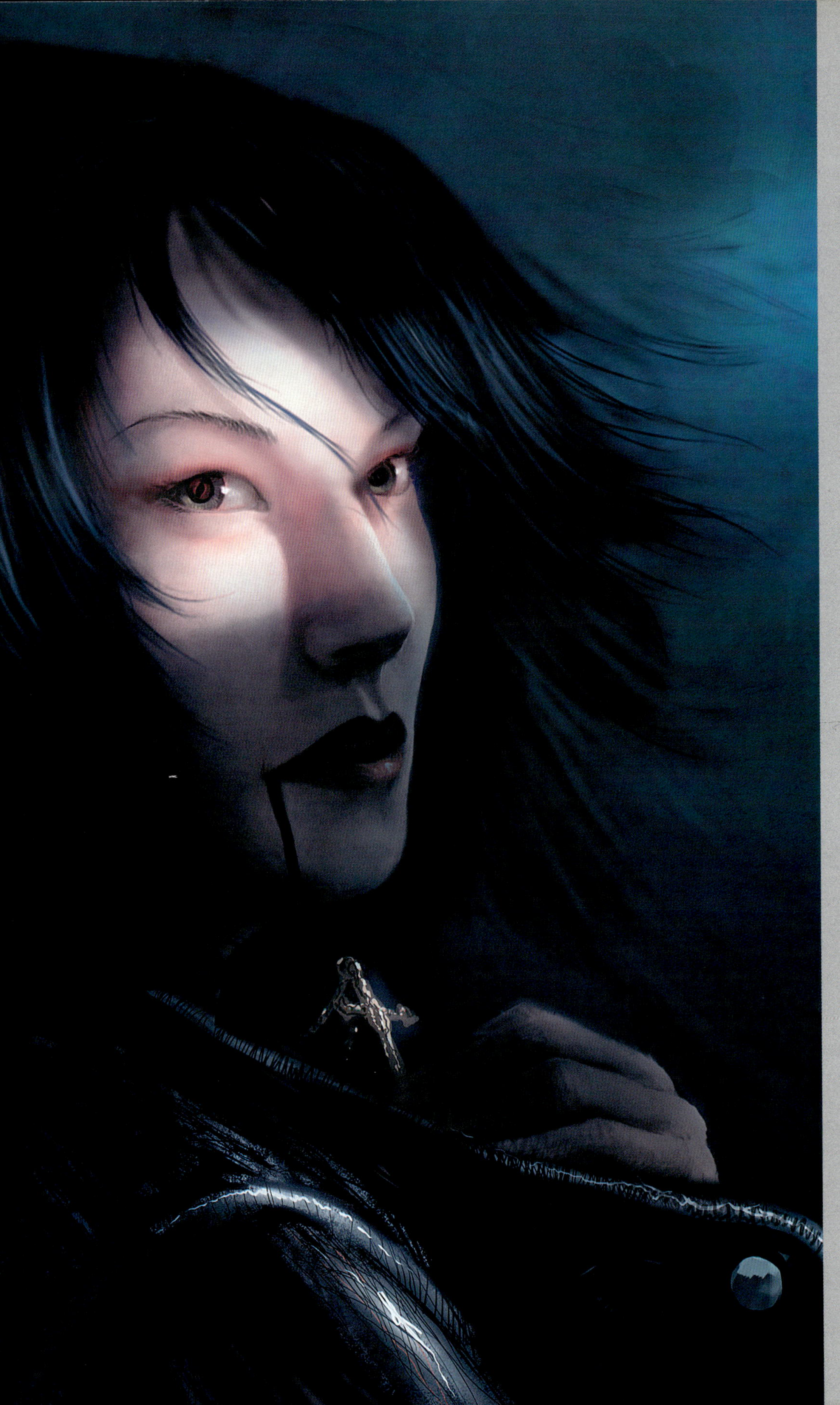

◀ **Blood Drinker**
Matt Bradbury
Digital painting
www.mattbradbury.epilogue.net

This piece is a study in lighting and a new approach to the Gothic standby—a beautiful vampire. Bradbury explains: "I've always found vampires quite interesting as they appear enigmatic and powerful, which makes them fun to paint. In this portrait the light across the eyes of the figure is supposed to draw in the viewer."

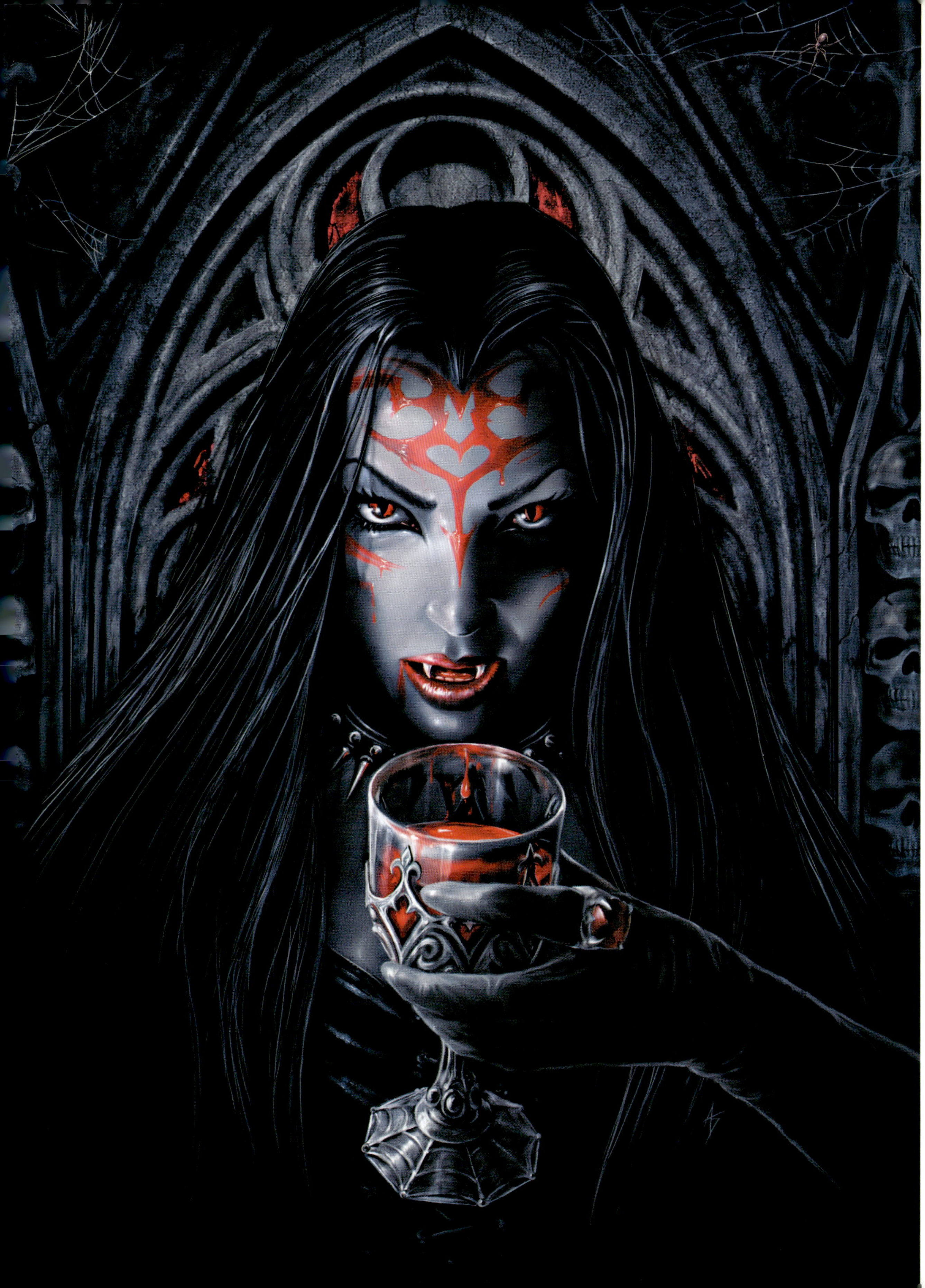

◀ **Vampire**
Anne Stokes
Digital painting
www.annestokes.com

What could be more Gothic than an enchantingly beautiful vampire, drinking blood in front of an arched window? Stokes explains: "Commissioned by ***Magazine Exchange*** *for use on a* ***MAX Protection Deck Box****, this vampire lures the viewer to drink from her glass. The limited color range of this painting is designed to emphasize the Gothic look. Painted in Adobe Photoshop, the details in the architecture line up to suggest there are horns on her head, which hint at the evil that lies behind this offer."*

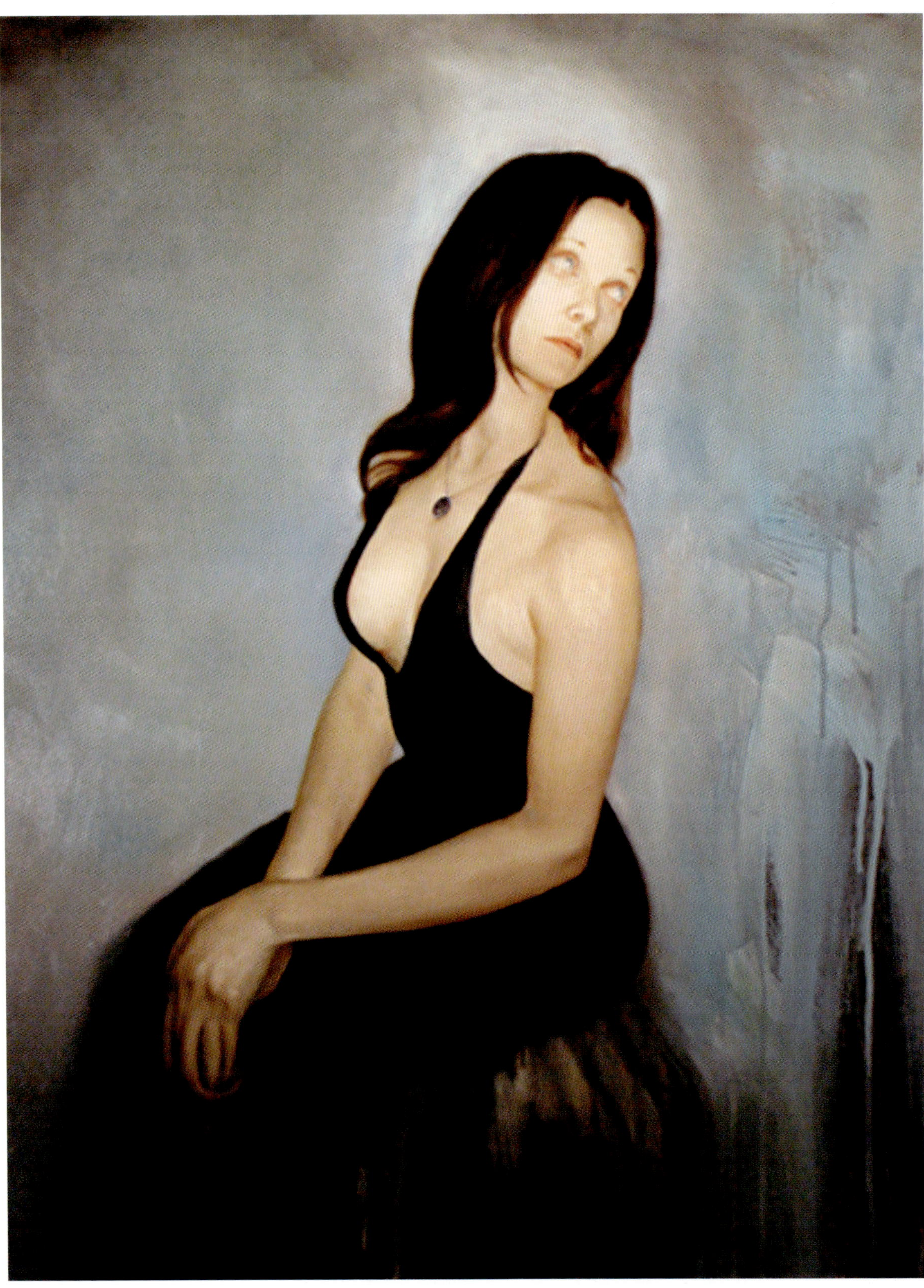

◀ **Seated Woman**
Michael Ryan
Oil on canvas
www.michaelryanart.com

Upon first glance, Ryan's ***Seated Woman*** *appears to be a dignified portrait of a beautiful woman, not unlike a traditional Sargent, Carolus-Duran, or Velázquez. But upon further inspection, her unusual, tentacle-like fingers and her haunting eyes show a sense of something darker... Ryan explains: "I paint from drawings or cartoons that are created from studies of models or photographs."*

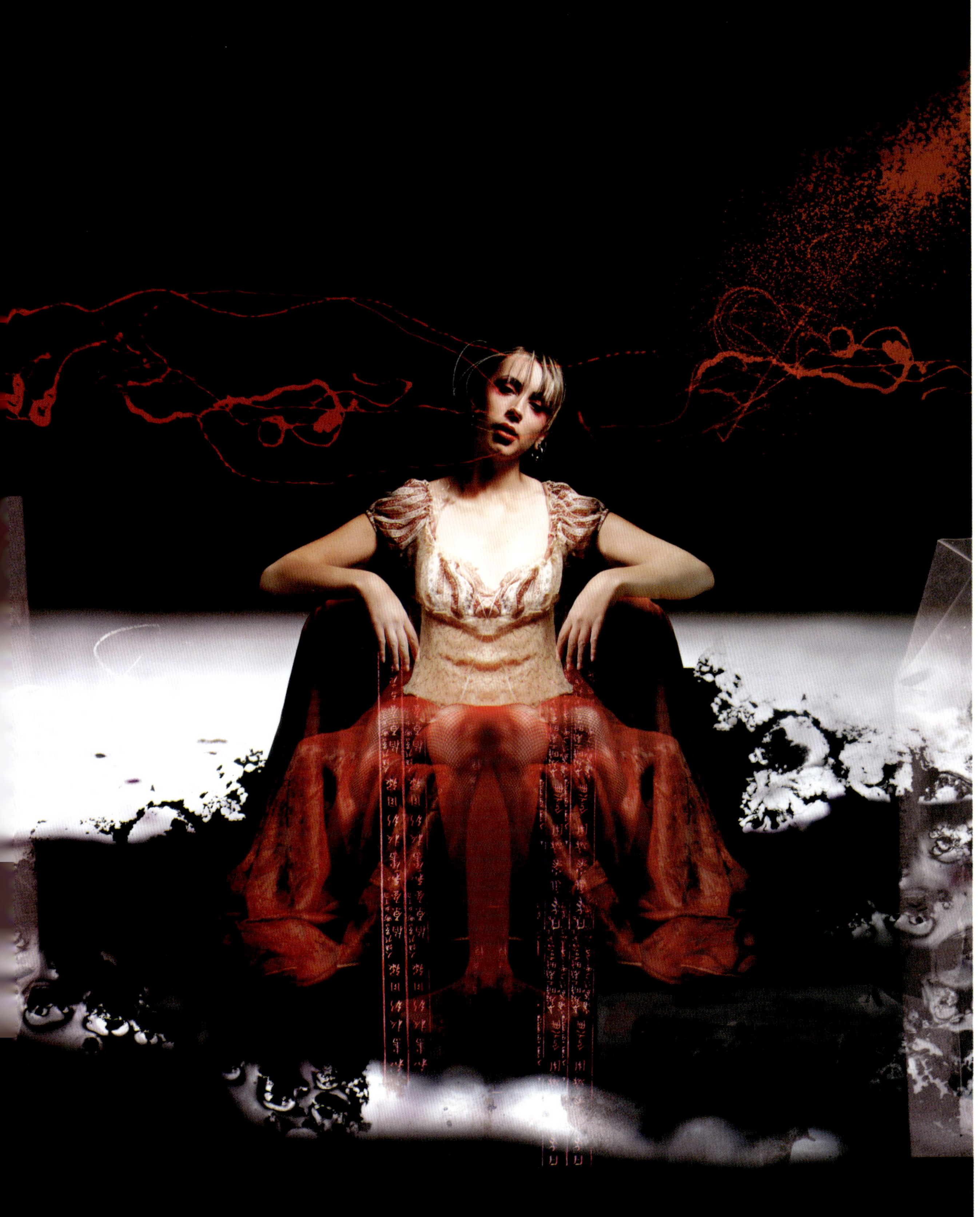

◀ **Speak**
Shannon Hourigan
Photography and
digital manipulation
www.shannonhourigan.com

Speak *is another mixed media, Adobe Photoshop creation by Hourigan. The lighting emphasizes the girl in the center, with atmospheric swirls and organic shapes in deep red giving the impression, perhaps, of blood.*

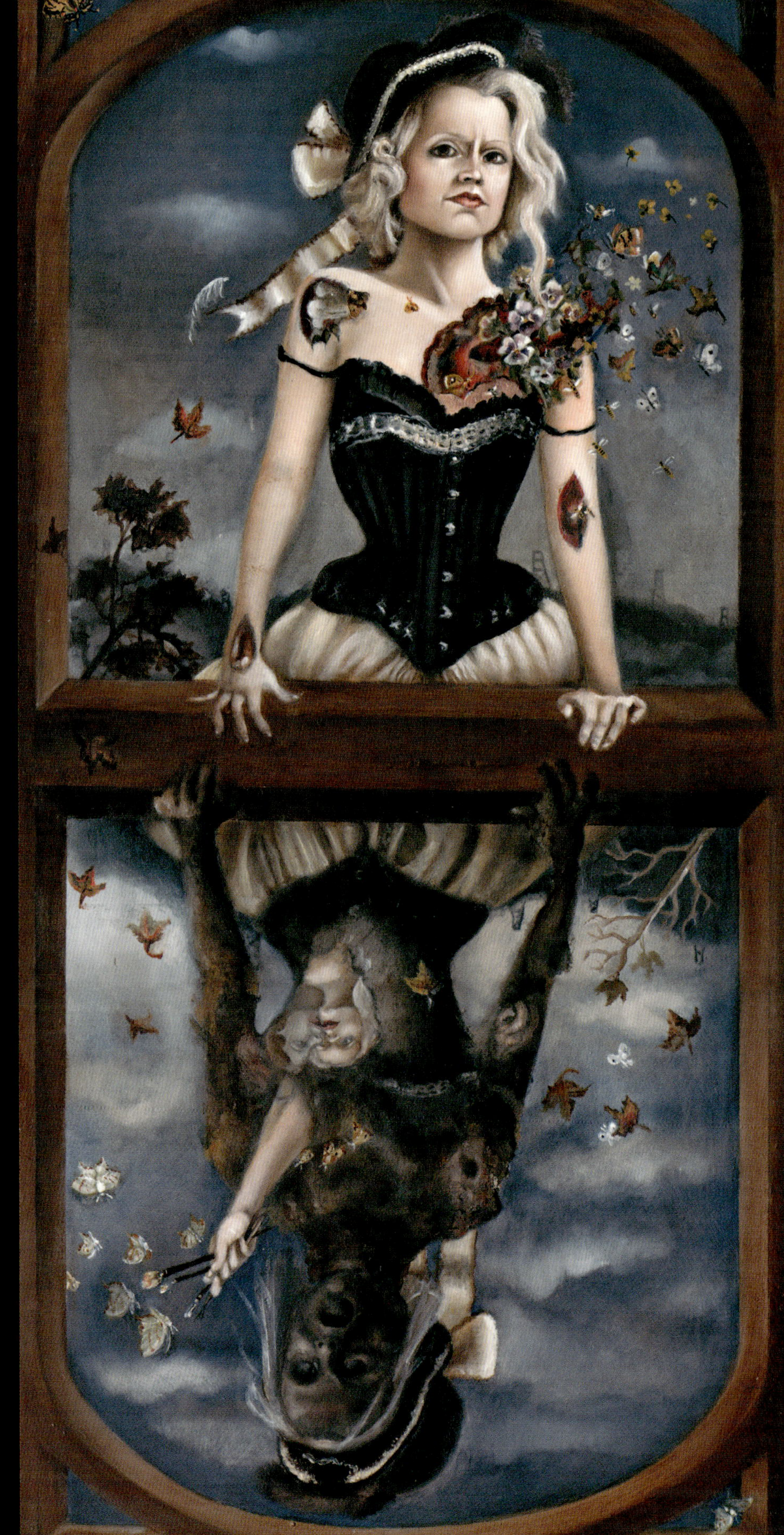

▶ **Youth is Wasted on the Young**
Tina Imel
Oil on wood
www.tinaimel.com

Imel's painting shows a beautiful youthful woman contemplating the decayed, decrepit corpse of her reflection: a juxtaposition of two contrasting self-portraits. Containing a message about enjoying life while you can, it nonetheless holds a few ominous overtones with the darker, surrealistic elements.

▶▶ **Bride of Lucifer**
Kuang Hong
Digital painting
www.zemotion.net

A darkly poetic piece, painted digitally by Hong in Corel Painter. "The story speaks of a young woman wanting to atone for her dead lover and clear his name. Sacrificing herself, she leaves with messengers of hell. Her will is so strong that on their way she plays a song which calls up to the seraphim."

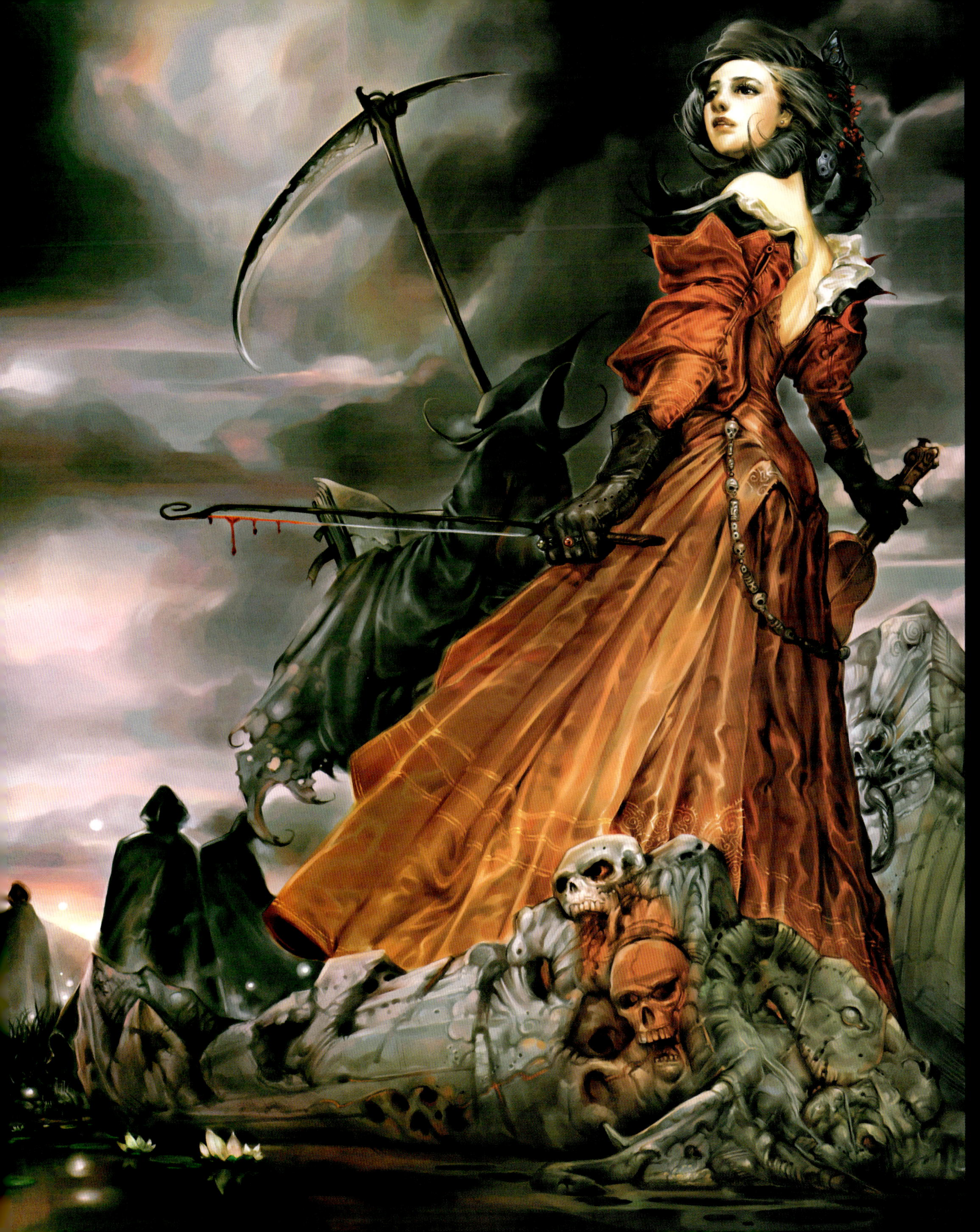

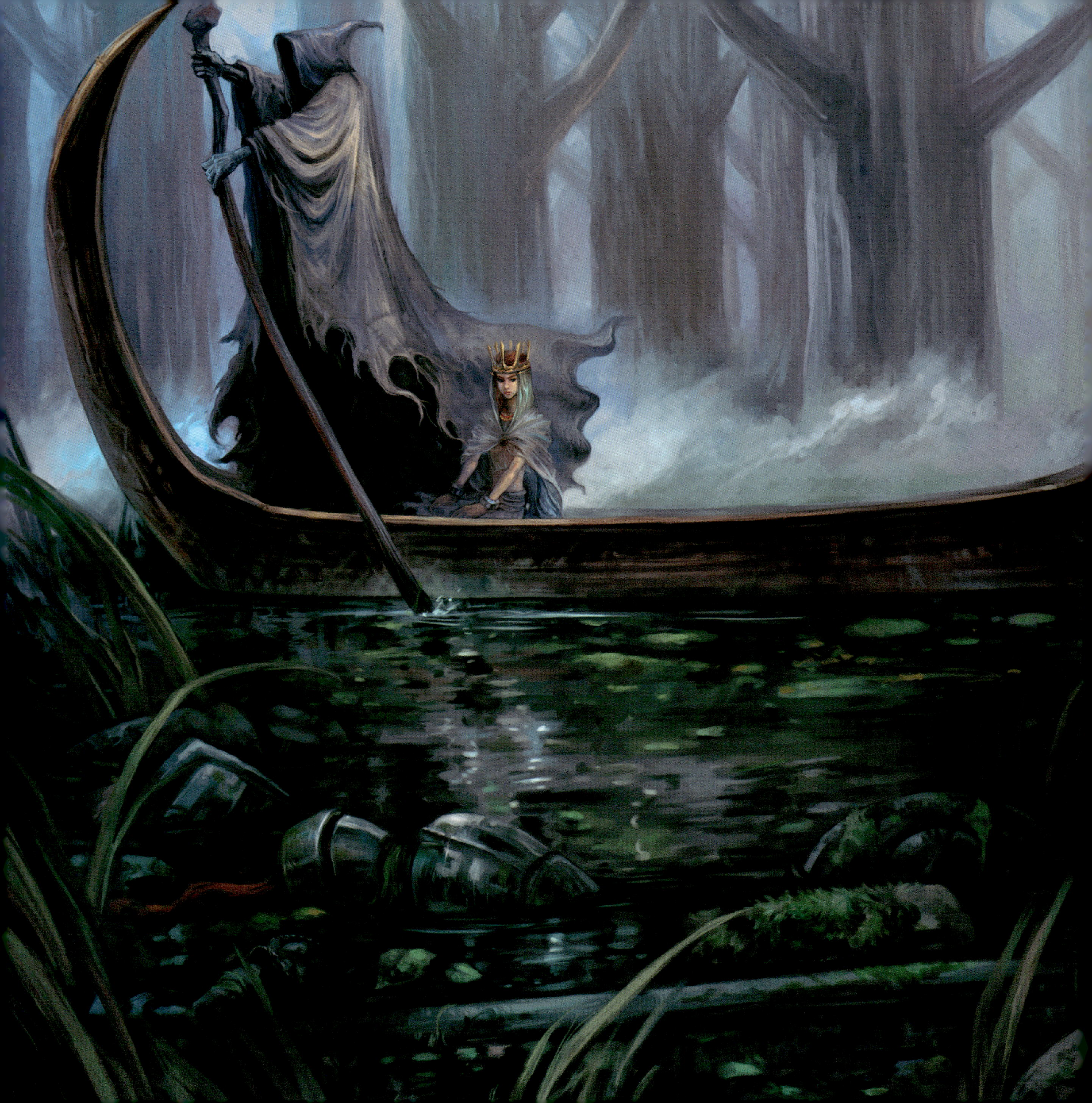

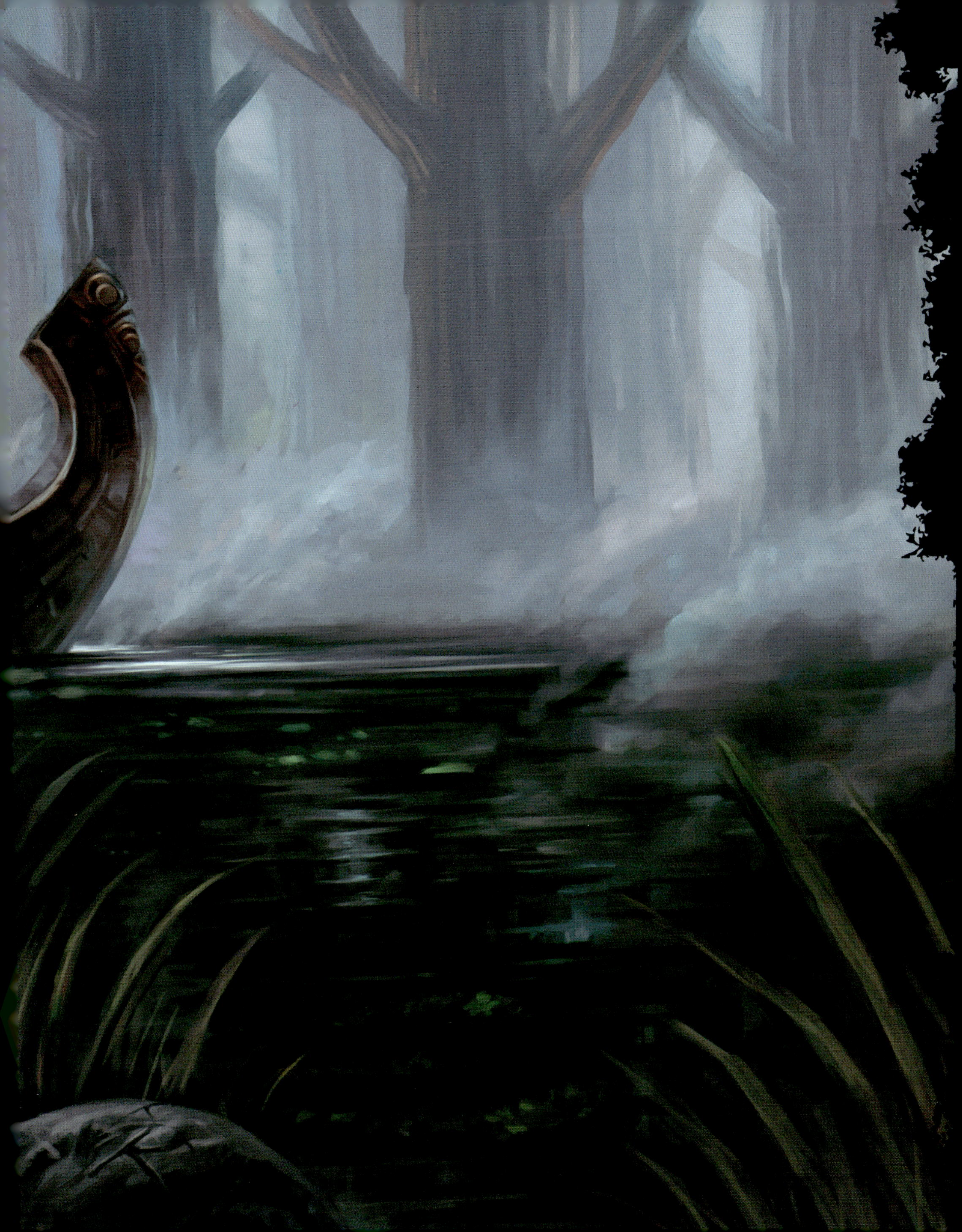

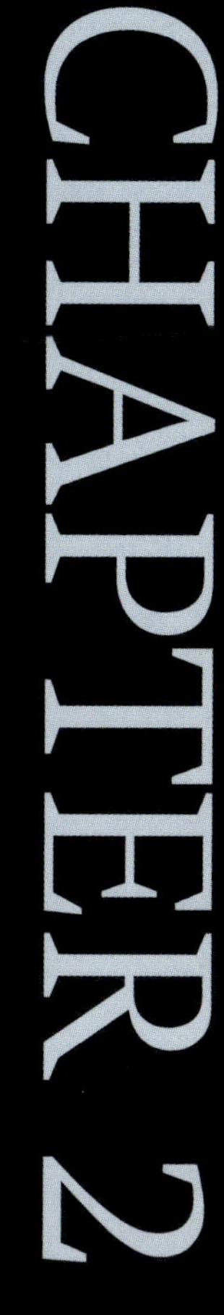

Go to Avalon
Xiao-chen Fu
Pencil, digitally painted
www.krishnafu.com

*A decidedly dreamlike piece, **Go to Avalon** was created in Corel Painter by the talented Xiao-chen Fu. "Avalon is a dream place with only one way to it: the ship manned by the god of death. A defeated shadow appears in the water. Although the dangers are hidden, nothing can stop you from venturing to Avalon, because you have a dream."*

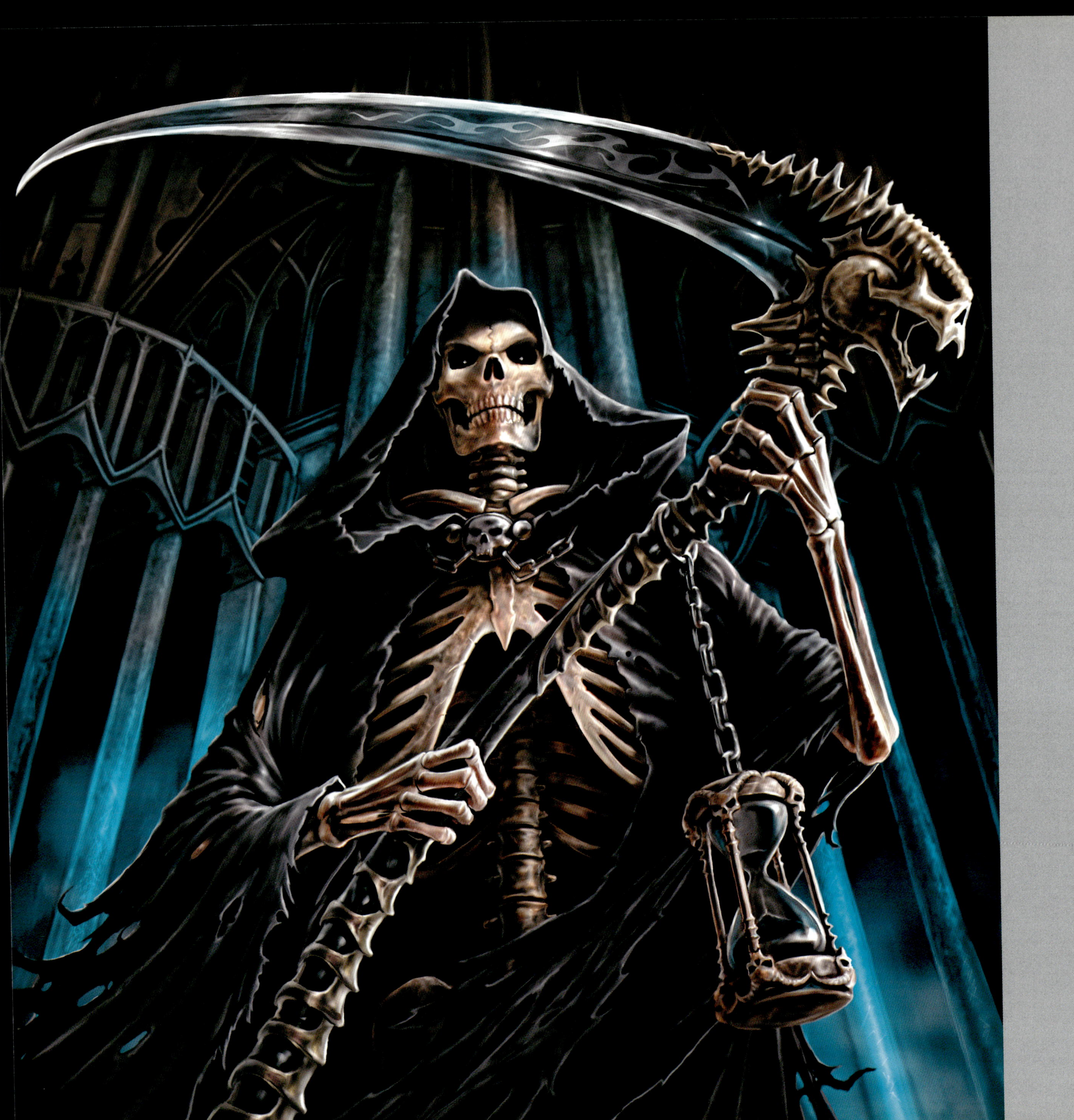

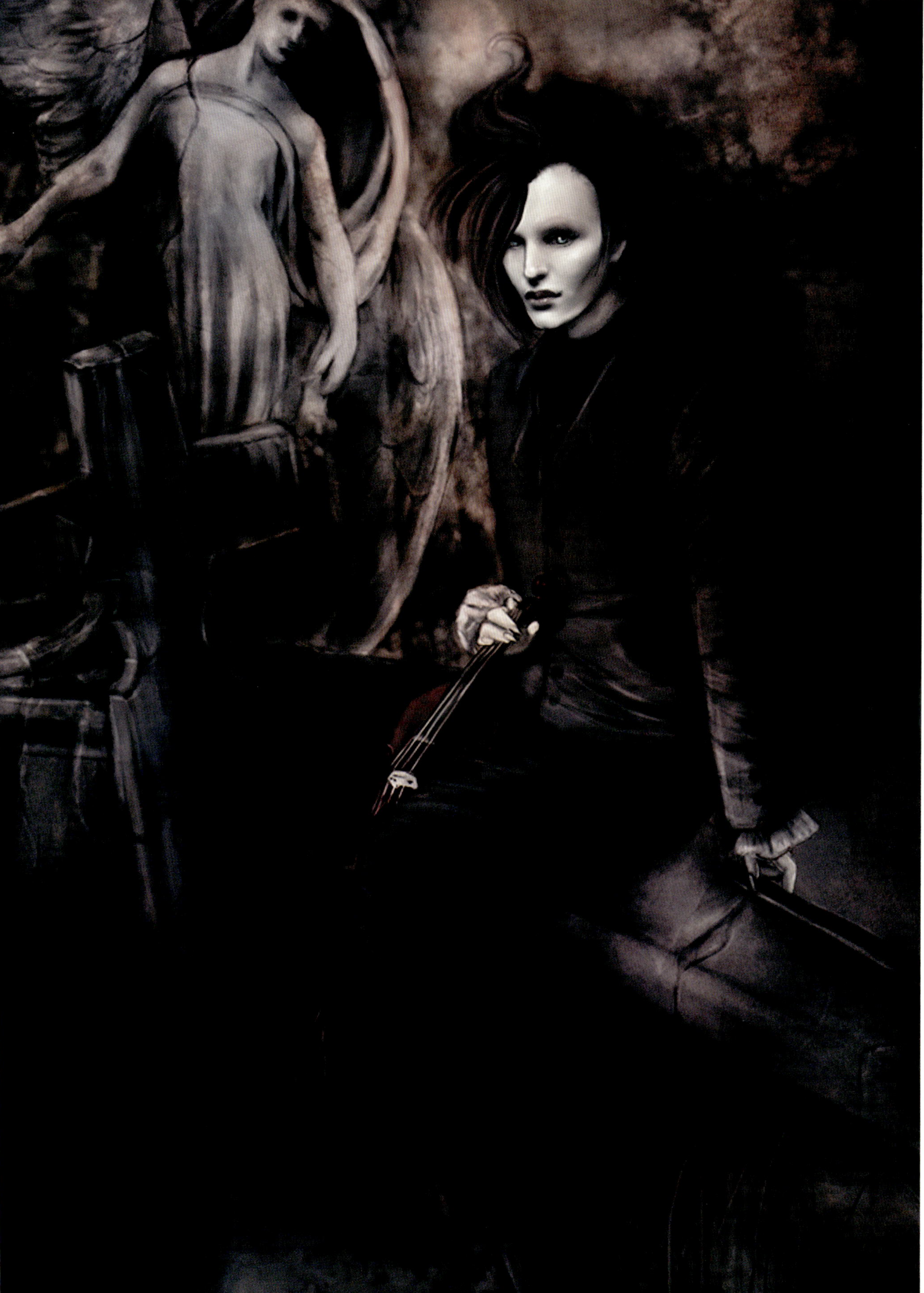

◀◀ **Lord of Time**
Anne Stokes
Digital painting
www.annestokes.com

A truly sinister, archetypal image—the Grim Reaper himself standing above the viewer (possibly his next victim?) "This image, painted in Adobe Photoshop, is a cover for Spiral's ***Dark Arts*** *calendar. A reaper is a good horror and time-related subject for this purpose. The details on the bone scythe and architecture add to the Gothic feel of the picture, and the viewpoint of looking up at the figure is designed to give an air of looming menace."*

◀ **In The Gaze of Angels**
Kimberly Myatt
Digital painting
www.beetlebones.net

An unabashedly Goth piece, with many Gothic elements: a dark-haired, pale-faced figure, cemetery imagery, and a lone violin. "This is an illustration of a character from one of my novels. I wanted the painting to be dark, luminating the vampire's skin. I used Adobe Photoshop to paint fine detail in black and white, and then painted the color beneath. I also used textures of stones and trees I had taken prior to this painting to give it a little extra punch."

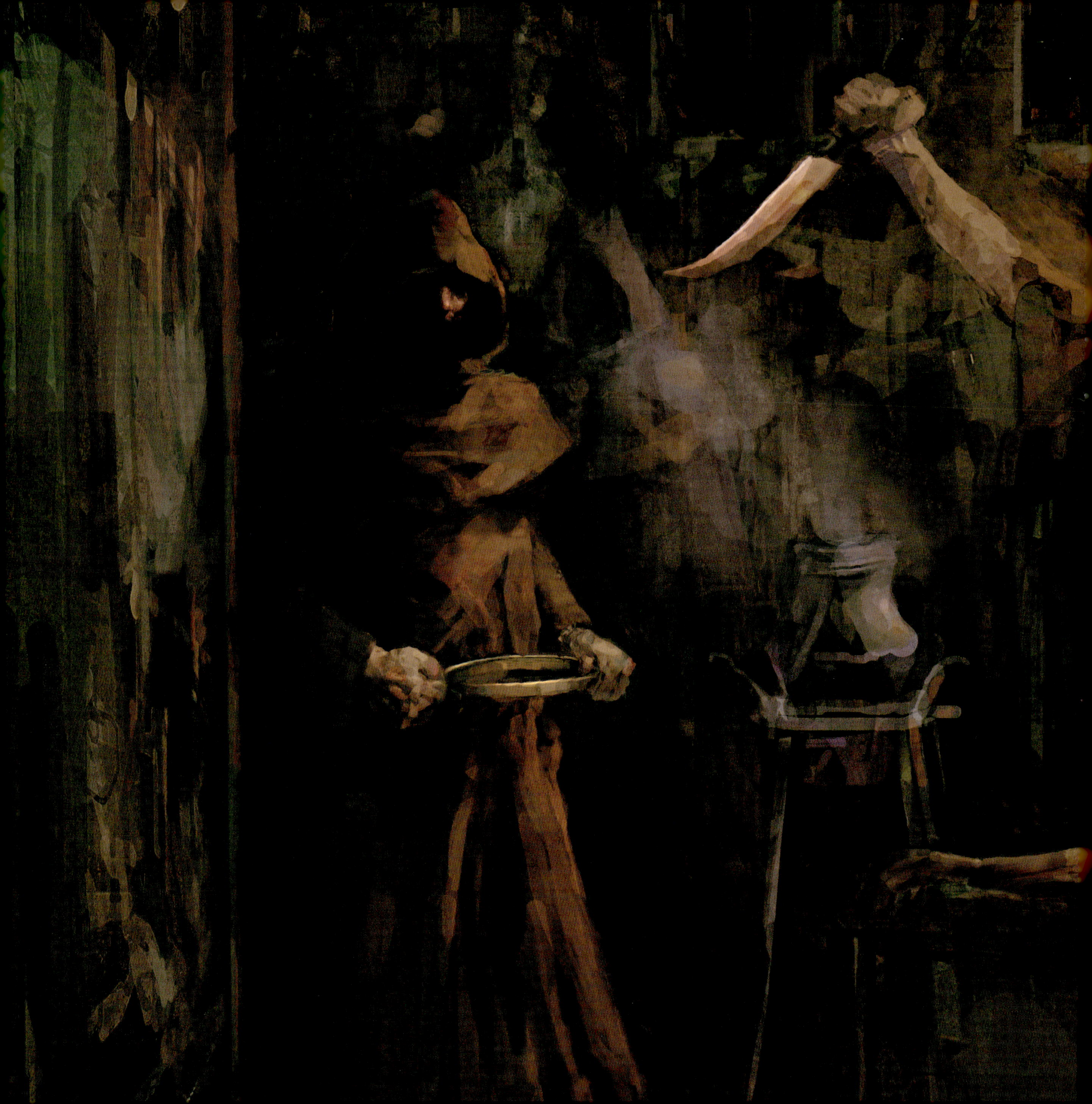

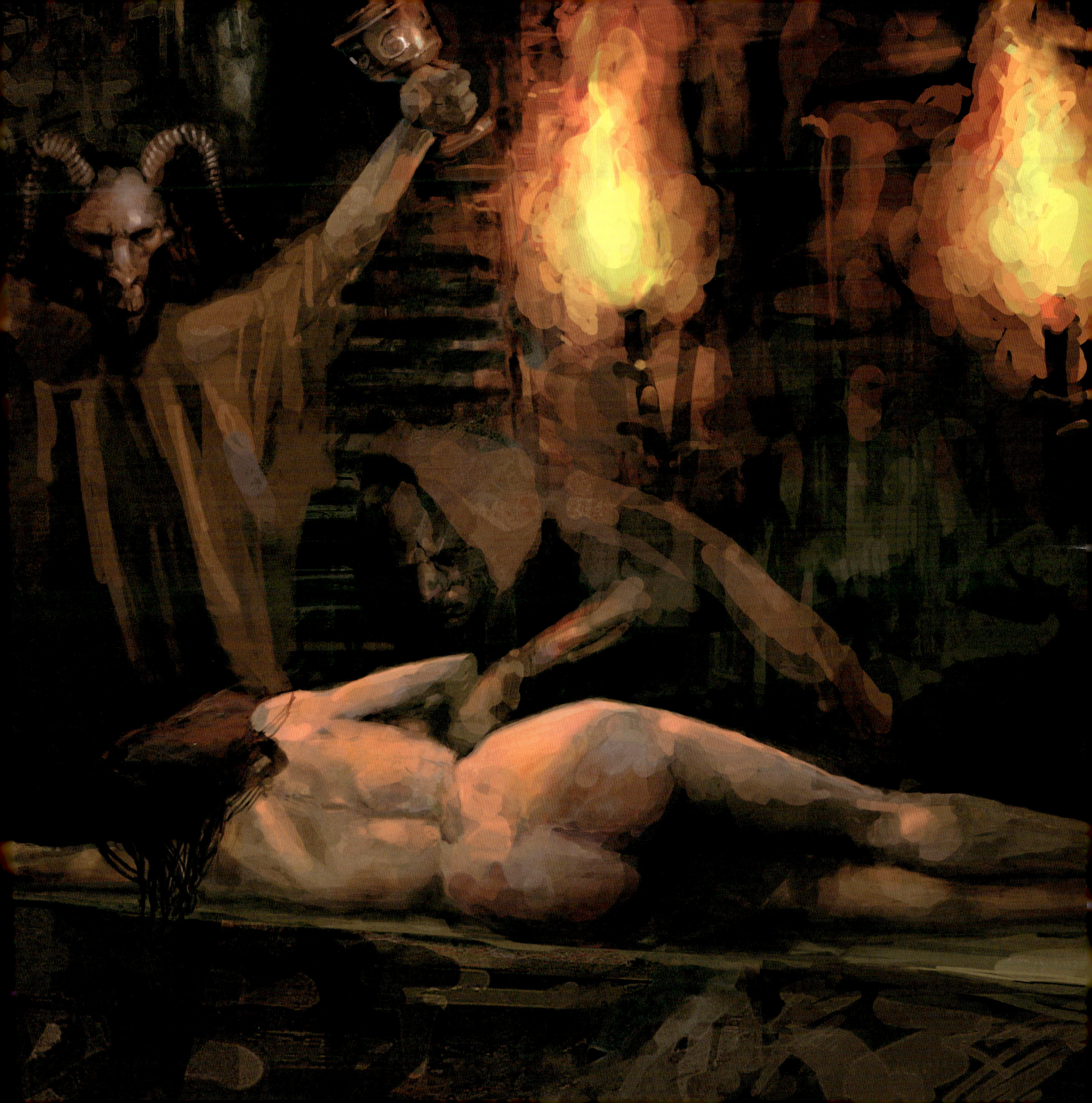

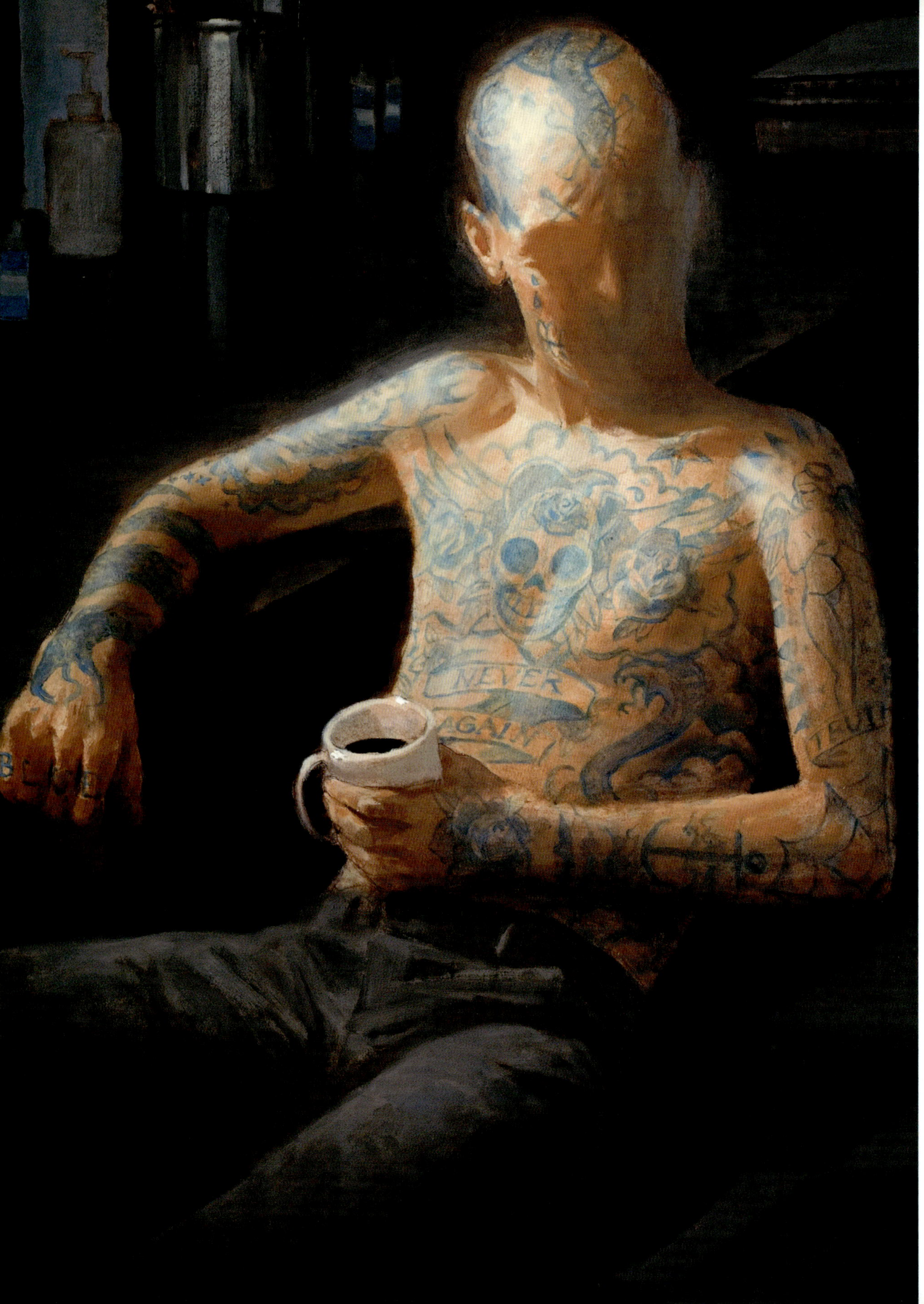

◄◄ **Sacrifice**
Kyri Koniotis
Digital painting
www.kyri.epilogue.net

A dramatic sacrificial scene painted digitally by Koniotis. "I have always been very influenced by Gothic and horror imagery, particularly by the films of directors like Jean Rollins, Amando Ossiorio, and Lucio Fulci, with hugely atmospheric scenes. I was also attracted to the work done for Warren in the '70s and '80s; magazines like ***Creepy****,* ***Eerie****, and* ***Vampirella****; with artists like Manuel Sanjulian, Enrich Torres, and Frank Frazetta."*

◄ **Blue Tattoo**
Chris Rahn
Oil on board
www.rahnart.com

Body modification is a mainstay of the Gothic subculture, and the man in the image has taken it to the extreme! Rahn explains: "For this piece, my only assignment was to paint blue."

► **Anguish**
George Patsouras
Digital painting
www.mkrevolution.net

A highly emotive piece, the anguish of the creature in the painting can truly be felt by the viewer. "I wanted this piece to be all about emotion. I chose a fairly dark, desaturated blue color palette to help convey the mood of this piece, combined with subtle rain. I wanted very dark and depressing vibes to represent anguish, and lots of time went into perfecting the creature's expression."

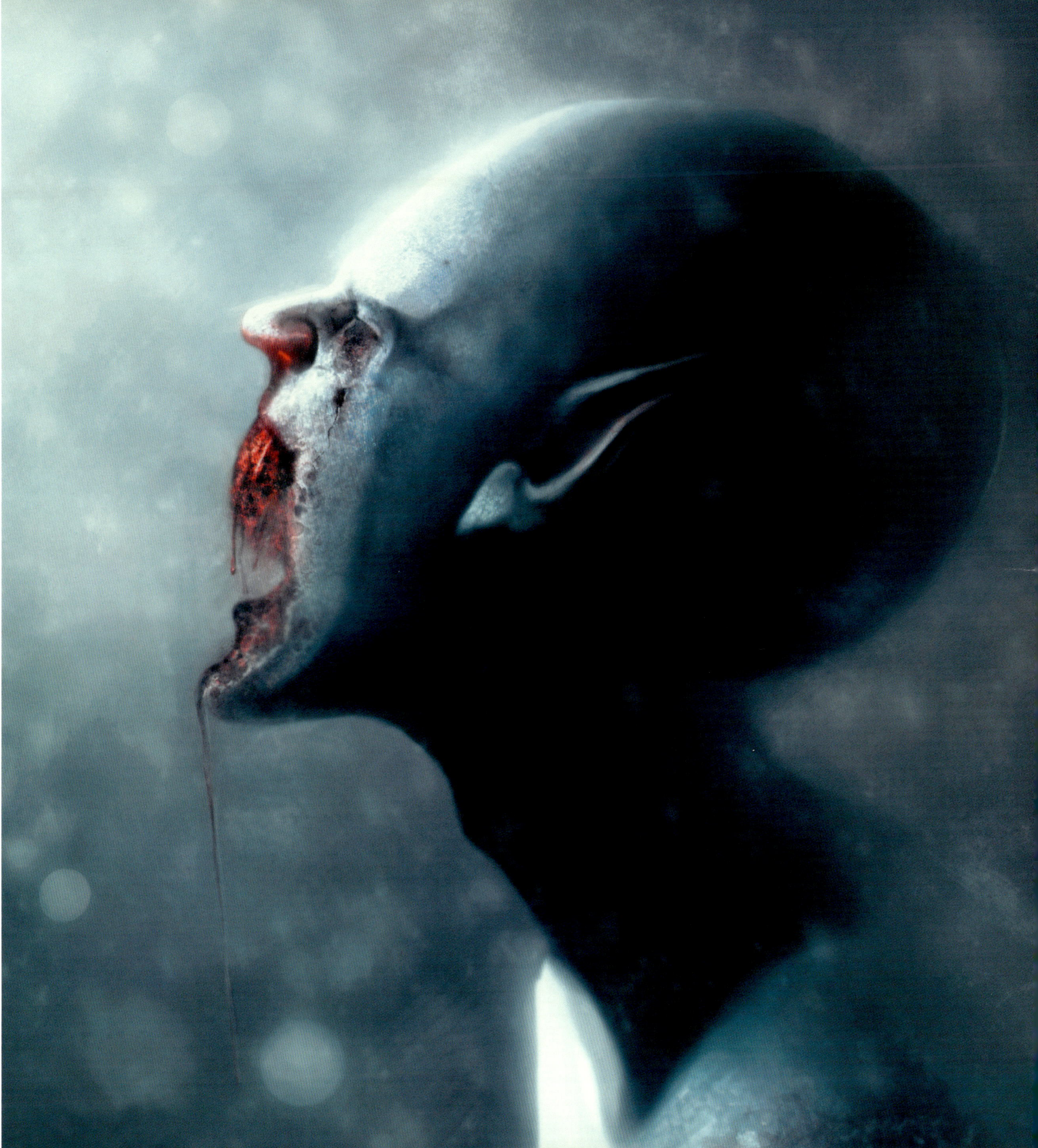

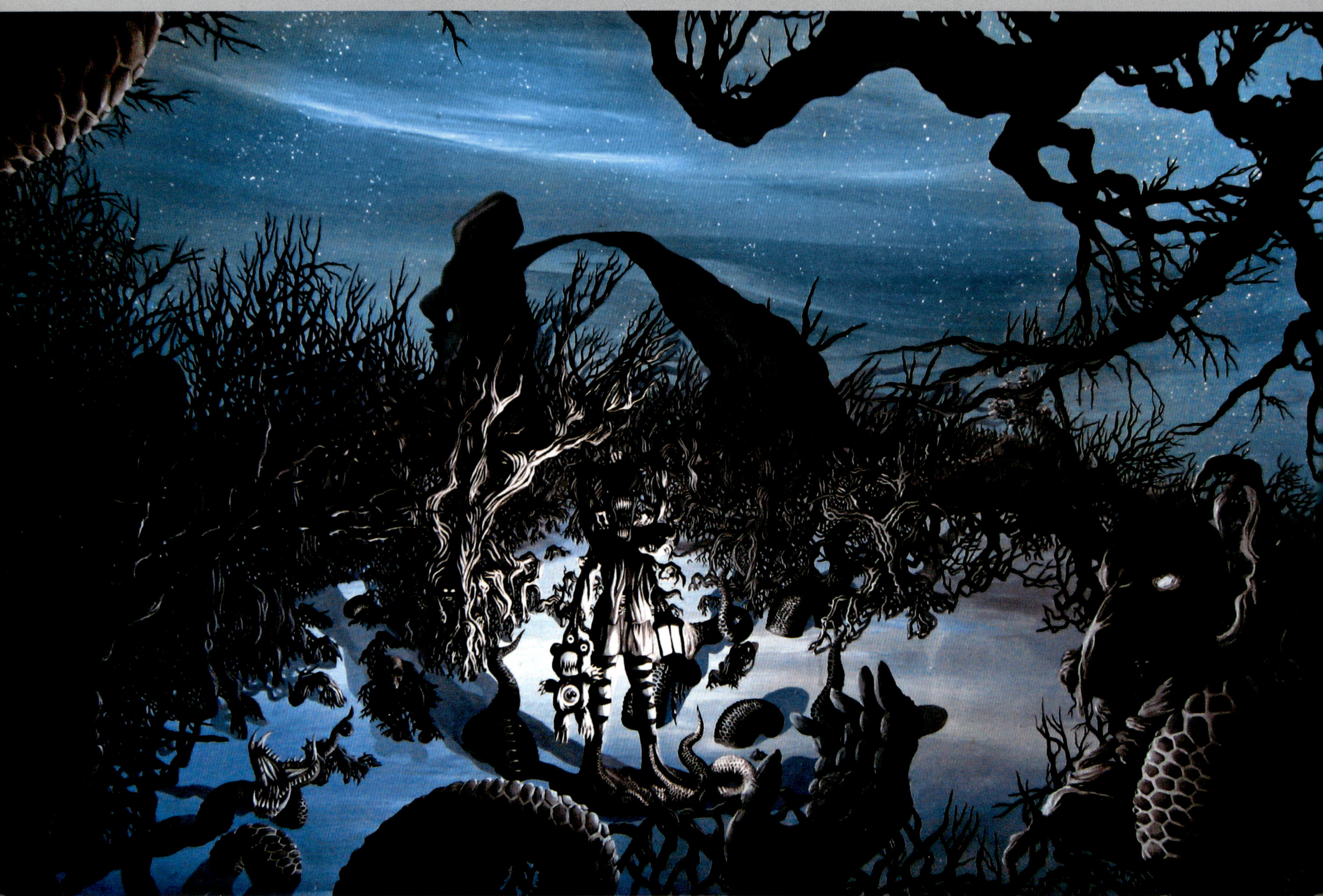

▲ **Hope (The Light at the End)**
Myke Amend
Acrylic on canvas
www.mykeamend.com

"This image is based on the concept behind the saying 'a light at the end of the tunnel,' or 'every cloud has a silver lining,' and was painted using acrylic on canvas. It includes a rather odd lure-fishing creature, and topsy-turvy surroundings with purposefully weird light and shadow effects to confuse the eye, to create an overall disturbing feel to the piece."

▶ **Talisman of Death**
Martin McKenna
Digital painting
www.martinmckenna.net

McKenna has created an ominous scene, both iconic and sinister. "The idea came from the text of the book, ***Talisman of Death****, which describes a black horse and hooded rider: 'A massive black stallion, its eyes pits of fire, snorting clouds of glowing cinders as it strains at the bit. Its rider, a dark spectral figure, is hunched and twisted.' I envisaged the horse rearing, almost in silhouette, against a full moon, the rider a Death-like figure with points of light for eyes. Tim Burton's* ***Sleepy Hollow****, and the Nazgul from* ***The Lord of The Rings*** *were the obvious references."*

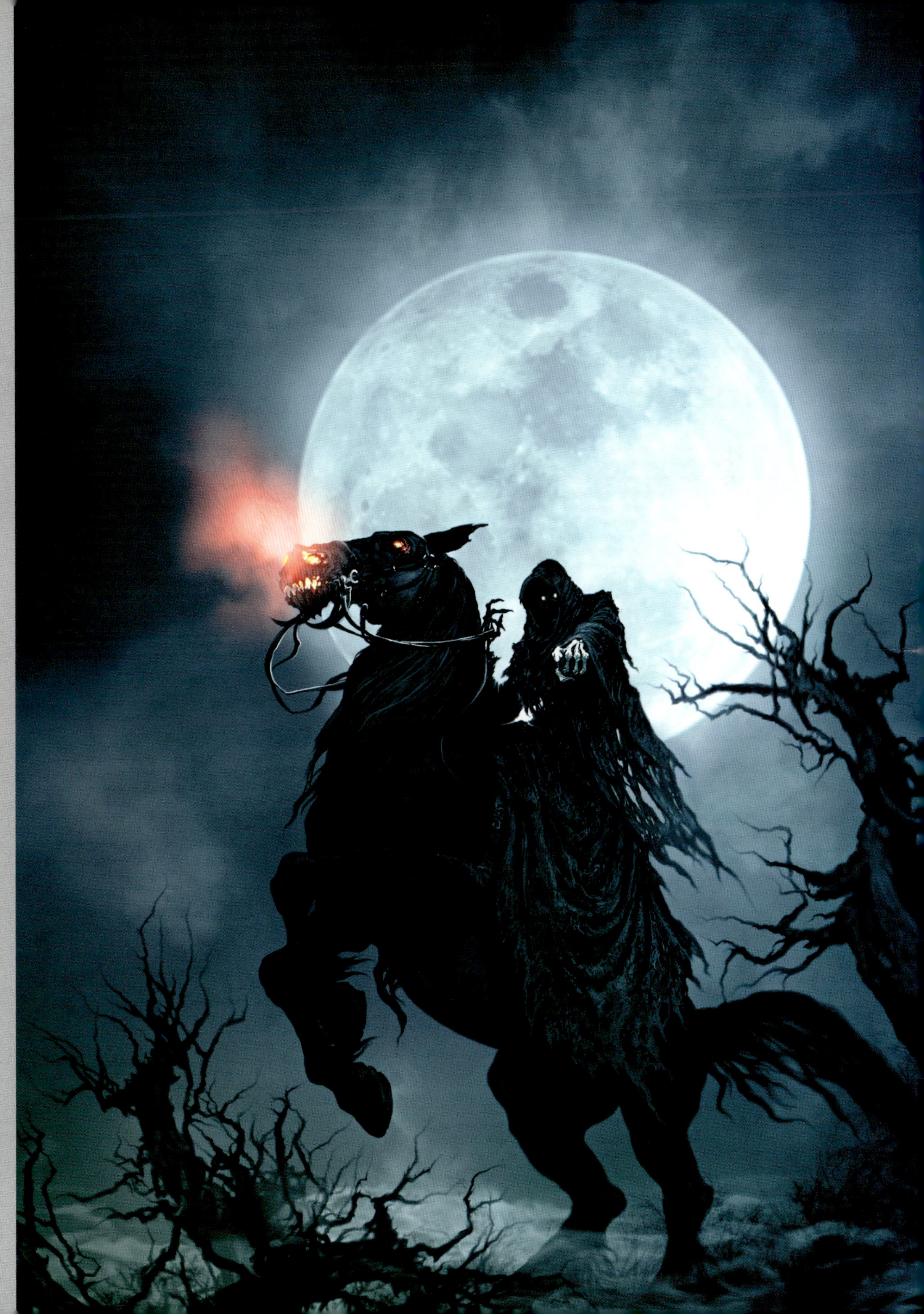

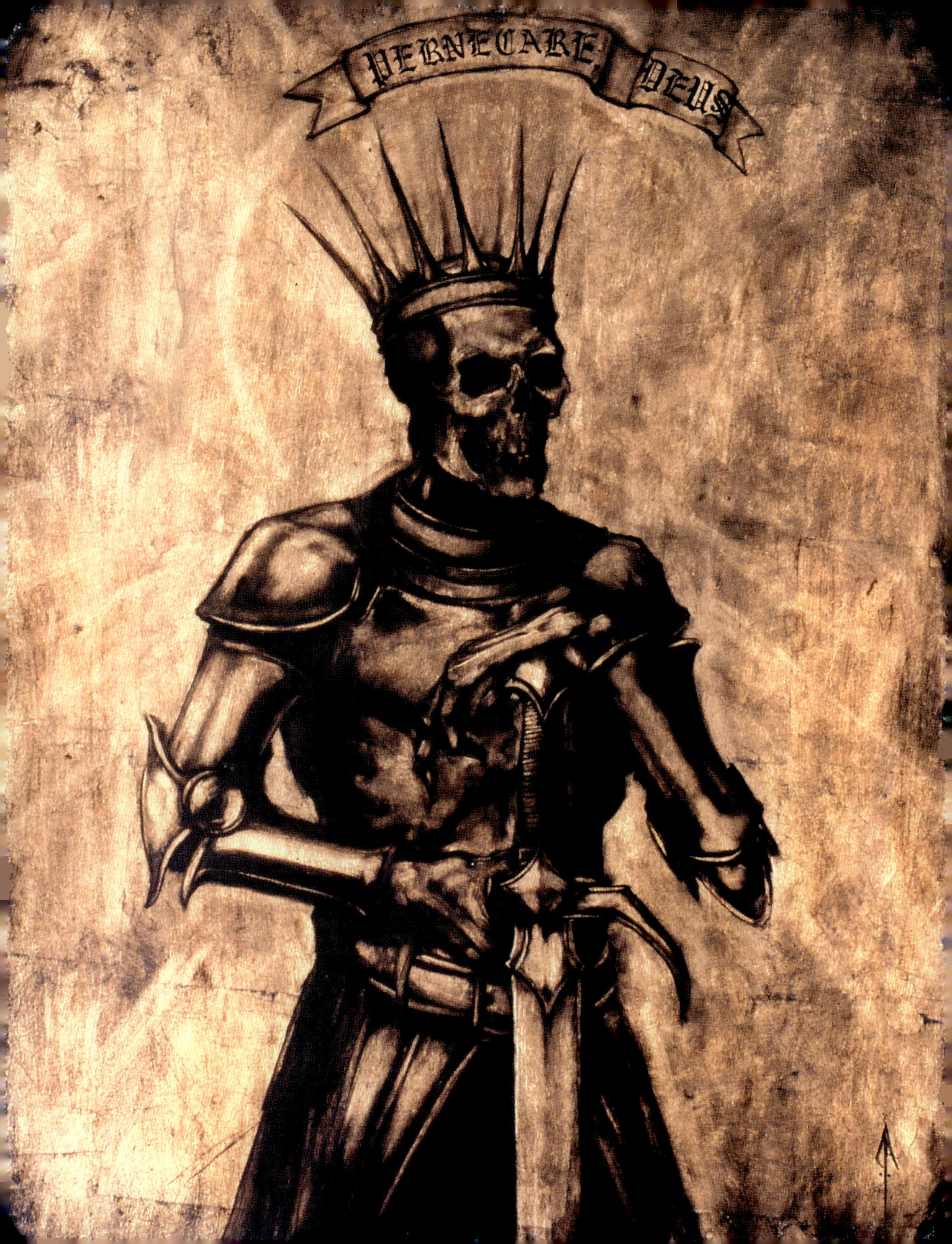
VERNECARE DEUS

◀ **Pernecare Deus**
John U. Abrahamson
Oil on gold-leafed paper
www.JohnUA.com

*"**Pernecare Deus**, translated from Latin means 'to kill God,' and is an expression of my lost faith. Deeply religious as a young adult and intimately involved in the services as an acolyte, my fall came after the tragic deaths of several friends in succession. The medium is oil paint on gold-leafed print paper. I painted the entire surface black and, with a wipe-away technique, I simply took away what was not the image I had in my head."*

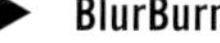

BlurBurn
Patrick Arrasmith
Essdee scraperboard
www.patrickarrasmith.com

*Arrasmith's striking image, **BlurBurn**, features a flame-headed man in the midst of an industrial wasteland. A meticulous work in the medium of scraperboard, Arrasmith has hand-etched this piece out of the blackness, revealing the fine white surfaces below. "This comes from a story I've been hoping to write. The main character is being confronted with a terrible situation that's out of his control."*

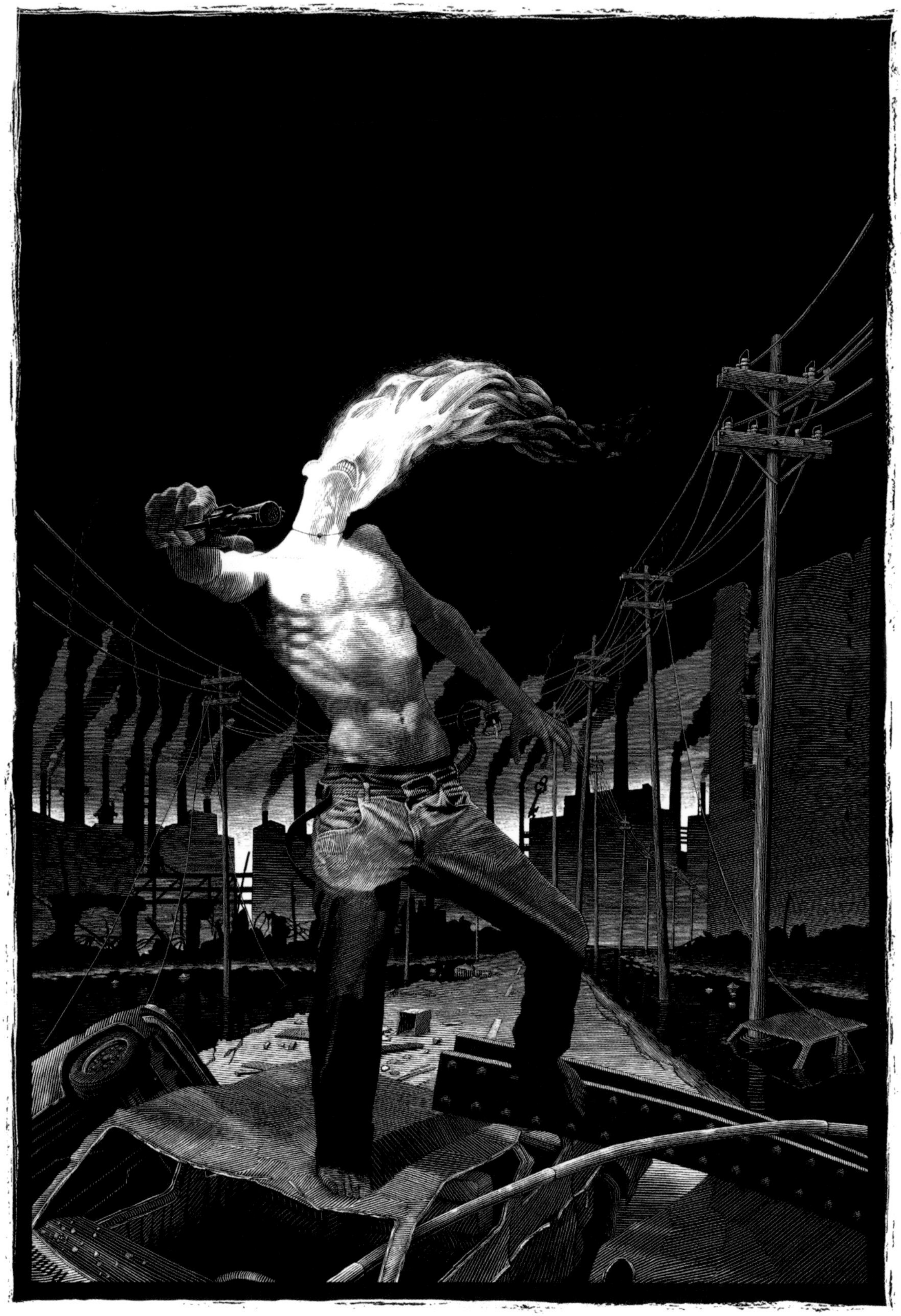

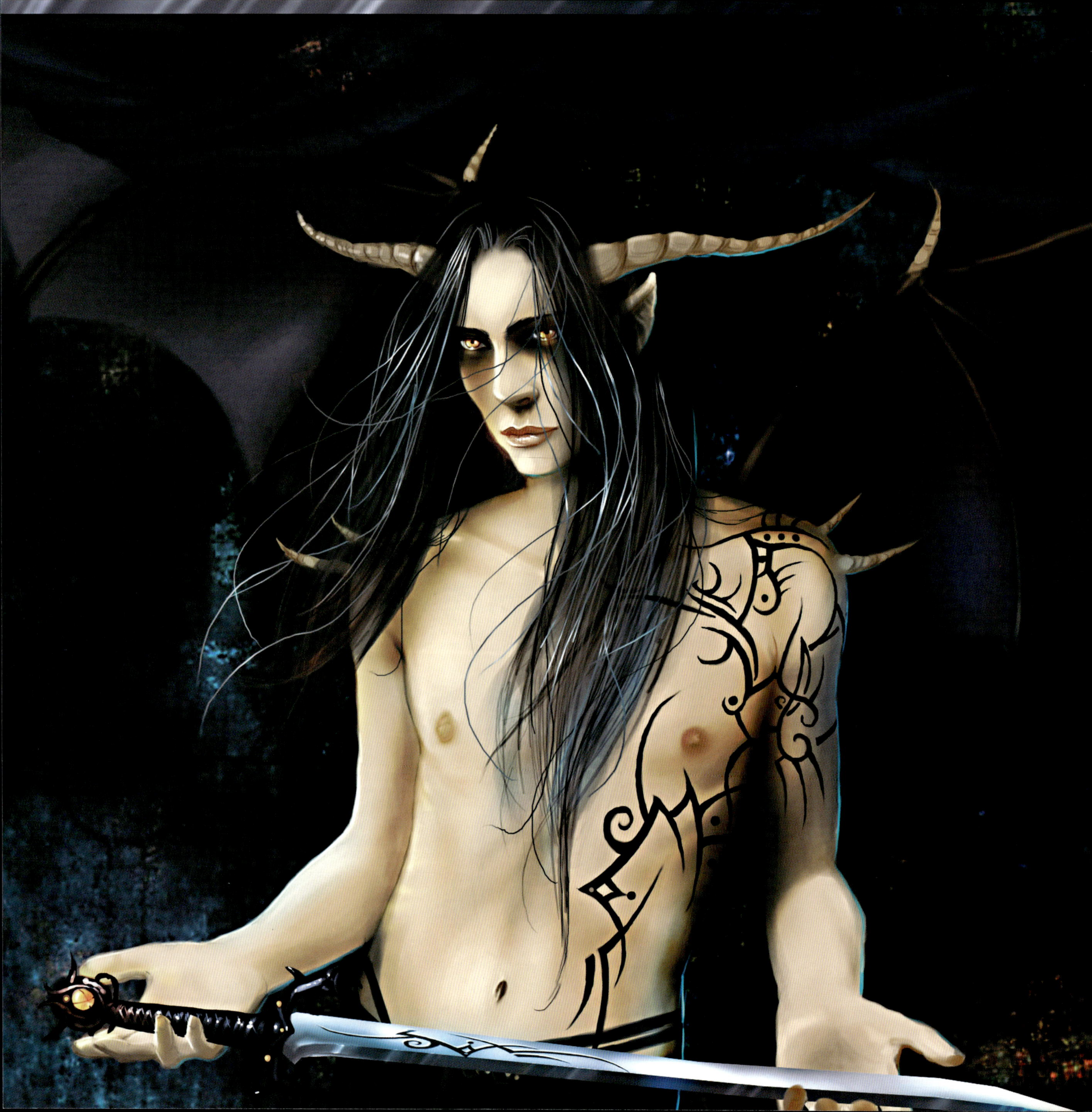

◀ **Meraphis**
Ulrike Kleinert
Digital painting
www.dreamaddiction.de

A winged male creature named ***Meraphis*** *by Kleinert, painted in Adobe Photoshop with a Wacom Graphics Tablet. "I drew this from scratch in Photoshop, using a collage of reference photos. I blocked in the shapes and some basic shading on a new layer, starting with the main figure of the demon, and added background colors and details later. The hair was last because I wanted it to flow over his body and give the whole picture a somewhat airy feeling despite the static pose."*

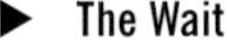
The Wait
Myke Amend
Acrylic on canvas
www.mykeamend.com

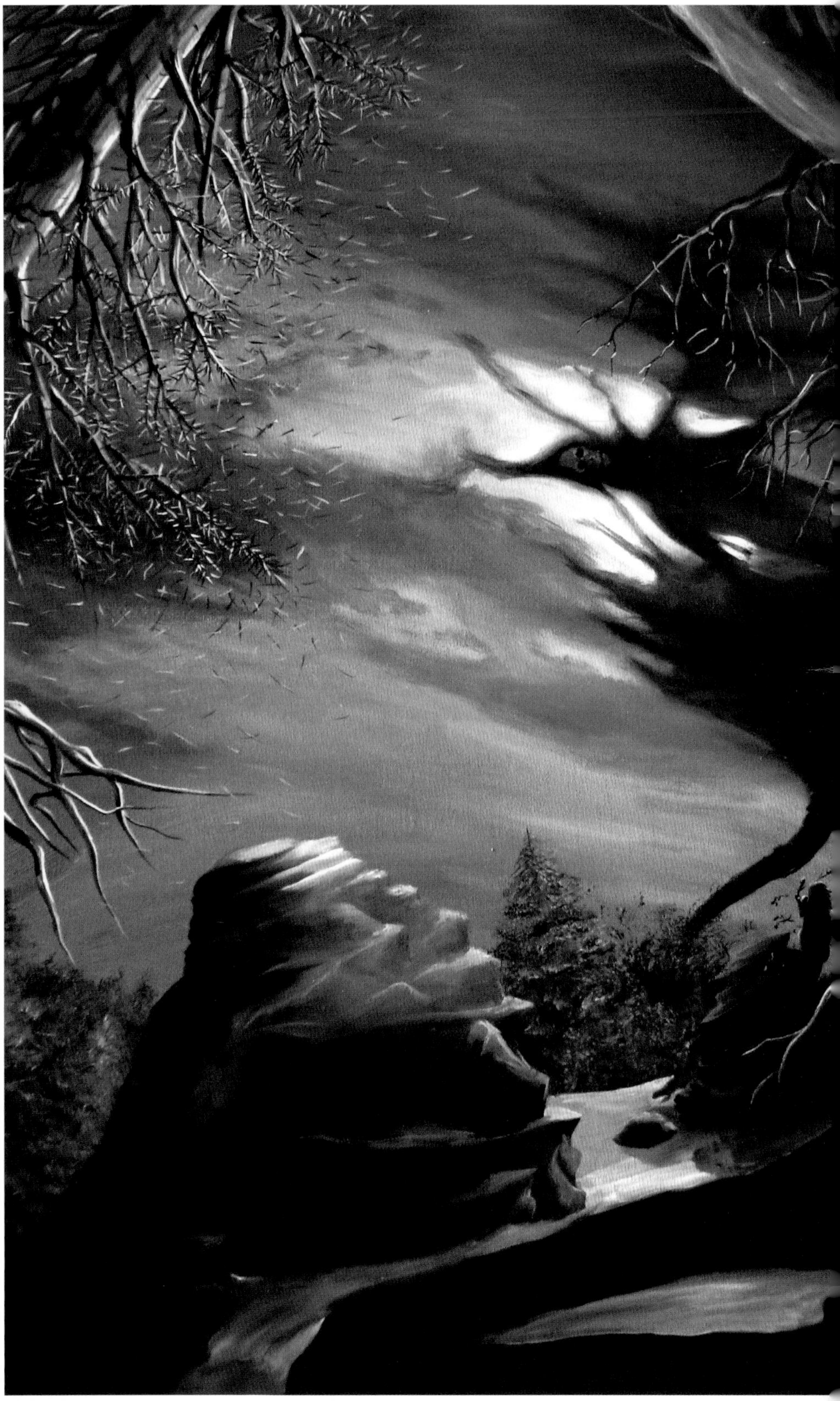

"I prefer to work with an odd mix of the serene and chaotic. I would say that if anything defines my style, this would be the one binding factor in all the mediums I work with. This piece, an acrylic painting, is no exception to the rule. It is a symbol of a mourning person, waiting patiently for death to come, inspired by its awesome presence."

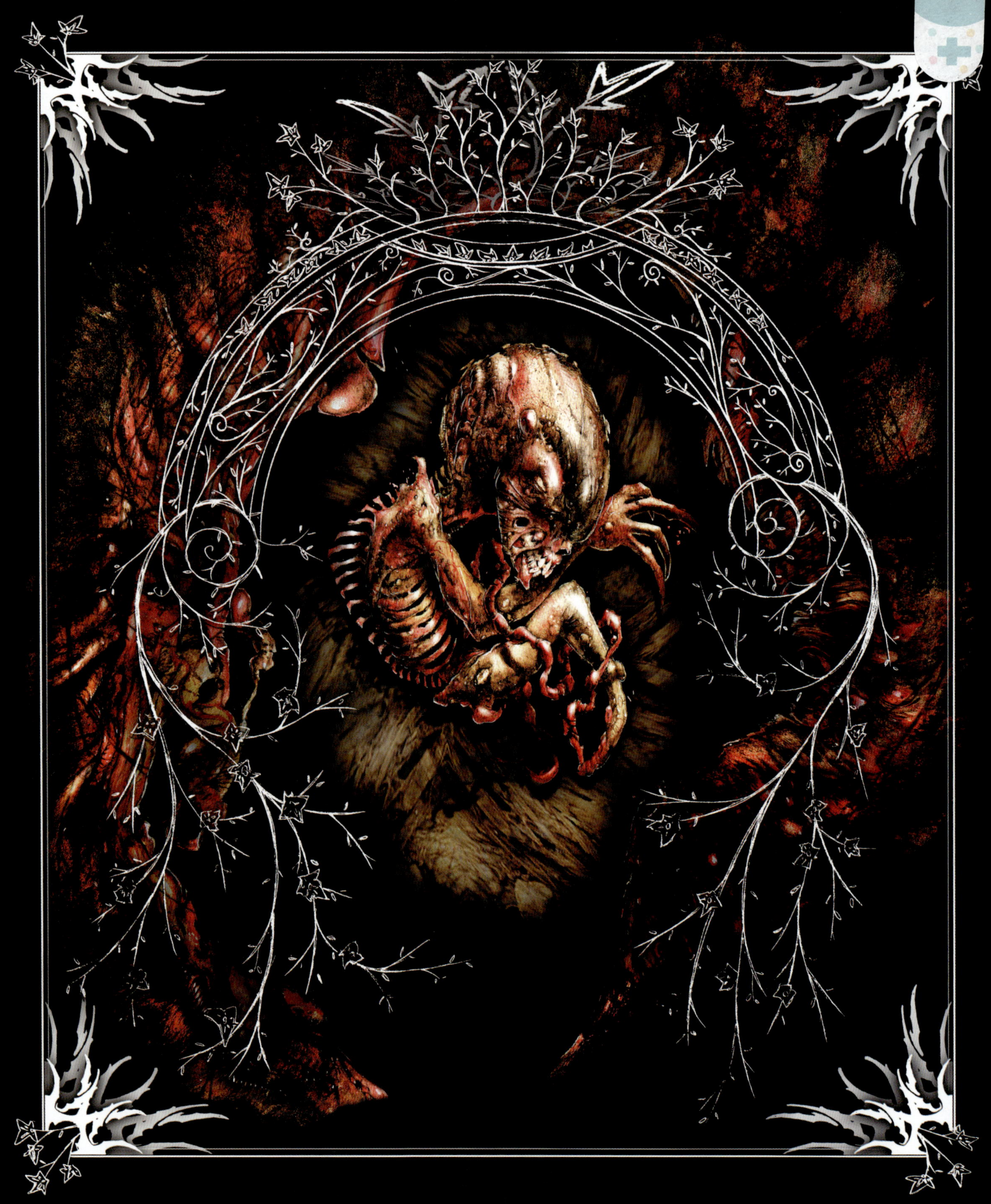

◀ **Ascension Study**
Kevin Crossley
Mixed media
www.kevcrossley.com

A disconcertingly alien-looking fetus from Crossley. The rich gore-soaked textures are well-balanced by the delicate design of the overlaid details. "This began life as an old watercolor painting, and was scanned into Adobe Photoshop along with a few pencil line doodles that I turned white and overlaid. I wanted to update the piece, but not lose any of the original watercolor texture, so any digital painting was kept to a minimum. It's a bit of a hybrid and makes me feel uncomfortable… but I'm not sure why."

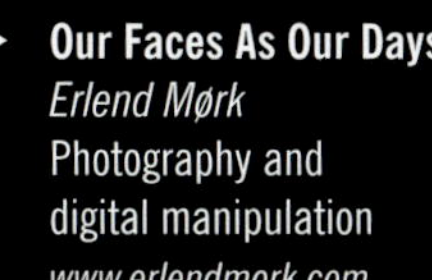

▶ **Our Faces As Our Days**
Erlend Mørk
Photography and digital manipulation
www.erlendmork.com

An infernal musical trio, Mørk's ***Our Faces As Our Days*** *features three attenuated, cadaver-like beings, seemingly enraptured with their music. Mørk constructed this picture "from many individual photographs, assembled using Adobe Photoshop."*

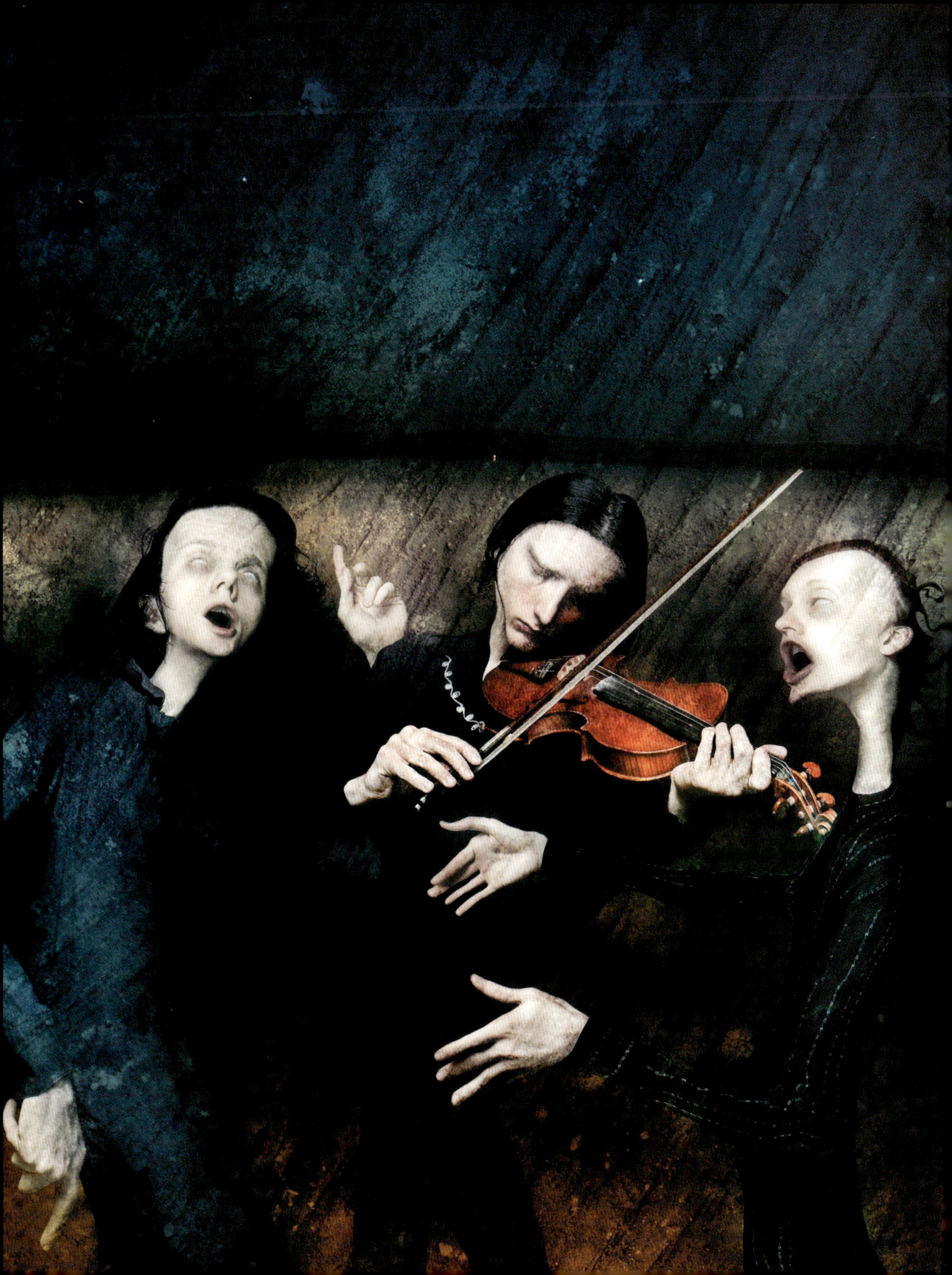

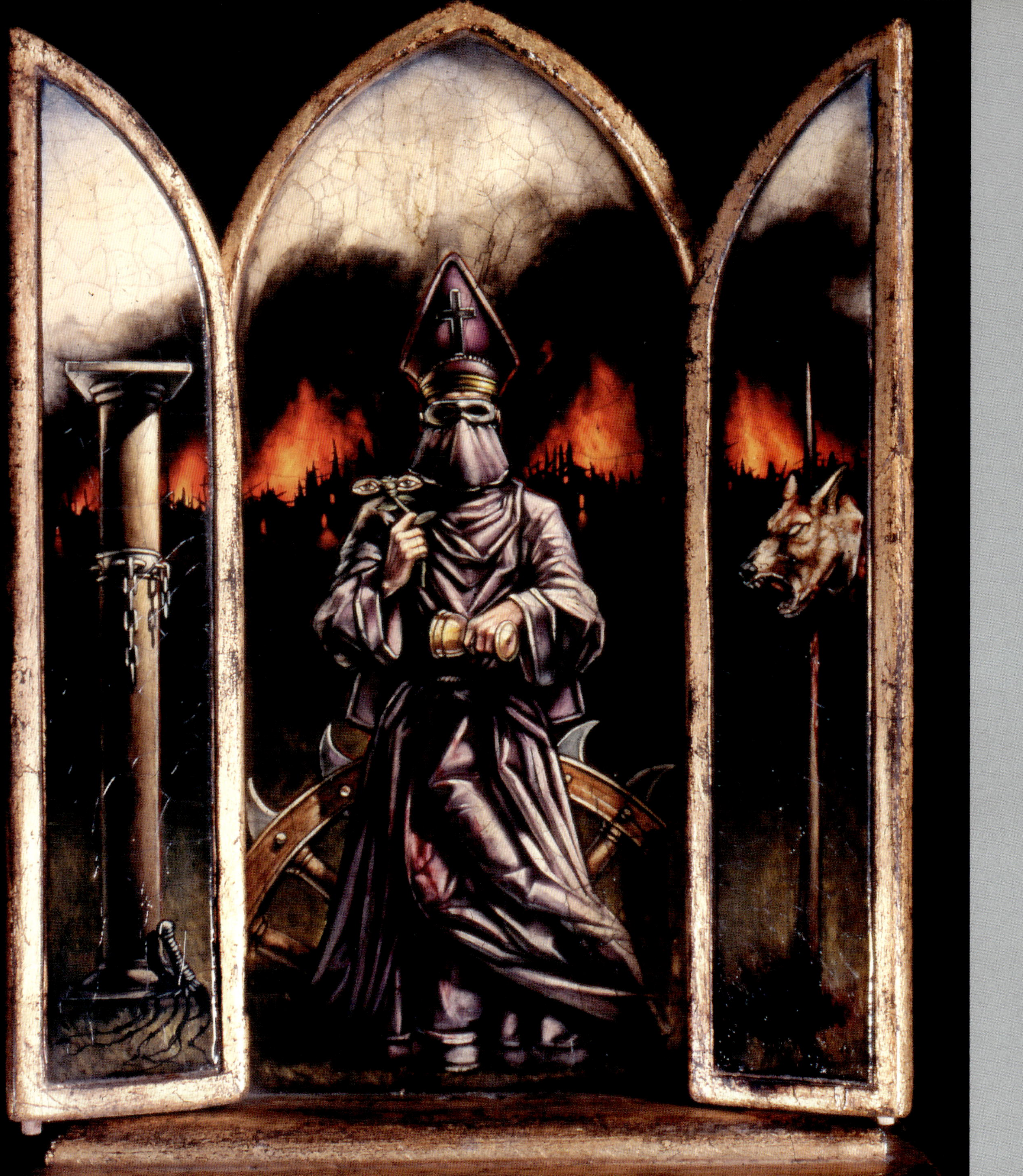

◀ **Vates**
John U. Abrahamson
Oil on gold-leafed wood panel
www.JohnUA.com

*An icon-like folding triptych from Abrahamson. The style of panel and medium used (oil on wood) is evocative of religious altarpieces of centuries past. Various religious elements as well as instruments of torture (such as the spiked wheel, cat of nine tails, and impaling spear) are backlit by hellish flames. "**Vates**, translated from Latin means 'Prophets.' The icon was a self-portrait."*

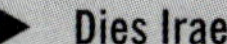

▶ **Dies Irae**
John U. Abrahamson
Oil on gold-leafed wood panel
www.JohnUA.com

*Abrahamson paints his nightmarish visions in traditional oil paints on wooden panels. "**Dies Irae**, translated from Latin, meaning 'Day of Wrath,' was painted in reaction to the horrible massacre at the Columbine High School. The incomprehensible acts of the two murderers cut into all of us. I gave that pain a voice."*

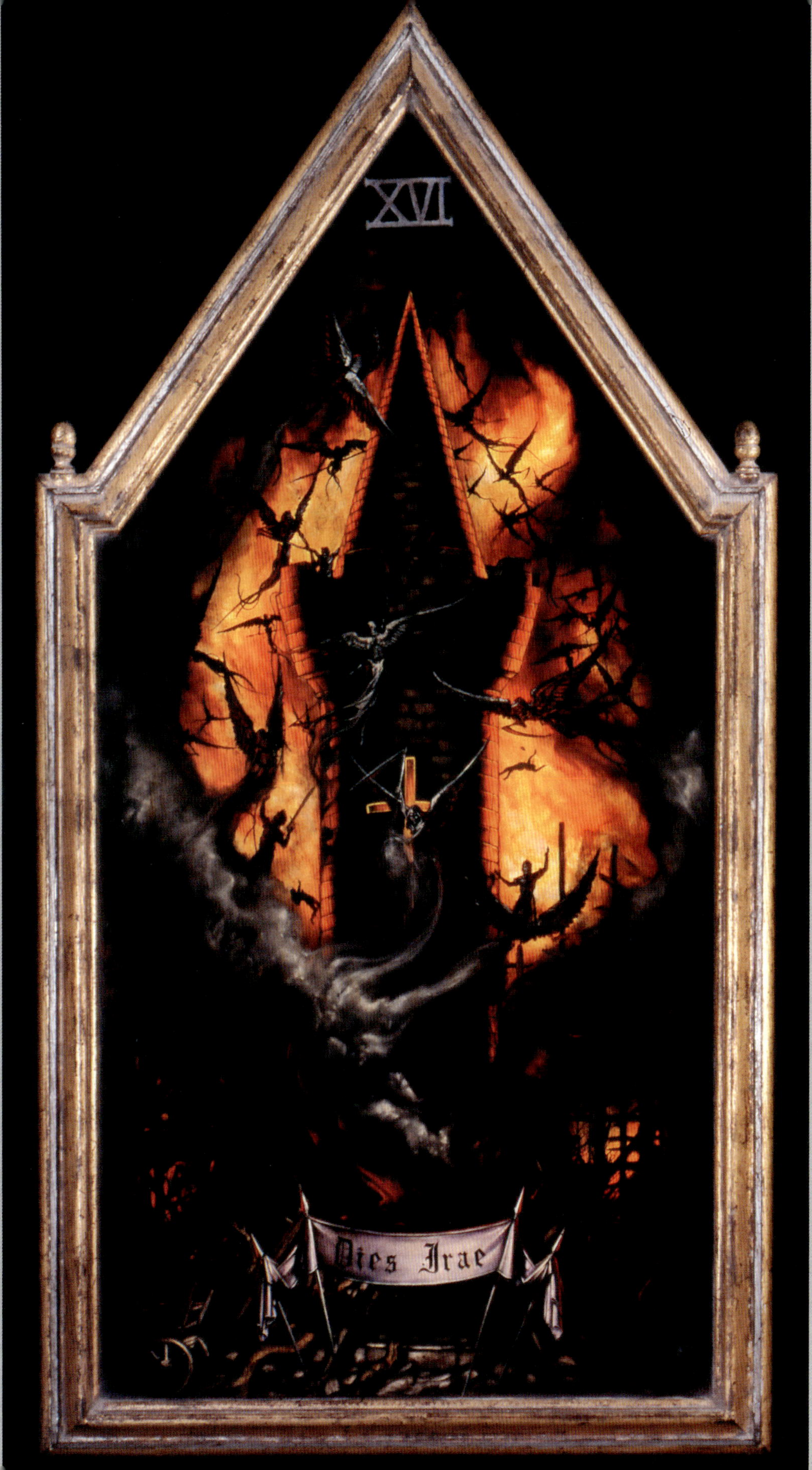

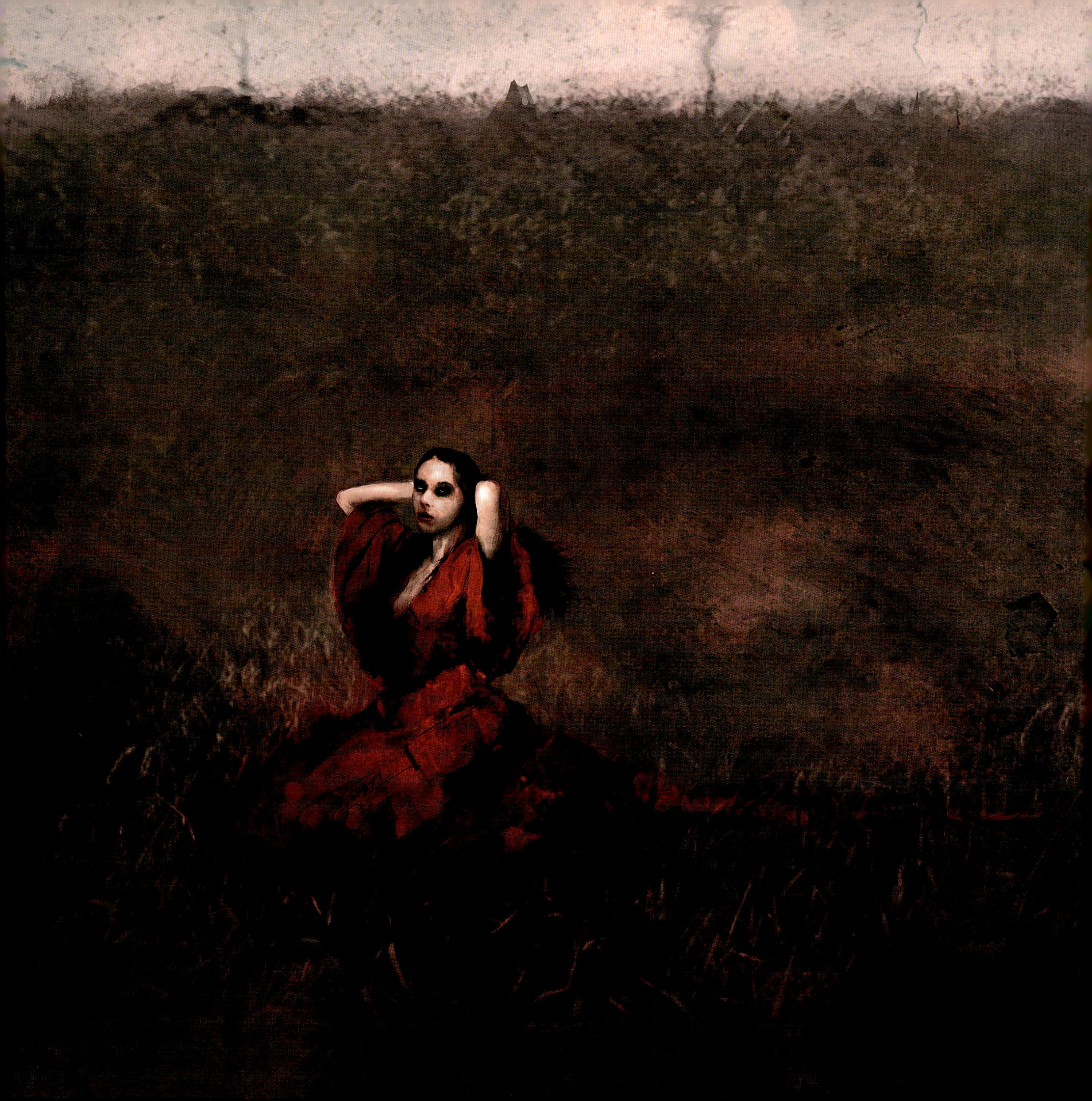

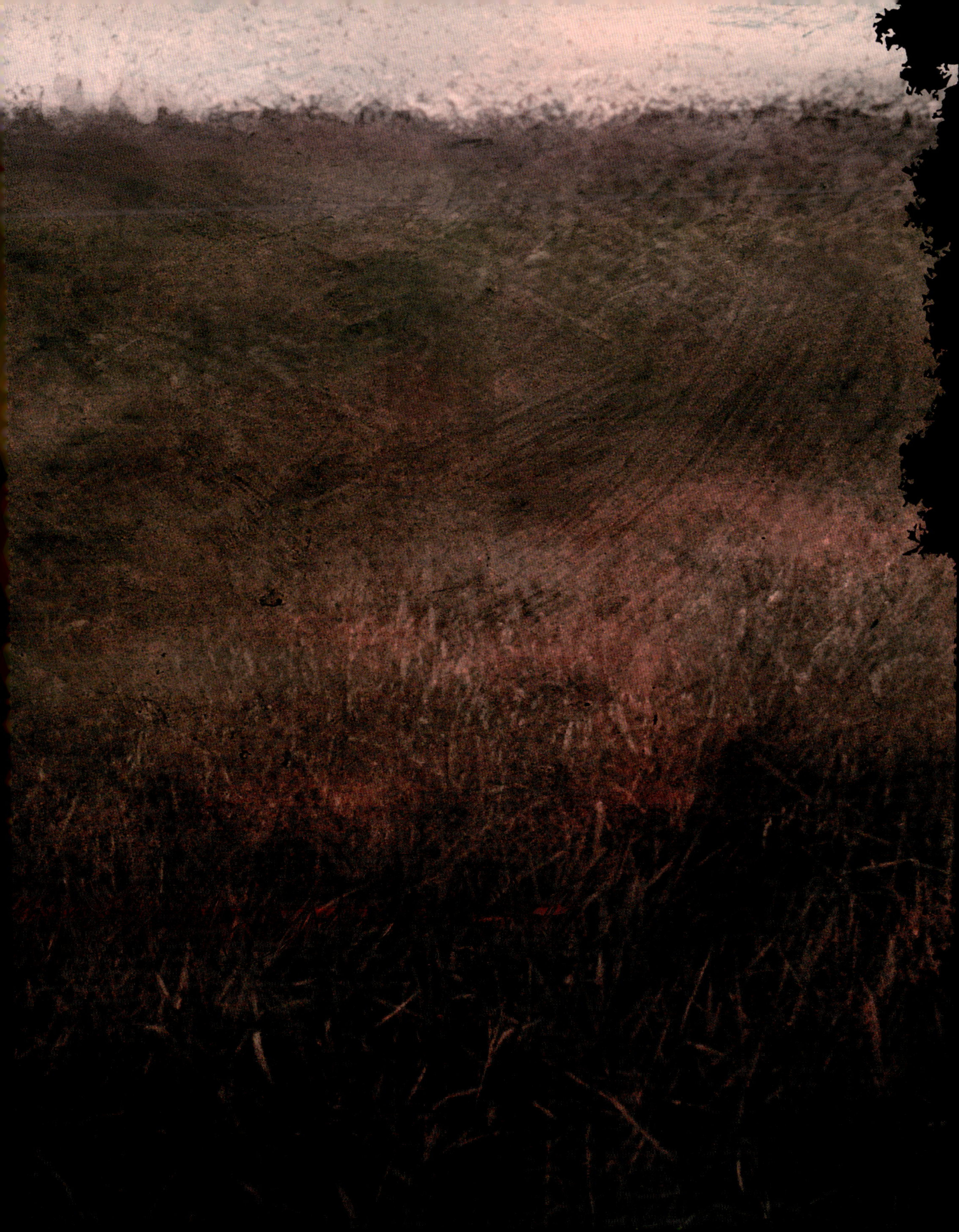

CHAPTER 3

GOTHIC ELEGANCE

◄ **Rapacious**
Samuel Araya
Mixed media
www.samael.epilogue.net

The pale, red-clad figure in Araya's painting stands out against the muted background with striking effect. "I started with an acrylic underpainting, added photographic elements, and painted over the composition using Adobe Photoshop. It's a small tribute to Baudelaire, and his poem ***The Fountain of Blood****, and is featured in the CD booklet of the band* ***Saboath****."*

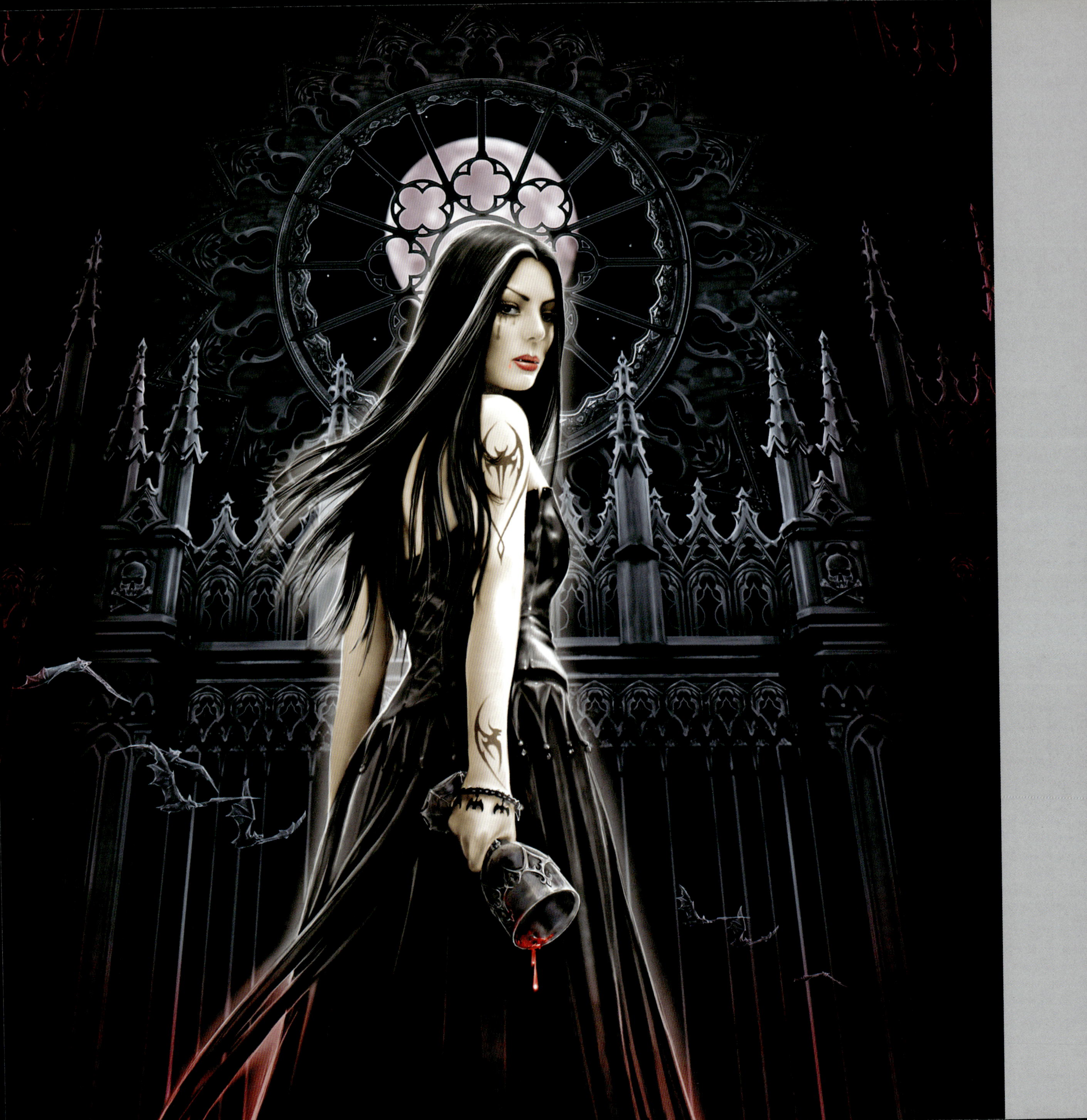

◀ **Gothic Siren**
Anne Stokes
Digital painting
www.annestokes.com

"This image was painted digitally using Adobe Photoshop for Reinders Posters. The piece incorporates classic Gothic imagery. The vampire girl hopefully prompts the viewer to think about what might have happened before the scene. A faint trickle of blood from her mouth, and the empty cup, combined with signs of tears in her smudged mascara, might indicate strife between her need as a vampire to drink blood, but her remorse at having to do so. The window frames her head in a play on the religious imagery of a halo."

▶ **Apsara**
Patrick Arrasmith
Essdee scraperboard
www.patrickarrasmith.com

An intricate scratchboard etching by Arrasmith, ***Apsara*** *is a study of darkness and light. "This piece started as a small figure study and portrait, but was developed with the background on a larger scale after I went to Cambodia and saw the temples of Angkor Wat. The sculptures of the celestial dancers that adorn the temples were the inspiration behind the piece."*

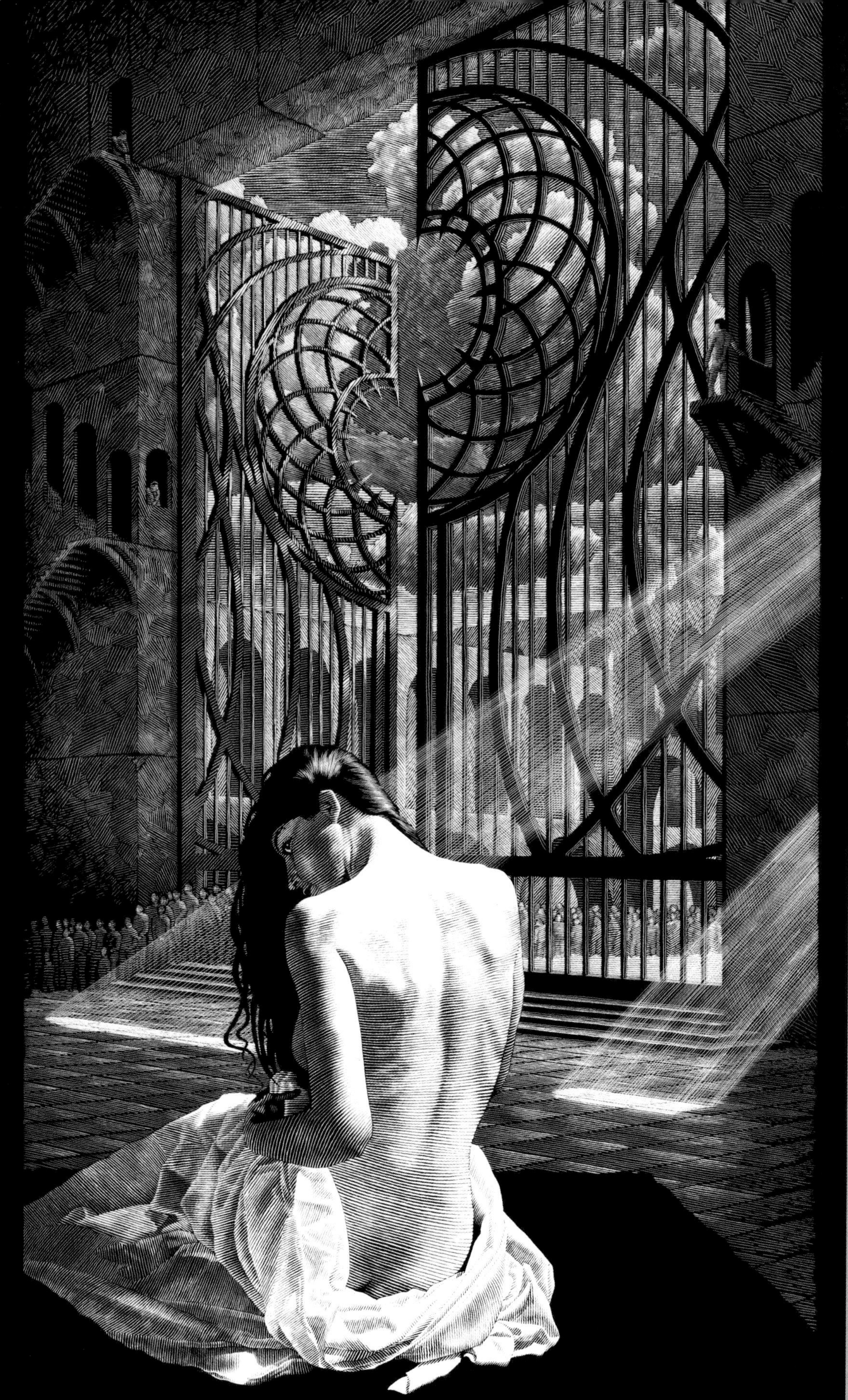

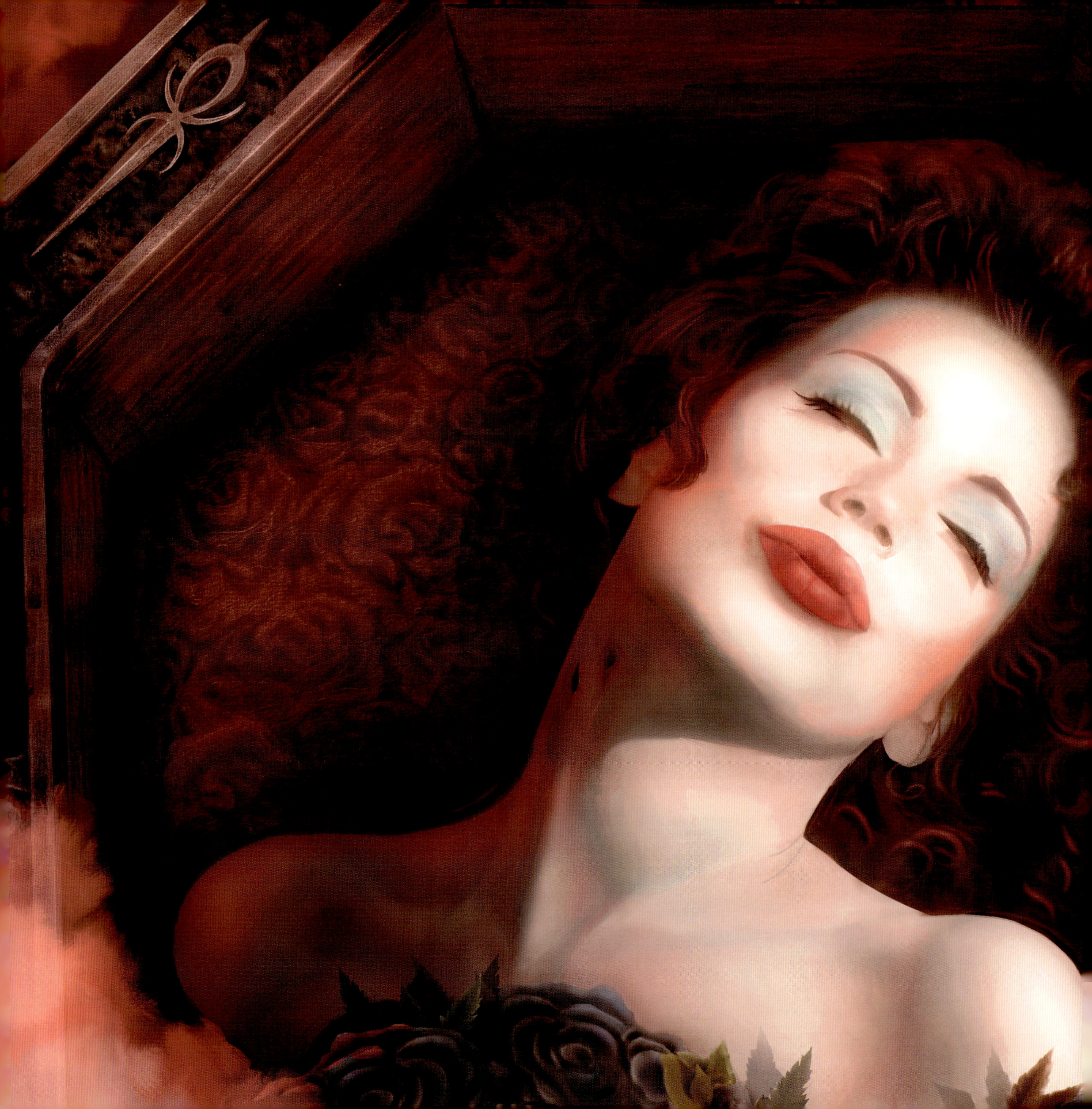

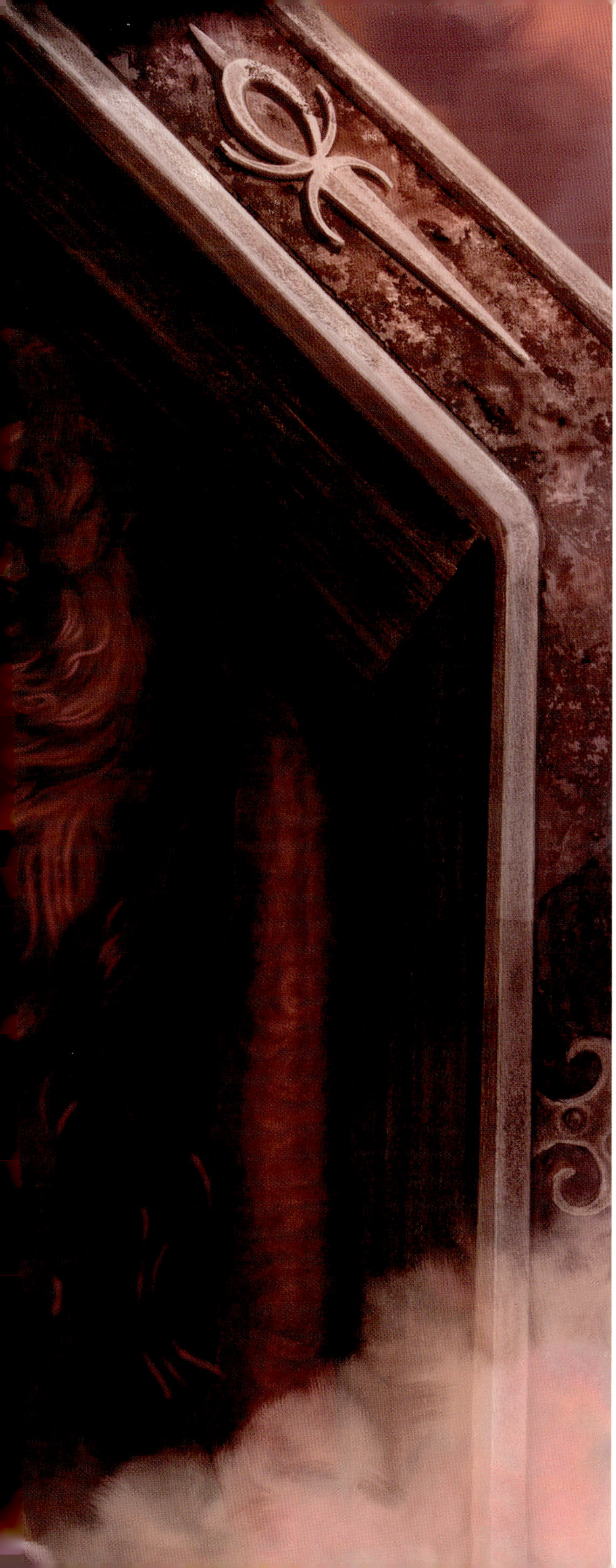

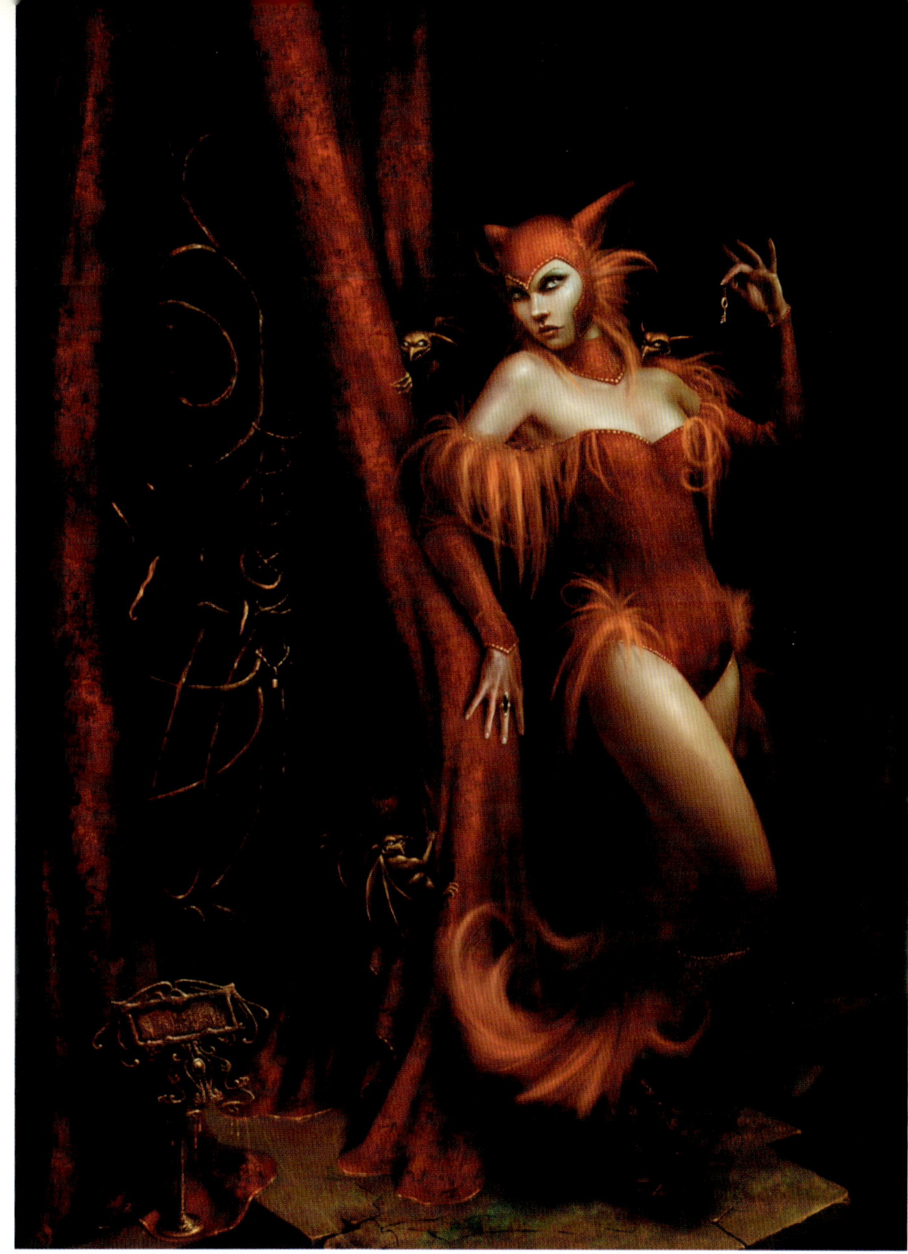

◀ **Black Roses and Bite Marks**
Tom Lavelle
Pencil, digitally painted
www. portalrun.epilogue.net

A vampiric vixen from Lavelle. "I was trying to portray the birth of a vampire. I wanted the character to appear like a dark angel entering a euphoric state, set in a dreamlike atmosphere. This started as a pencil study on Bristol board, using a photo of a model for reference, and was then painted using Adobe Photoshop."

▲ **Jadefox**
Benita Winckler
Digital painting
www.eeanee.com

*A seductive image of a sly female, digitally painted using Adobe Photoshop. "**Jadefox** is one of my shaman characters, in her human form, with jade-green eyes and the weightless step of a fox. I envisioned her in an old place underground, with endless corridors; the walls veiled in red cloth, hiding the edges of the abyss.*

▶ **Twofold**
Leslie Ann O'Dell
Photography and digital manipulation
www.shyble.com

A disturbing yet beautiful concept piece, combining photography, digital painting, and scanned roots and weeds. ***Twofold*** *shows duality with a corrupted aesthetic. "The concept for this piece is the duality of light and darkness. One extreme cannot exist without the contrast of the other. I believe a state of total illumination is as good, or as bad, as a state of total darkness. To achieve unity there must be a balance."*

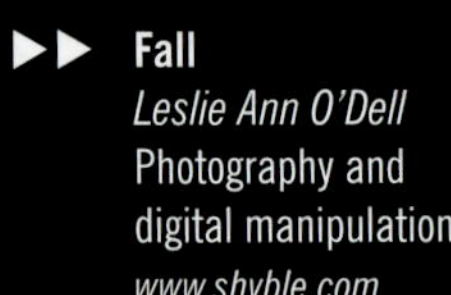

▶▶ **Fall**
Leslie Ann O'Dell
Photography and digital manipulation
www.shyble.com

Finding beauty in nature, O'Dell has used a combination of textures, photography, and scanned flowers to create ***Fall****. "This piece is about the transitions of two seasons: the end of fall and the beginning of spring, both merging together, discarding winter; and of mother nature waiting comfortably to awaken the new season."*

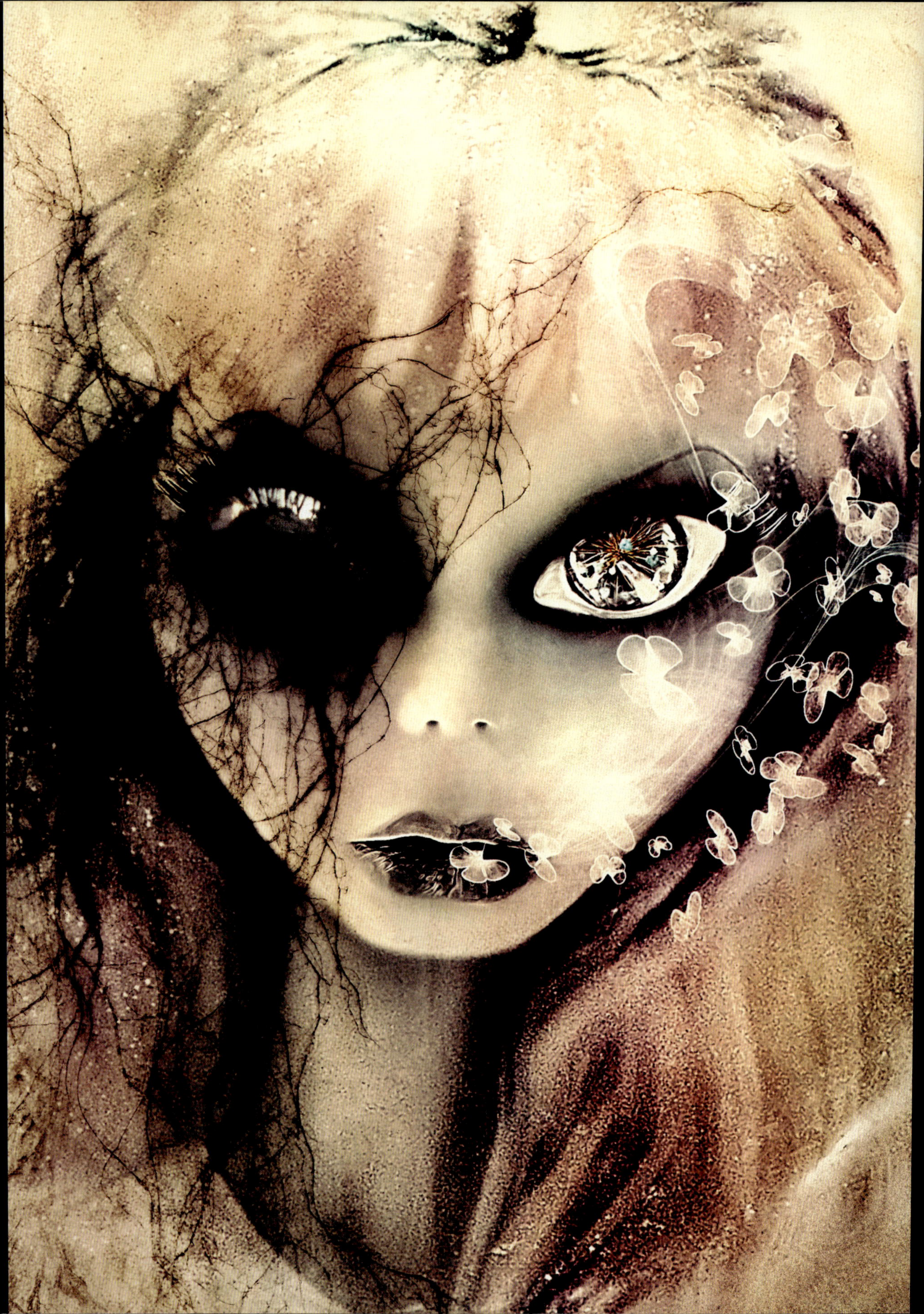

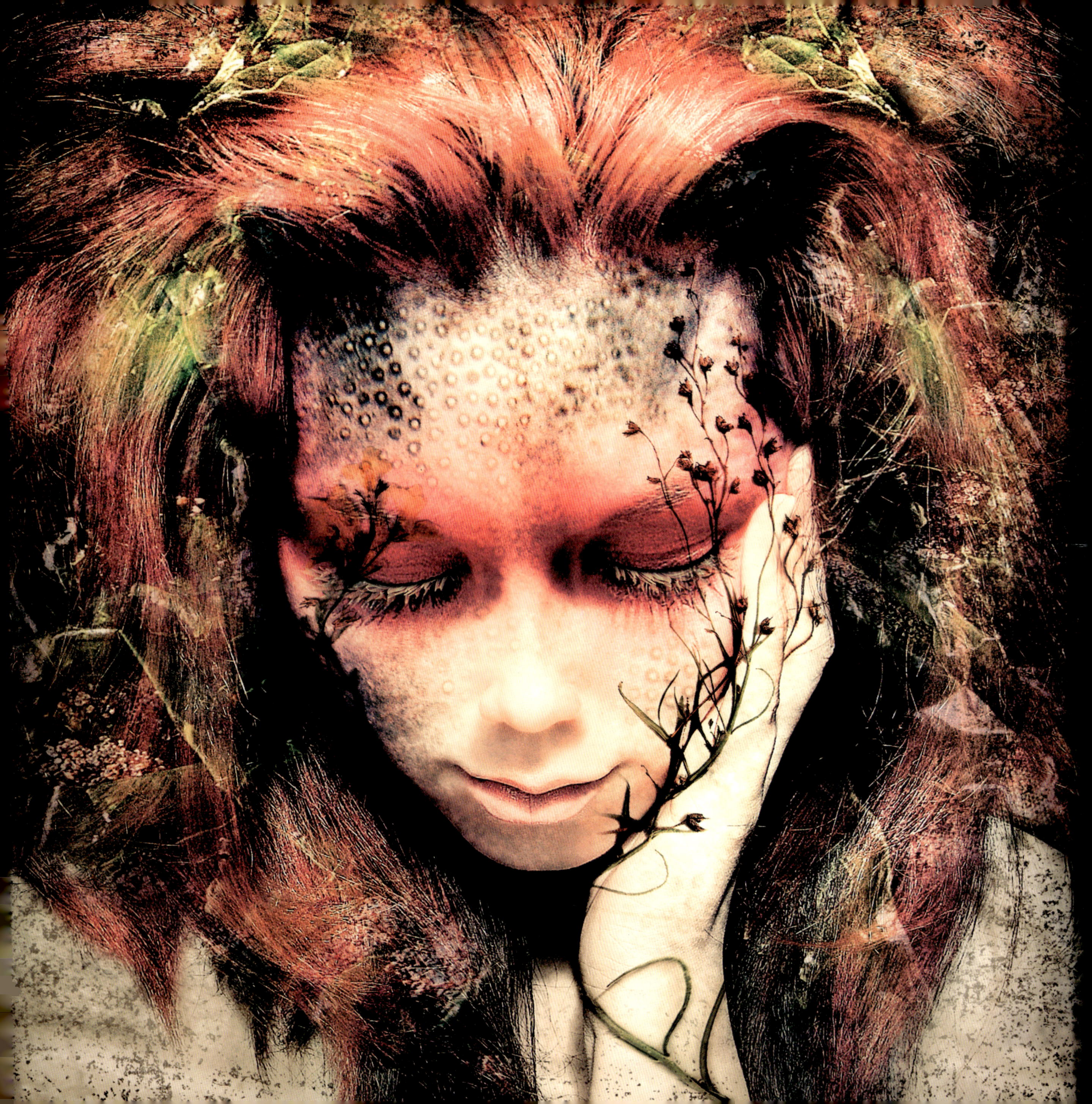

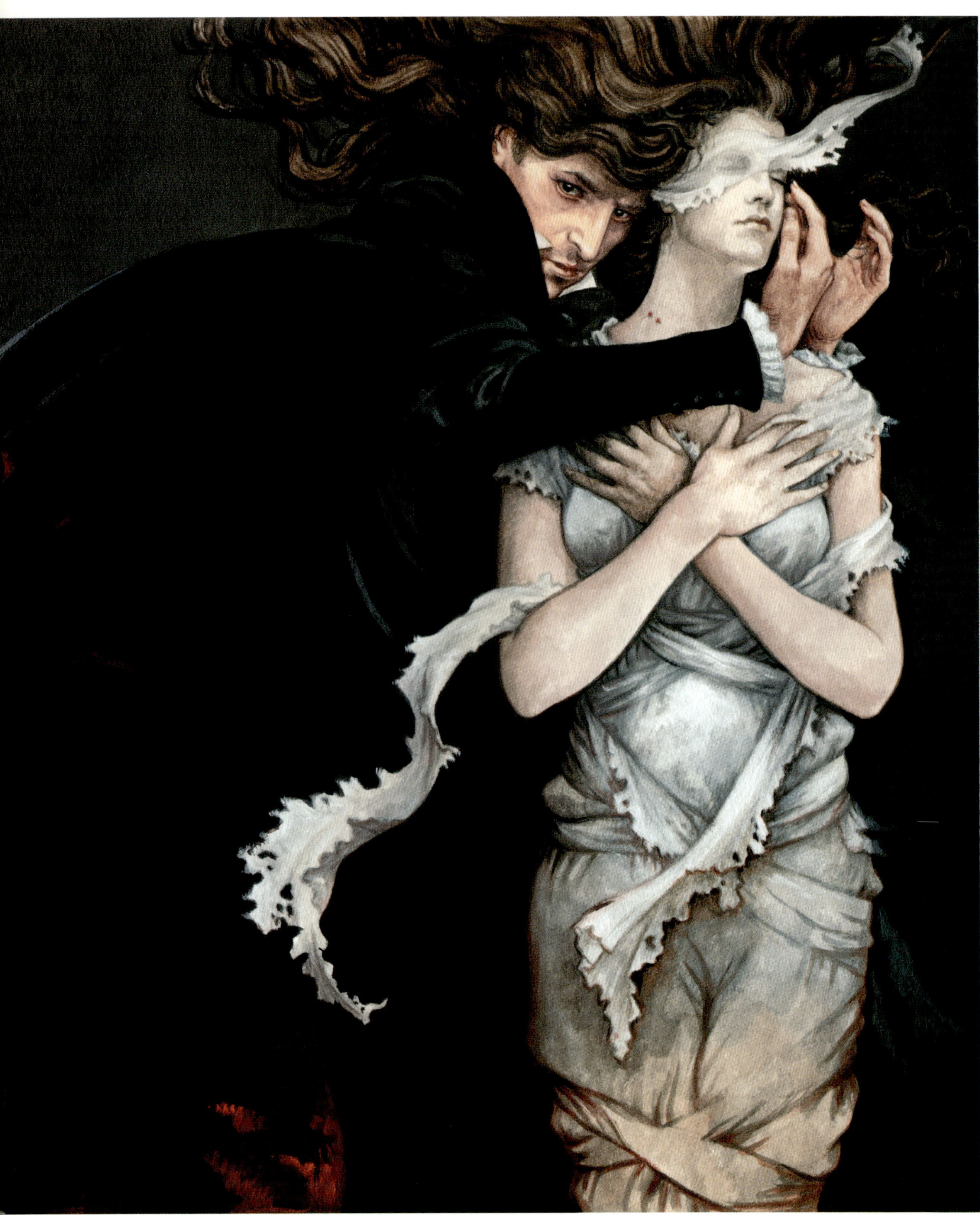

◀ **Dracula**
Anne Yvonne Gilbert
Acrylic on canvas
www.yvonnegilbert.com

An iconic Gothic image—here is Gilbert's painting of the seductive ***Dracula****, embracing a beautiful female victim. "Painted using acrylic on canvas, this was conceived as a sample piece to explore an idea for a forthcoming book. I feel the subject should be at least as romantic as it is horrific—the book being primarily a love story. I wanted to create a mood, rather than show the image in detail, so it was painted quite starkly using no reference material."*

▶ **The Price of Honey**
David Bowers
Oil painting
www.dmbowers.com

Fraught with delicately painted symbolism and dark portent, Bowers weaves metaphors with this transcendent piece. The artist explains: "Women who pursue the luxuries that life has to offer may find that there is a price to be paid. In this painting the figure's swollen, bee-stung hands are proof of this girl's willingness to suffer to gain life's sweet pleasures."

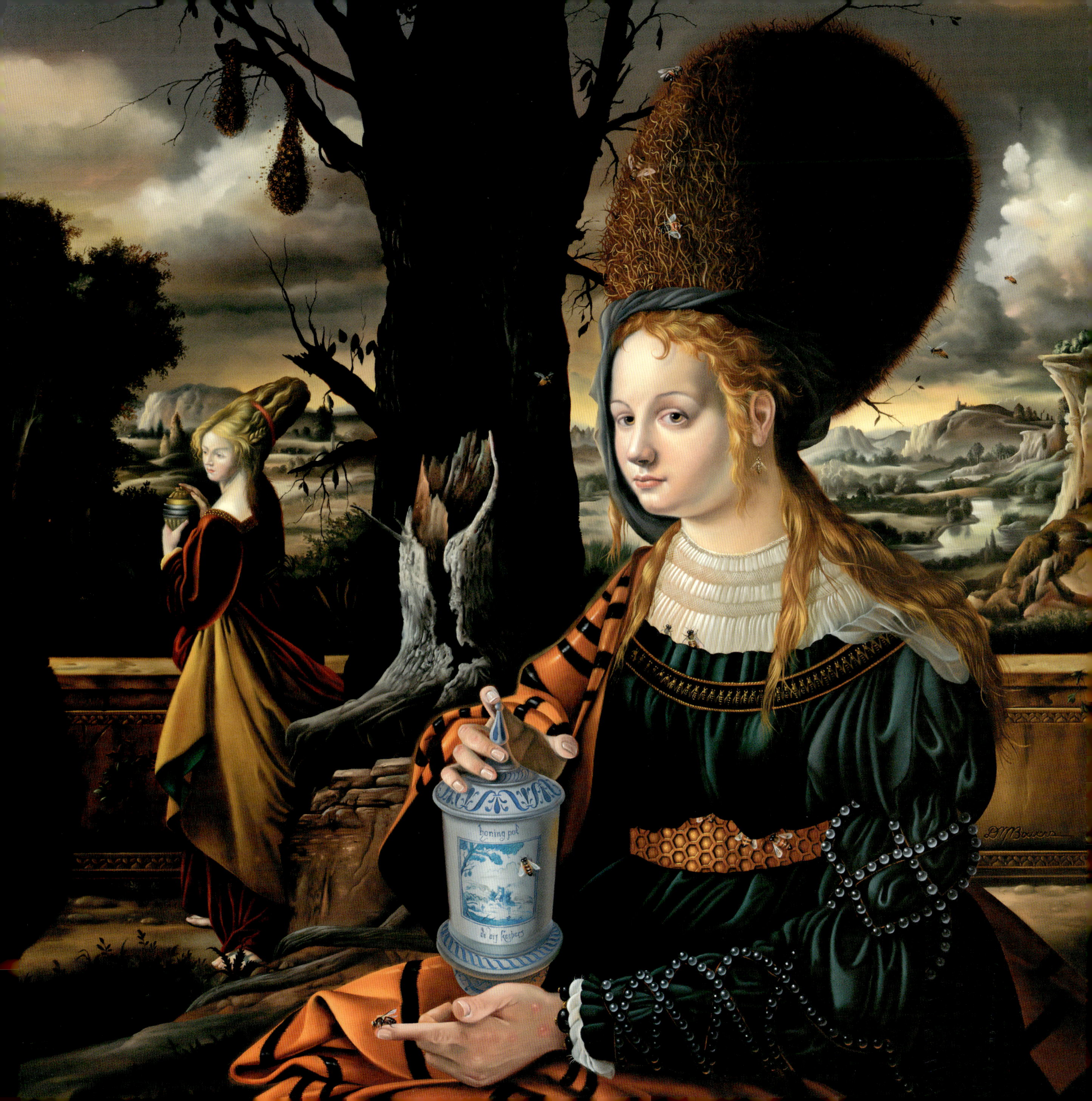
honing pot
de bij keepers
DMBowers

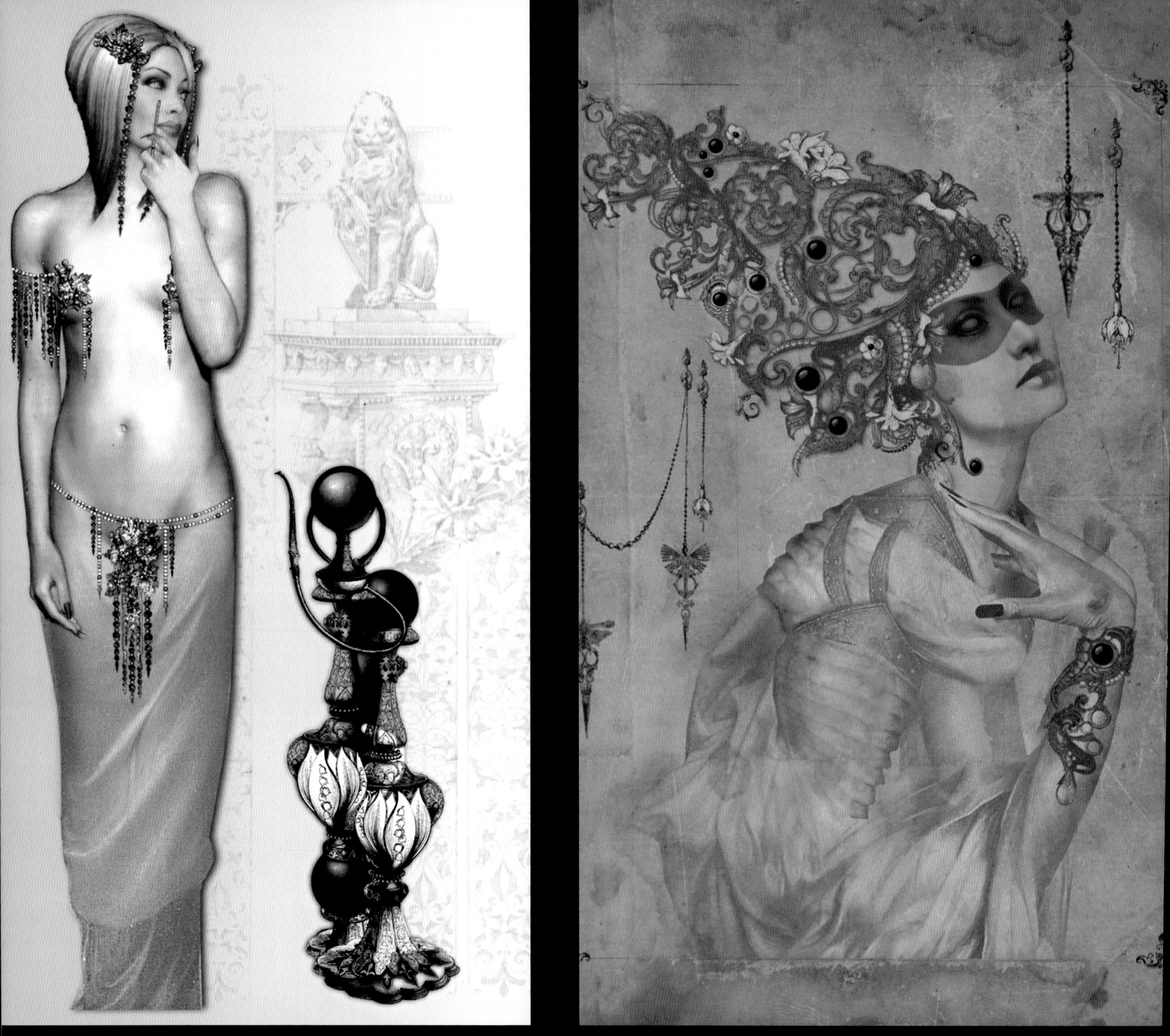

◀◀ **Lux**
Bethalynne Bajema
Mixed media
www.bajema.com

"The figure started out as a photograph I had printed on heavy paper. I added detail to the body with pencil and paint, recreating the face and hair. I used inks to detail her beaded clothing, basing it on traditional pen and ink artwork. I scanned, and added it to a collage of old ink works, including an inked hookah of mine. ***Lux*** *is a creature from my* ***OE519*** *comic, and one of my absolute favorite characters."*

◀ **Sepia Stain**
Bethalynne Bajema
Mixed media
www.bajema.com

"The woman in this image represents the Empress in the major arcana of my Tarot collection. The image is a mixed media piece. The original image was sketched in pencils on drawing paper, with inking done on the head piece. The designs in the head piece are based on traditional pen and ink drawings. I scanned this and added more detail digitally using a program called Picture It. After placing it on the cover of a very old scanned book, I had the work printed on thick canvas paper. Finally I went over it with watercolors and tea water to fade it. I used pencils for extra detailing."

▶ **Lady Death**
Laurie Lipton
Pencil on paper
www.laurielipton.com

Astonishing detail and delicate lace contrast sharply with the hard bleached bone of ***Lady Death*** *(also known as Doña Sebastiana or La Santísima Muerte) in Lipton's pencil drawing. "The lovely Lady of Death appears frequently in Mexican folk art. This was very painstakingly difficult to draw. I had to draw around the white lace and halfway through it I thought, 'why am I doing this to myself?' It nearly (metaphorically) killed me, which would have been very appropriate."*

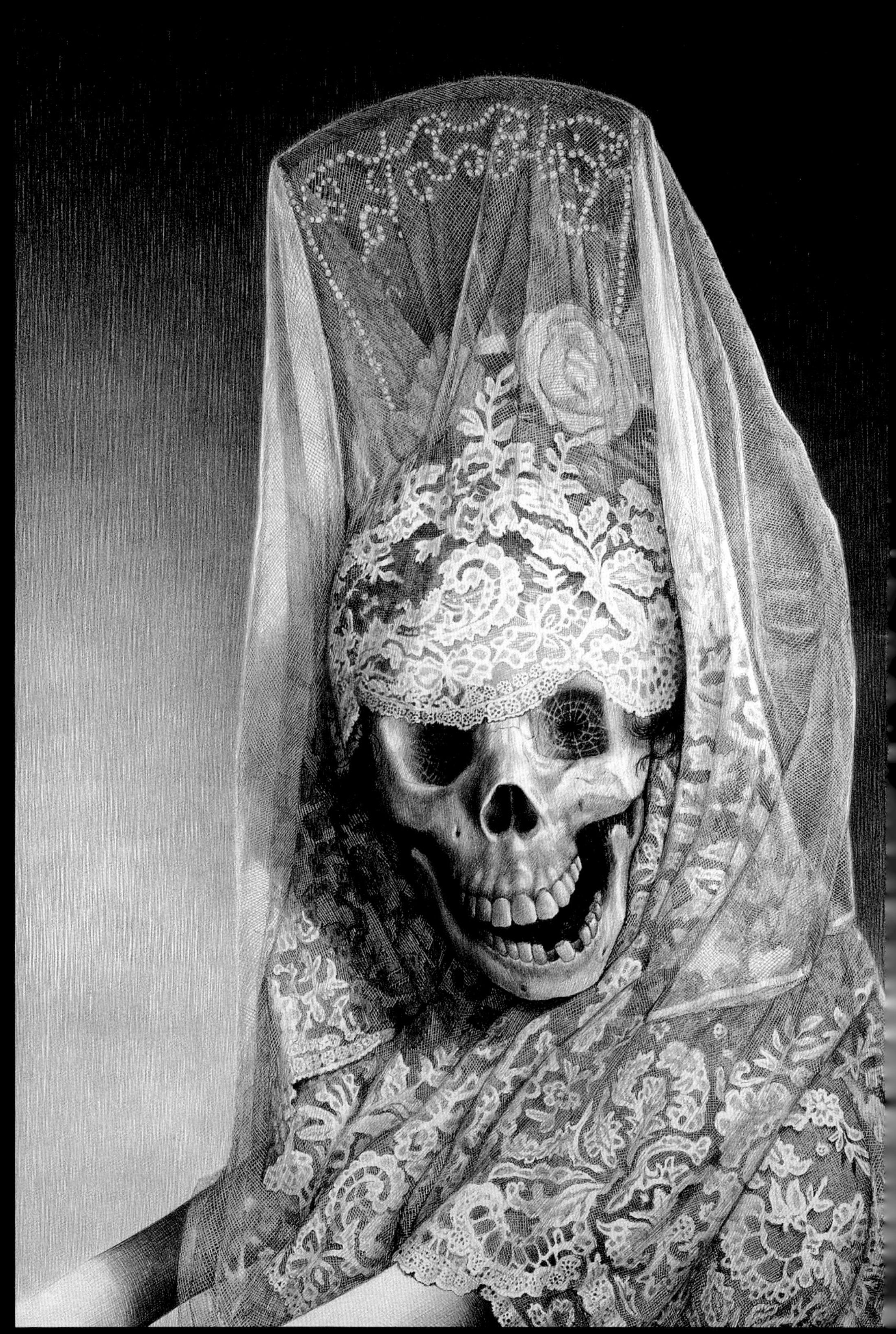

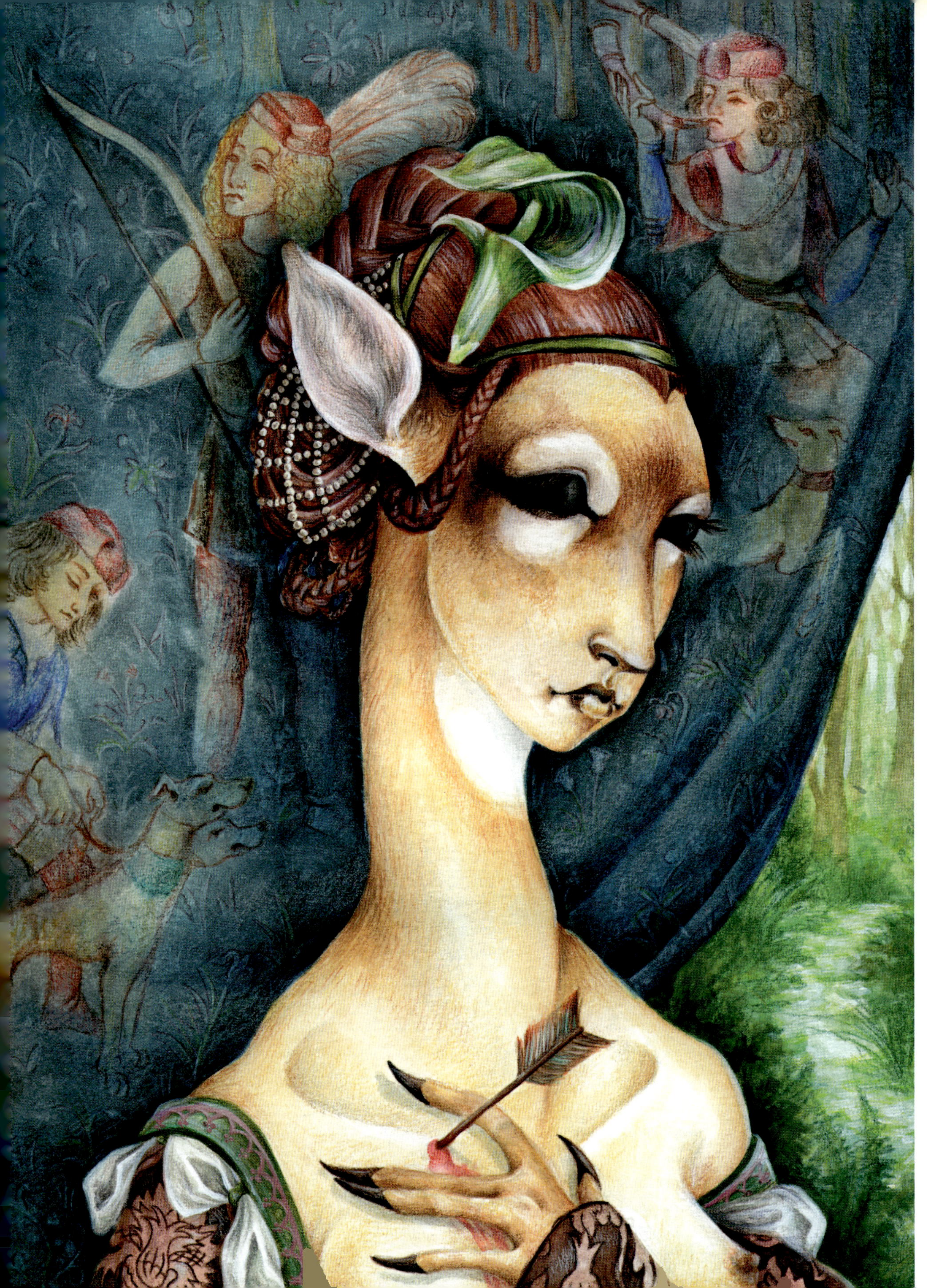

◀ **Deer Woman**
Desirée Isphording
Mixed media
www.sphinxmuse.net

"A maiden is caught between two forms: that of a graceful doe and that of a girl. She is a shape-shifter, a creature who lingers at the edges of the Veil. She does not completely belong to either the realm of Faery or of mortals. She wears the finery of human aristocracy as well as a Jack-in-the-Pulpit (Arisaema triphyllum) in her hair. A tapestry, woven with human hands, bars her from the forest, the haunt of her faery kin. That same tapestry may also hold a clue—hunters with their dogs and spears are searching the forest for game."

▶ **Rafinesque Awaiting Sleep**
Desirée Isphording
Colored pencil
www.sphinxmuse.net

Transforming a Gothic Renaissance-style woman into a bat-like creature, Isphording has used colored pencils to compose this fanciful chimera of a portrait. "I discovered a species of bat, known as Rafinesque's big-eared bat, and immediately knew that Rafinesque was to be her name. Although she has delicate fangs, she is (generally) not of the blood-sucking variety, and carries a little butterfly for a snack in a glass bauble pinned to her garment. Since dawn is approaching, she is readying to drape herself in her wings and wait for slumber."

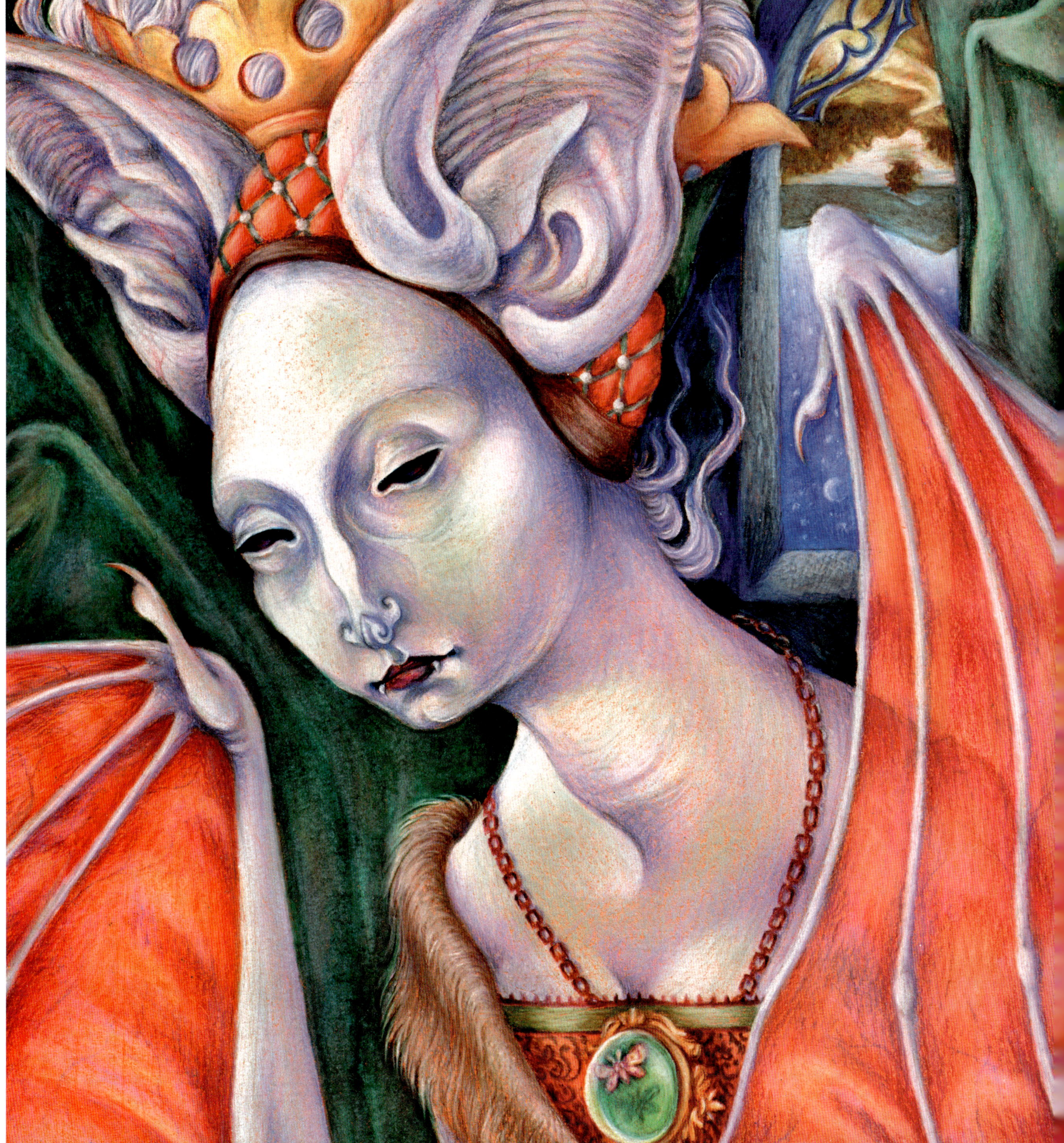

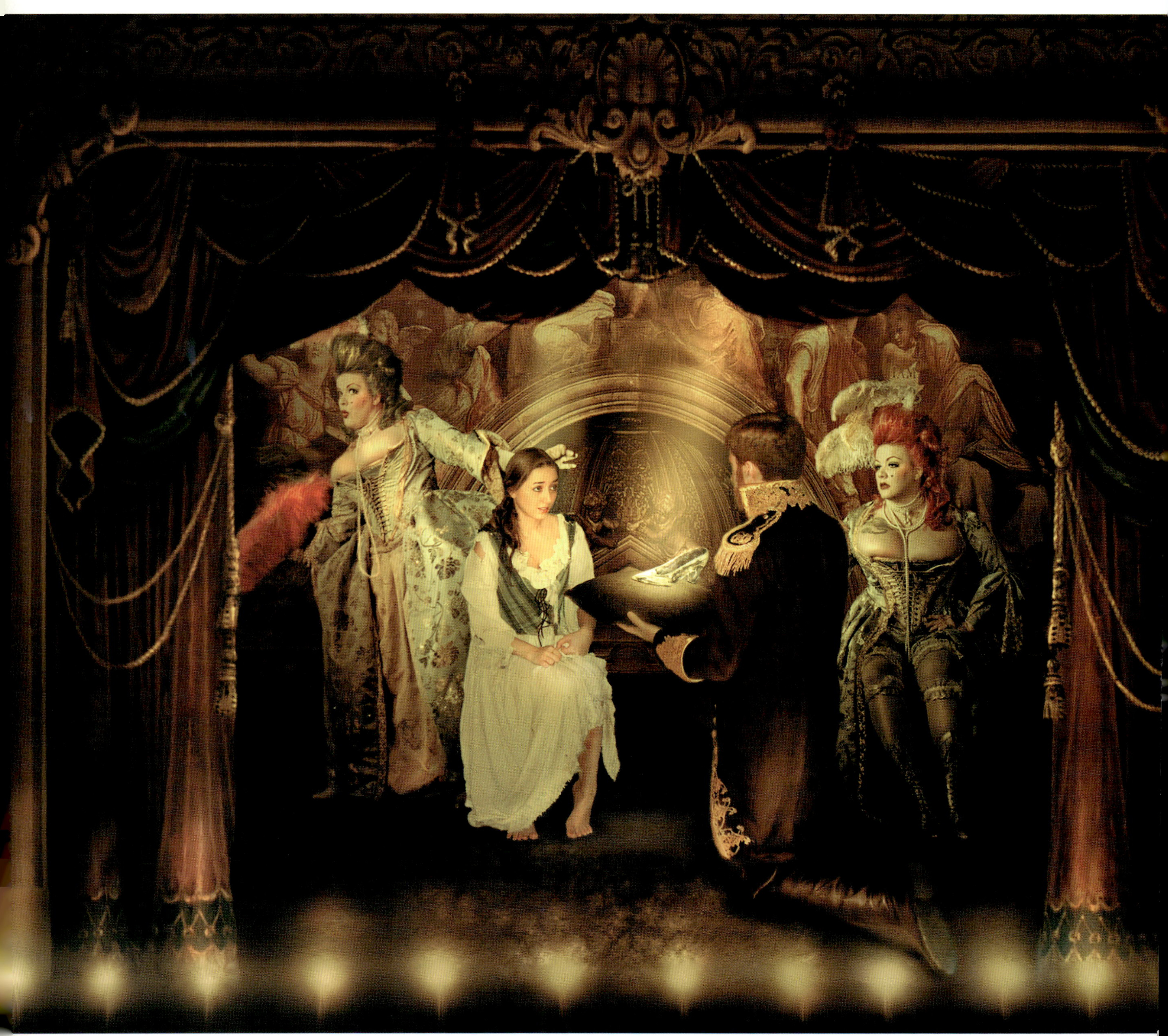

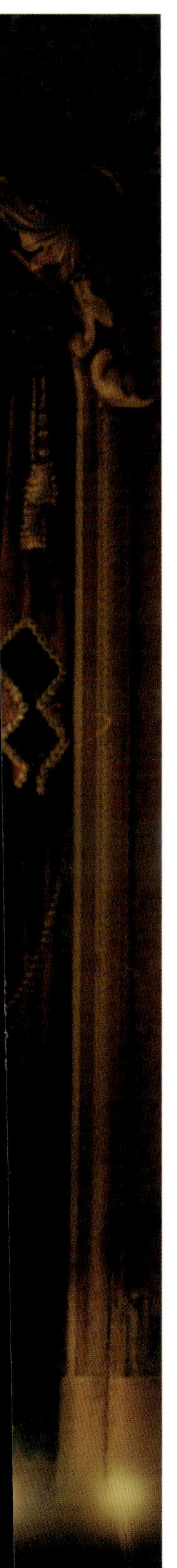

◀ **Limelight**
Pat Brennan
Photography and digital manipulation
www.moonmomma.co.uk

*Brennan's **Limelight**, created in Adobe Photoshop, gives a Gothic twist to a Cinderella stage play. "I attempted to recreate the look of an old Victorian pantomime theater. The thespians among you will see I haven't got a clue about lighting a stage. I was going for the Victorian theater lime-lit look."*

▶ **Indecision**
Pat Brennan
Photography and digital manipulation
www.moonmomma.co.uk

Brennan uses Adobe Photoshop to its best advantage, creating a truly beautiful work of art. "I was experimenting here with using very old sepia images and blending them with my own photography." Conveying a rite of passage, Brennan explains it is "the moment before taking the final step into life, womanhood, and all that goes with it. The girl has no real choice, it will happen whether she chooses to pick up the key or not."

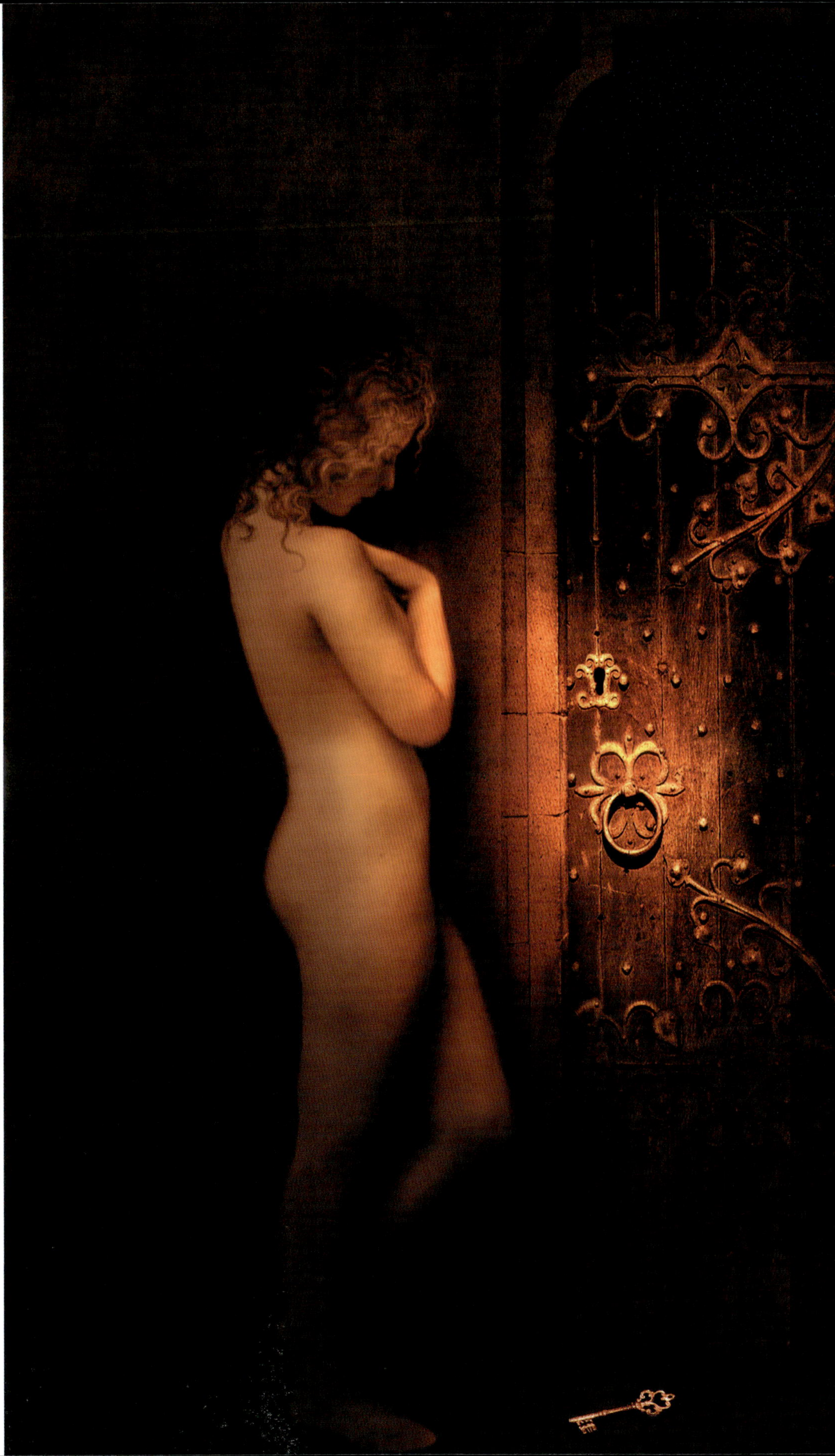

▶ **Her Future has Already Begun**
Caniglia
Mixed media
www.caniglia-art.com

Cangila's mixed media piece was created using watercolor, acrylic, and gouache paint, as well as ink and pencil. "This painting deals with the different ways in which society sometimes views women," Caniglia explains. "I feel that society pushes the sexualization of girls from a very early age, before they are emotionally and physically ready. It is sad how woman are sometimes seen as sexual objects, rather than people with independent thoughts and behaviors. The red mark across the eyes represents rejection. It is the mark of the woman who fights for her beliefs. When someone stands up and fights for their beliefs, then their future has begun."

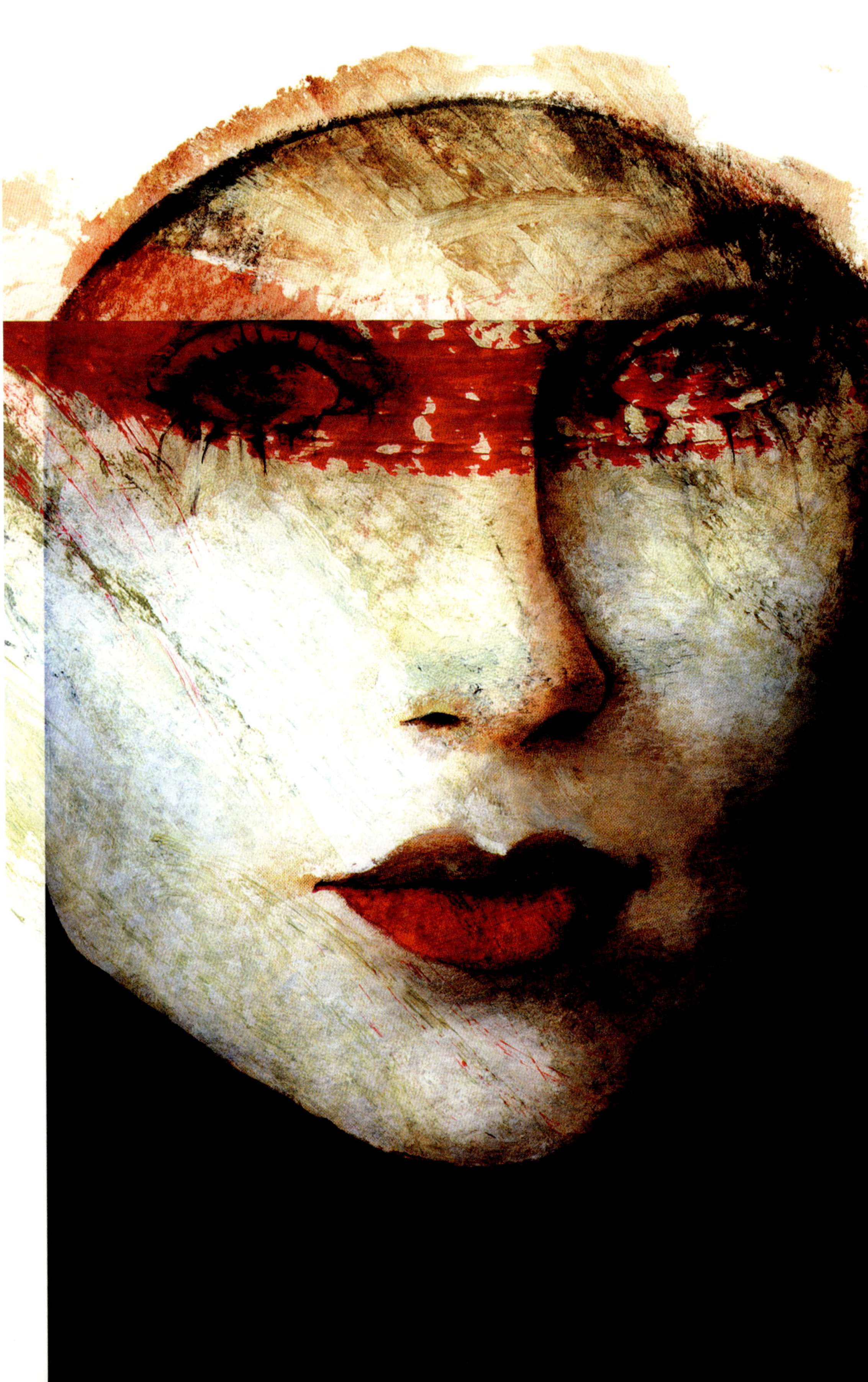

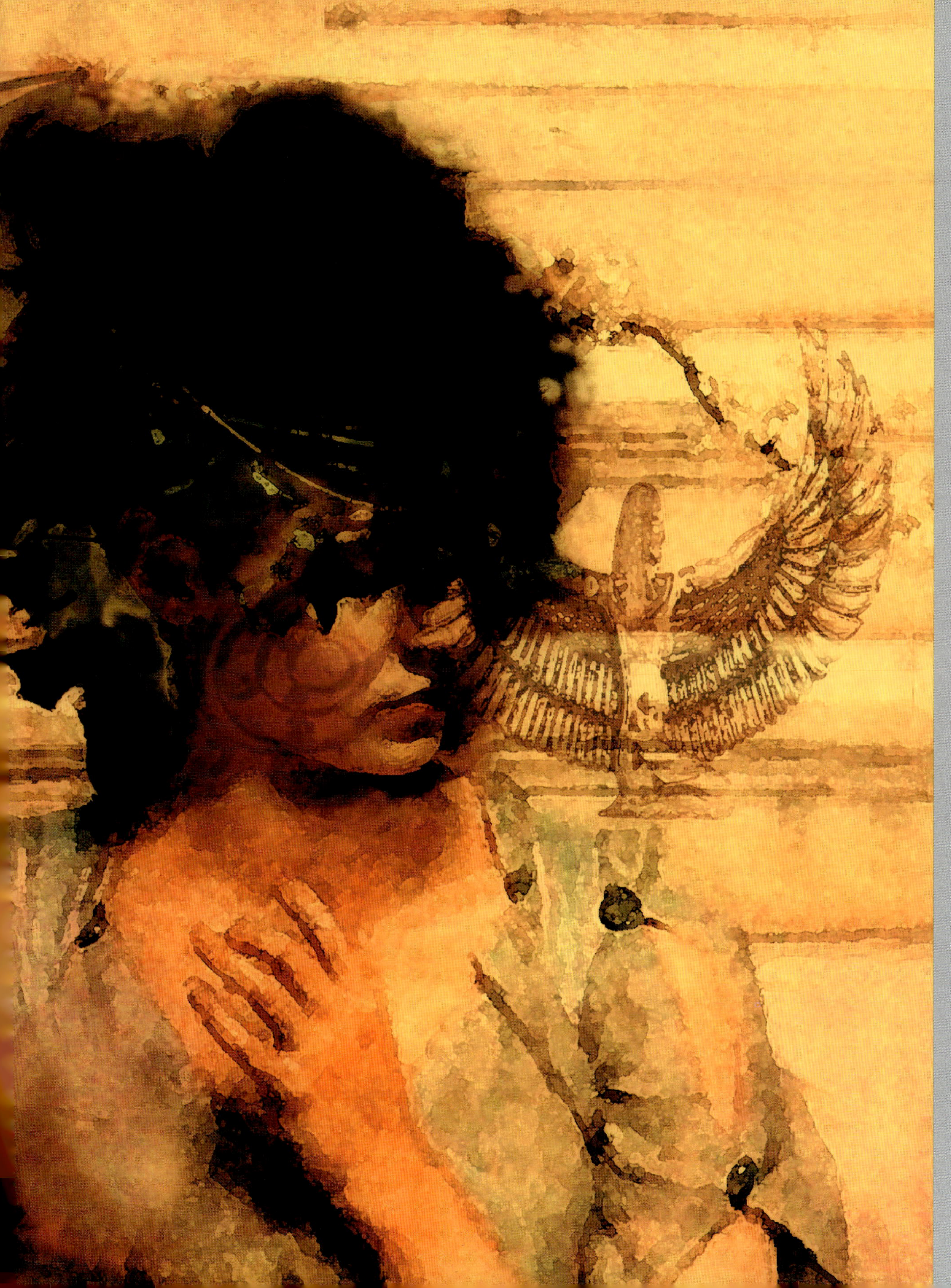

◀ **Pandora**
Eric Scala
Digital painting
www.ericscala.com

An appropriate cover piece for master of Gothic fiction Anne Rice's book **Pandora** *— Scala's painting evokes a cryptic and ancient feeling. Egyptian and masquerade imagery add to the general air of mystery. "I made this piece using Adobe Photoshop and Corel Painter. I had to find a style for the series and I wanted it to look like a painting."*

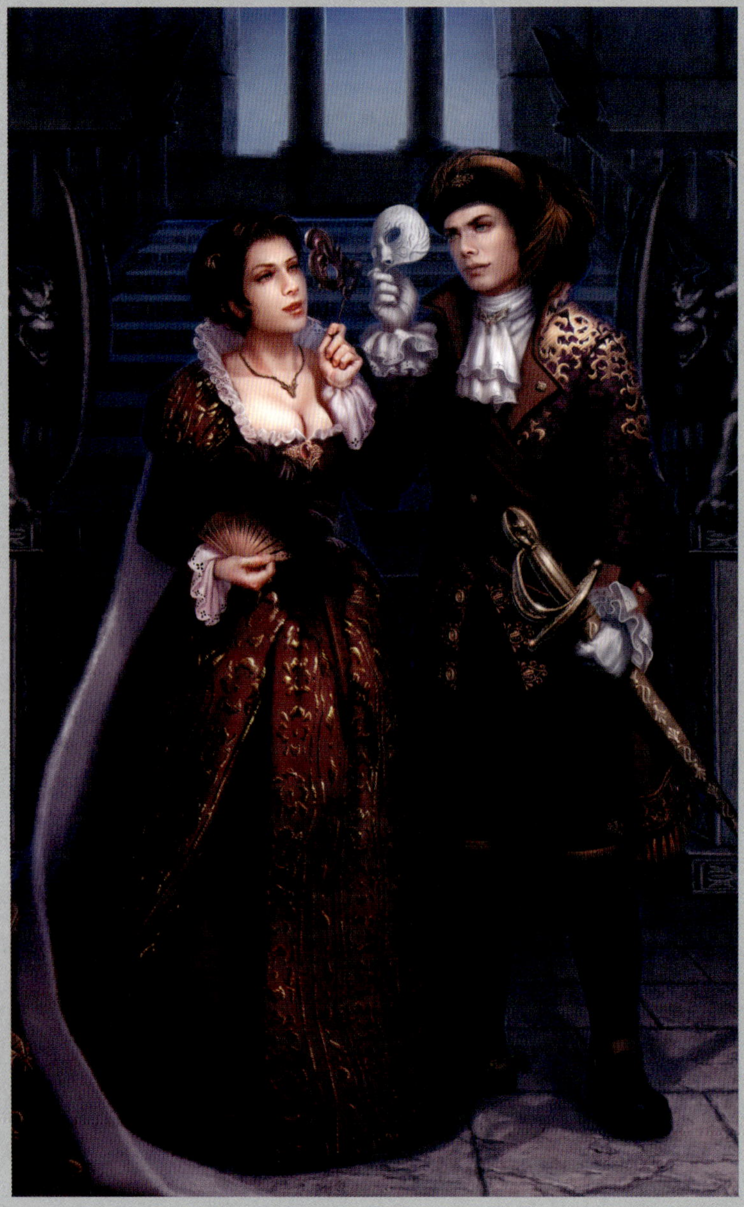

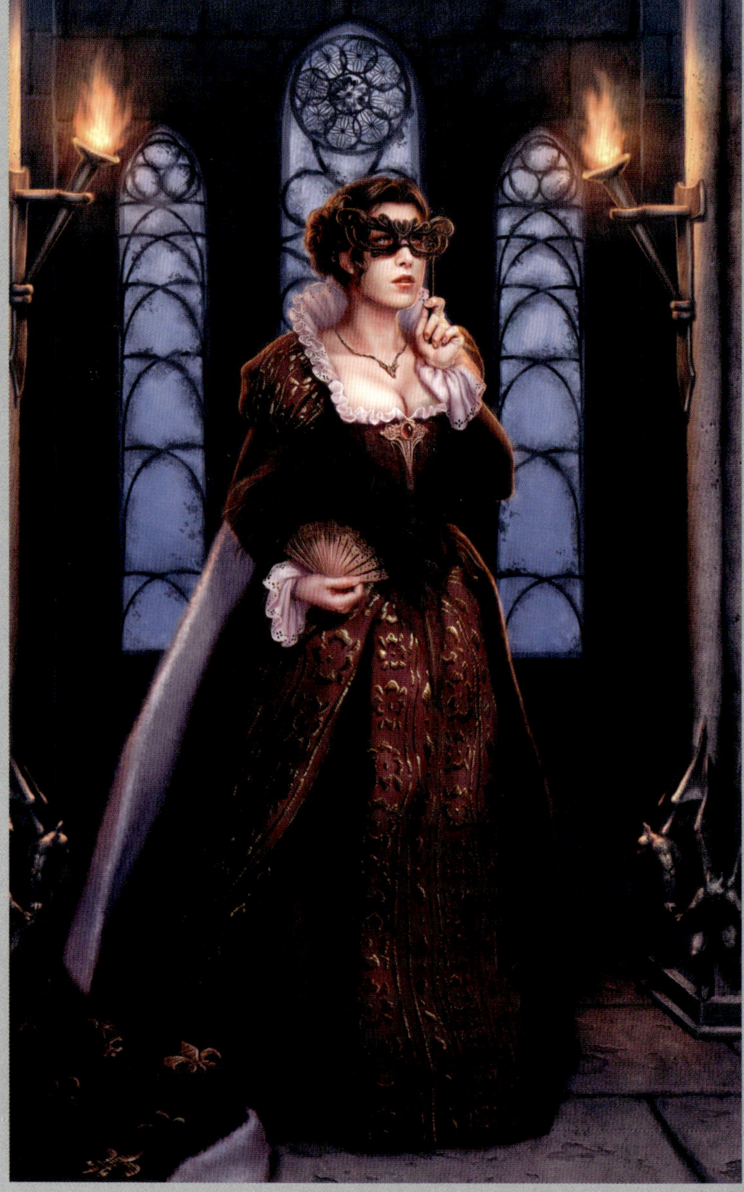

▲ **Master and Mistress**
Camille Kuo
Digital painting
www.camilkuo.com

The picture of Victorian Gothic elegance: this couple is at the height of romantic fashion. Seemingly preparing for a masquerade ball, both pause to stand for a portrait in their mansion, replete with a gargoyle-festooned staircase. "This was created for MedicaSpa LLC who wanted to emulate the style of the Romantic Victorian/ Elizabethan Gothic appearance, to promote a perfume."

▲ **Mistress**
Camille Kuo
Digital painting
www.camilkuo.com

Gothic aristocracy at its finest. The Mistress, in a sumptuous gown, has an air of gloomy nobility about her. Kuo has created this upper-crust example of Gothic sensibility digitally, with careful attention to lighting and detail. "It is painted freehand, using references for the figure, bar the circle patterns at the top of the middle window and the royal shape on the cape."

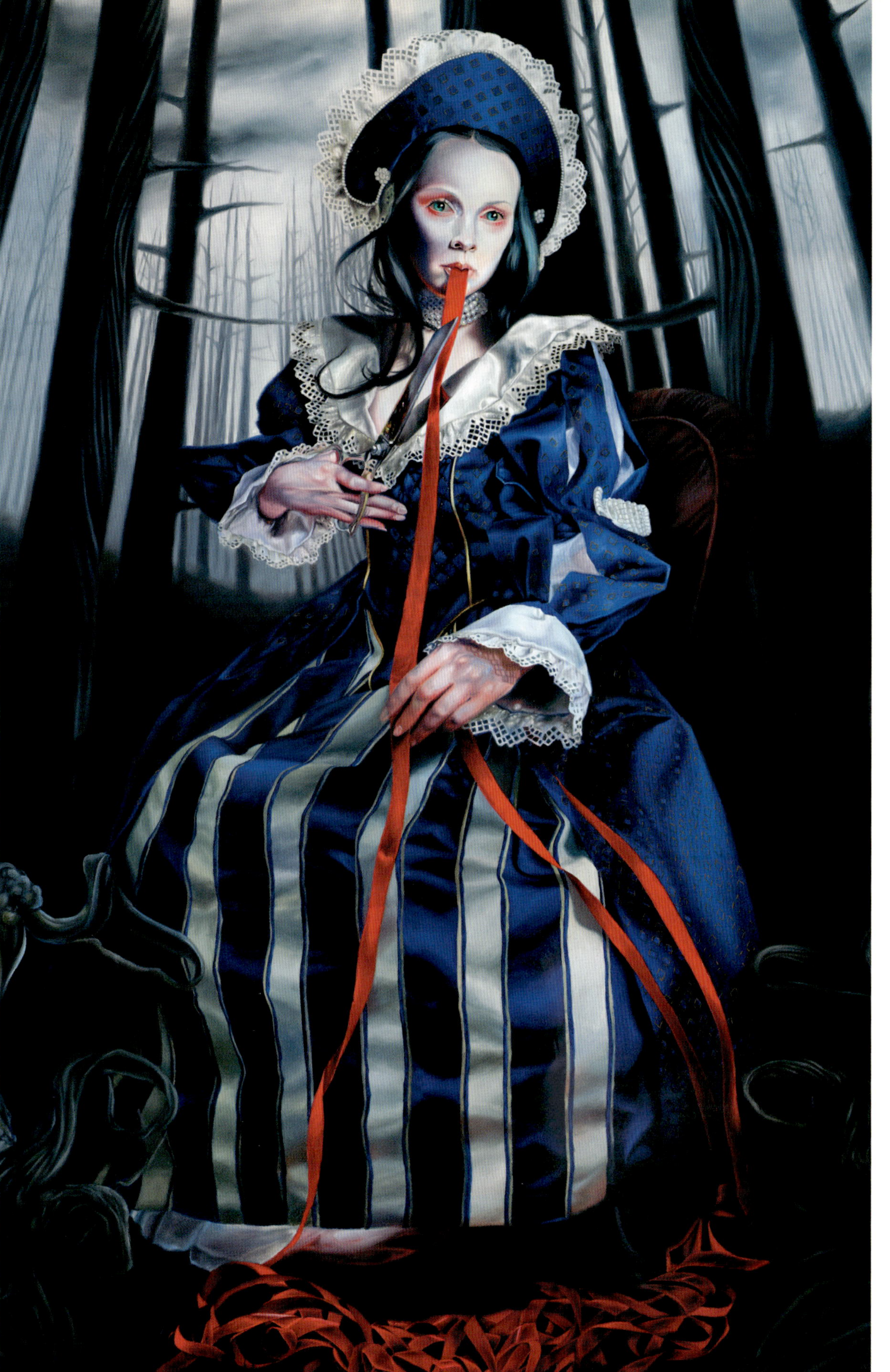

◀ **Red Ribbon**
David Stoupakis
Oil on board
www.davidstoupakis.com

Stoupakis's oil painting shows his masterful use of the medium with the delicately painted fabrics and features of the central figure. "The theme was inspired by my wife's favorite childhood story of a young lady who tells her boyfriend he can never remove her red ribbon necklace. One day they go beneath an old oak tree for a picnic and she falls asleep. Curiosity gets the better of him and he undoes the necklace. To his horror her head falls off."

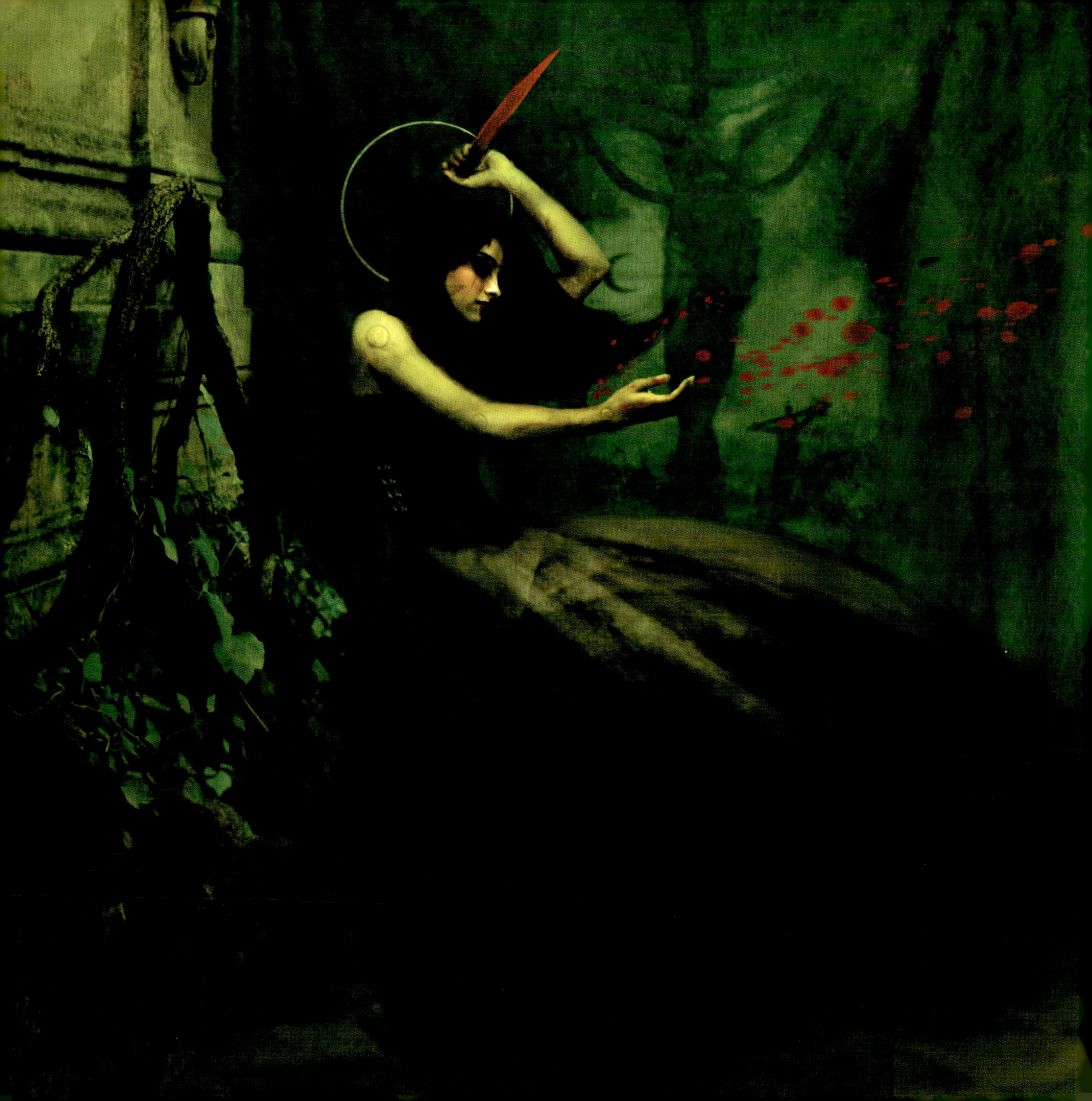

◀ **Dread The Fallen**
Samuel Araya
Digital painting
www.samael.epilogue.net

A beautiful female figure in a grimly green setting holds a bloody knife in Araya's digital painting, ***Dread the Fallen****. Subtle religious overtones and darker symbolism in this work nod to the heavy metal inspirations behind this piece. "A piece for the band* ***Cradle of Filth****. Music, especially black metal, has been a heavy influence in my work since my early days. This image tries to reflect upon the dynamic aspects of that style."*

▶ **Inferiority Complex**
Ryohei Hase

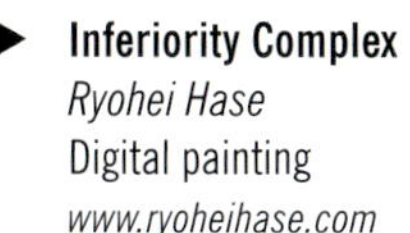

Digital painting
www.ryoheihase.com

An exquisite digital painting by Hase. A female figure, ripe with decay, appears to try and hide it with beautiful things: flowers, ribbons, and lace, but to no avail. "This is an image of a woman who wants and tries to be beautiful, but things are not going well for her."

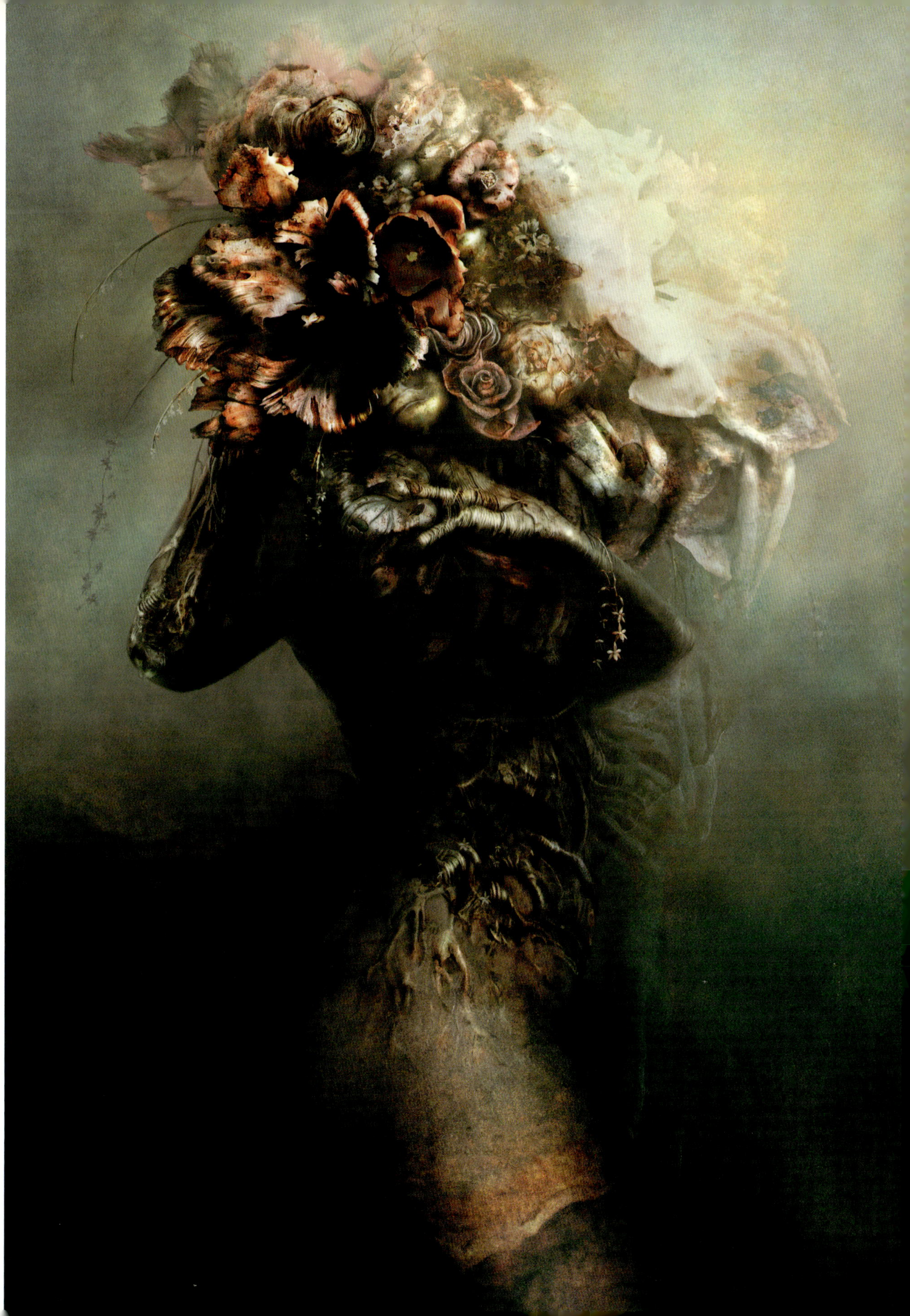

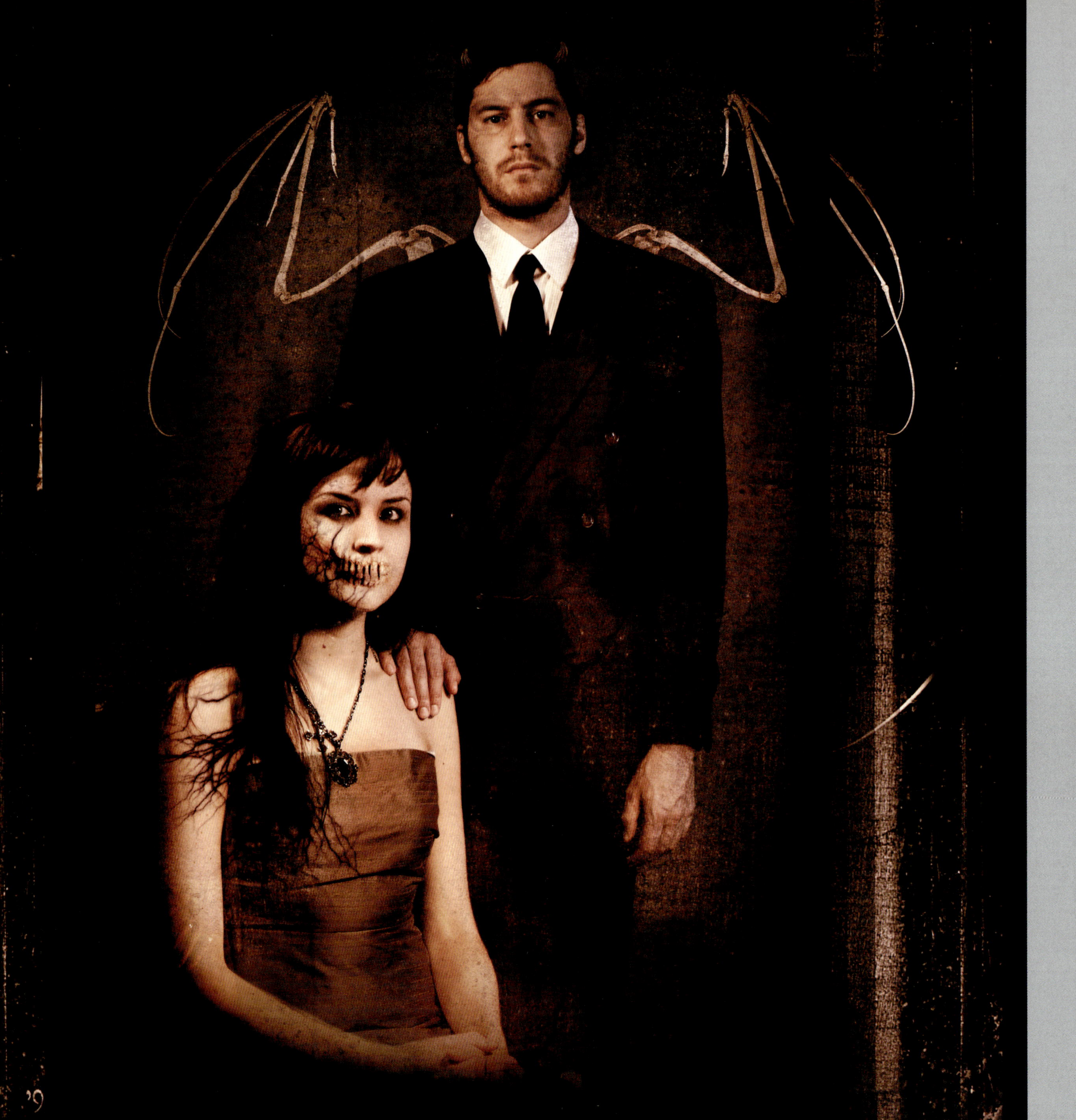
'9

◀ **Portrait**
Shannon Hourigan
Photography and
digital manipulation
www.shannonhourigan.com

A seemingly traditional formal portrait, but with a creepy twist. Hourigan has created this piece in Adobe Photoshop by manipulating her own photography. She explains: "This is a self-portrait with filmmaker Travis Betz."

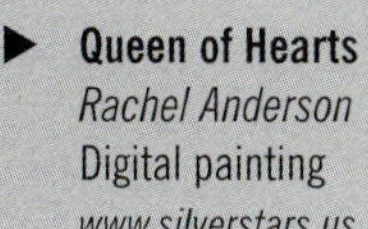

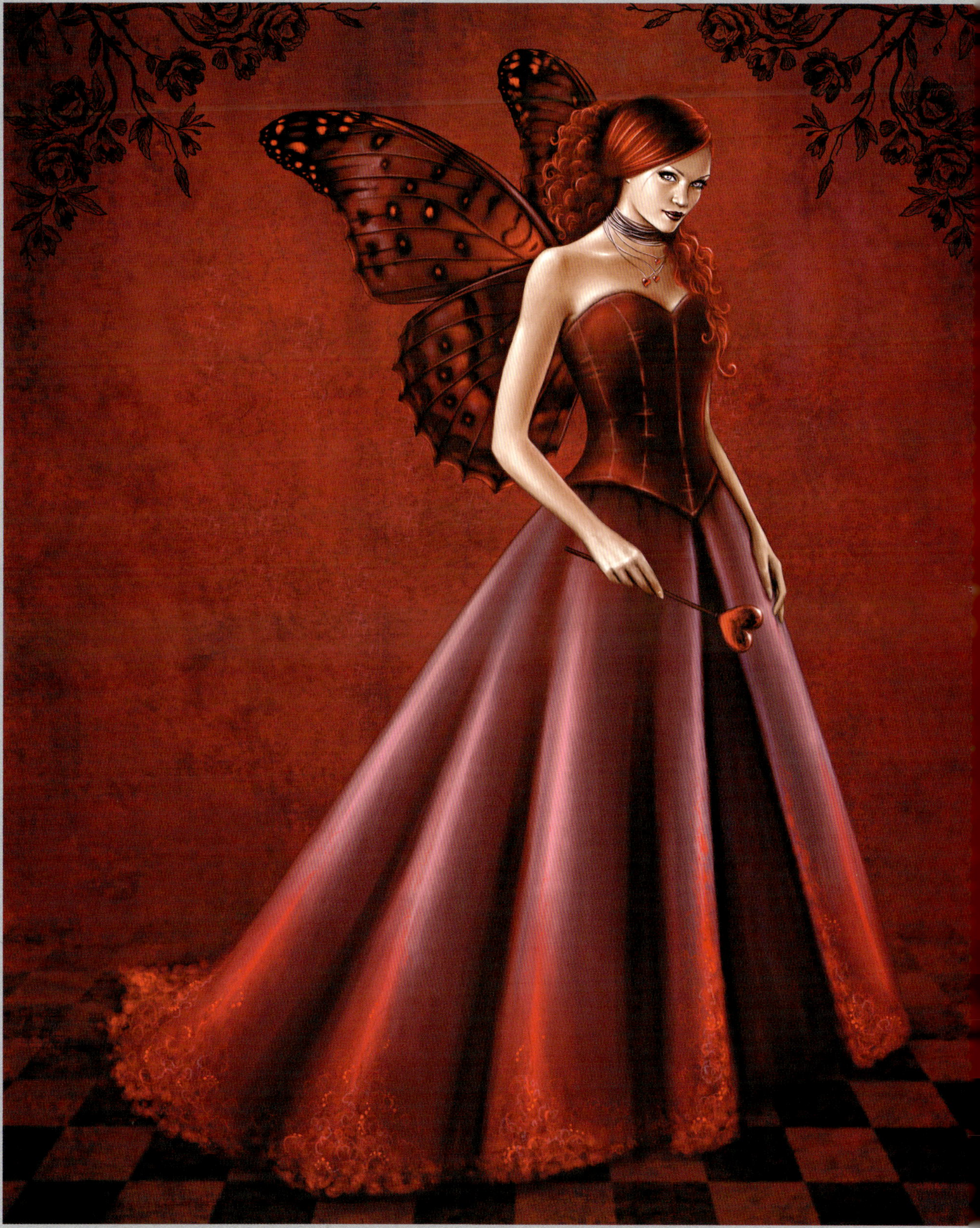

▶ **Queen of Hearts**
Rachel Anderson
Digital painting
www.silverstars.us

Anderson paints a dark fairy queen, draped in blood-red clothes. "I painted this piece from scratch in Adobe Photoshop and Corel Painter. I wanted to create a character that at first glance is pretty and sweet, but a closer look reveals a mischievous glint in her eye. Love is like that sometimes."

Swan Maidens of Charenton
Tina Imel
Oil on wood panel
www.tinaimel.com

Here we have Imel's triumph of Victorian Neo-Surrealism. ***Swan Maidens of Charenton*** *is a truly stunning oil painting with elements of Gothic Victoriana, burlesque and vaudeville shows, traditional theater, and many dreamlike oddments. Hand-painted with amazing detail, the Swan Maidens give the impression of a forgotten era with the faded glory and shabby splendor of the torn stage backdrop. Ironically, in addition to being a famous company, Charenton is also the name of a 17th-century French insane asylum that once held the Marquis de Sade.*

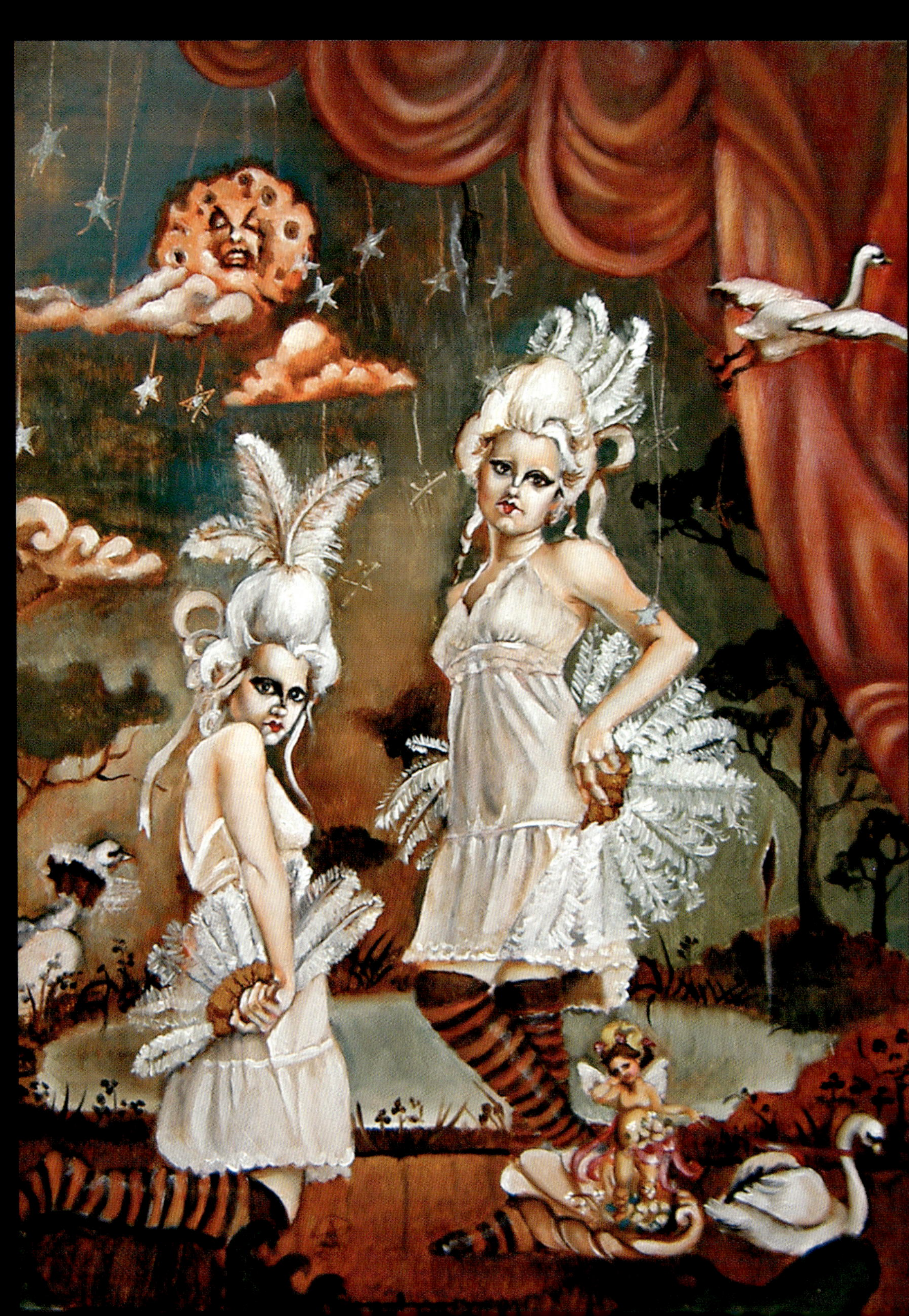

▶ **Love at 5am**
Tina Imel
Oil on wood panel
www.tinaimel.com

Tina Imel's delicate oil painting is an example of her Neo-Surrealist leanings with Gothic Victorian tendencies. The beautiful artist in the painting wears a clearly Victorian outfit, replete with corset, while the whole image is skewed to give the impression that one is looking through a Victorian convex oval glass frame.

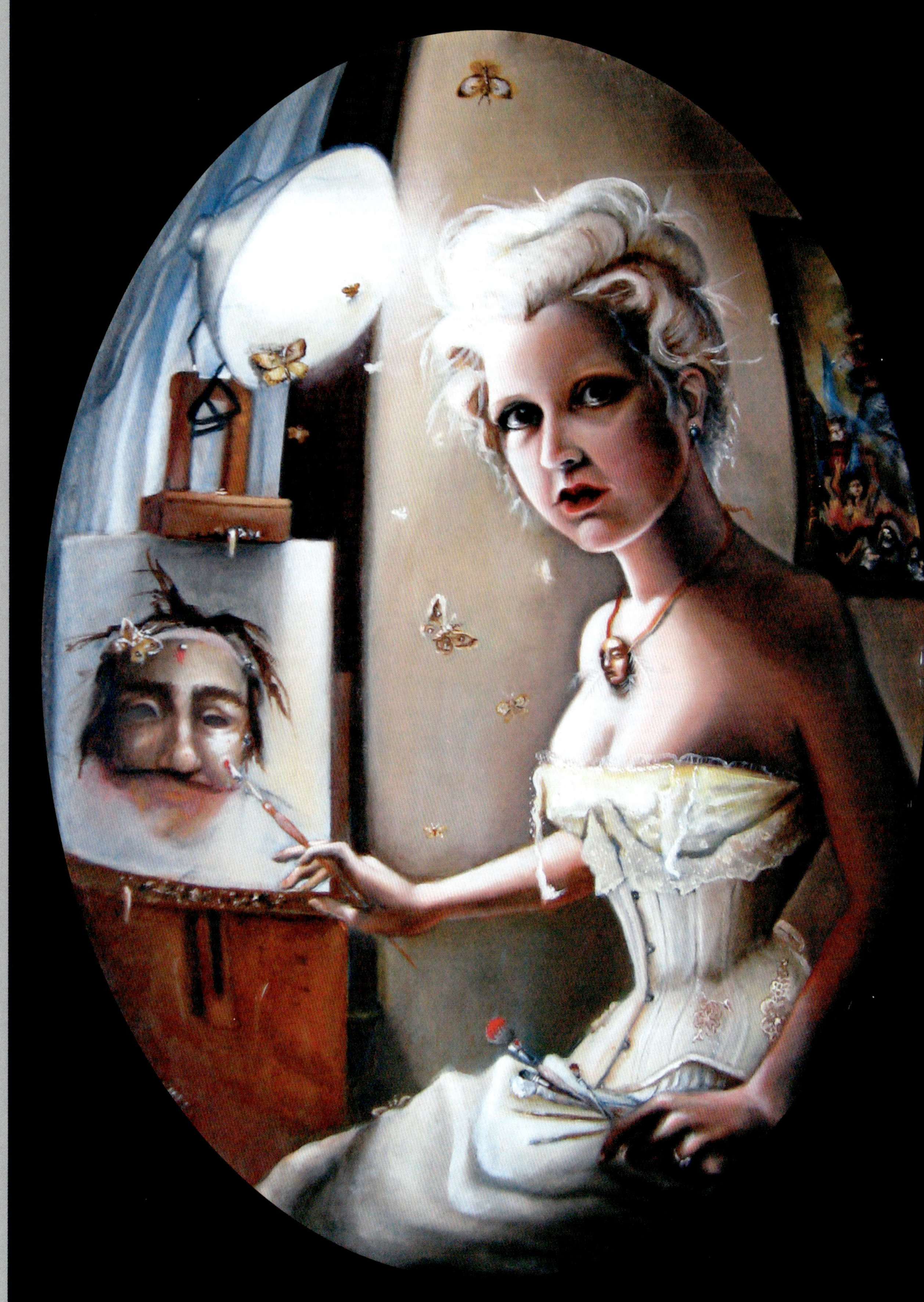

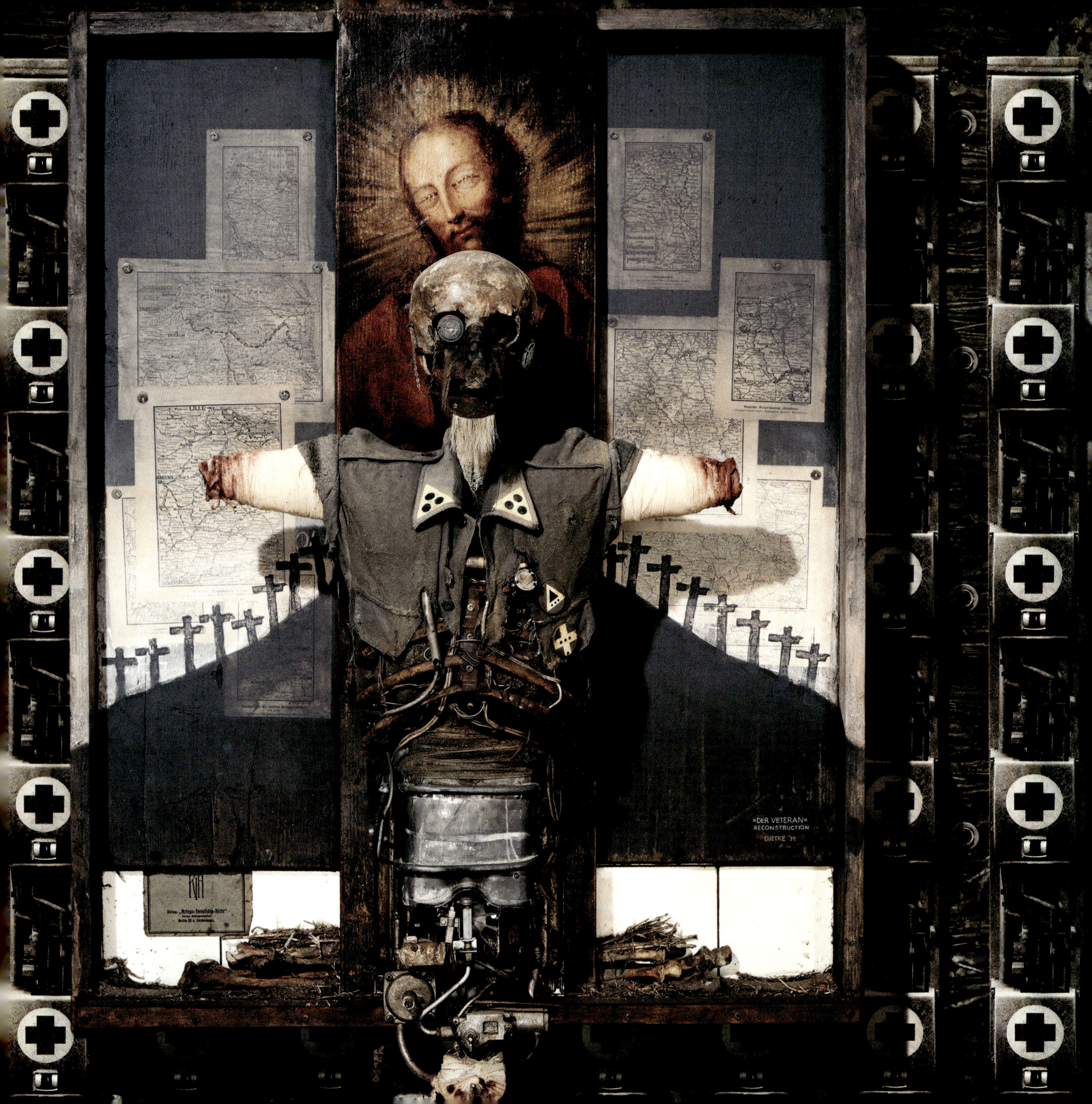
»DER VETERAN«
RECONSTRUCTION
LUETKE '94
„Kriegs-Invaliden-Hilfe“

CHAPTER 4

INDUSTRIAL GOTH

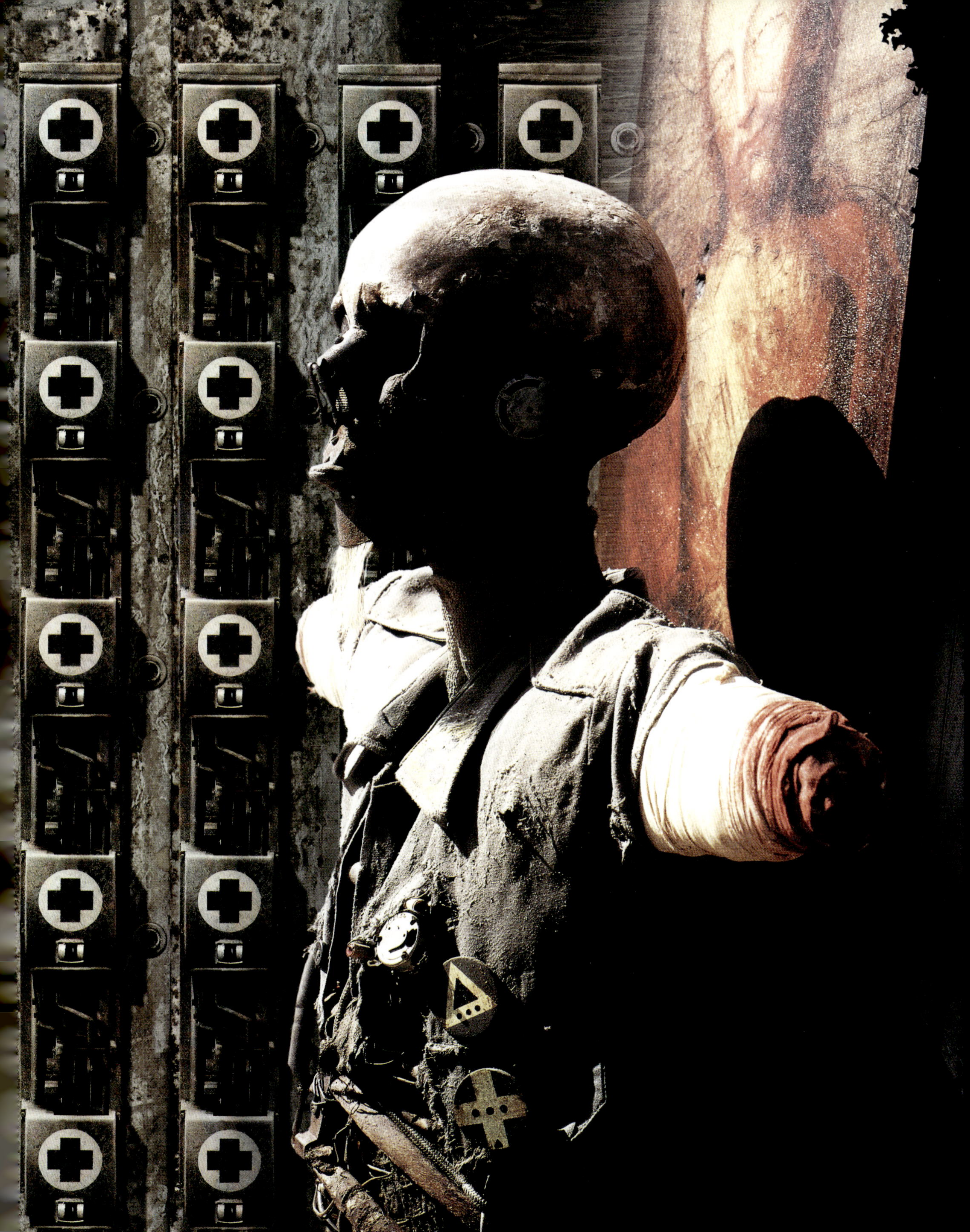

◀ **The Veteran**
Joachim Luetke
Sculpture
www.luetke.com

Images of war, religion, and technology are integrated into a phenomenal sculpture by Lueteke. "Created from scrap, this sculpture aims to imitate the overall look of idols used with voodoo rituals. It's an attempt to simulate the reassembling of fragments, or remains of the western culture decrypted by so-called 'primitive people.' Although this sculpture is static, it seems to imply its purpose while standing still."

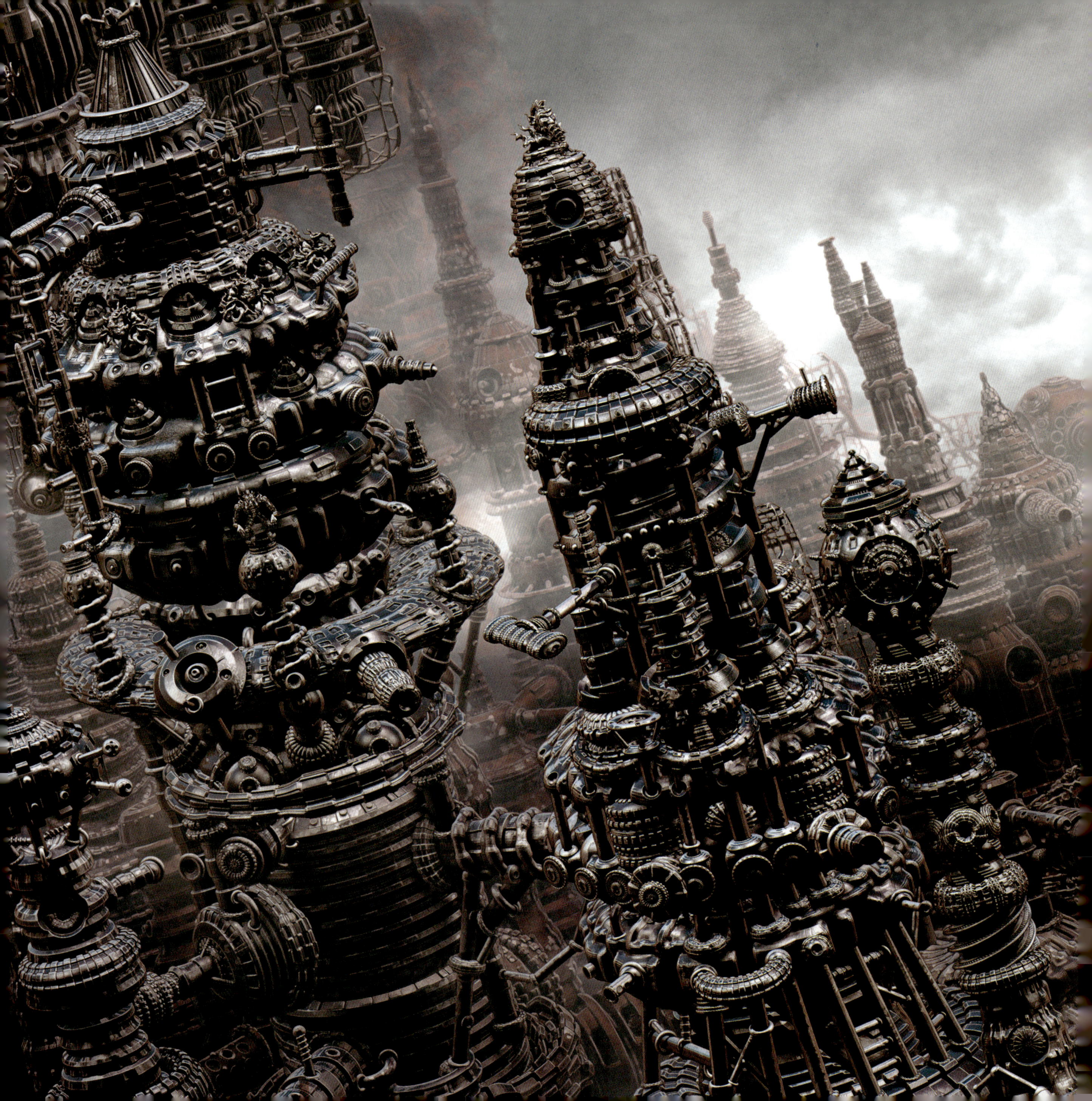

◀ **Primitive City**
Meats Meier
Digital image
www.3dartspace.com

A joyless, intricate scene created by Meier, of an industrial-looking landscape. The silver, metallic tones, and smoggy-gray sky give a cold, impersonal feel to this piece. Meiers explains: "A snapshot of an alien primitive city."

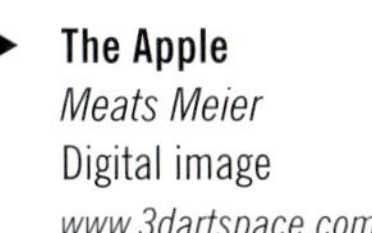

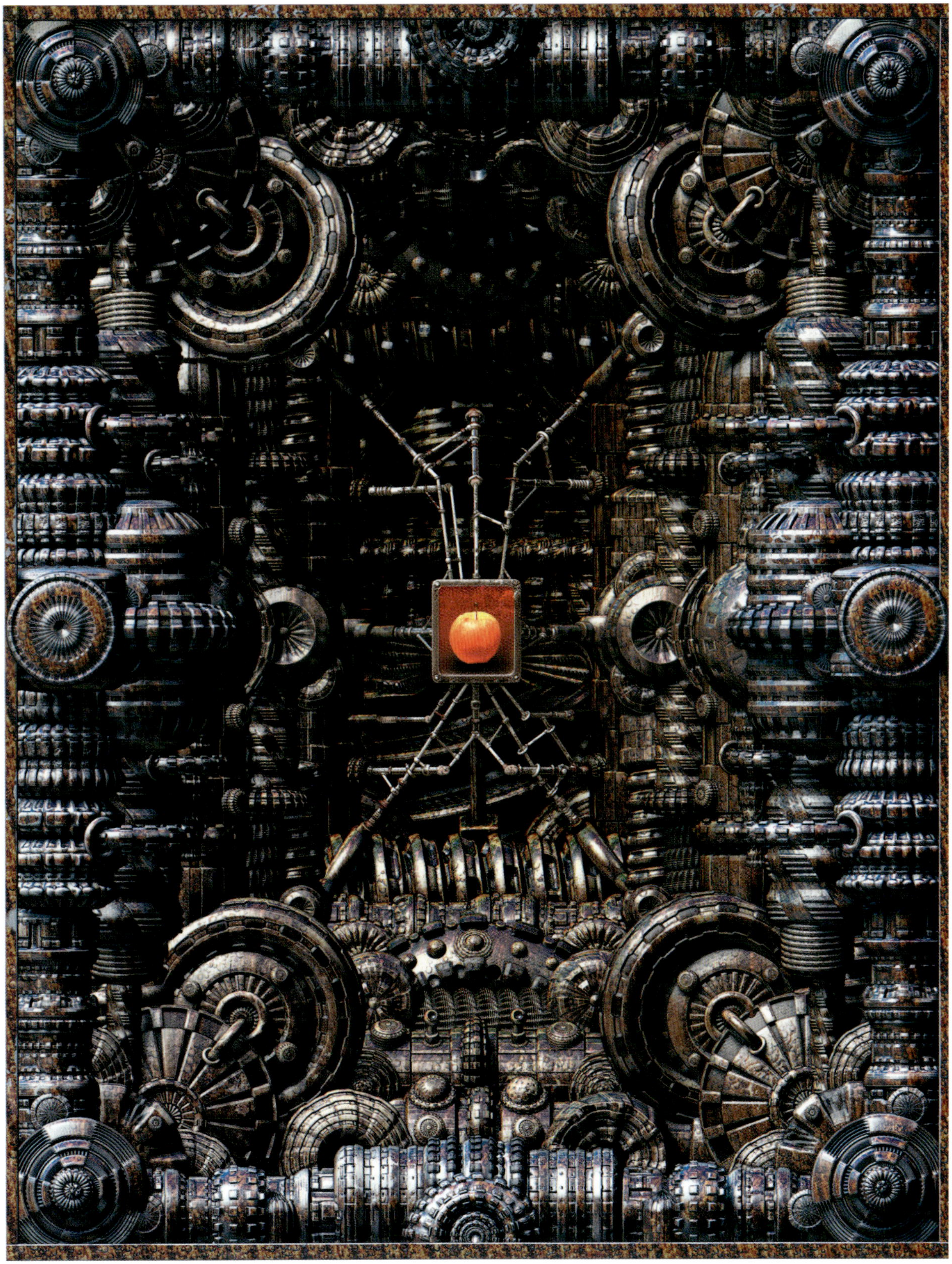

▶ **The Apple**
Meats Meier
Digital image
www.3dartspace.com

In the heart of the dark industrial equipment lies a single, bright-red apple. The contrast between the grim mechanical implements and the brilliant, life-giving apple gives a strong feeling of an organic presence even within the cold, inanimate metal. "A natural apple powers the machinery. This digital 3D art was created using the programs Maya, Zbrush, and Adobe Photoshop, as was the piece ***Primitive City****."*

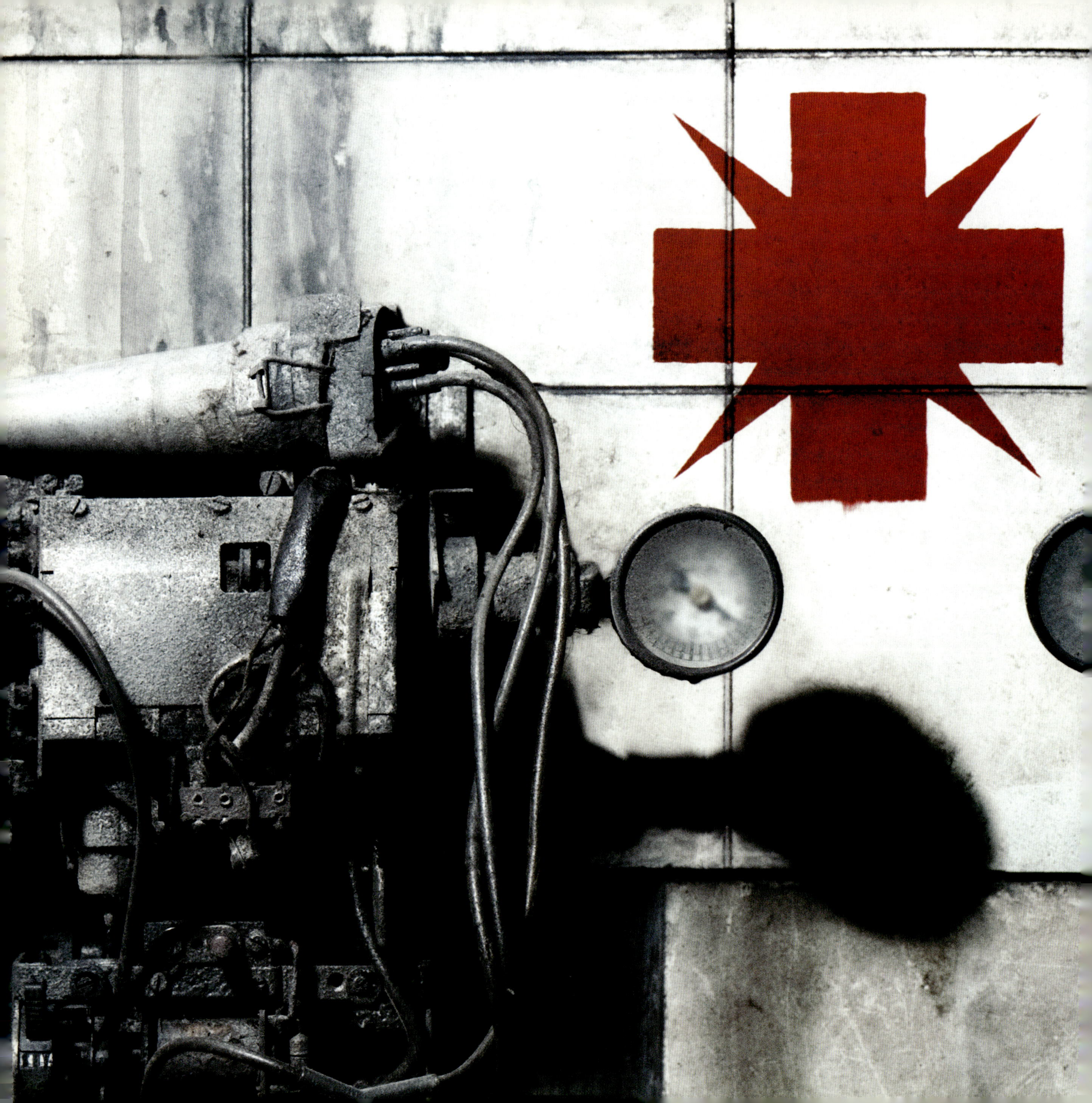

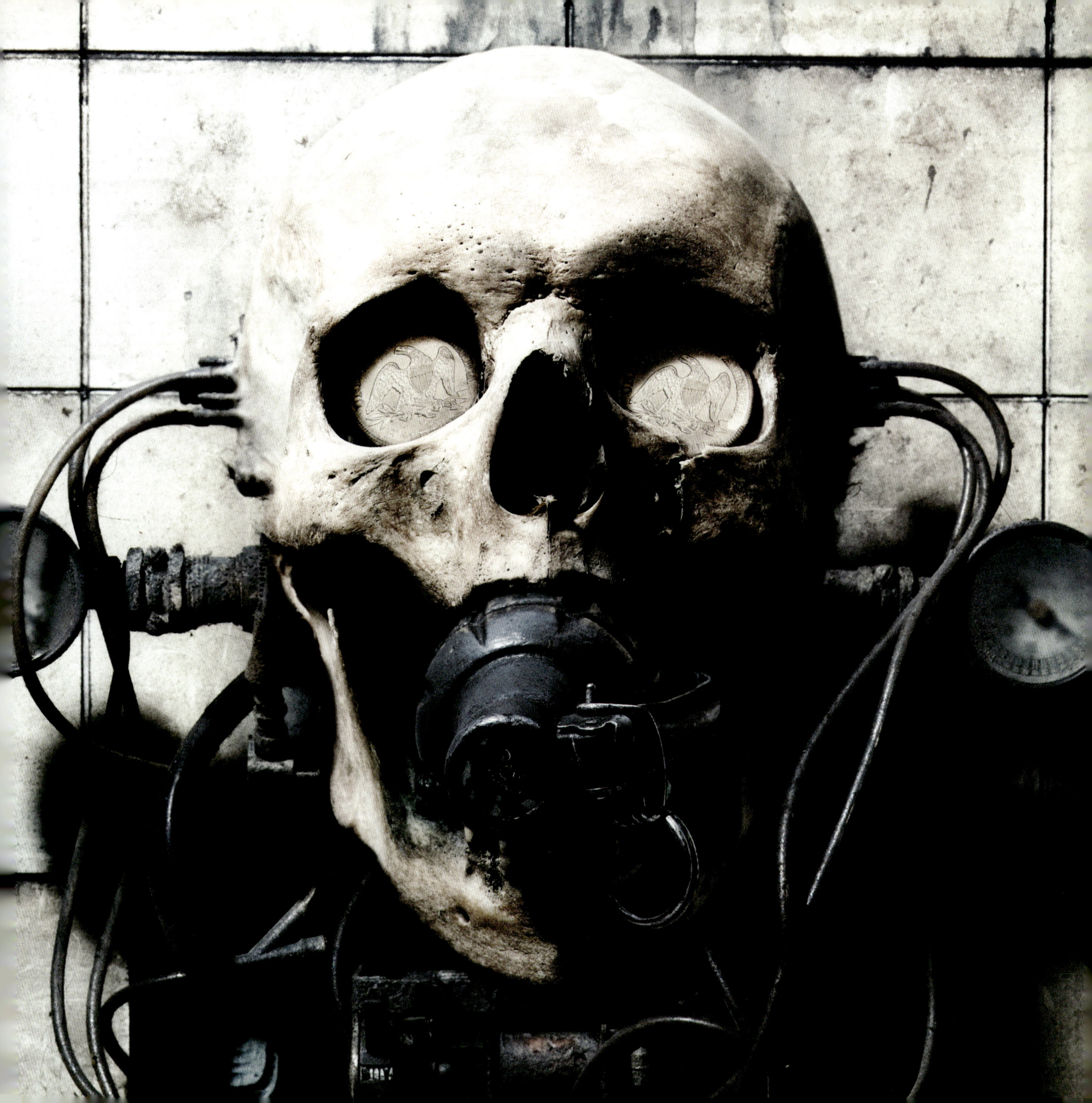

◀◀ **Divine Heresy**
Joachim Luetke
Mixed media
www.luetke.com

Luetke's heavily symbolic sculptural compositions incorporate many beautiful (but sometimes troubling) elements. His ***Divine Heresy*** *weaves human skulls with industrial elements (pumps, gauges, tubing) against a clinical, tiled wall. An oppressive red symbol looms ominously. "This mixed media piece was created for Dino Cazares's debut album."*

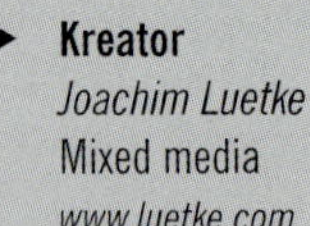

▶ **Kreator**
Joachim Luetke
Mixed media
www.luetke.com

Cold mechanical technology blends with soft organic human tissue before a godlike being in Luetke's ominous ***Kreator****. "Like* ***Divine Heresy****, his piece is a combination of sculptural elements and photography, assembled in Photoshop, and finalized in Painter. It was designed for Kreator's* ***Enemy of God*** *album."*

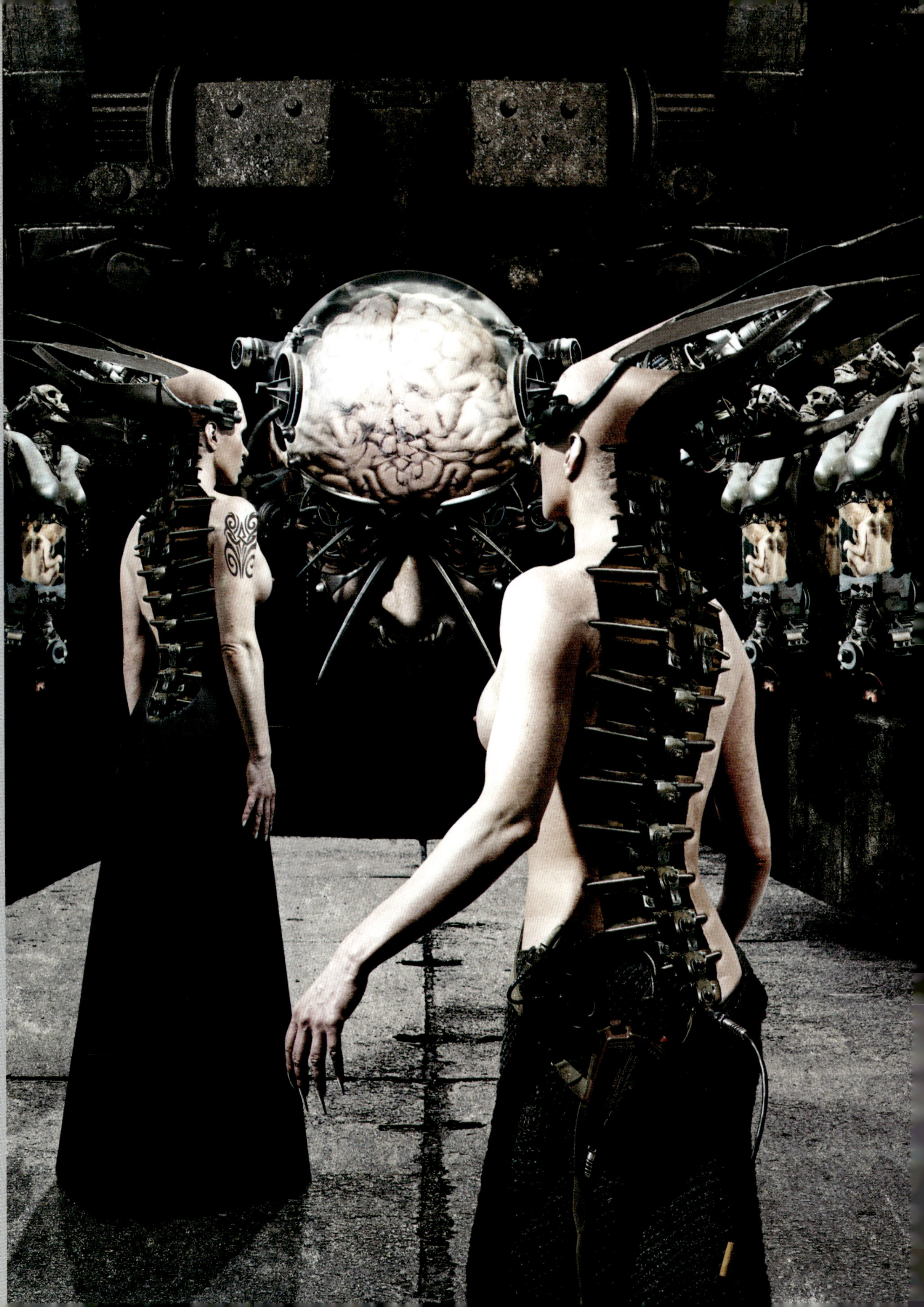

▶ **Aracnoid**
Anne Stokes
Digital painting
www.annestokes.com

*Stokes's **Aracnoid** represents her overwhelmingly biomechanical vision, with spidery Gothic overtones. "This painting was originally commissioned for Biomx merchandise produced by Spiral. It was painted digitally in Adobe Photoshop and combines sci-fi elements inspired by the Borg and horror imagery, with a dose of spider-like features thrown in for good measure. The image has strong design elements in its symmetry and costume."*

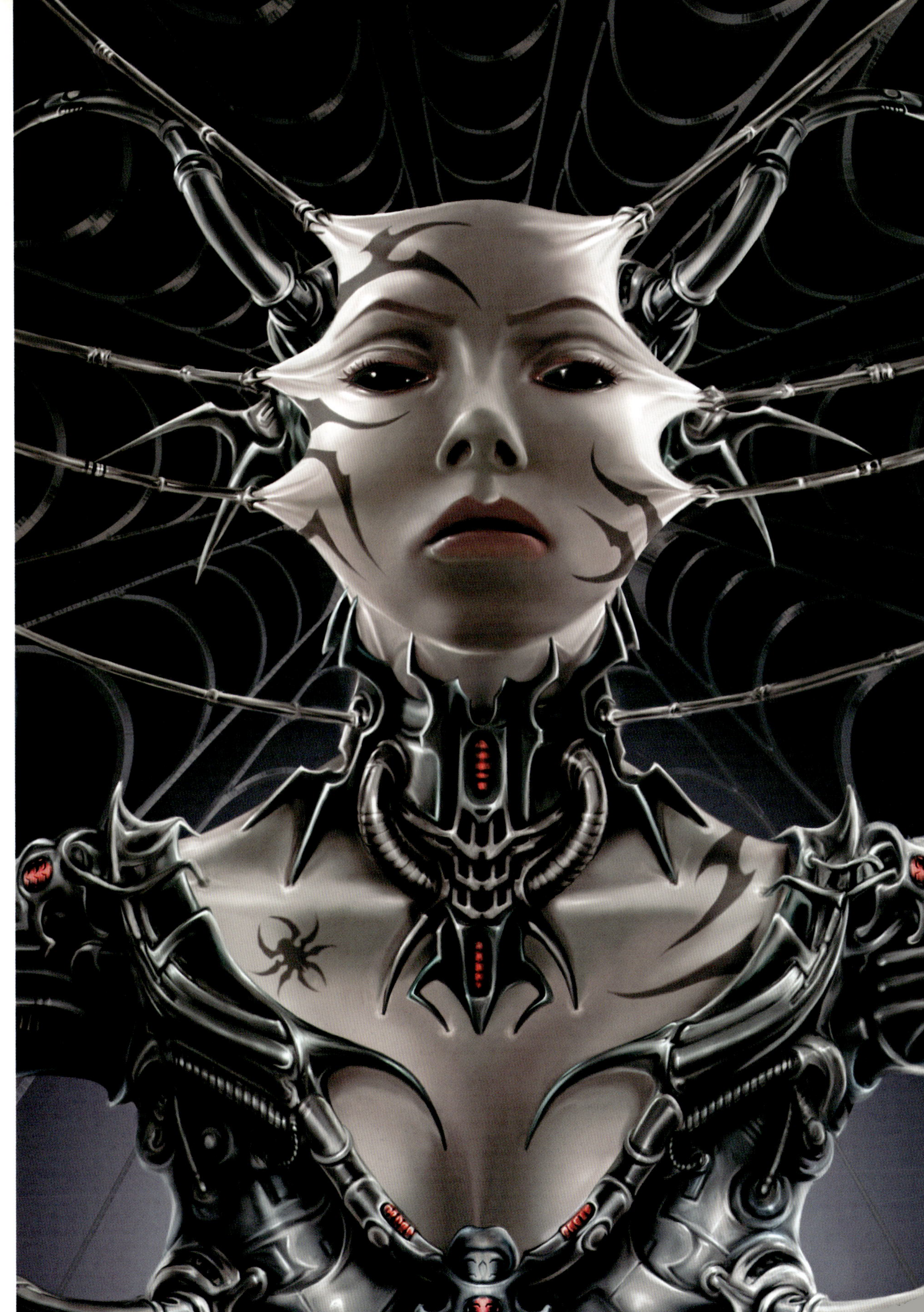

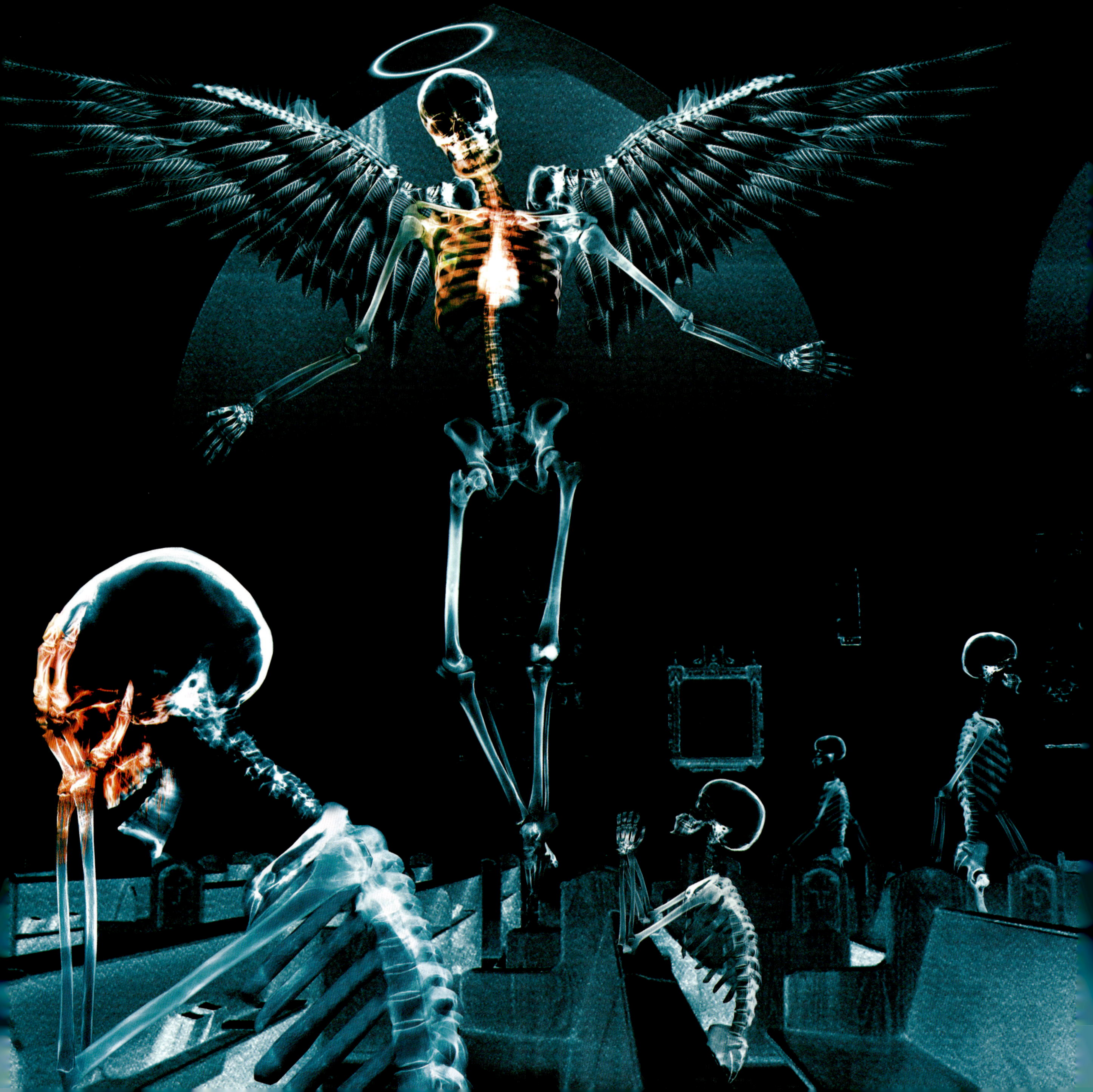

◀ **X-Ray Angel**
Patrick Byers
Photography and digital manipulation
www.101industries.ca

X-Ray Angel *is a combination of photography and digital manipulation from Byers's* ***Angelos*** *series. The "filmy" quality and coloration gives an X-ray feel to the piece, which was created by altering, and layering, hundreds of photographs in Adobe Photoshop. Byers explains: "It's about how angels know how to find the one they will serve and protect."*

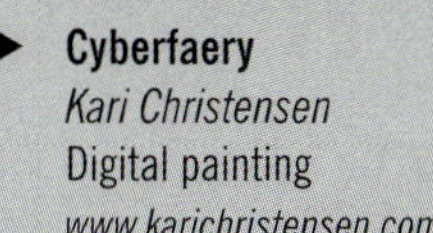

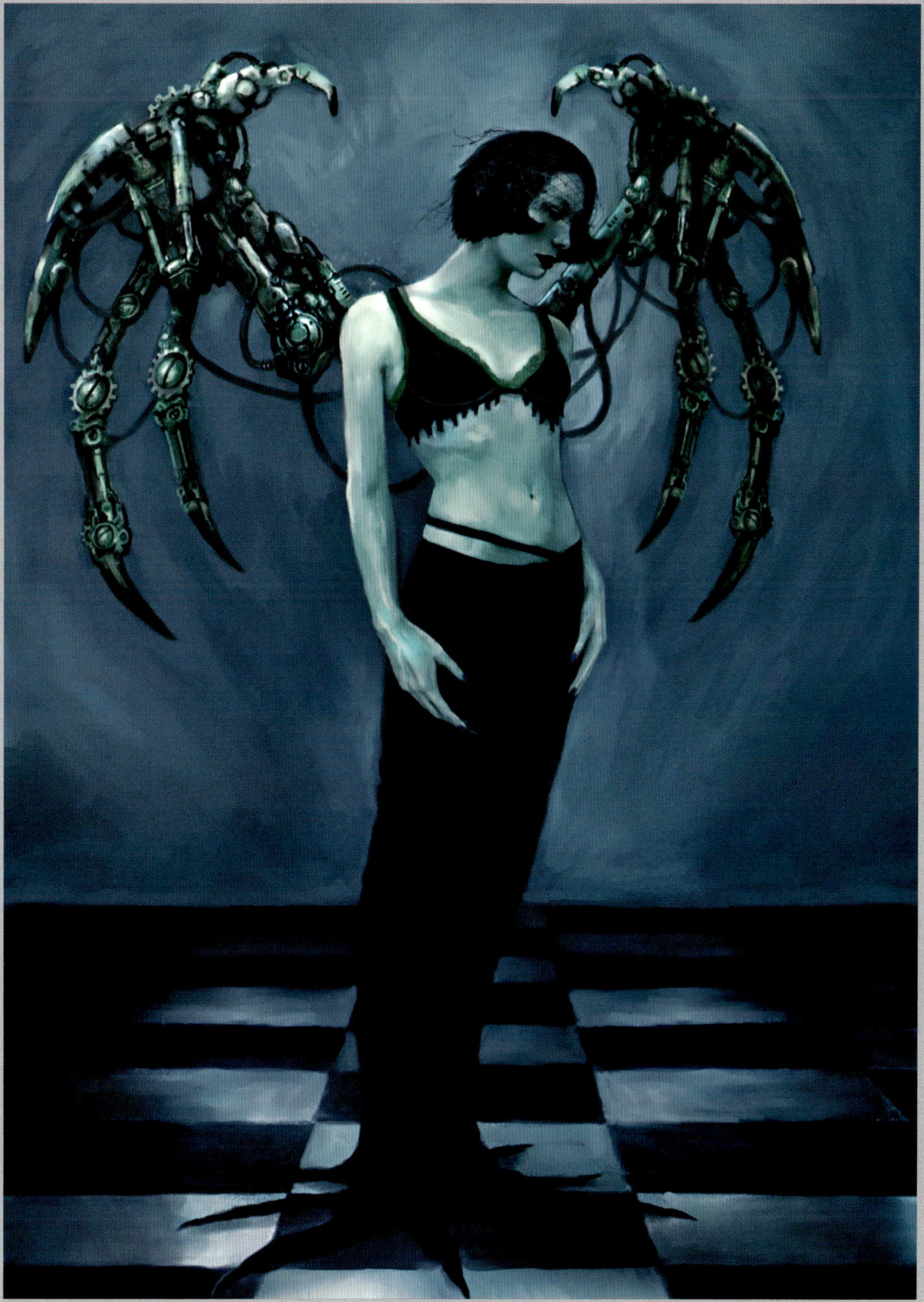

▶ **Cyberfaery**
Kari Christensen
Digital painting
www.karichristensen.com

A beautiful digital painting of an industrially enhanced, statuesque fairy creature by Christensen. "I combined three of my favorite things in this painting; Gothic and industrial elements, with a fairy-tale character."

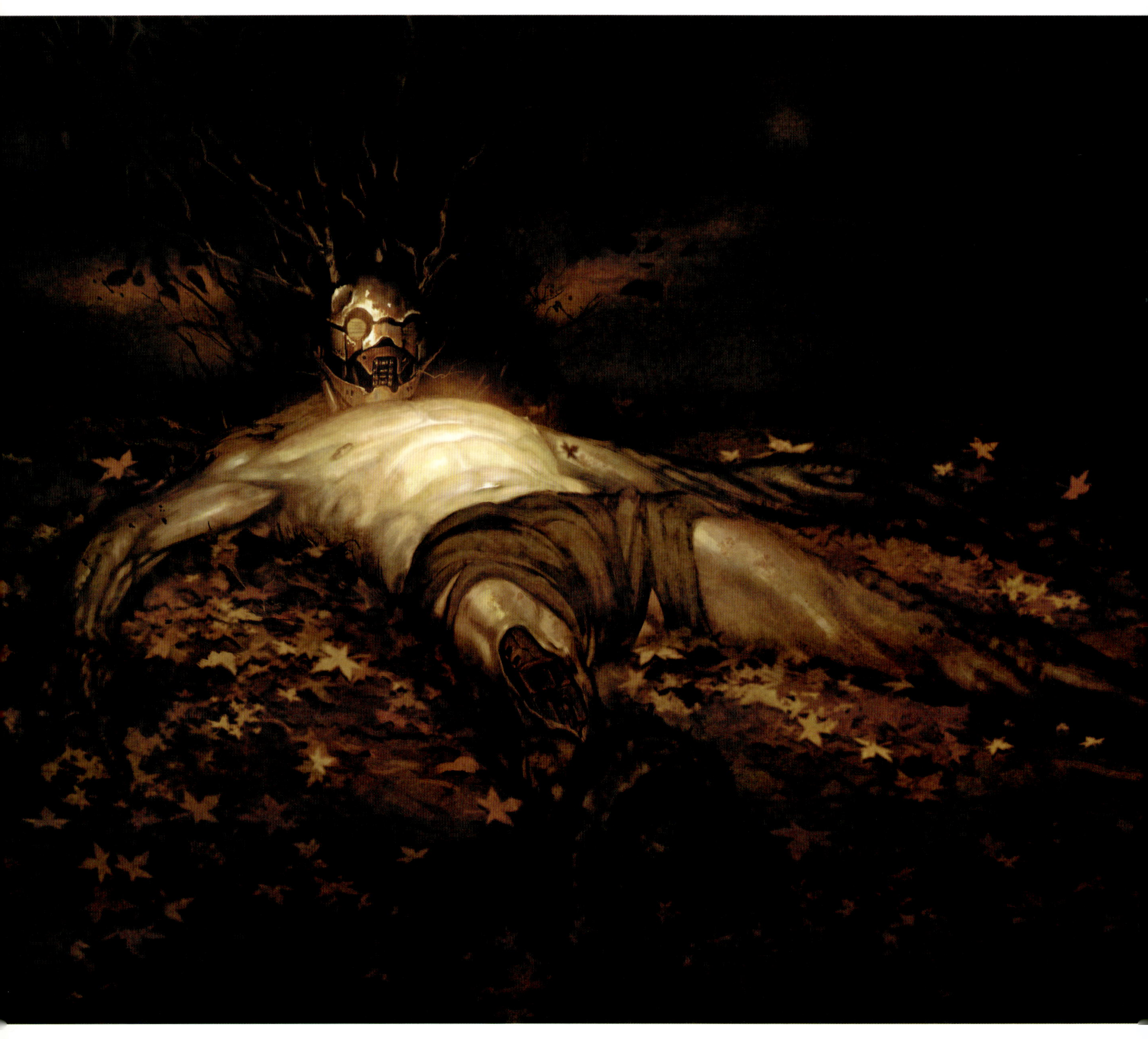

◀ **Stationed**
Christian Alzmann
Pencil, digitally painted
www.christianalzmann.com

A rich color scheme and attention to detail lends a sense of realism to this piece. It is rife with decay and stagnancy, giving it a truly disquieting aura. "This started out as a drawing, using pencil on paper, which I scanned and painted using Corel Painter and Adobe Photoshop. This piece is about growing roots in life and feeling trapped. The style is inspired by old photography. It almost has a painterly quality to it, coupled with warm, rich palettes of the old masters."

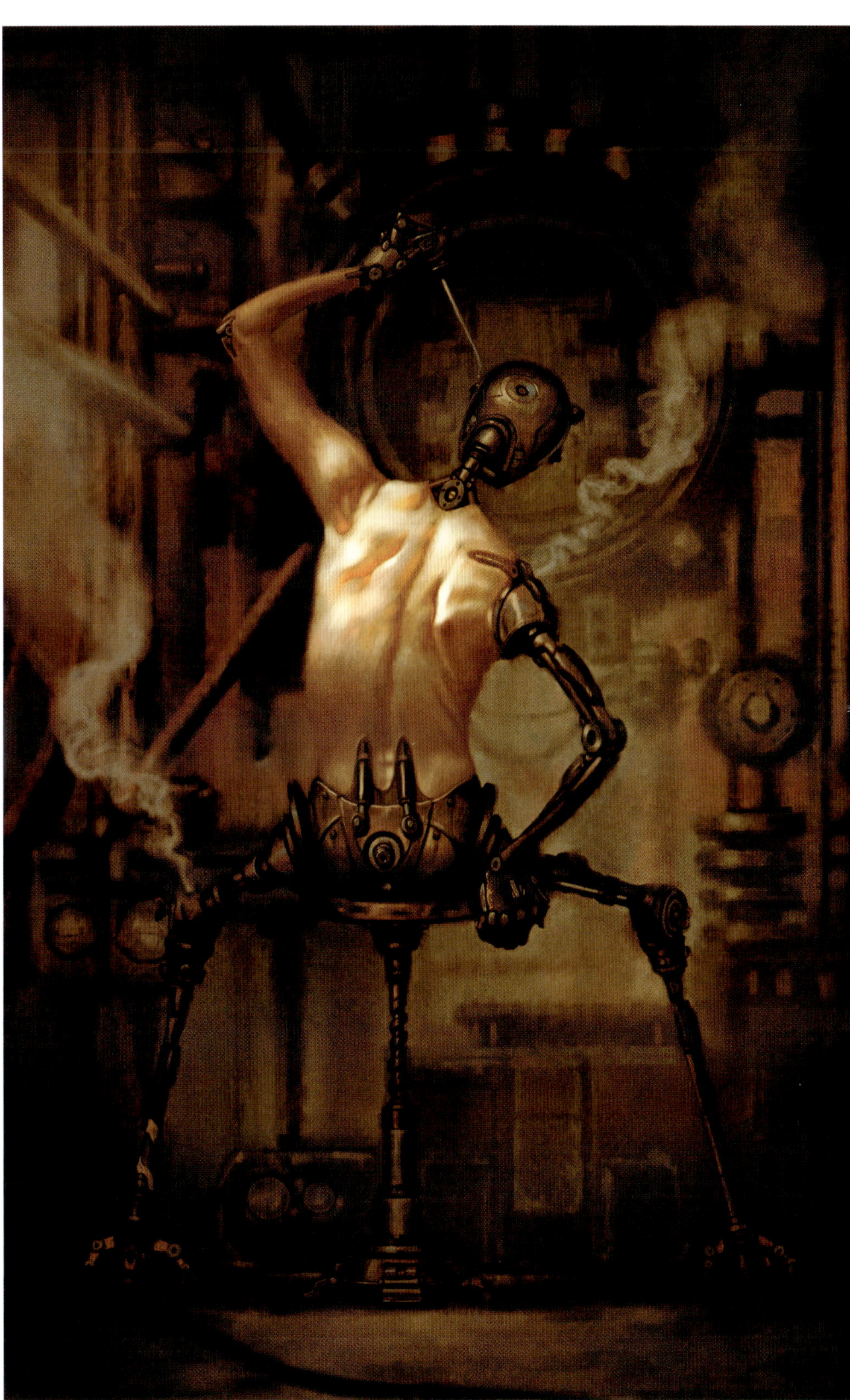

▶ **Maintenance**
Christian Alzmann
Pencil, digitally painted
www.christianalzmann.com

*The Gothic subgenre of steampunk biomechanics is afoot in Alzmann's curious painting. "**Maintenance** was created using pencil on marker paper, then scanned in, and painted using Corel Painter and Adobe Photoshop. I use Painter to get the brushwork, textures, and forms, and Photoshop to balance the color and values. Old photography inspired me, and the thought of this half-robot half-man who is all alone, and has to take care of himself. We are looking at the back of him because he prefers his solace, and we aren't supposed to be there."*

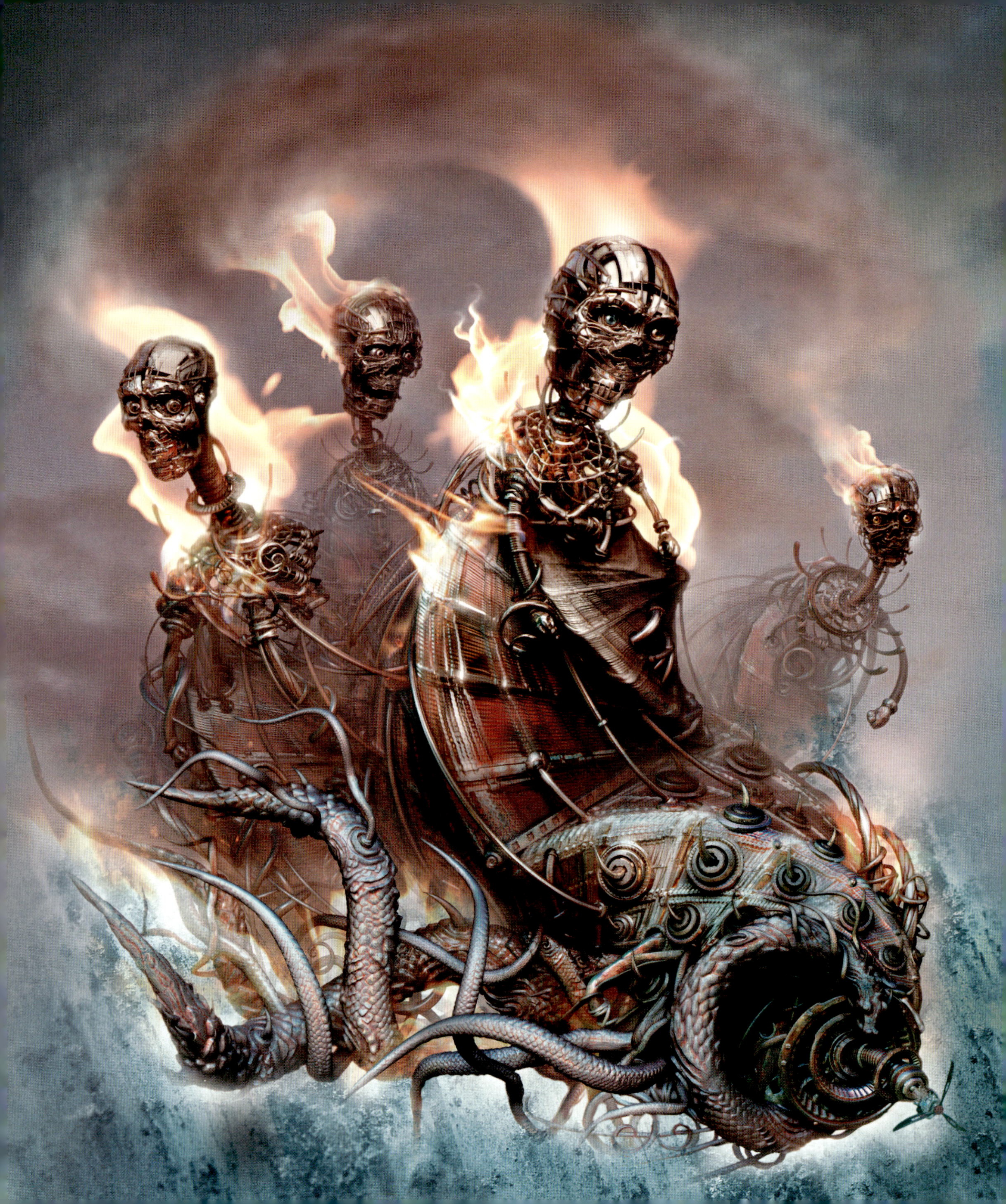

◀ **Four Horsemen**
Meats Meier
Digital image
www.3dartspace.com

Meier used his digital wizardry to create his apocalyptic vision of the ***Four Horsemen****. His masterful use of the programs Maya, Zbrush, and Adobe Photoshop is reflected in this technological depiction of a long-held myth. "The four horsemen of the apocalypse ride in to deliver their justice."*

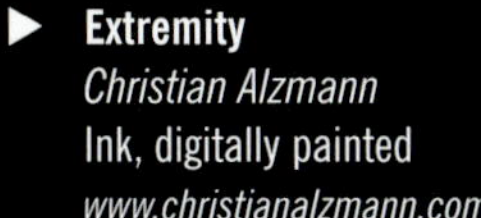

▶ **Extremity**
Christian Alzmann
Ink, digitally painted
www.christianalzmann.com

A sinister, biomechanical female figure, nearly monochromatic in palette, and starkly Gothic in feel. "I started with an ink drawing on a Post-it note. I scanned and painted it using Corel Painter and Adobe Photoshop. I wanted to make something that was pretty and regal-looking, but dark and dangerous at the same time. I also wanted to have graphic curves in this composition, hence she has a snakelike quality."

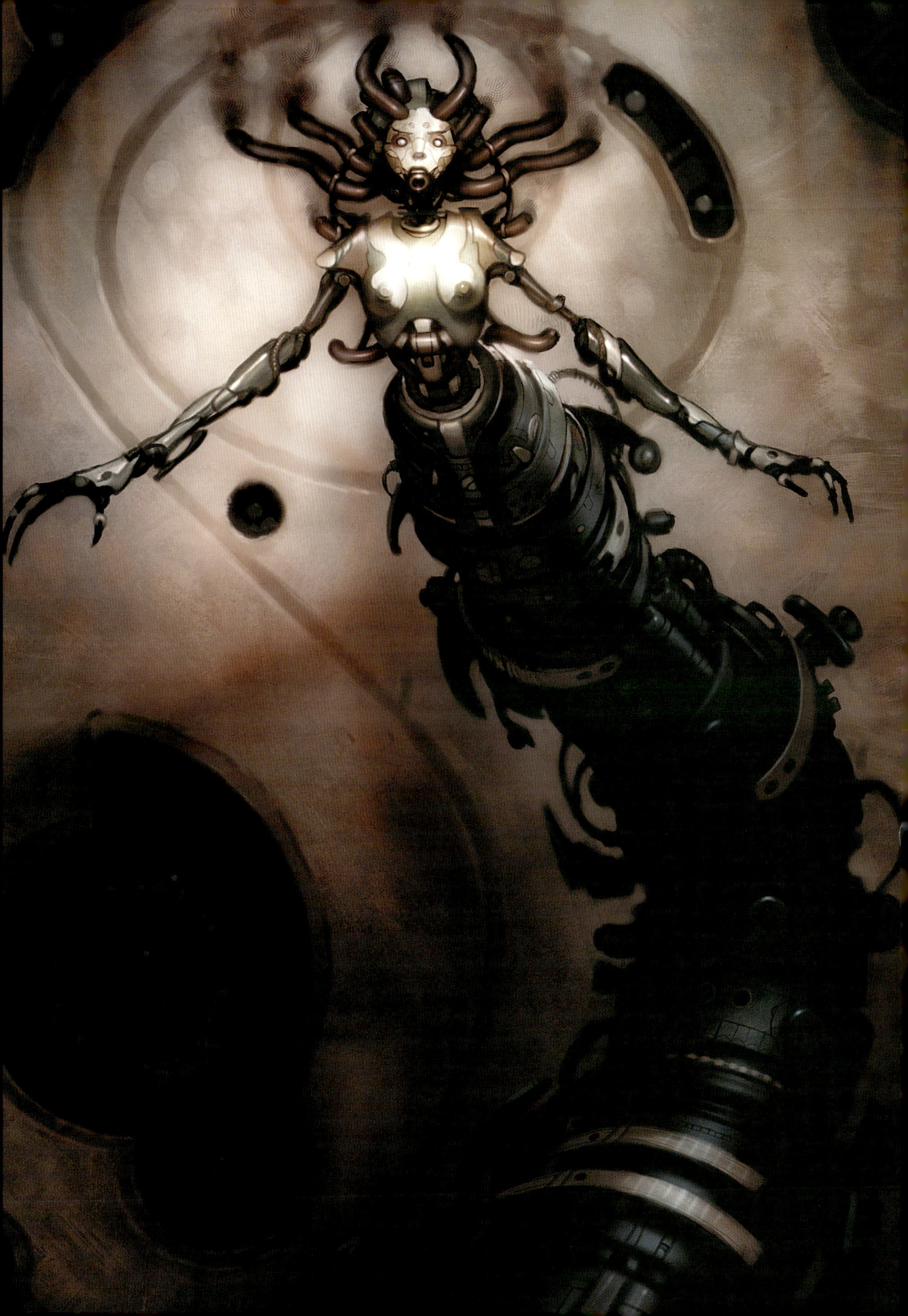

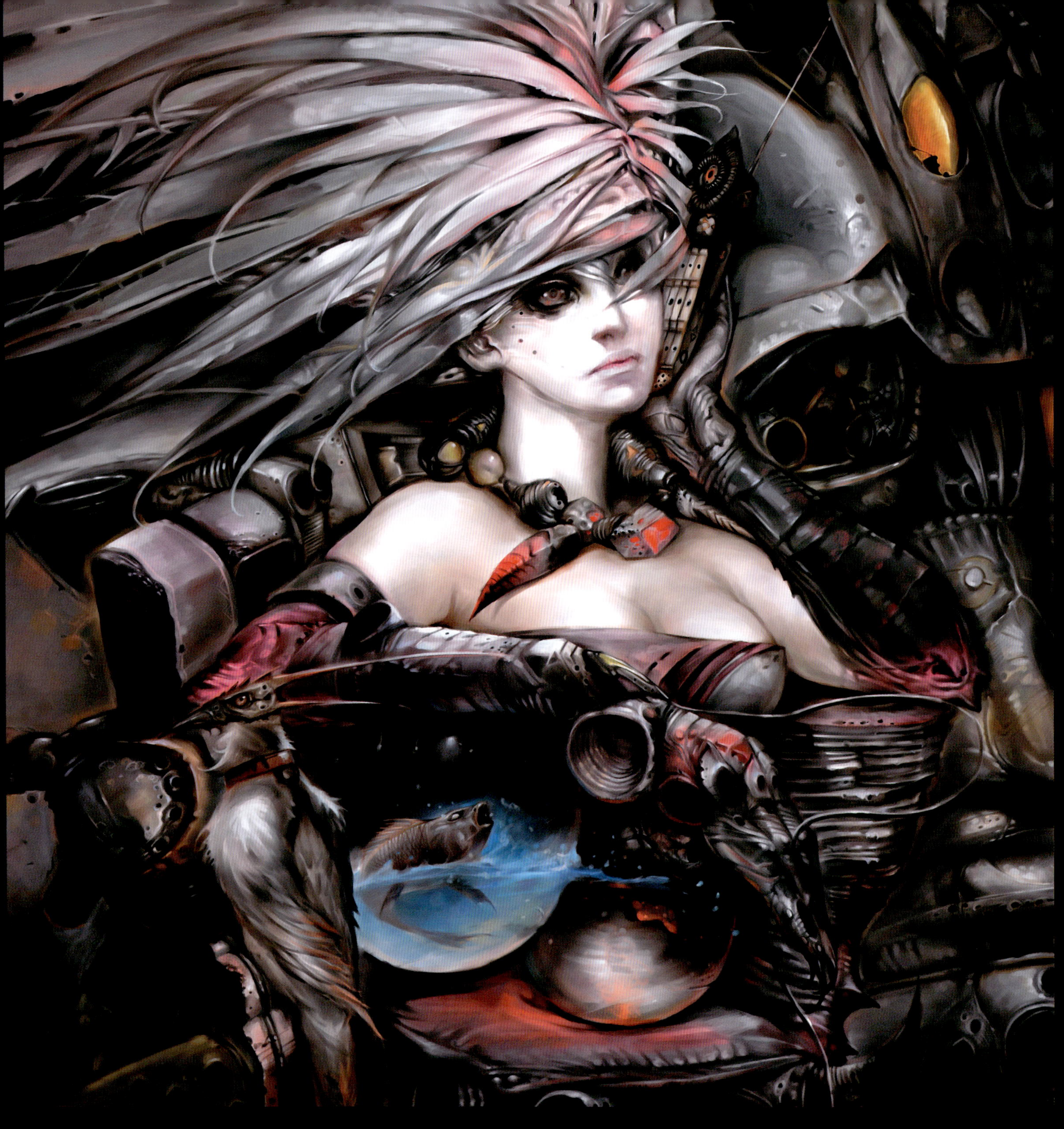

◀ **My World**
Kuang Hong
Digital painting
www.zemotion.net

Influenced heavily by biomechanical elements, Hong's **My World** *features a tender humanoid female embraced by the cold steel of cybernetics. Signs of natural life are underlined by the presence of the fish and the bird. Hong created this digital painting using Corel Painter. "This is a personal work that was inspired by an older piece, entitled* **Butterfly**. *It illustrates a unique and independent world, mixing themes of ancient and contemporary fads."*

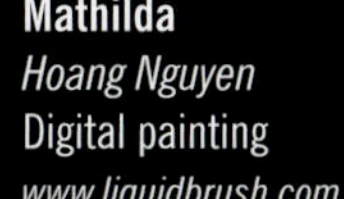

▶ **Mathilda**
Hoang Nguyen
Digital painting
www.liquidbrush.com

Conjuring a particular sense of melancholy and despair from a bygone age, Nguyen has used Adobe Photoshop to compose his **Mathilda**, *lost in landscape obscured by clouds of smoke, the light hitting her bruised and saddened face. "I was inspired by the World War I era and wanted to capture the mood and the sense of loss. I also wanted to bring a fantastical element to the piece, to give it a 'what if' feel."*

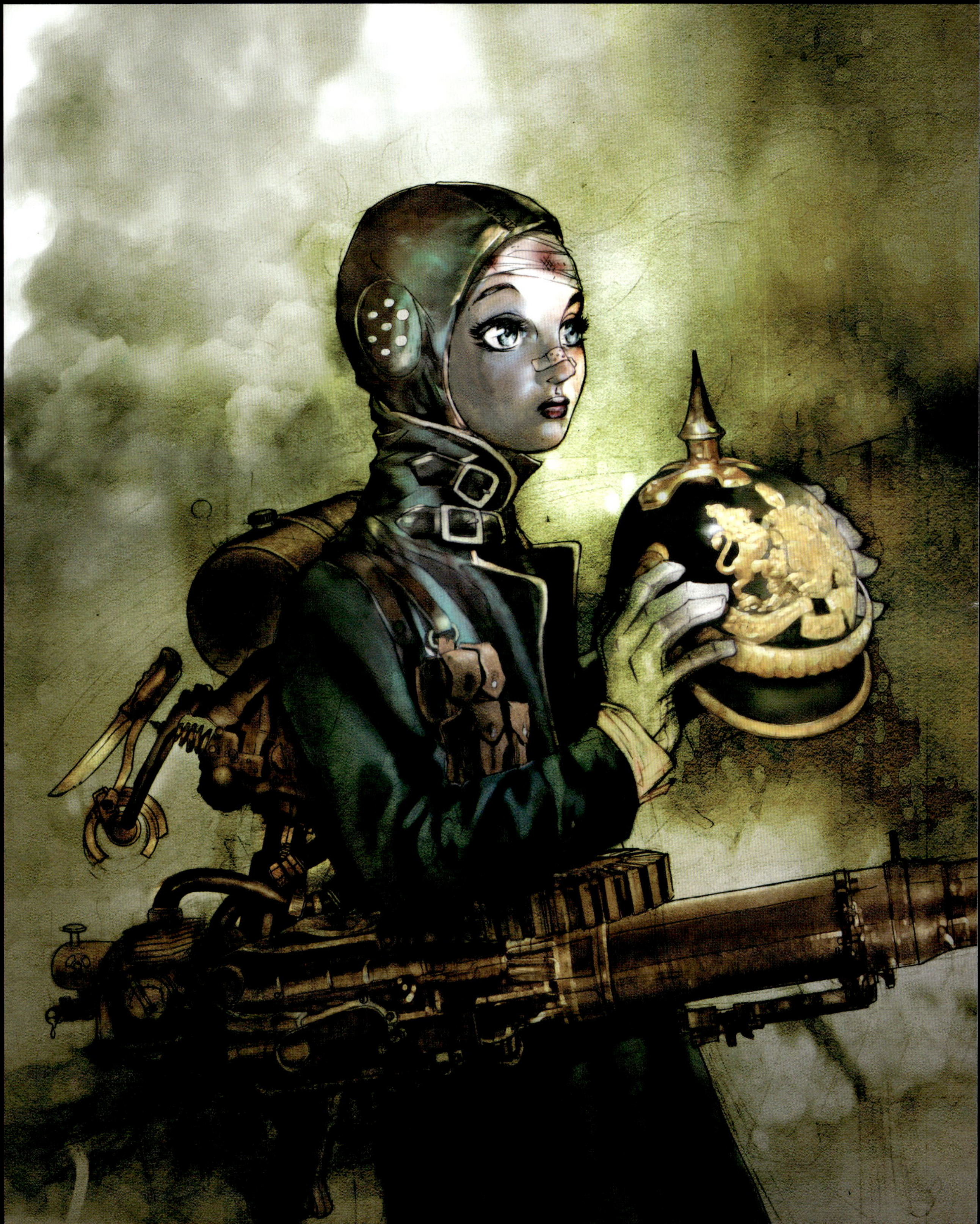

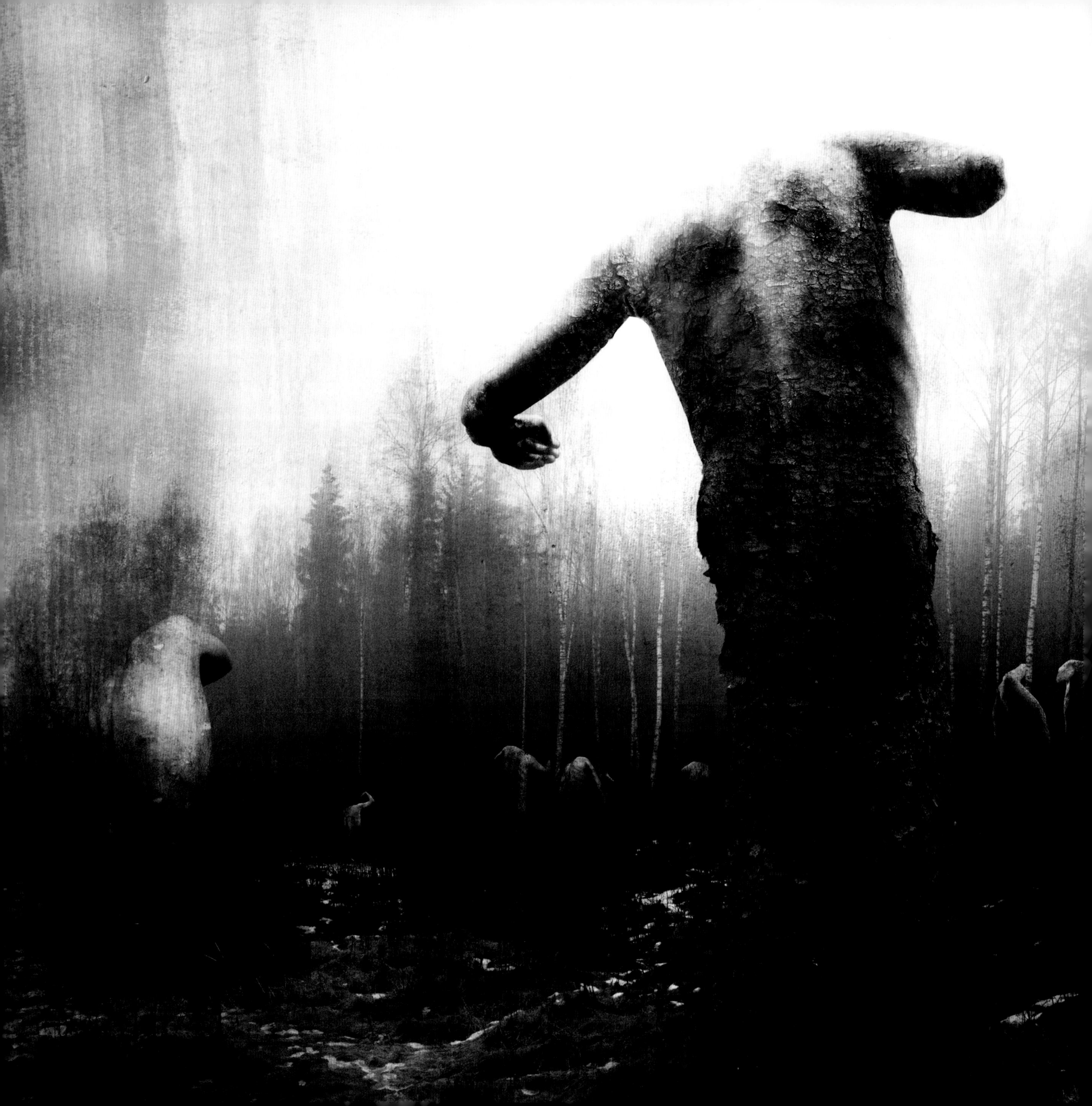

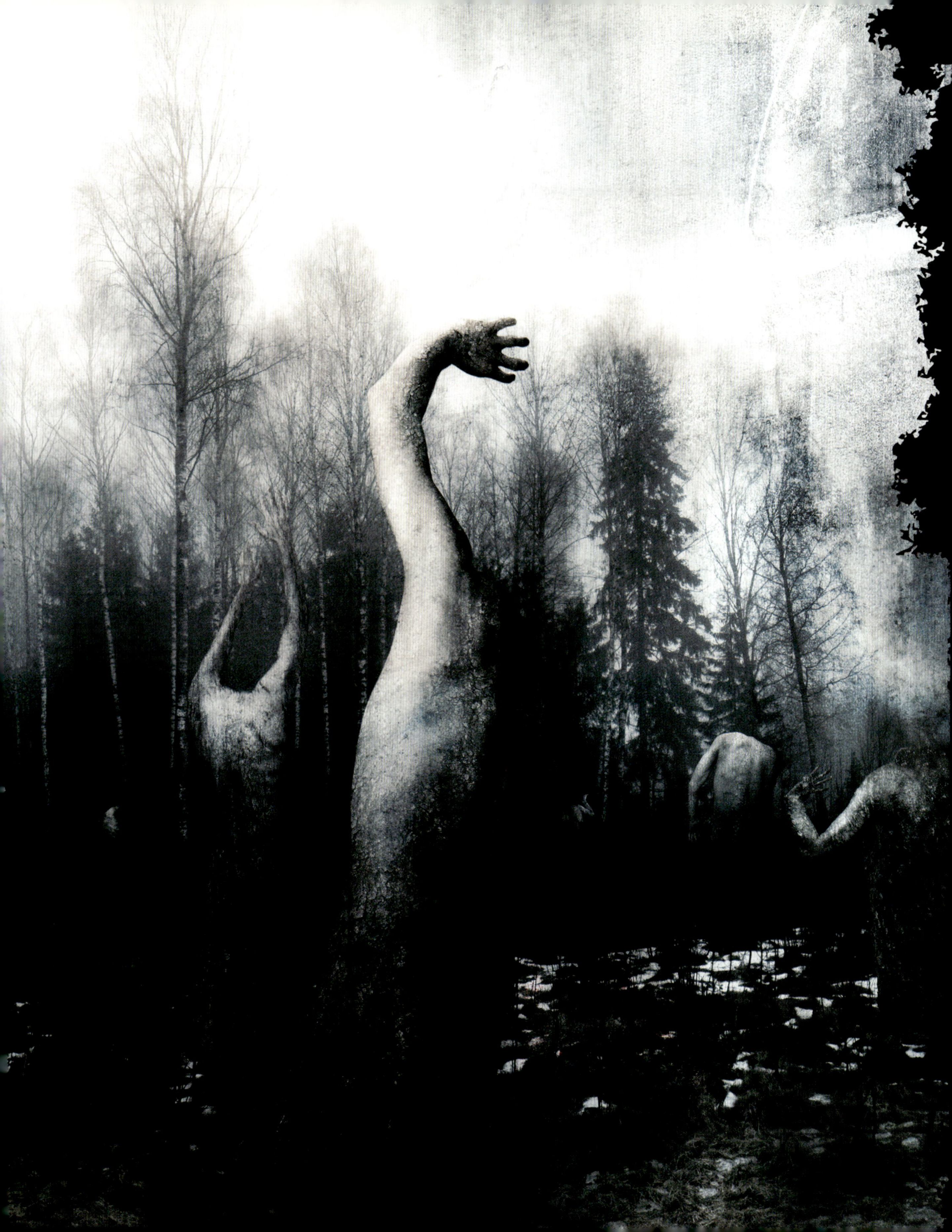

CHAPTER 5

LURKING HORROR

◀ **Birthmark**
Erlend Mørk
Photography and
digital manipulation
www.erlendmork.com

Mørk's nightmarish photographic masterpiece, ***Birthmark****, features humanoid figures amidst a bleak landscape. He created his vision digitally, assembling many photographs in Adobe Photoshop. The limited palette gives a blighted and desperate feeling to the piece.*

Dunce
Gus Fink
Mixed media
www.gusfink.com

An ingenious take on an antique postcard, Fink has fabricated this powerful image of a rather pitiful creature. "This dunce is a baby born into a world of entertainment and exposure. The baby doesn't want to be a clown, so it's forced to look like one — giving it the ultimate punishment of being the Dunce forever."

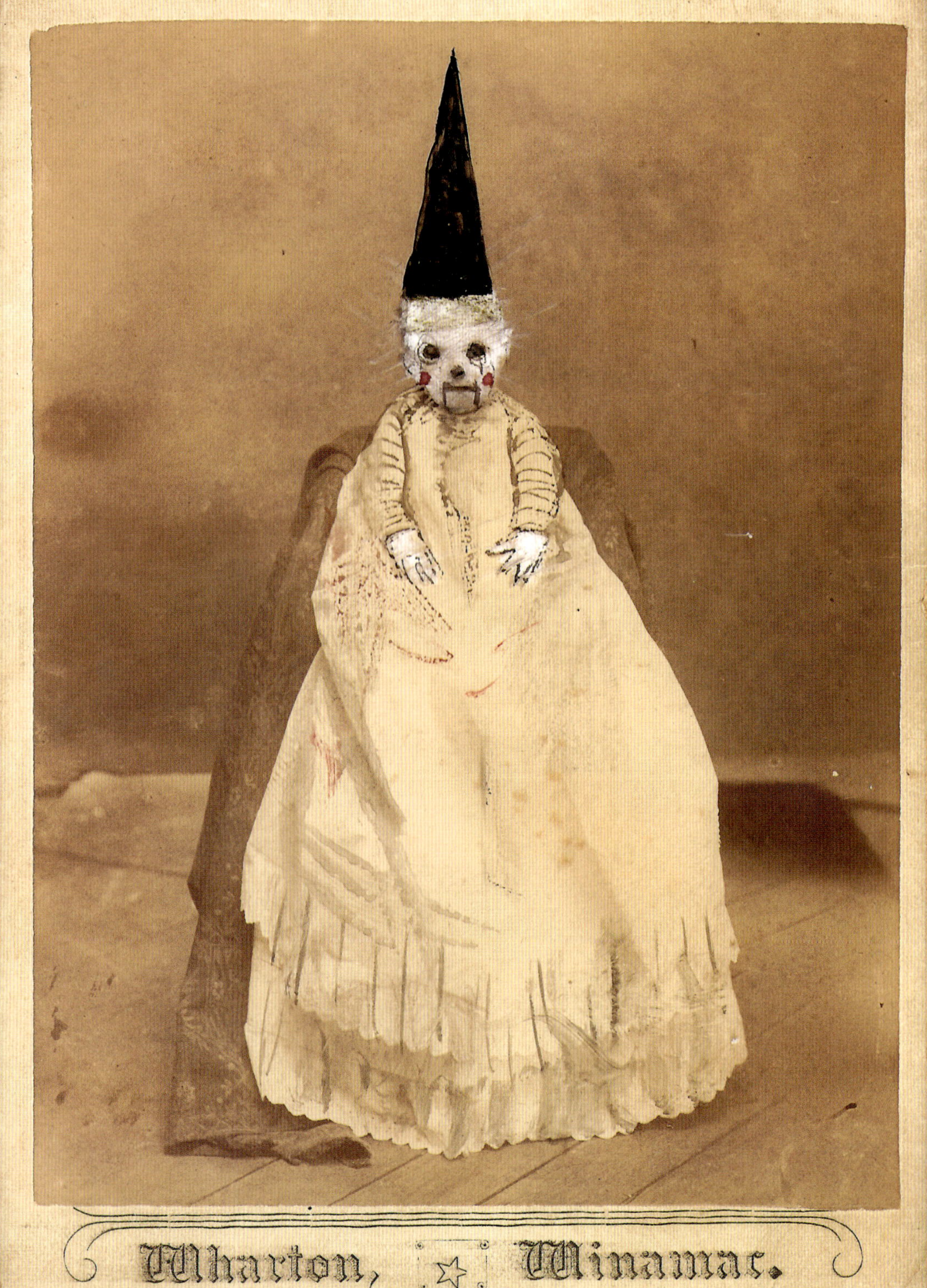

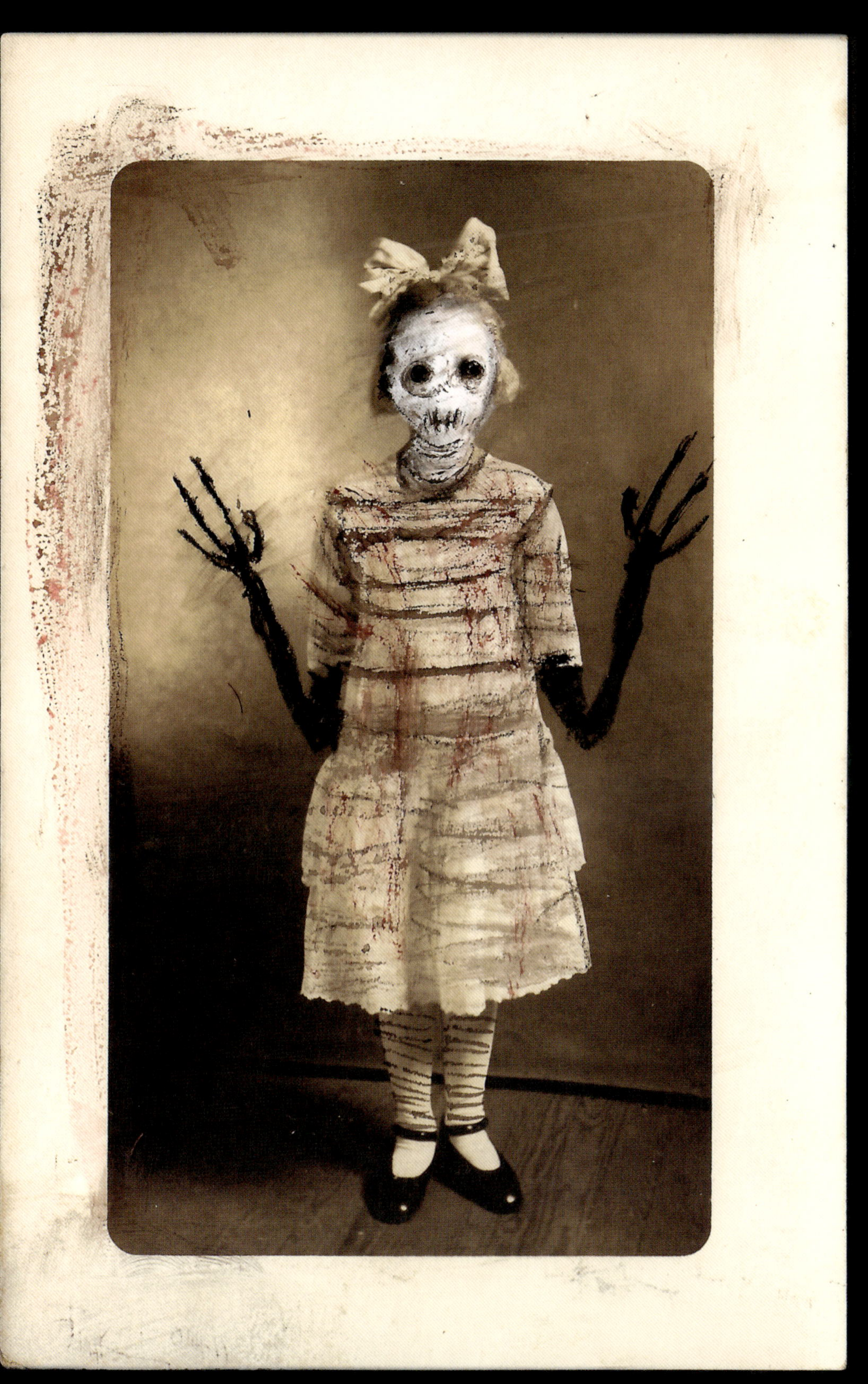

◀ **Stick Girl**
Gus Fink
Mixed media
www.gusfink.com

*Another inspired piece — this time Fink has made a "Stick Girl" out of an antique postcard. Fink's unique visions often include elements of creeping horror, humor, and even a little thoughtful insight. "**Stick Girl** is made of sticks and stones. She called so many girls so many names that instead of others throwing them at her, karma turned her into them!"*

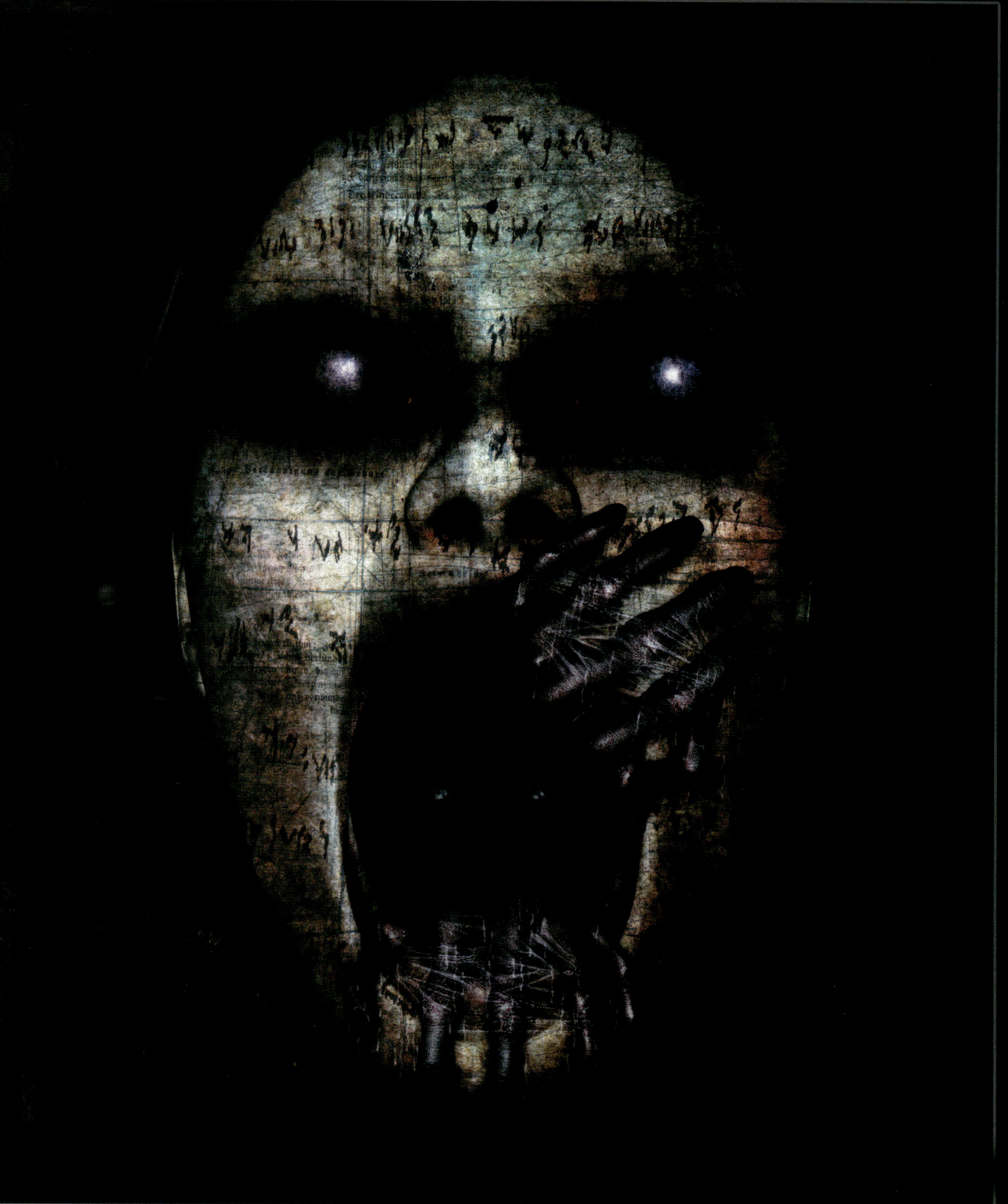

◀ **Something Inside**
Charli Siebert
Digital painting
www.unimaginative.org

A digital creation composed by Siebert in Adobe Photoshop and Poser. ***Something Inside*** *depicts a ghastly, contorted face with a pair of hands coming out from within. Diabolical runes are etched upon the mask-like features, and cobweb-like textures adorn the hands.*

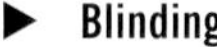

Blinding
Charli Siebert
Digital painting
www.unimaginative.org

Despair and claustrophobia abound in Siebert's ***Blinding****. Created digitally using Adobe Photoshop and Poser, Siebert has composed a dismaying scene of a blinded figure in a dank space. The nearly monochromatic color scheme and scratched surfaces give the image a forgotten and desolate look.*

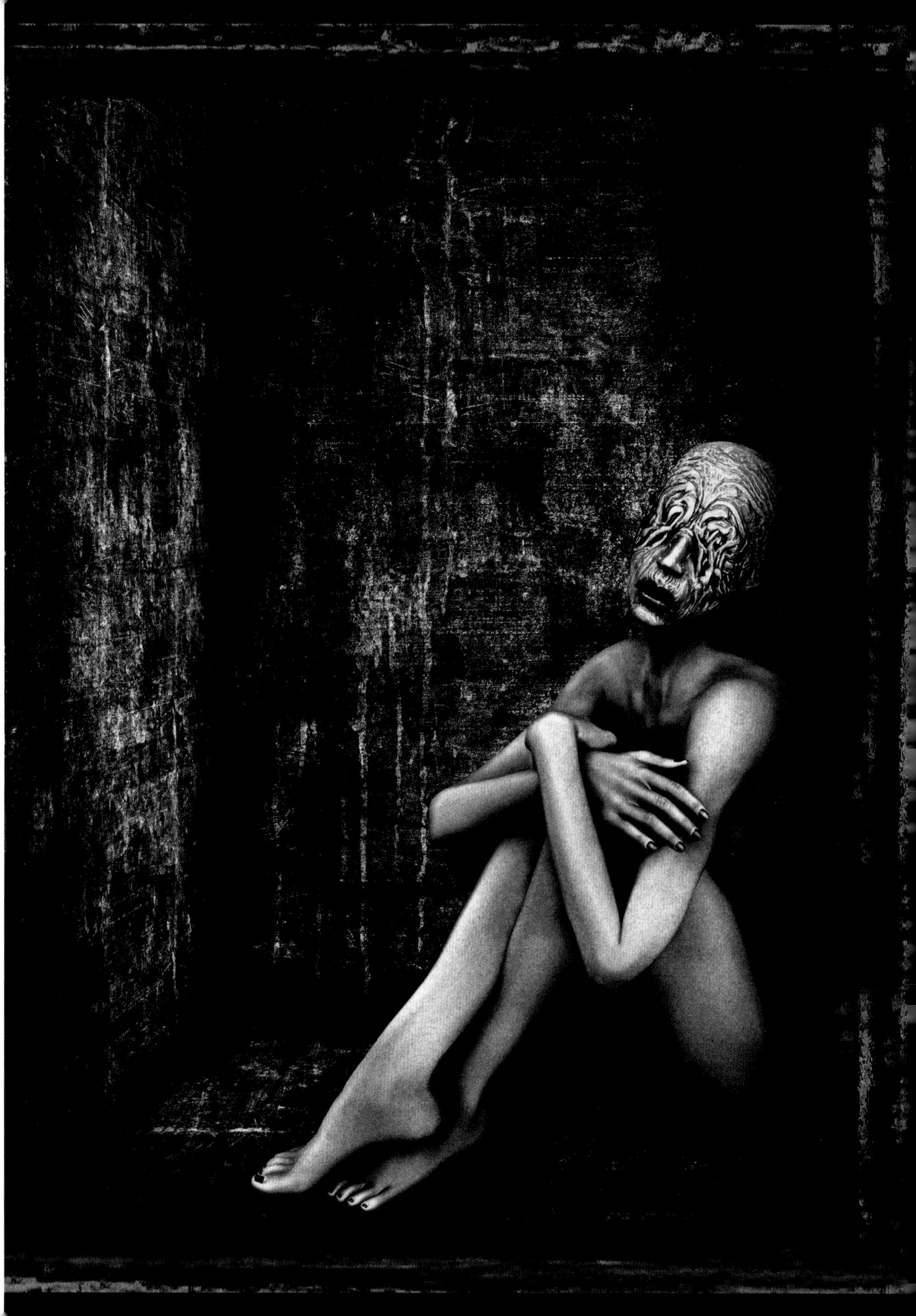

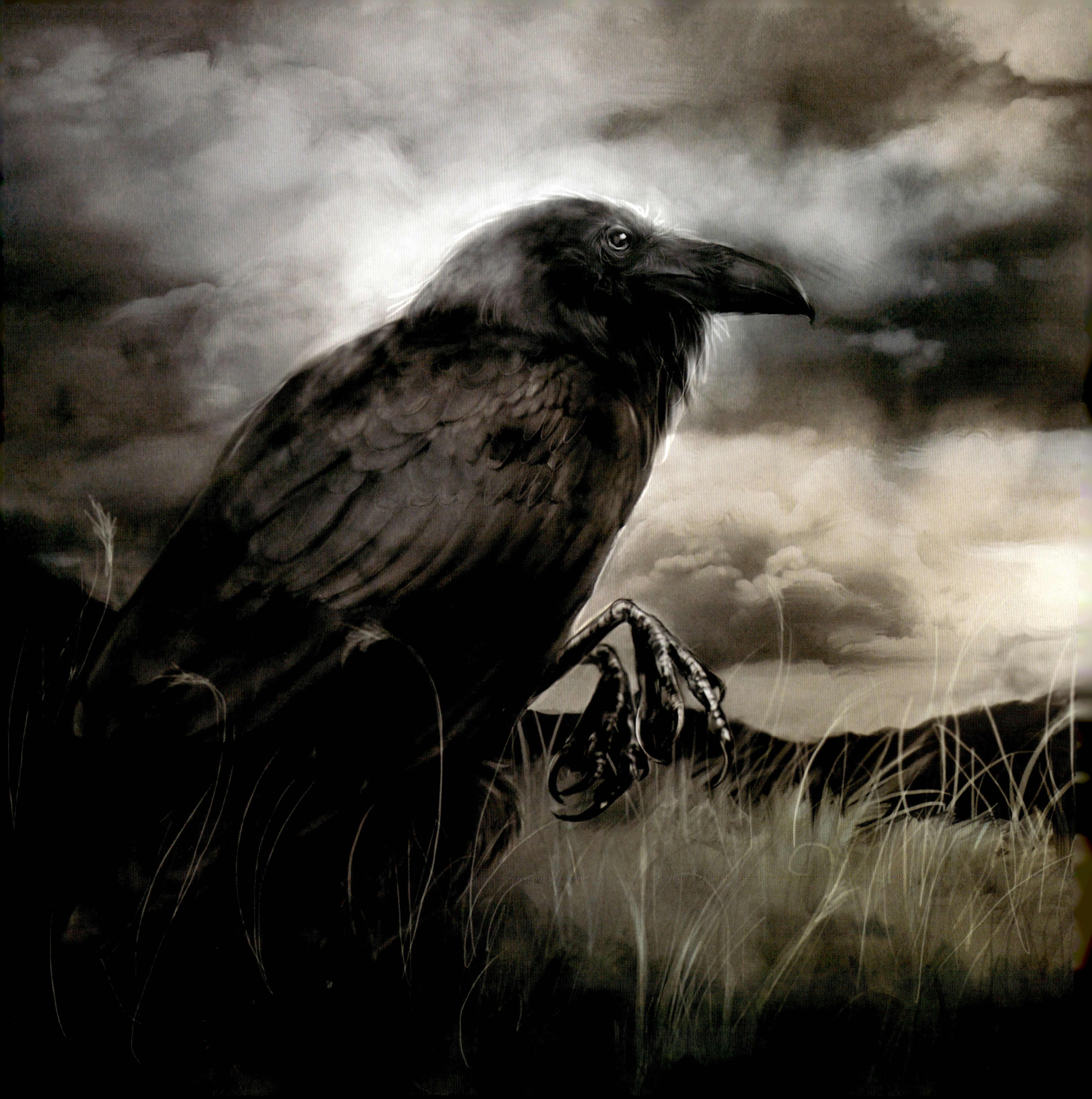

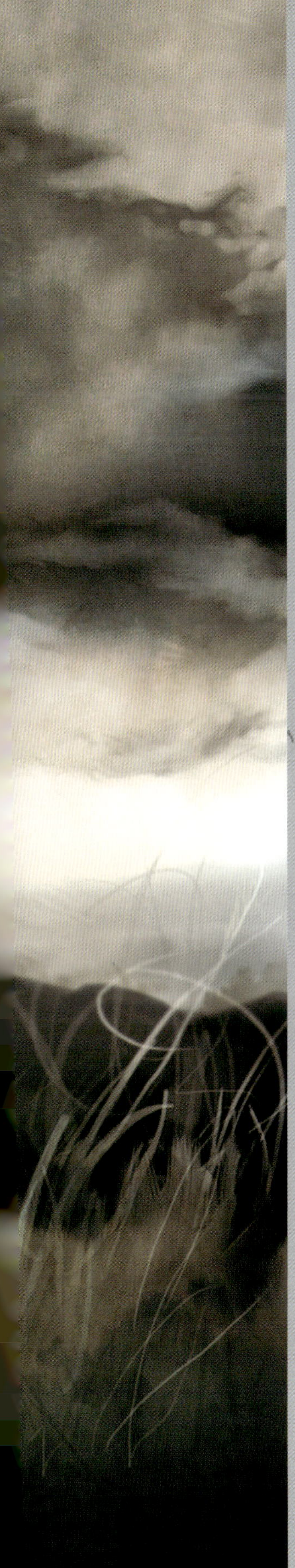

◀ **Watcher**
Kimberly Myatt
Digital painting
www.beetlebones.net

A moody, atmospheric piece featuring a different sort of raven... "This piece often confuses people. It takes a while to notice that the raven has four legs, it seems. I used a lot of references for the raven, including a close-up of talons I found in a book. I wanted this piece to be a bit less refined than some of my other work, so the black-and-white foundation was loose and free-flowing. It was tightened up with detail once I had placed the color on a layer beneath, and flattened the image."

▶ **Tear Down Heaven**
Camille Kuo
Digital painting
www.camilkuo.com

A vivid and vicious self-portrait, Kuo expresses a moment of inner-torment through her stunning artwork. The combination of natural colors with the brilliantly obscene red and yellow setting brings an aura of desperation and madness to the piece. "All people have hard times in their lives, as do I. I had a bad mood and with it came this inspiration. It's all painted freehand from scratch, using a photograph of myself as reference."

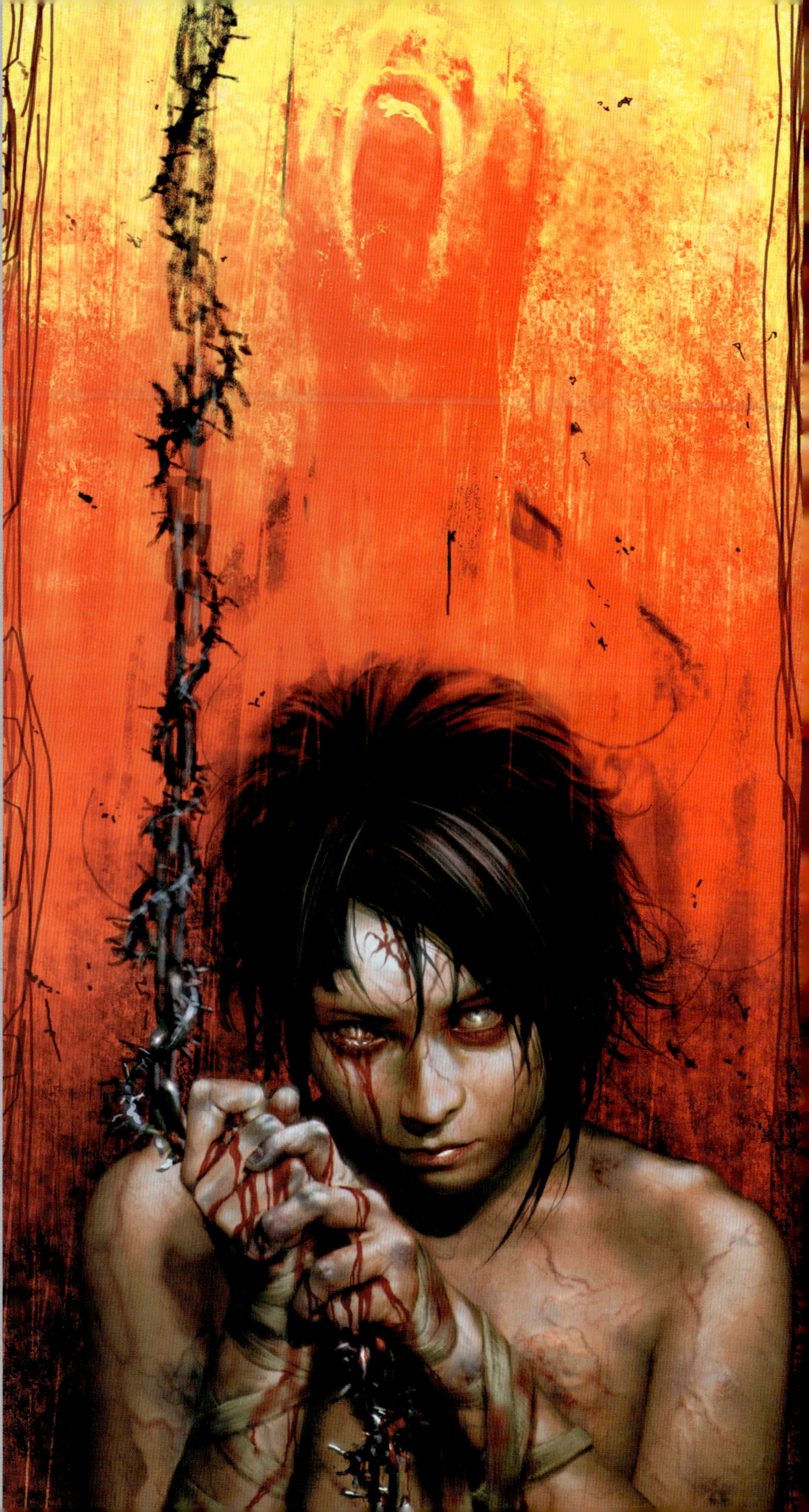

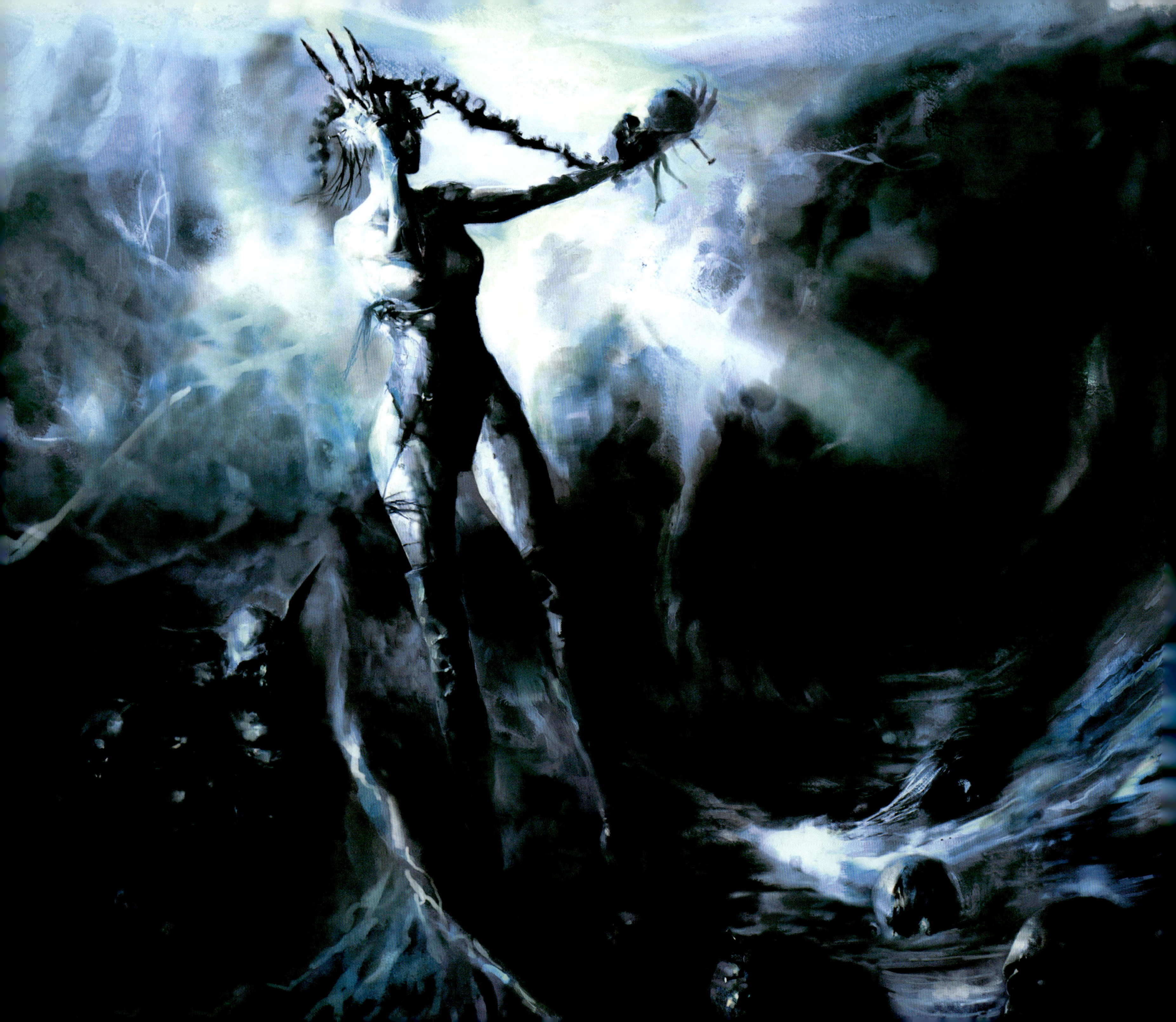

◀ **Descent Into Darkness**
Kyri Koniotis
Digital painting
www.kyri.epilogue.net

"When I originally sketched this scene in my pad the idea behind it was to try and portray a dying man's vision of hell. It went through a lot of changes before it got to the finished, digitally painted, version you see here. I was very much influenced by Simon Bisley and H. R. Giger at the time, as well as horror films, and themes of sex and religion."

▶ **Save Us**
George Patsouras
Digital painting
www.mkrevolution.net

A powerful image of a statue weeping bloody tears. "I have always wanted to paint a statue crying tears of blood because of the striking imagery involved. I based this on a photograph of myself, so it is a self-portrait in a sense. I wanted the light to come from the top, to help bring out the anatomy of the figure. When I painted this with Adobe Photoshop, I started in grayscale and added colors later."

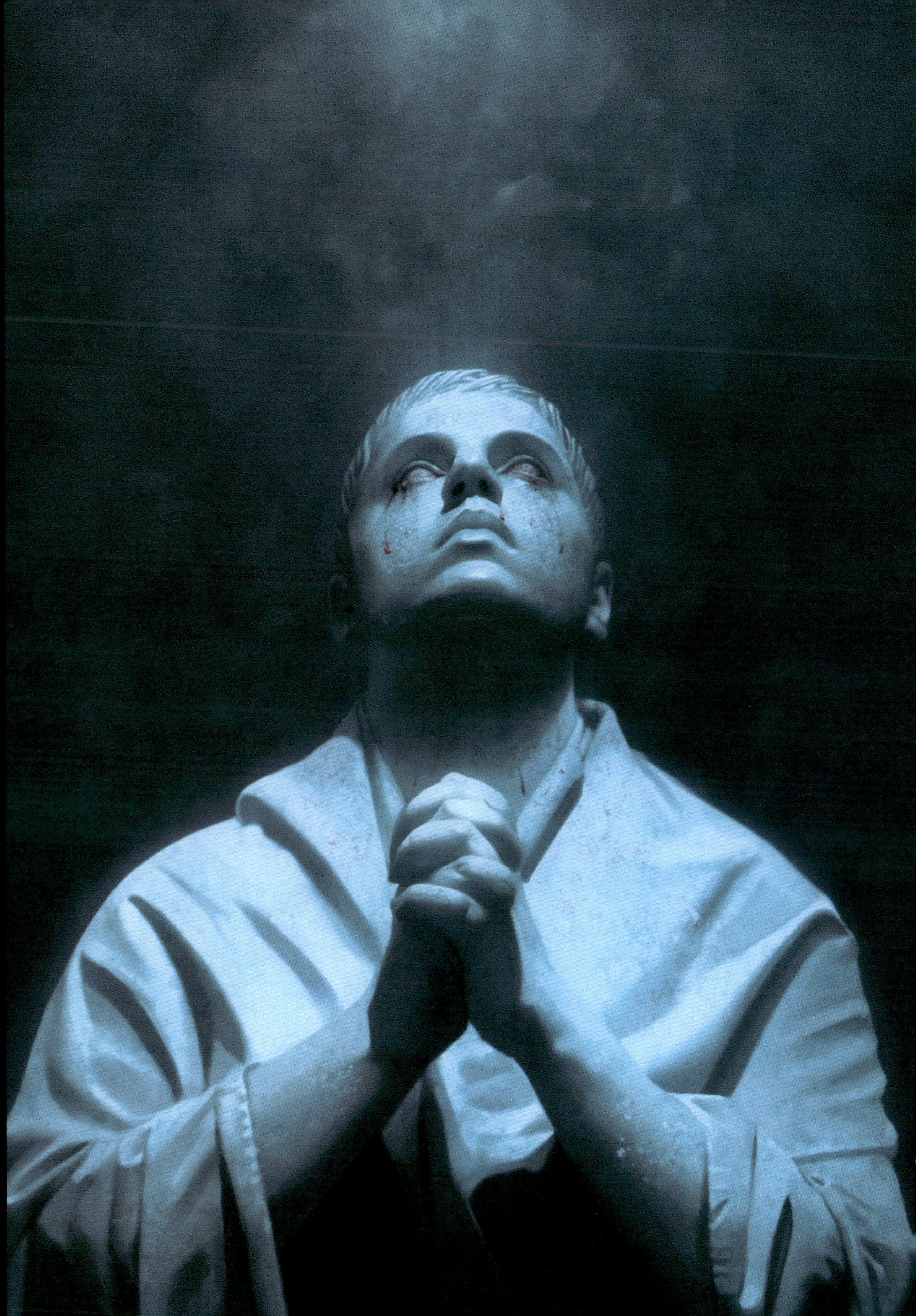

▶ **House of Discord**
Erlend Mørk
Photography and
digital manipulation
www.erlendmork.com

A gaunt figure is the centerpiece in Mørk's horrific ***House of Discord*** *— a disturbing vision indeed. "Although I work digitally, I consider my approach very much based around working in the traditional photographic darkroom. Though it is not important for me what things are or were, 99.8 percent of what you see is different photographed objects."*

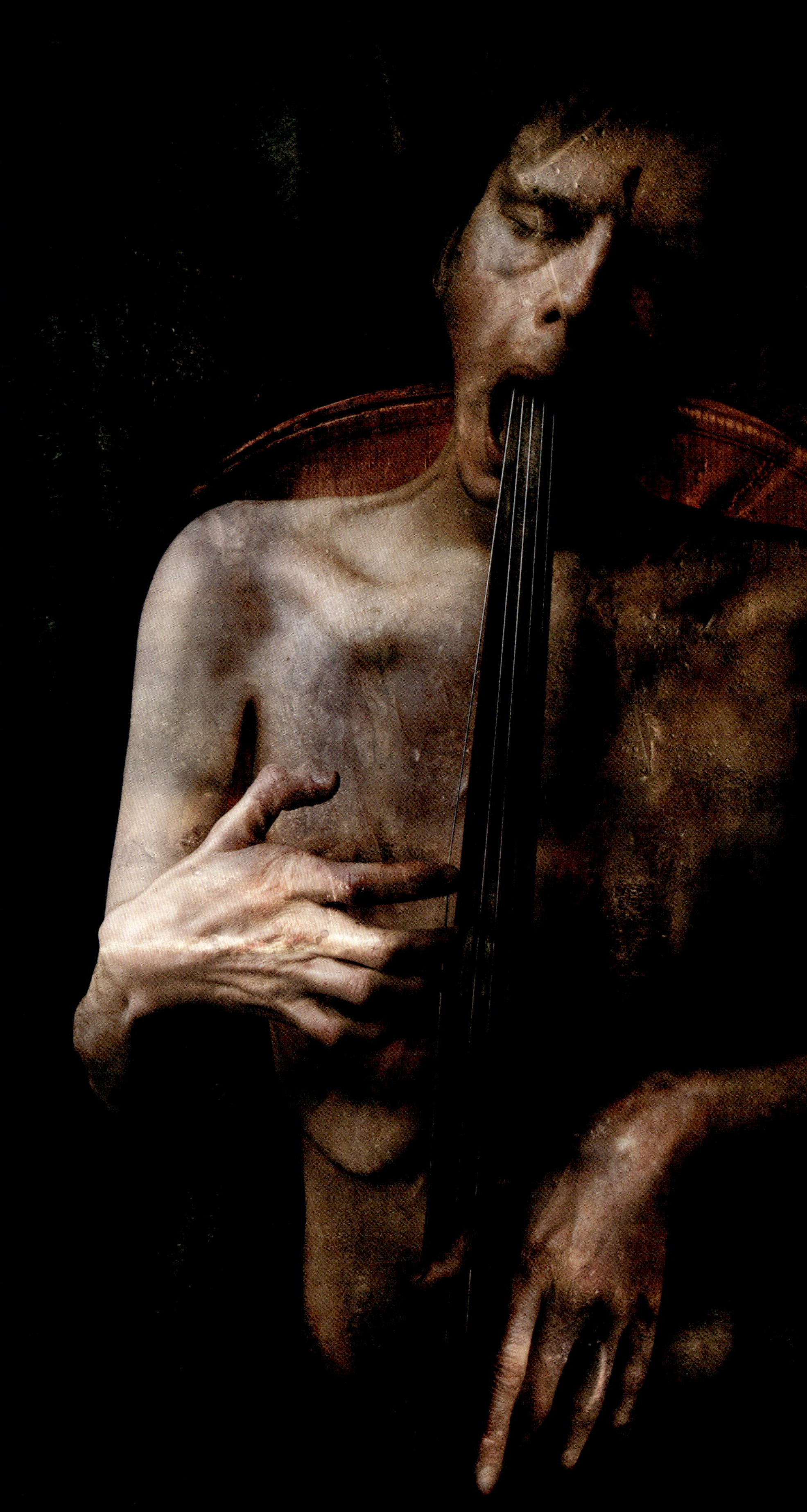

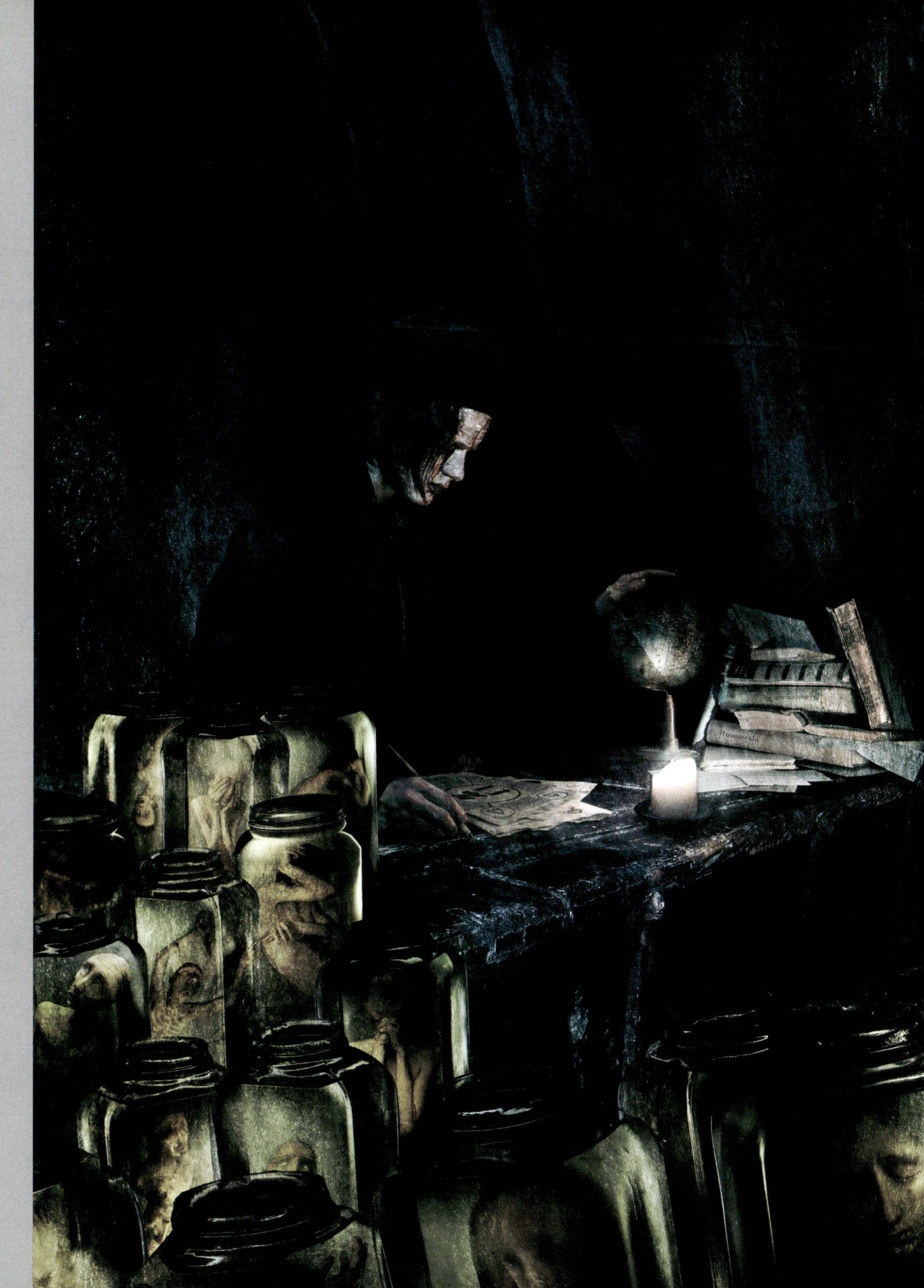

▶ **Narrentraum**
Erlend Mørk
Photography and digital manipulation
www.erlendmork.com

Narrentraum *— a fool's dream — perhaps a diabolical alchemist, in his laboratory, with specimen jars containing his monstrous experiments? An intriguing piece from Mørk, finely crafted by the artist from countless original photographs. "Every step is digital, from camera to print. They end up as limited edition pigment prints."*

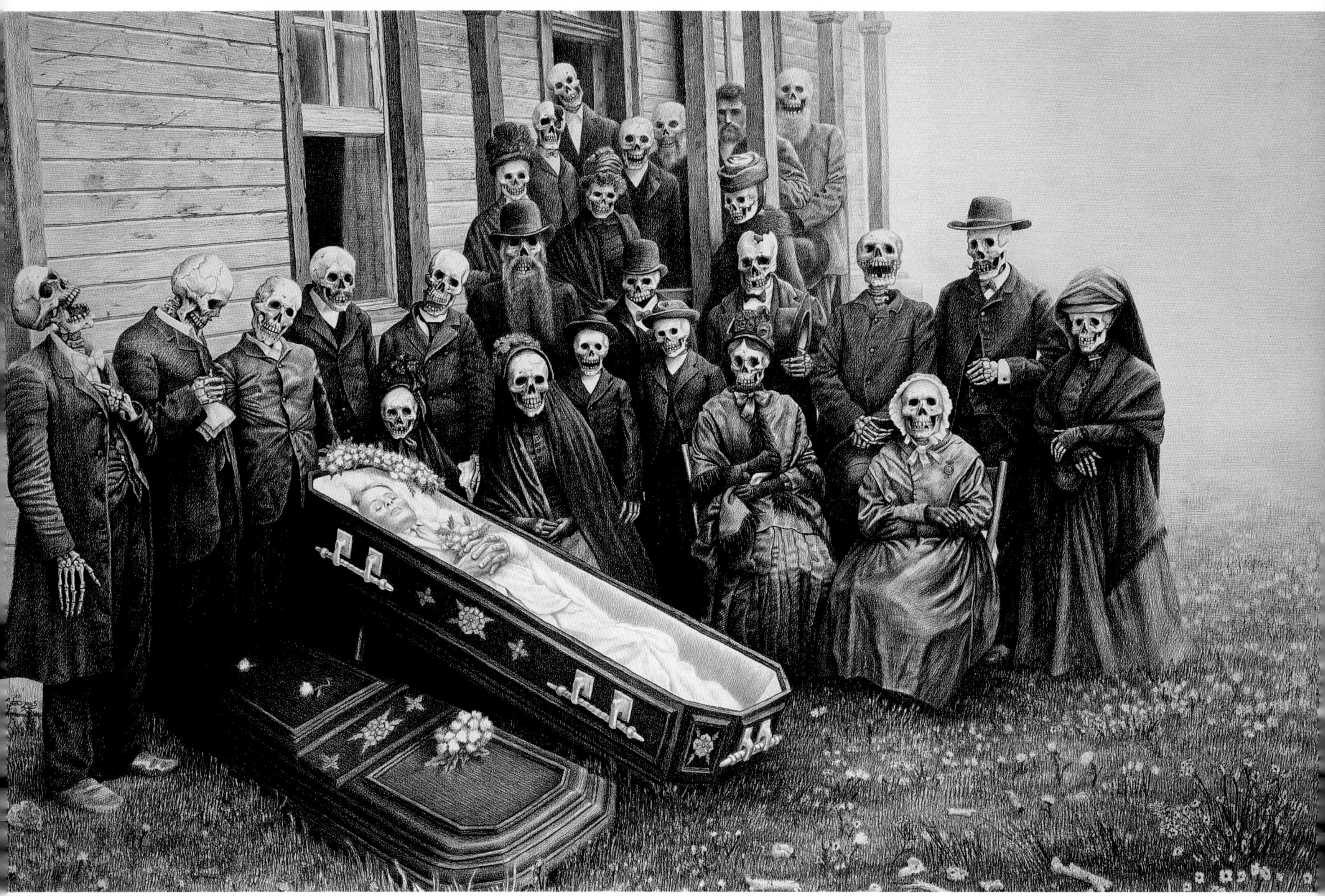

▲ **Family Reunion**
Laurie Lipton
Charcoal and pencil on paper
www.laurielipton.com

An amazingly detailed drawing from the talented Laurie Lipton, inspired by the Mexican tradition of Dia de los Muertos. "This was part of a 'Day of the Dead' show I did, inspired by a trip to Mexico. Many Mexicans believe you join your ancestors when you die. This is what I thought a family reunion would look like on somebody's Death-day. It's also what some of my own family reunions feel like."

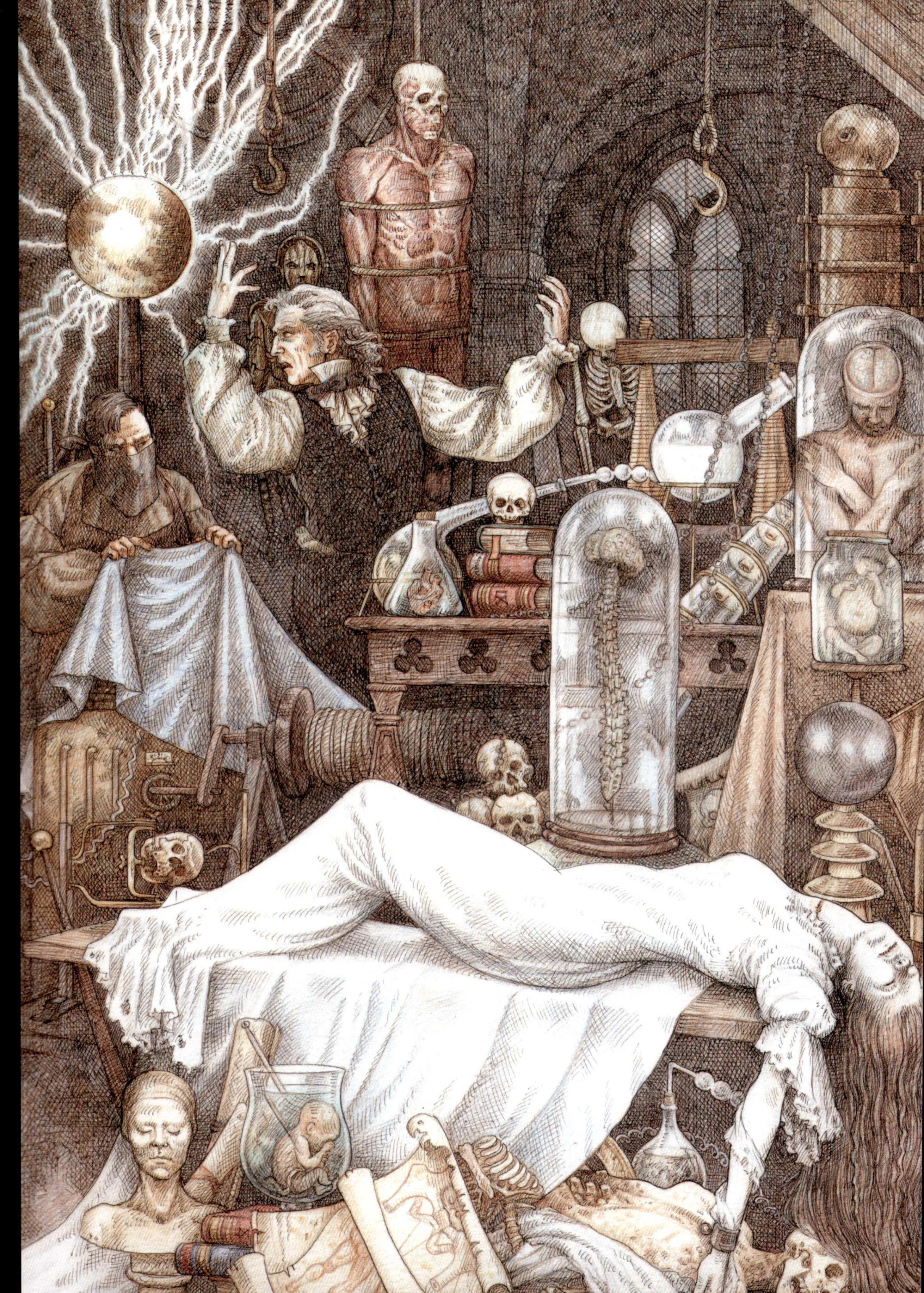

Bride of Frankenstein
Anne Yvonne Gilbert
Pen and ink drawing
www.yvonnegilbert.com

An erotic scene of Gothic horror. Gilbert has drawn this baroque scene of Dr. Frankenstein's laboratory "For the first time in my career I have been exploring Gothic themes in a, what can only be described as decorative picture-book style. My drawing tends to be delicate and my color subdued so I have been intrigued by its suitability to illustrate subject-matter which normally lends itself to a stronger, more graphic approach. As always the eroticism of the subject is what truly motivates me."

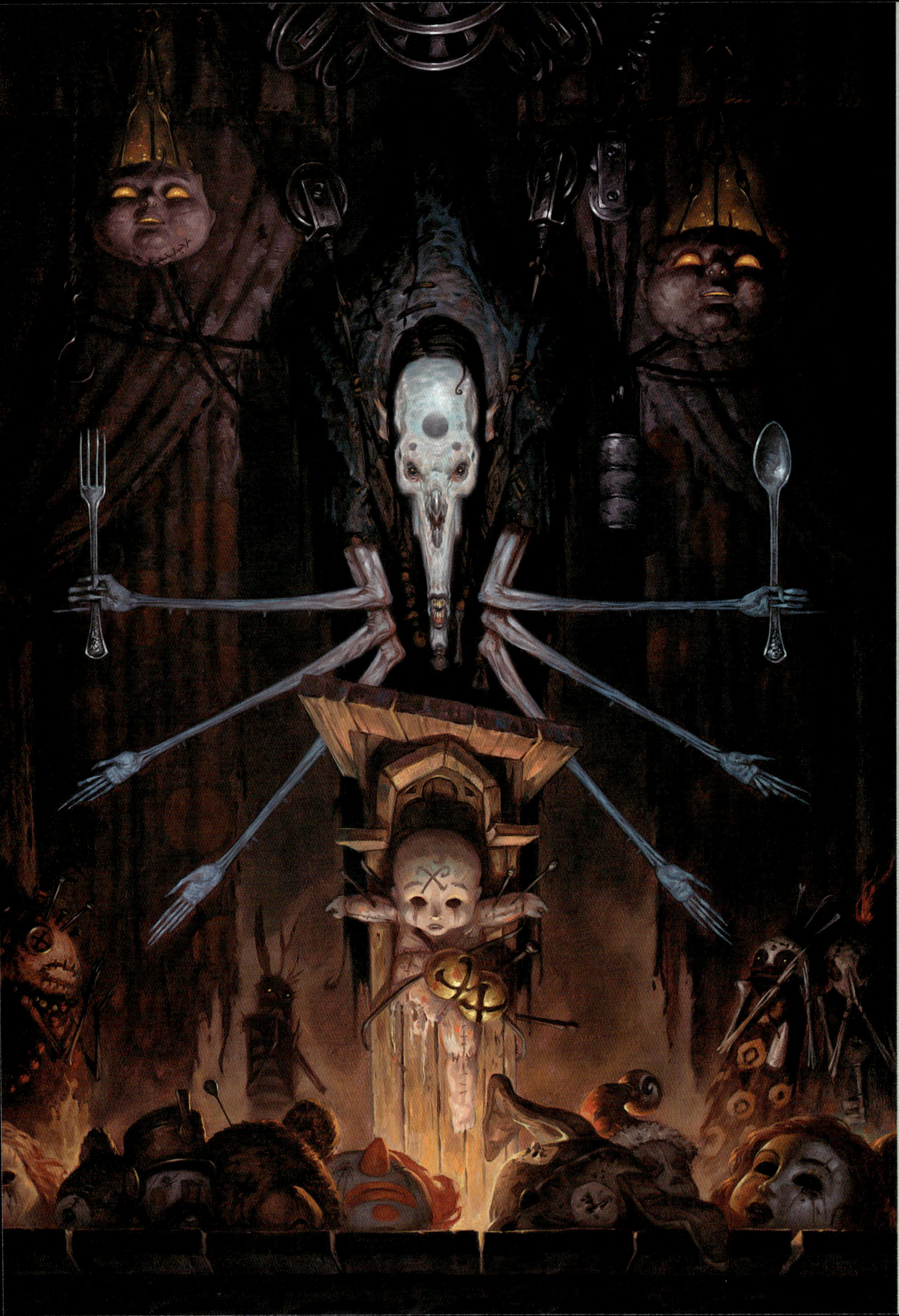

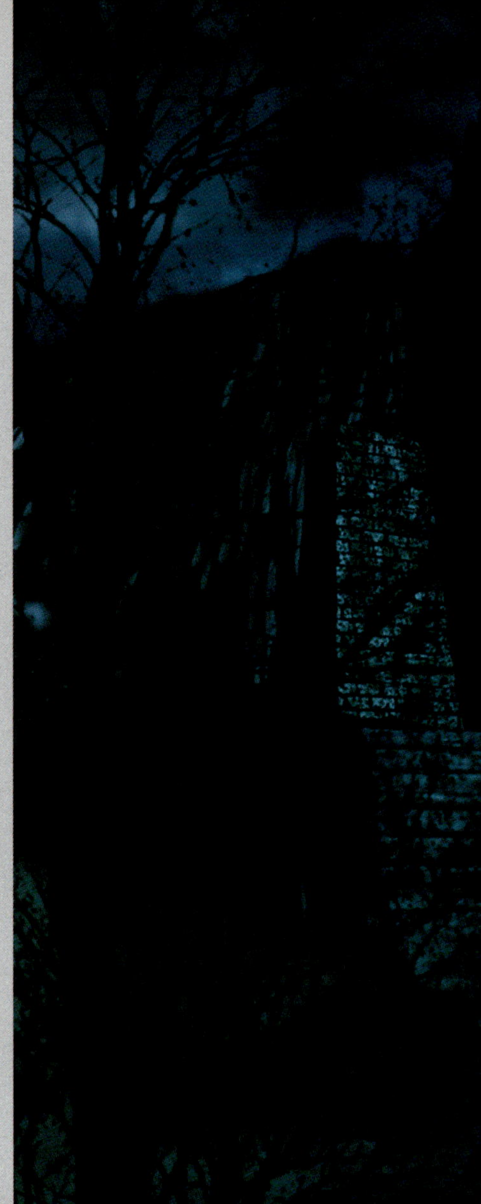

◀ **The Plucker**
Brom
Oil on illustration board
www.bromart.com

A seriously creepy character from Gothic art master Brom's book. The painting features a terrifying being surrounded by discarded and dismembered childhood toys. Brom writes: "The Plucker leaned down until its face hung a kiss away from Angel, peeled back its black lips and exposed the most sincere smile its rotting teeth would allow. 'You'll be such a tasty,' it whispered."

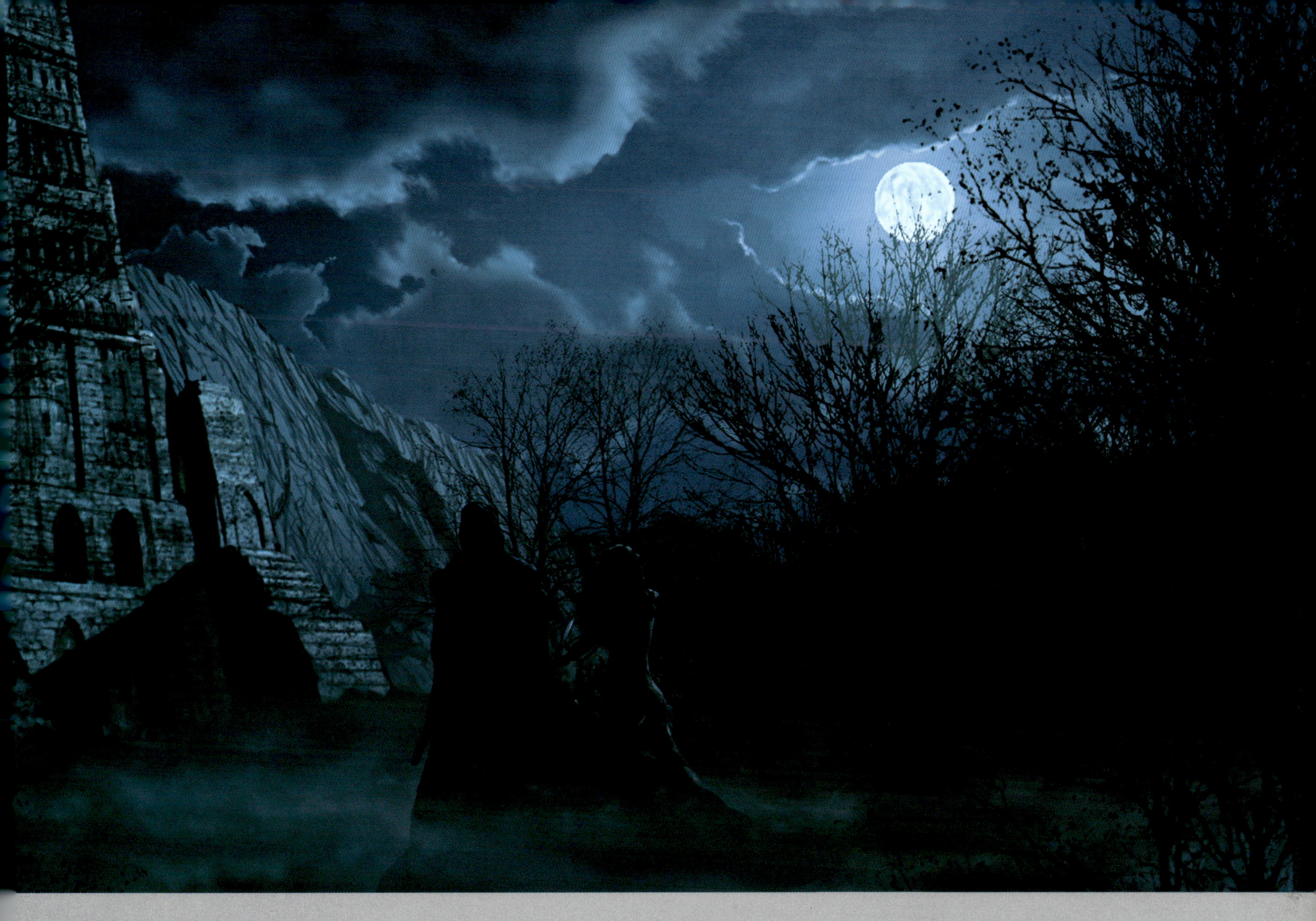

▲ **Tomb of the Night Terrors**
Matt Bradbury
Digital painting
www.mattbradbury.epilogue.net

*Matt's digital masterpiece is a classically Gothic scene — two nameless figures approaching an imposing necropolis by the light of the full moon. "**Tomb of the Night Terrors** was inspired by the movie **Van Helsing**. As I was painting, I imagined a little back story for these two heroes about to do battle with a brood of vampires."*

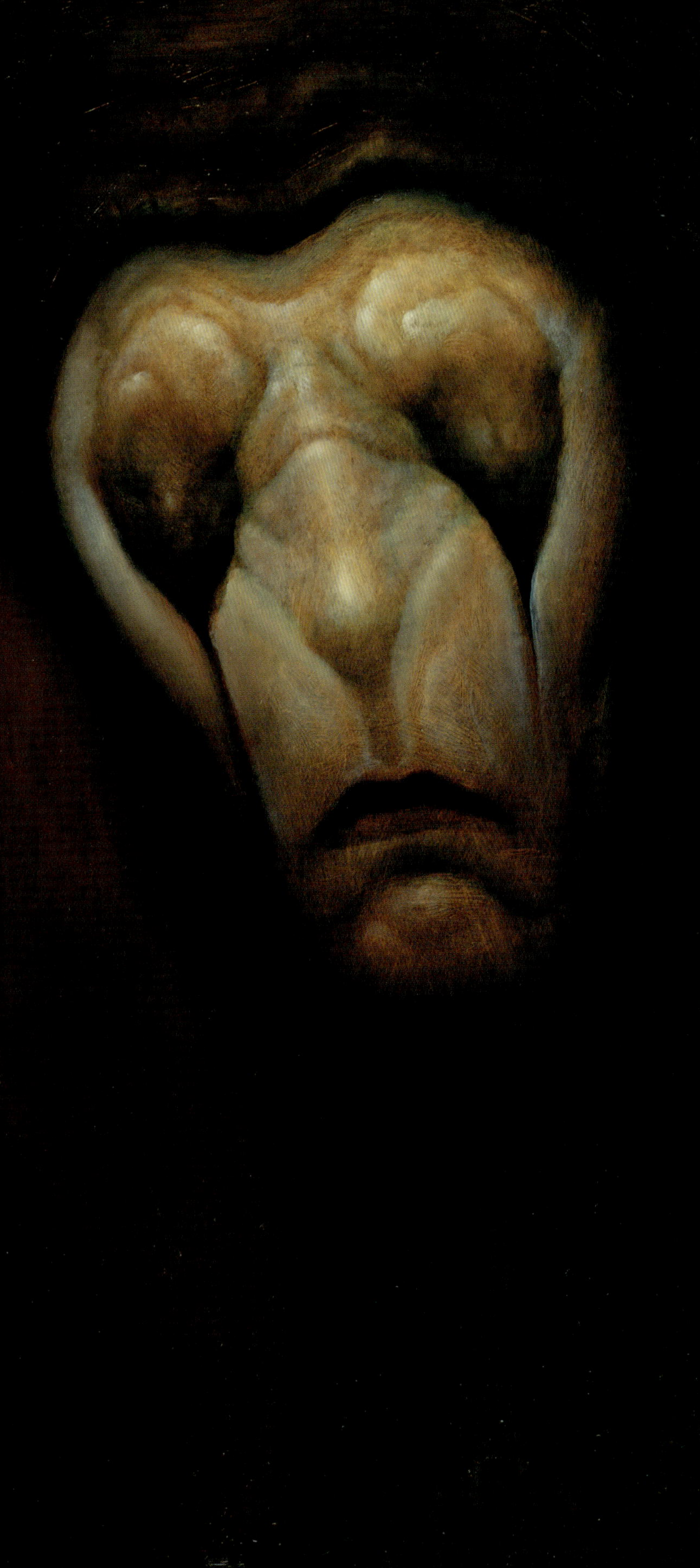

◄ **Sister**
Chet Zar
Oil on wood panel
www.chetzar.com

A hauntingly appealing piece, Zar's oil painting, ***Sister****, masterfully uses color and lighting to show the aura of forboding surrounding this distorted (yet still somewhat human) face. The skull-like visage peers out of the murky setting, a portrait of an unknowable person. "This was a companion piece to a couple of other paintings I did called* ***Mother*** *and* ***Father*** *(both of them have a very Gothic feel). It was painted for a solo show that took place in Berlin at the Strychnin gallery."*

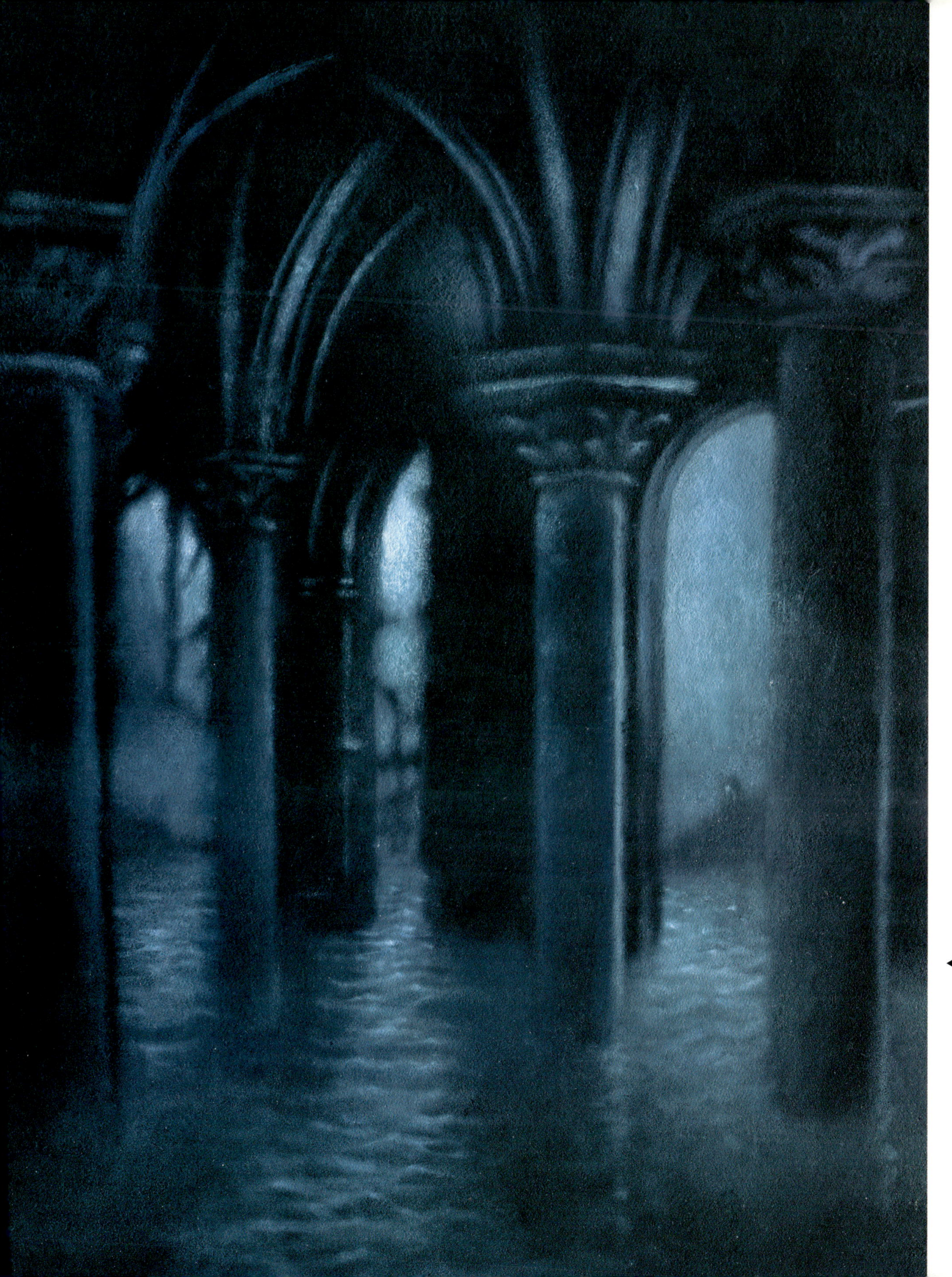

◀ **The Ruins of Ecclesia**
Linda Joyce Franks
Oil on paper
www.nimbvs.com

Gothic in mood as well as in architecture, Franks' ***The Ruins of Ecclesia*** *is a stunning image of a flooded cathedral. The deep blues in this painting and the unusual lighting scheme help create a somber feel with a surreal atmosphere.*

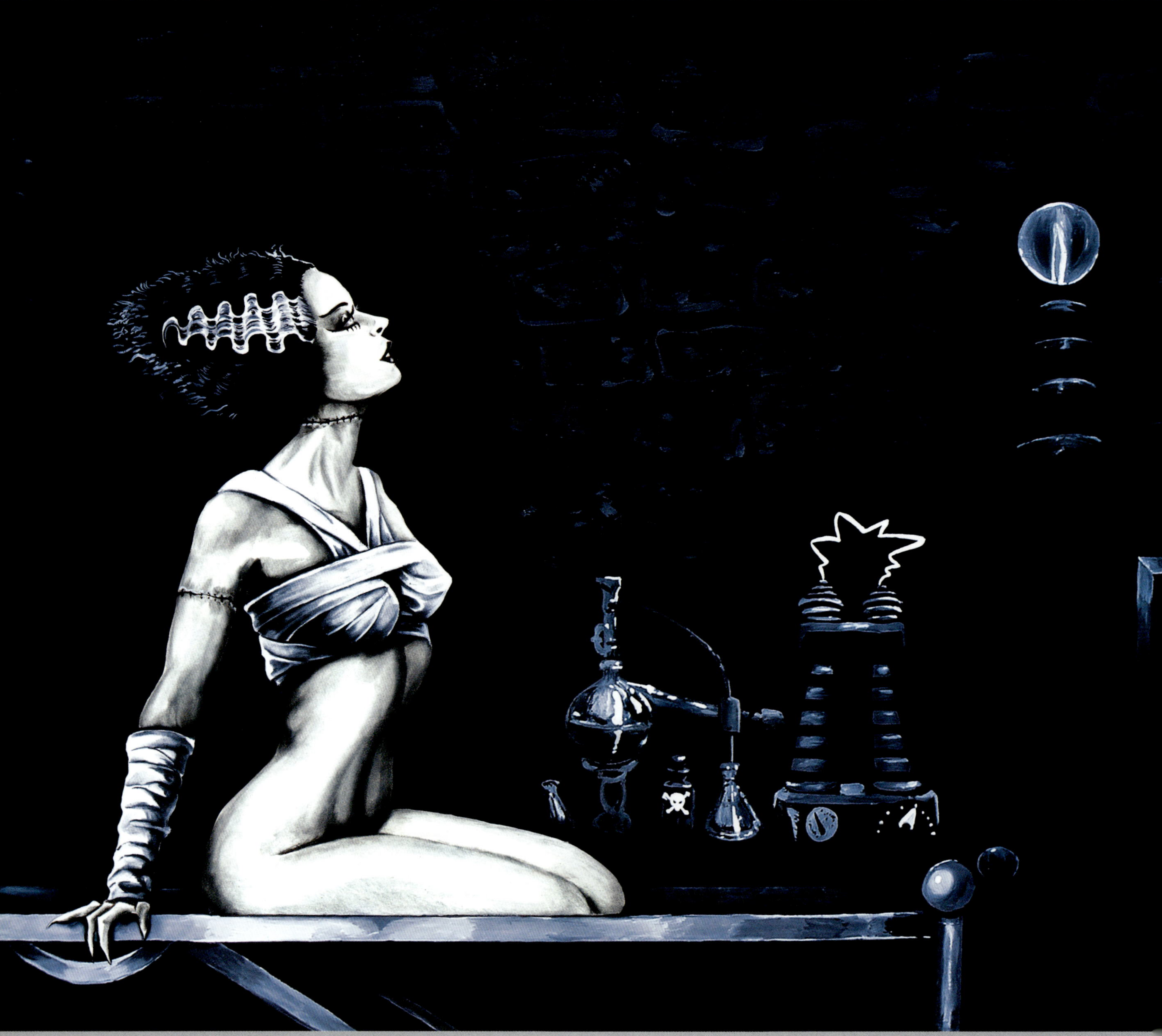

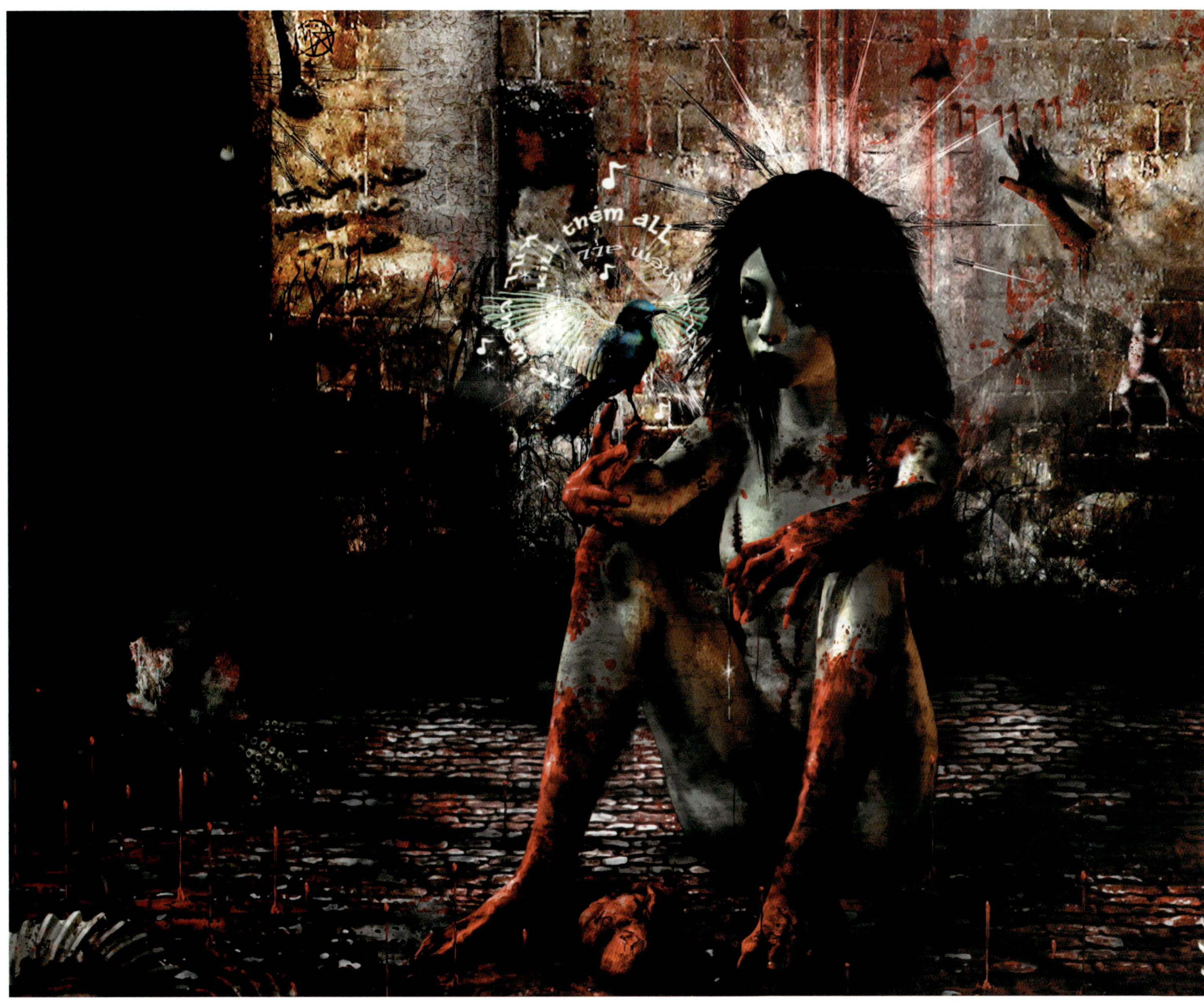

◀ **The Bride**
Michael Park
Pencil and acrylic on illustration board
www.myspace.com/michaelpark

"The flesh of the Bride was done with black and white Prismacolor pencils, and the rest using acrylic paint. I wanted to give the Bride a sexy look. I love to mix this media together to help make objects pop out—making her 3D. The lack of color was a key element, inspired by the black-and-white film ***The Bride Of Frankenstein****."*

▲ **Exterminating Angel**
Myke Amend
Mixed media
www.mykeamend.com

"A mixed media piece including photography, 3D modeling, pencil sketches, and digital paint. Like many of my digital pieces, the style is a weird mix heavily influenced by Dave McKean, Derek Riggs, and Michael Whelan. The character is dehumanized, symbolic of shaping oneself to do whatever is required for a greater purpose or destiny."

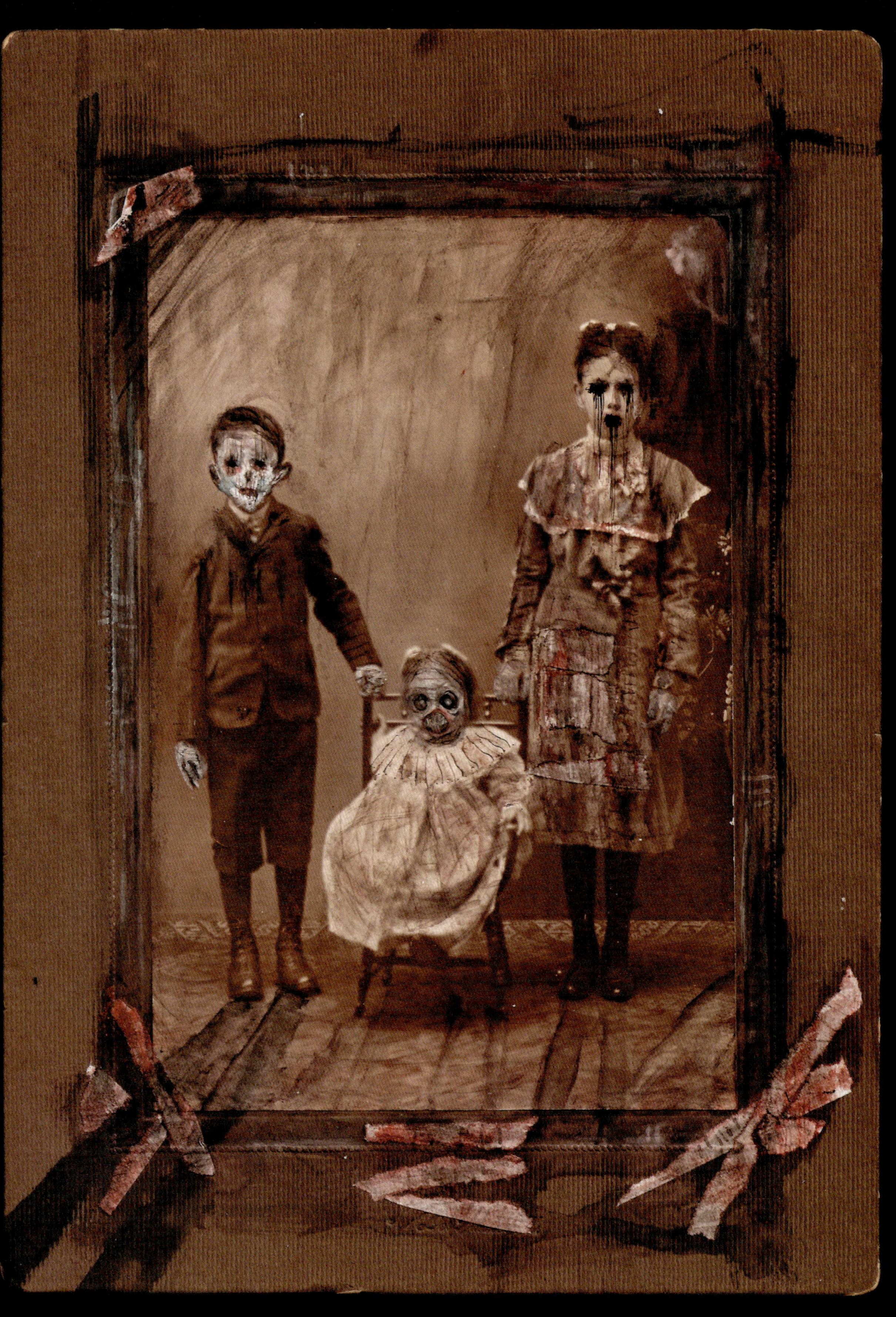

◀ **Children of Yesterday**
Gus Fink
Mixed media
www.gusfink.com

An altered photograph by Fink breathes new life (or death) into a found object. "These are the forgotten ones who paved the way of today, with hard work and the shedding of blood, sweat, and tears. Without them we wouldn't be where we are now. While technology is important to us, it still isn't truly used to benefit the world or those who live among it."

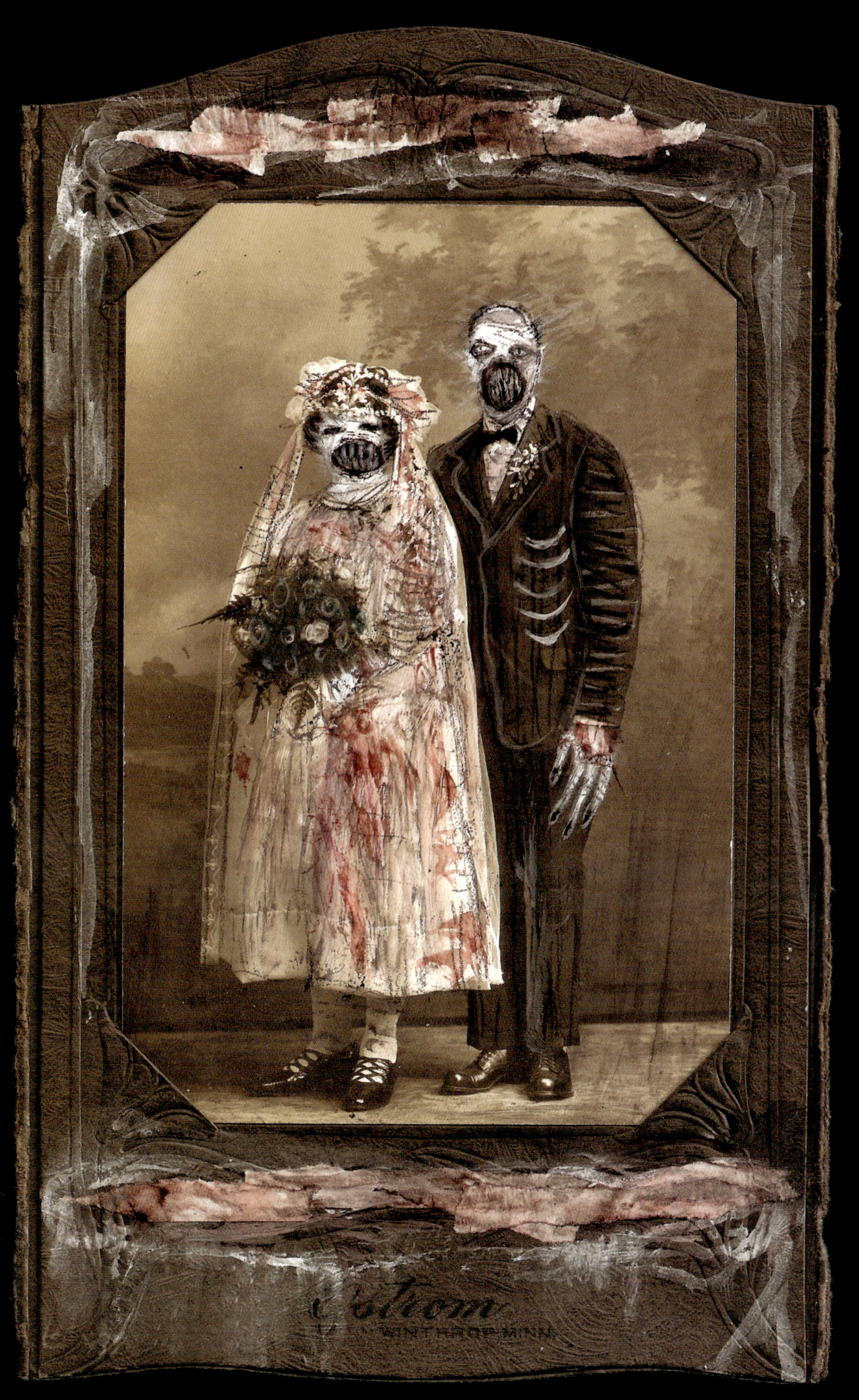

◀ **Mock Wedding**
Gus Fink
Mixed media
www.gusfink.com

Fink's original and decidedly creepy re-imagining of an antique wedding photo. "If a loving couple make a mockery of traditional wedding ceremonies in order to be wed under Satan this will bring them a life filled with money and success—but they will rot and die a horrible death."

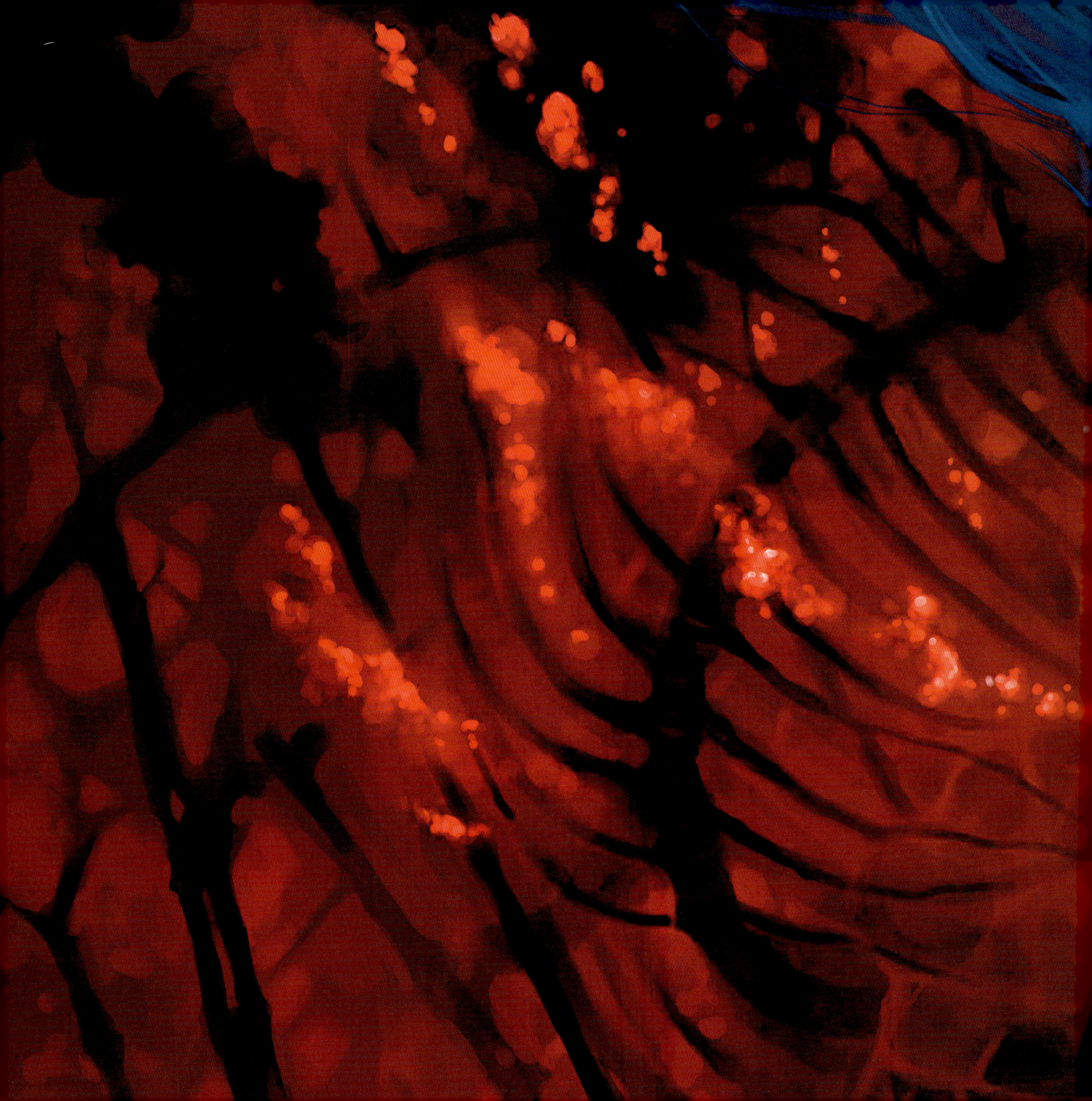

CHAPTER 6

DARK FANTASY

◀ **Nightmare**
Xiao-chen Fu
Digital painting
www.krishnafu.com

A vibrant blue and red color composition reveals subtle details upon further investigation. ***Nightmare*** *is part of Fu's* ***Dreamland*** *series. "When you sleep, dreaming begins. A fond dream is blue; the body is joyous like a fish in water. The nightmare is red; the red blood spreads from deep within the abyss till, slowly, you are flooded. The Dreamland's queen is smiling at you with her pet."*

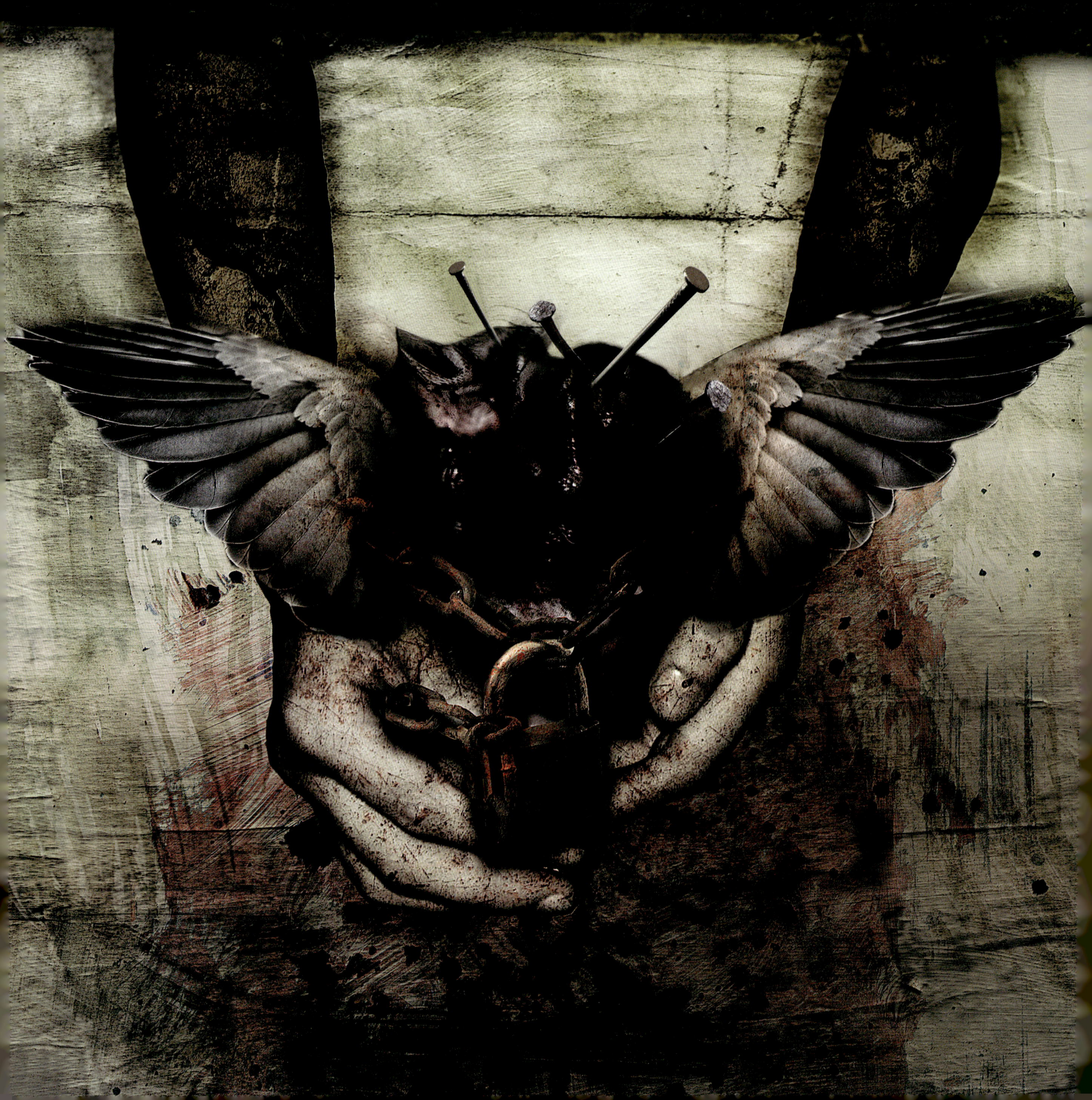

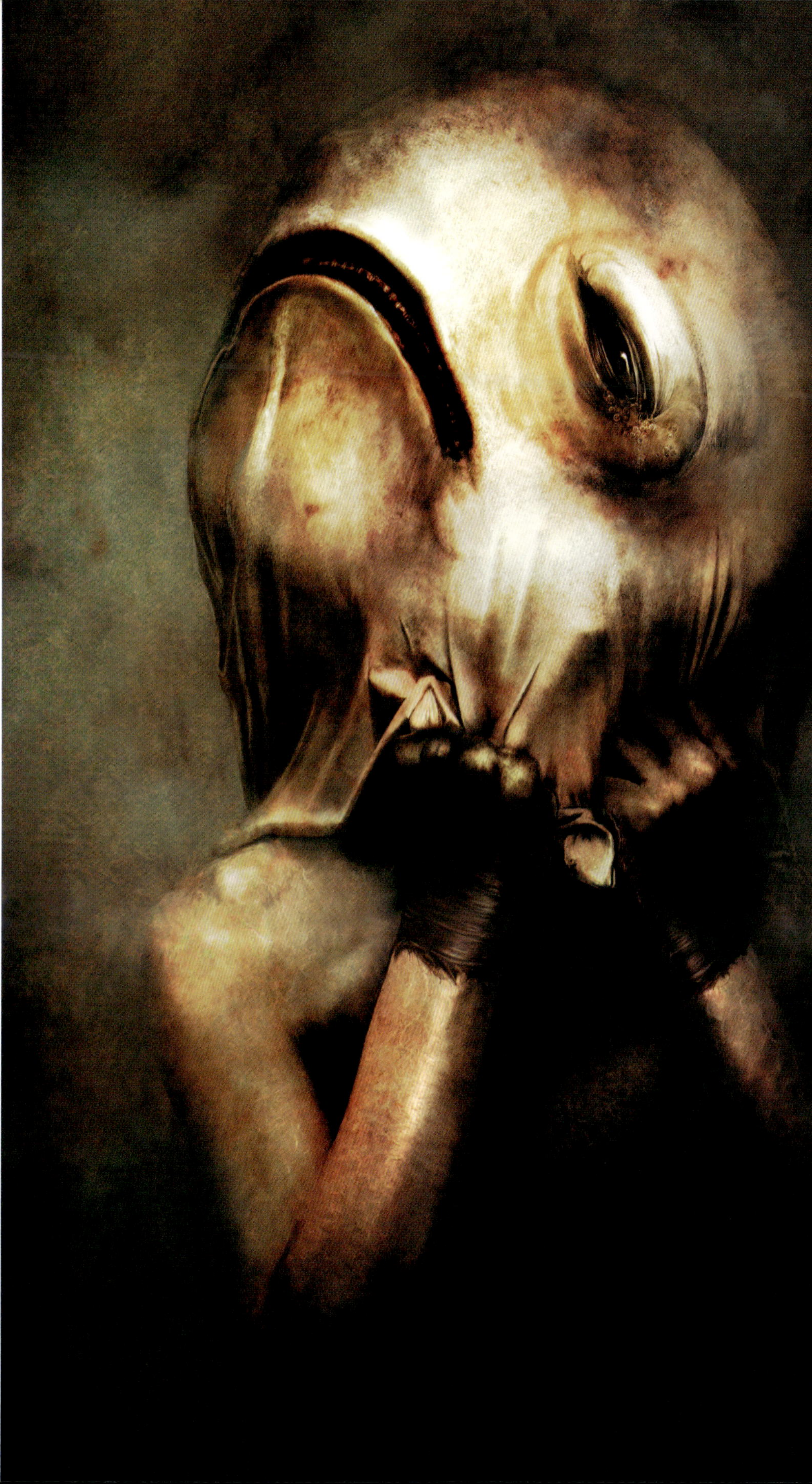

◀ **For I Have Sinned**
Antti Isosomppi
Photography and digital manipulation
www.isosomppi.com

Isosomppi used Adobe Photoshop to create this powerful piece. "I wanted to illustrate an ugly subject: the sickness of the mind. One who is suffering from this has a black lump for a heart. It can never be free as the owner of this heart is chained to perform evil deeds in the darkness. This was a very straightforward, thought-provoking theme, and was very enjoyable to work on. I wanted it to appear 'dirty,' using ugly, washed colors and rough texturing."

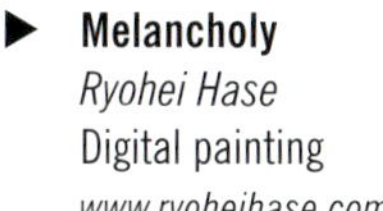

▶ **Melancholy**
Ryohei Hase
Digital painting
www.ryoheihase.com

Hase's ***Melancholy*** *shows a figure pulling a saddened visage over their own face in a rich and murky color palette. "This is an image from a series of initial work — a person who covers his face with melancholy."*

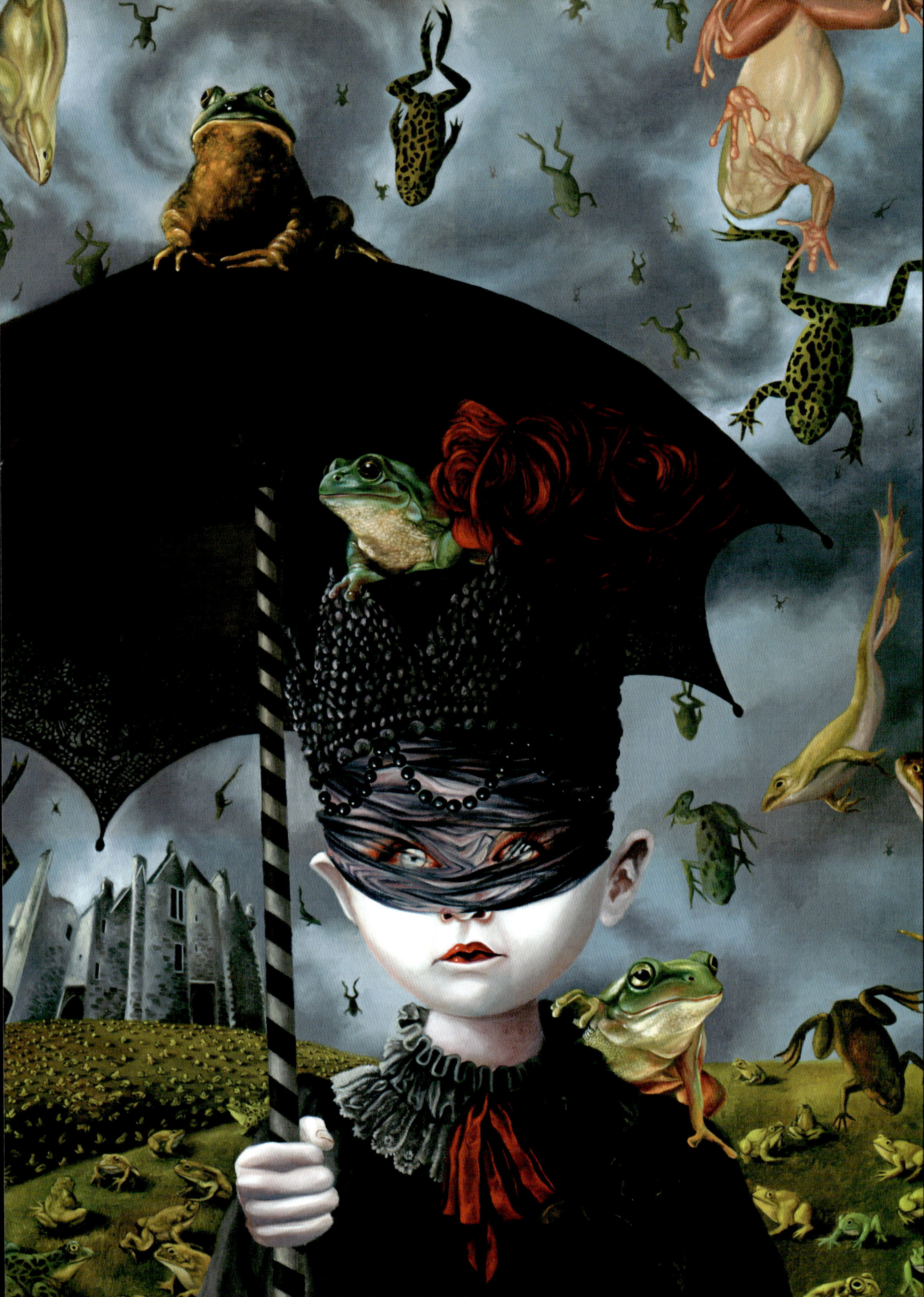

◀ **The Day the Frogs Rain Down**
David Stoupakis
Oil on board
www.davidstoupakis.com

A truly surreal scene inspired by a bizarre natural phenomenon. While a meteorological oddity may sometimes explain a rain of frogs, there seems to be more to the story in this oil painting by Stoupakis. The veiled child in the foreground and the foreboding mansion in the background give this piece a Gothic feel.

▶ **The Messenger**
David Stoupakis
Oil on board
www.davidstoupakis.com

*Stoupakis's **The Messenger** is a well-executed and striking image. It is an oil painting that features a seemingly triumphant child carrying a flaming globe—fire, destruction, and pestilence in her wake. It is perhaps a dark vision of things to come.*

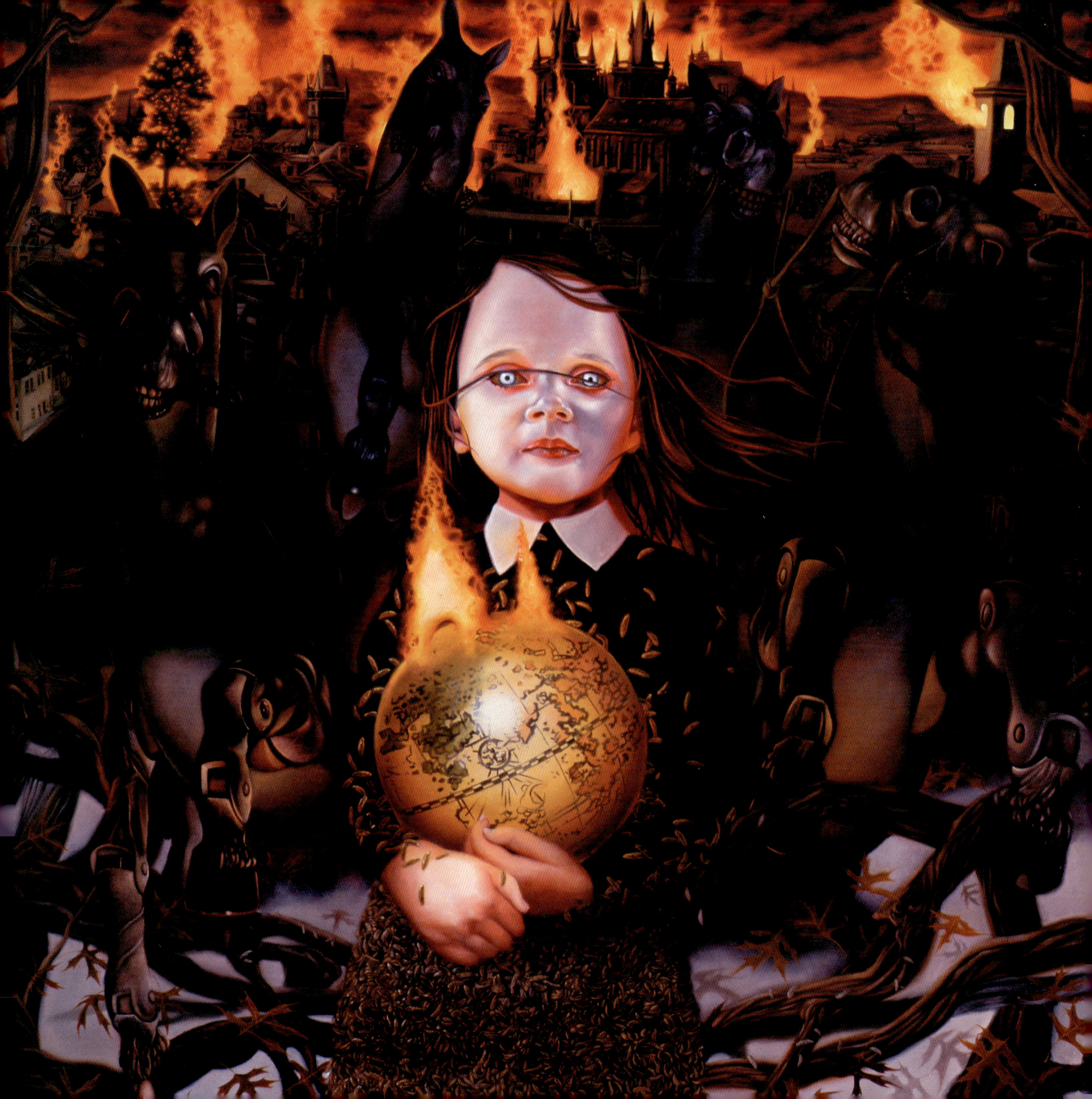

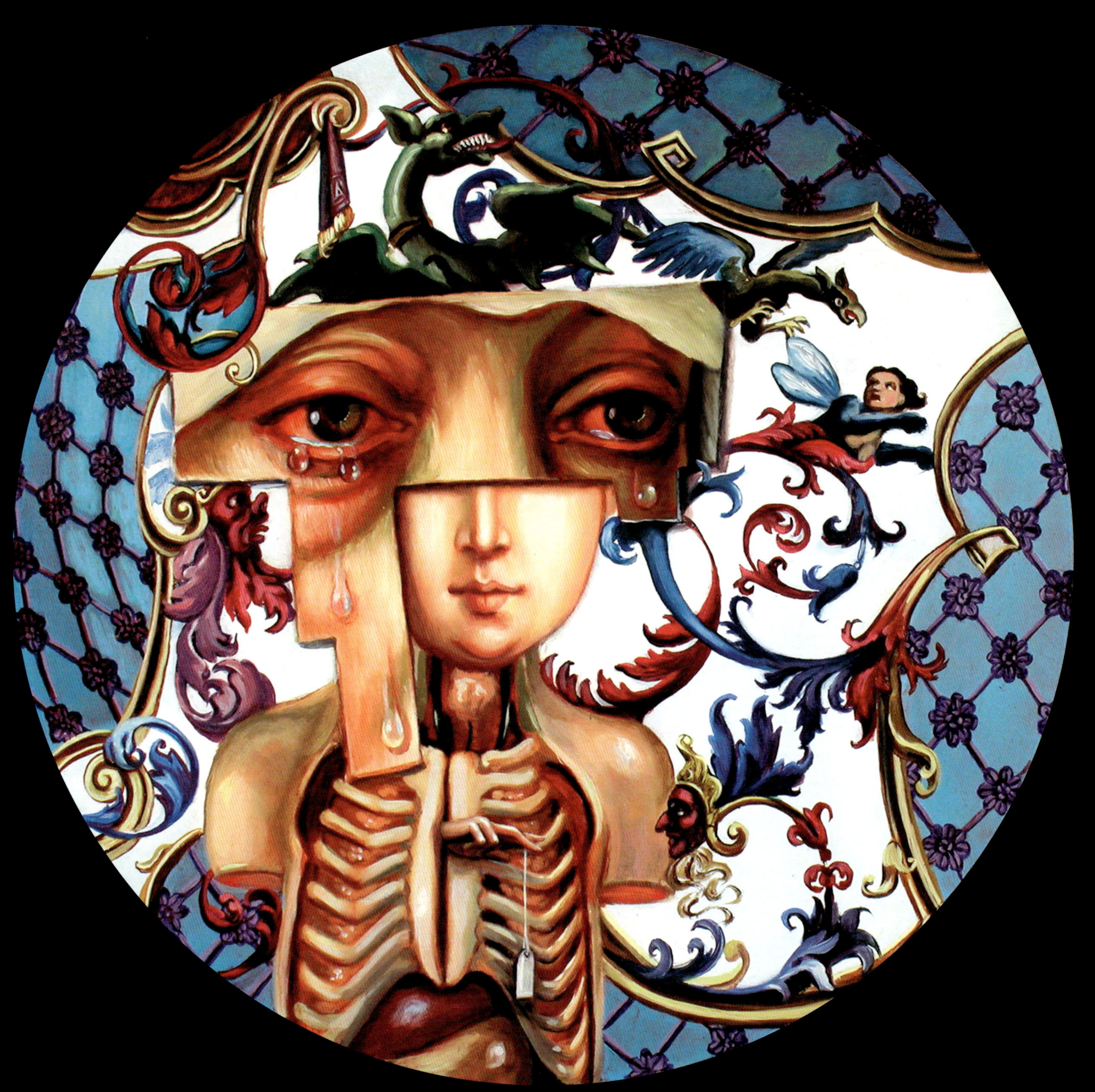

◀ **The Severance of Creeping Charlotte**
Carrie Ann Baade
Oil on copper
www.carrieannbaade.com

A sophisticated narrative oil painting from Baade. "Inspired by the troubled life of Charlotte Perkins, the author of ***The Yellow Wallpaper****, this painting explores loss of identity and potential madness, resulting from the failure of a relationship and the discord of marriage."*

▶ **The Ecstasy of Madam Dolorosa**
Carrie Ann Baade
Egg tempera and oil on panel
www.carrieannbaade.com

The conventional, devotional, weeping image of the Madonna Dolorosa (Our Lady of Sorrows) is played upon in Baade's ***Madam Dolorosa.*** *"In the tradition of the original this painting is a self-portrait that uses Christian symbolism to speak about the pain of love and loss. Have we not all felt as though we 'may die' from the pain of losing a love?"*

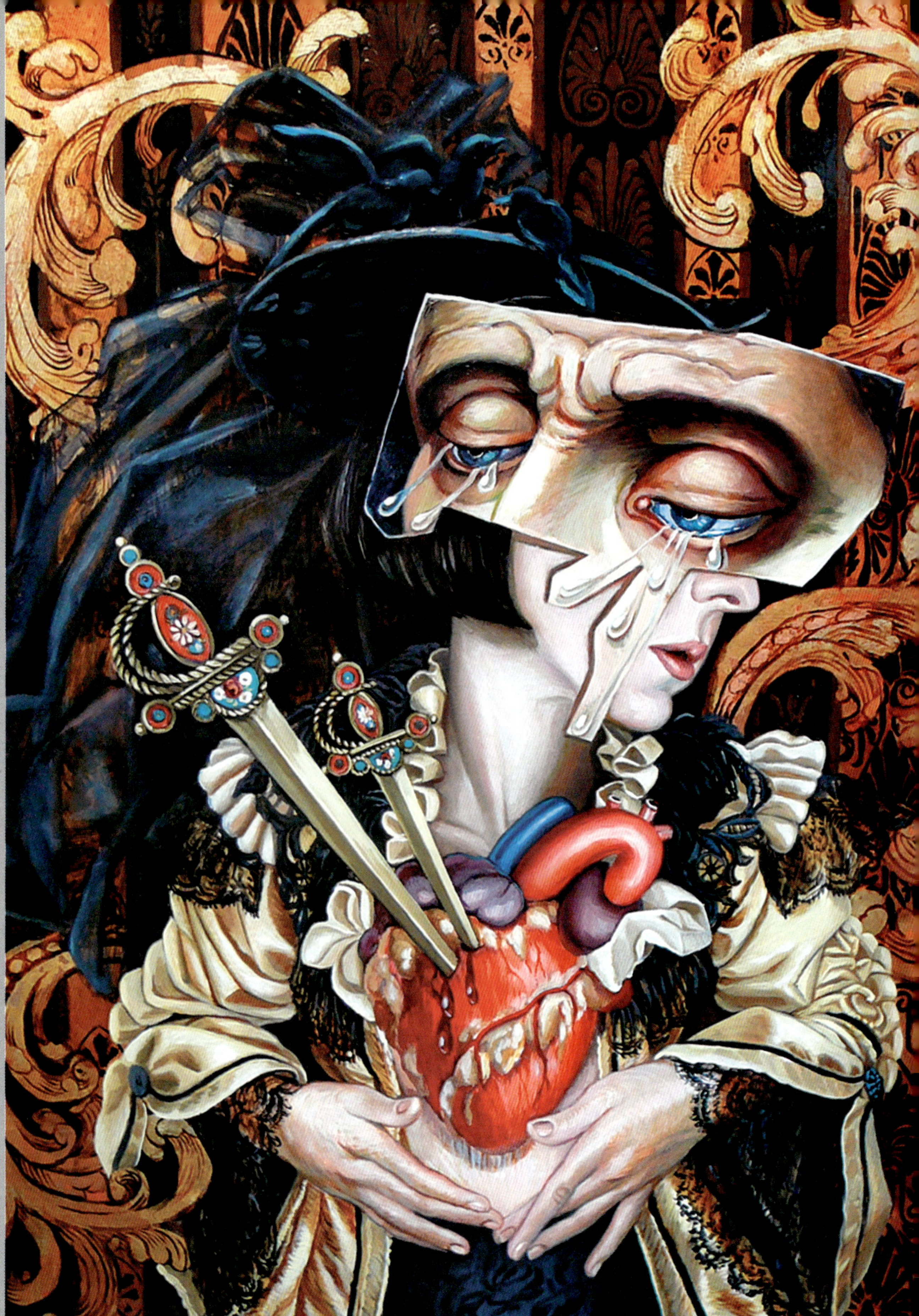

▶ **Nightspirit**
David Gough
Acrylic on canvas
www.davidgoughart.com

A surreal fantasy composed of a beautiful enchantress and some almost Hieronymus Bosch-like creatures, Gough has used his acrylic paints to best effect in ***Nightspirit****. "Loosely inspired by John Atkinson Grimshaw's* ***Spirit of the Night****, I recast my entity for my Victorian Gothic series, as a sort of pied-piper of nightmares. The being is collecting together all the diabolical manifestations of my fevered insecurities and vexations of the time."*

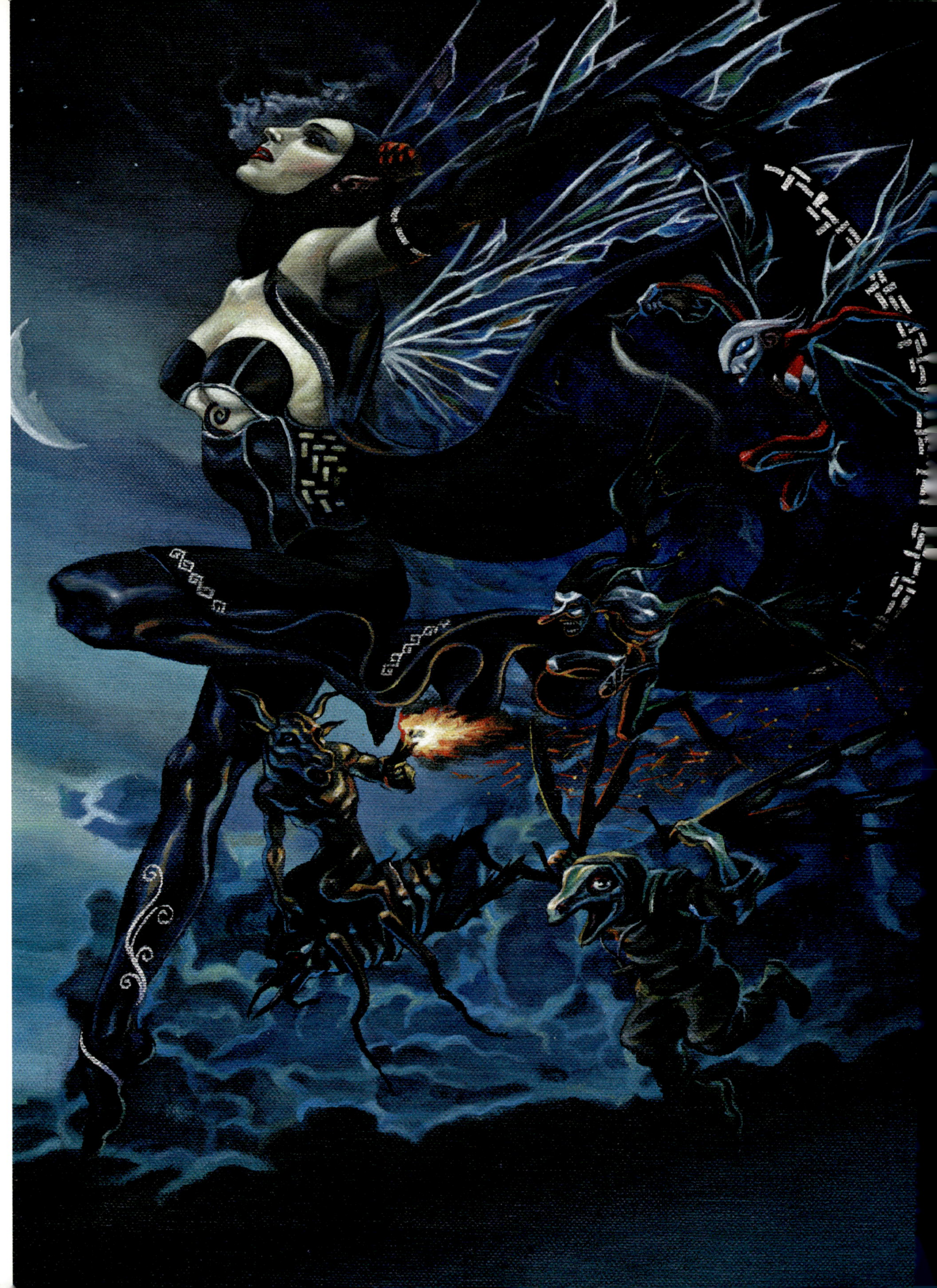

▶▶ **The White Doe of Nara**
Desirée Isphording
Mixed media
www.sphinxmuse.net

A compelling creature, with large dark eyes staring at the viewer. "My main cultural influence for this painting is Japan. I have long been captivated by ukiyo-e, Japanese woodblock prints, particularly by the Bijin-ga genre prints of Utamaro. Within Japan's indigenous religion of Shinto, Sika deer are regarded as sacred messengers from the gods. In addition to my usual mediums of colored pencil and watercolor, I experimented with printing and stamping."

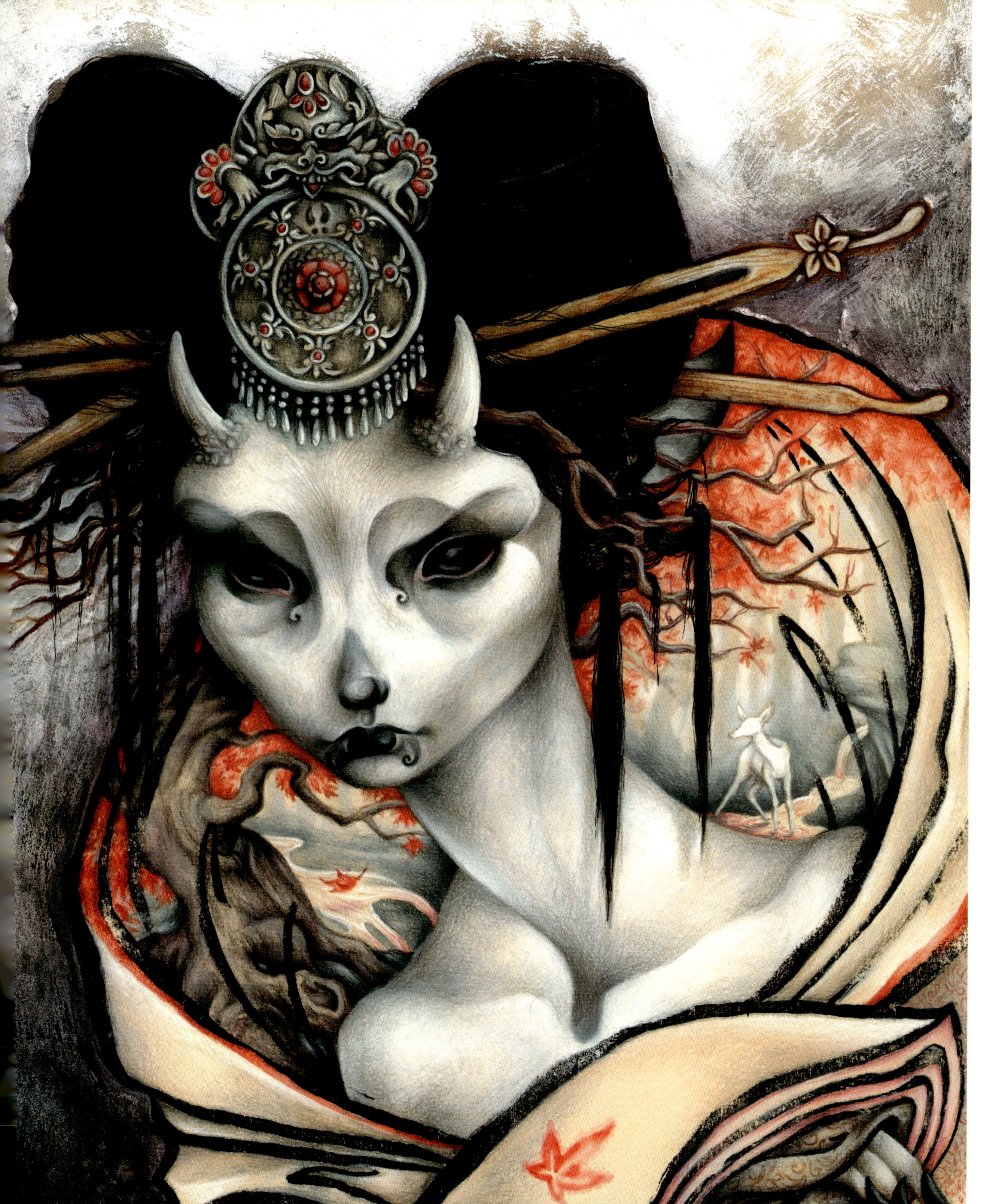

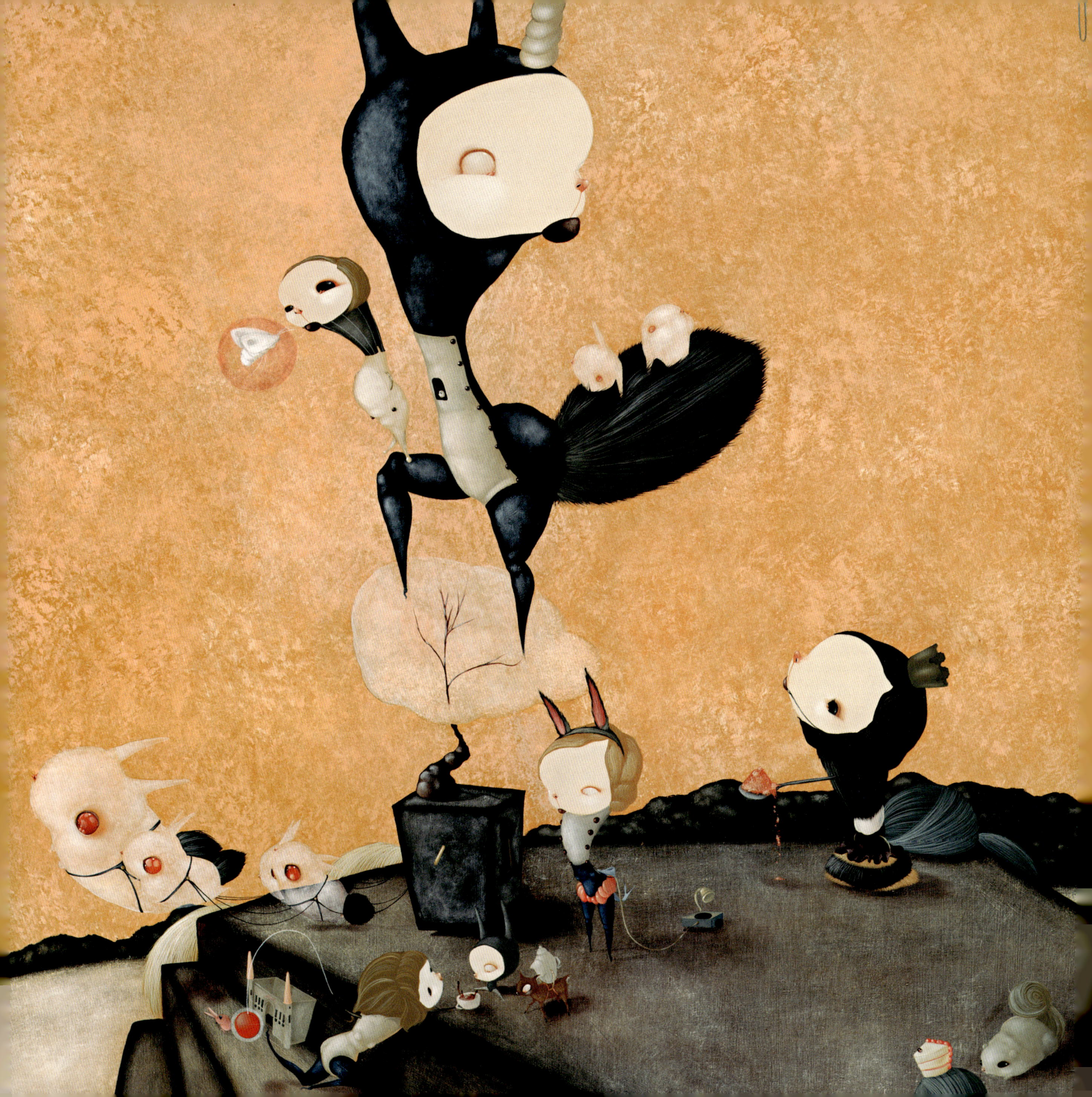

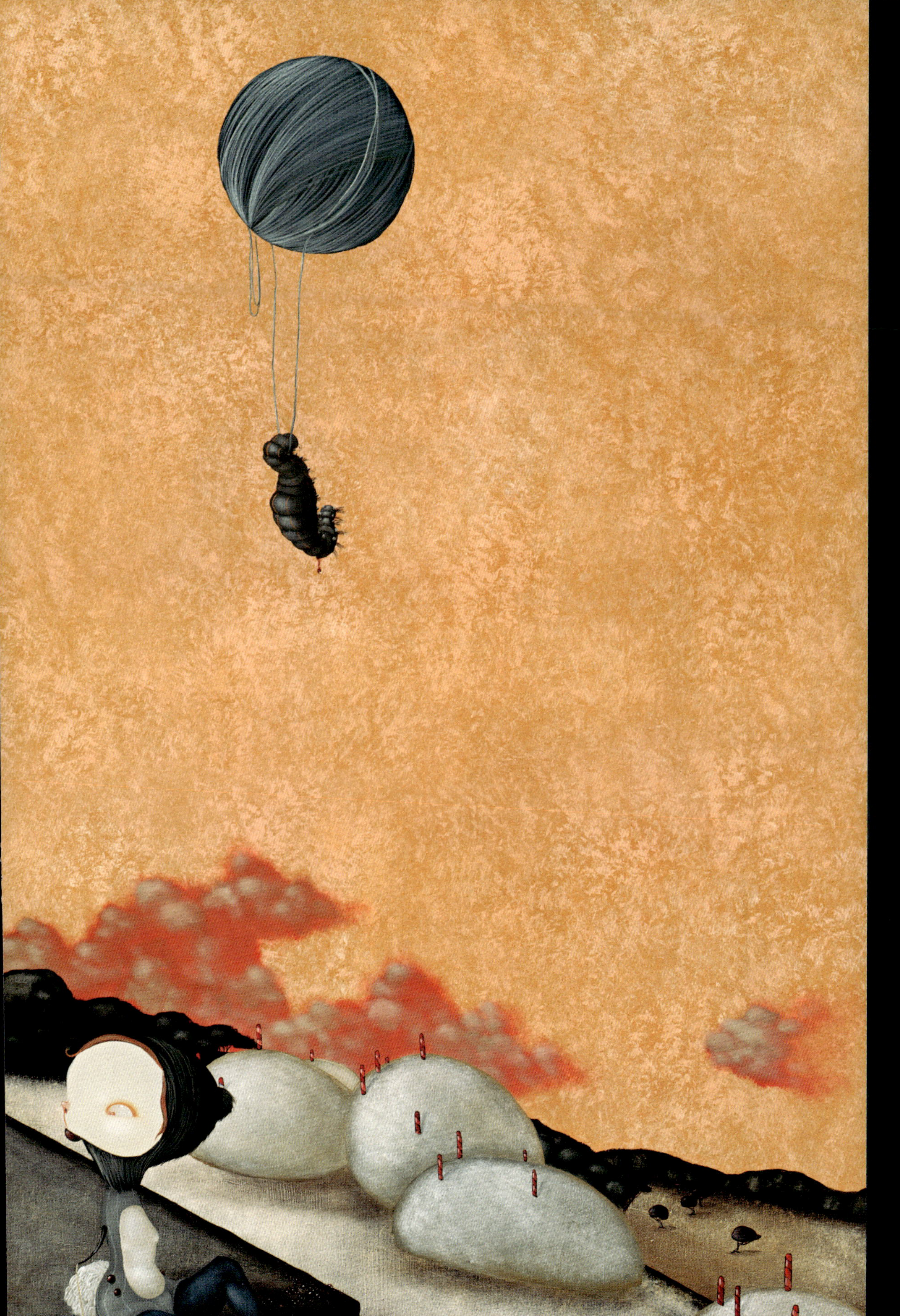

◀ **Where Owl Perched Pockets Hold All the Souvenirs**
Lola
Acrylic on panel
www.lolastrangeart.com

A surreal scene of Lola's strange creatures. "Our resting spot for self reflection – this haven is where we find all the answers to who we are and why. Where we are finally comfortable and have a complete understanding of our past. It is an incredible journey we should all endure."

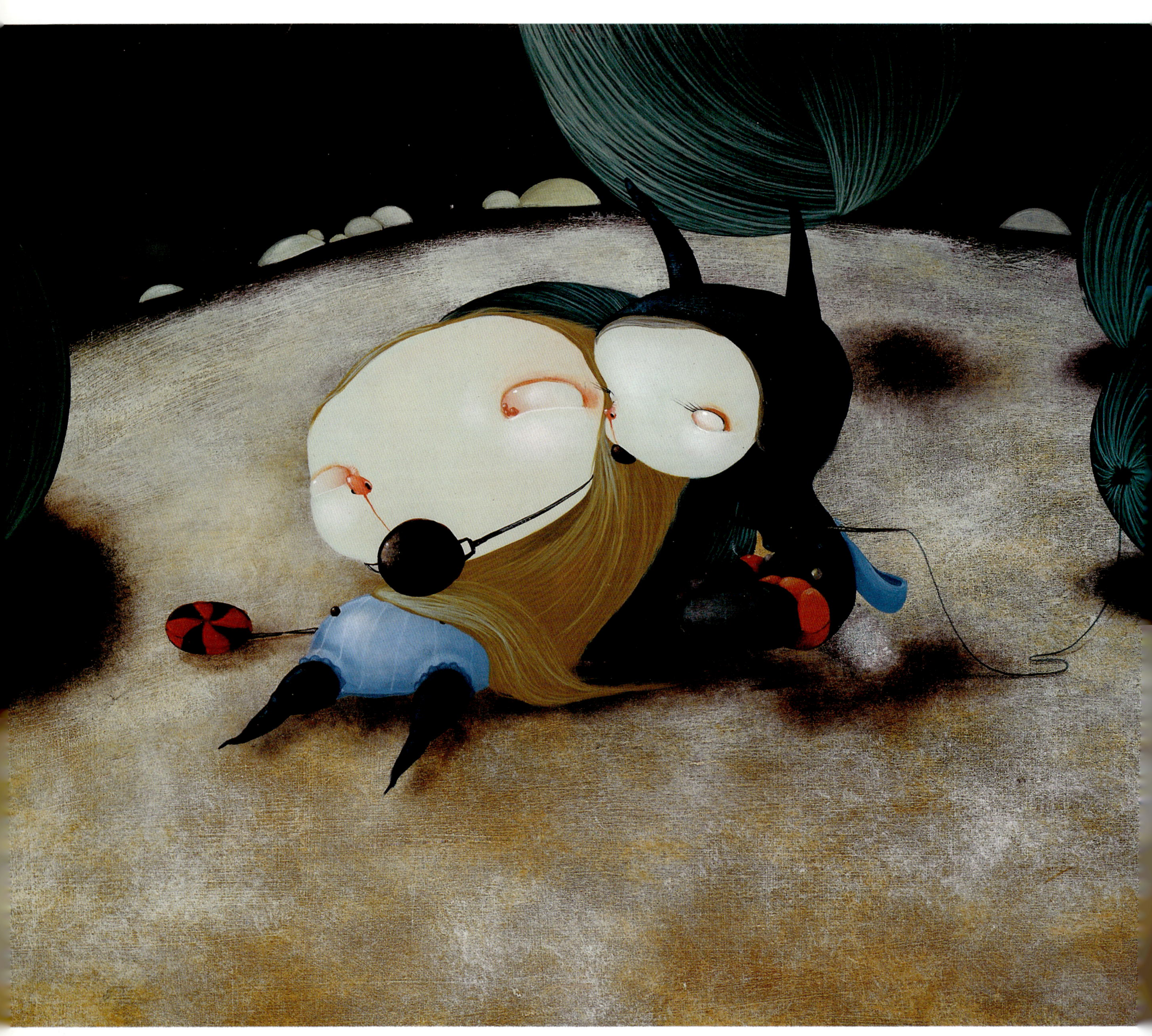

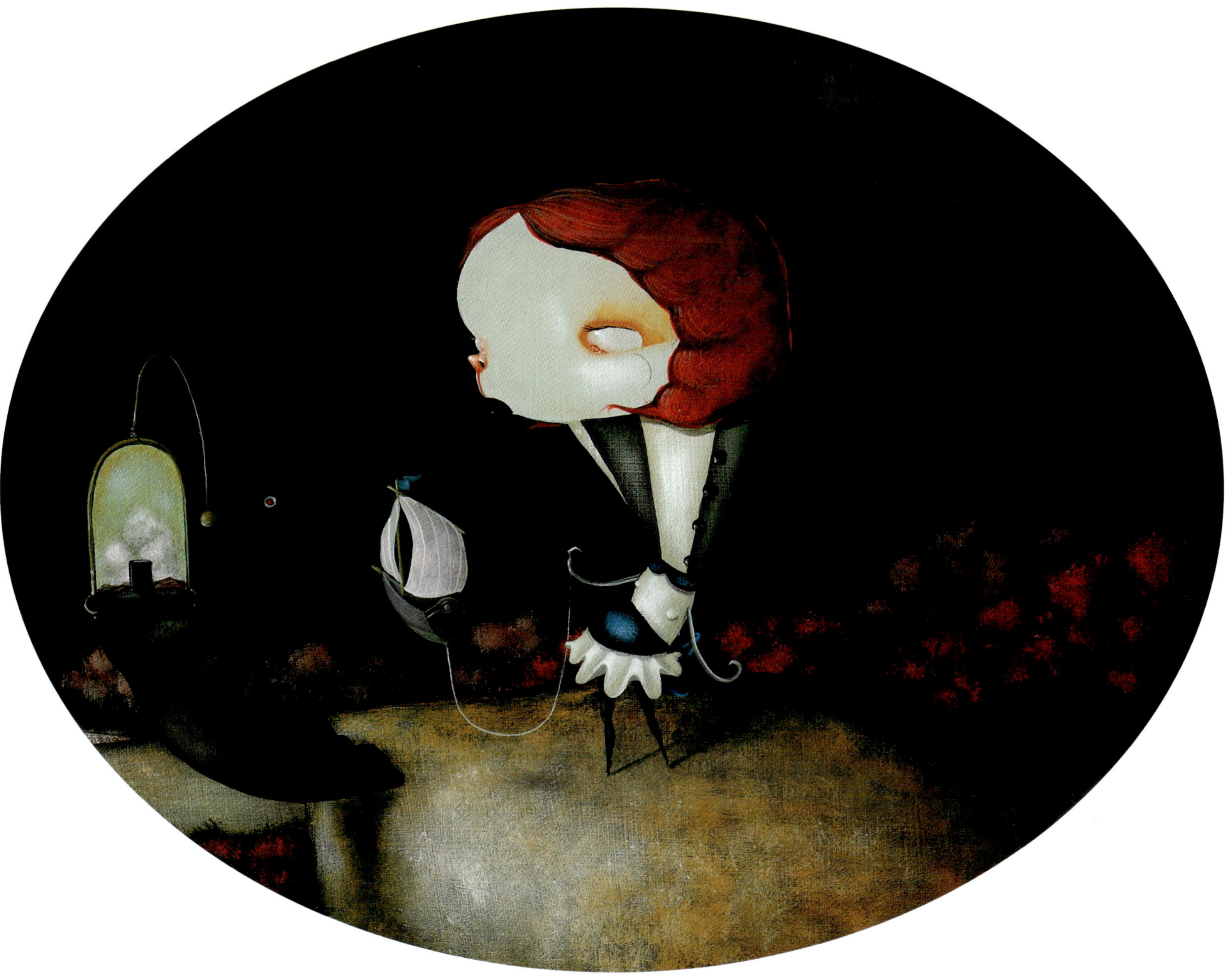

◀ **"Was That Too Loud?" She Whispered**
Lola
Acrylic on panel
www.lolastrangeart.com

A finely painted scene of two curious characters from the wonderful Lola. "Personal and intimate conversations have only the universe to respond. As we slip behind our curtains, our thoughts grow their own garden of comfort and habitual pattern, until the moment you decide to think differently."

▲ **Luminous Edge of Beginnings**
Lola
Acrylic on panel
www.lolastrangeart.com

A beautifully strange acrylic painting from Lola. "This piece is a reference to the great start of an important journey, where we are usually unaware of what lies ahead, and magically led by our most passionate feelings, never noticing the gift of the path we are on until we come to the end."

Fruit of the Secret God
John Santerineross
Photography
www.santerineross.com

*Neo-Symbolist photographer John Santerineross has created an elaborate scene for **Fruit of the Secret God**. The choice of models in Santerineross's work is not random. She (occasionally, he) has to have something special, something that works both for the photographer and the image. Santerineross holds each one in high esteem for offering their body for his art, and that often translates into a lasting friendship.*

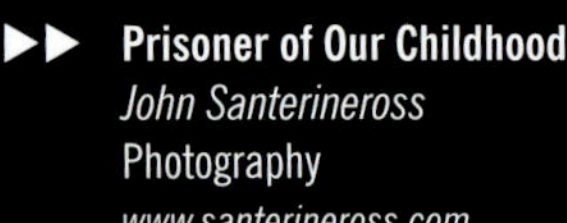

Prisoner of Our Childhood
John Santerineross
Photography
www.santerineross.com

There is nothing accidental in Santerineross's work — symbolism abounds and every tiny detail is a deliberate calculation. But don't expect to be told the meaning of the piece. One cannot be lazy when looking at his work because there are hidden messages and deeper understandings that would be missed by a casual glance.

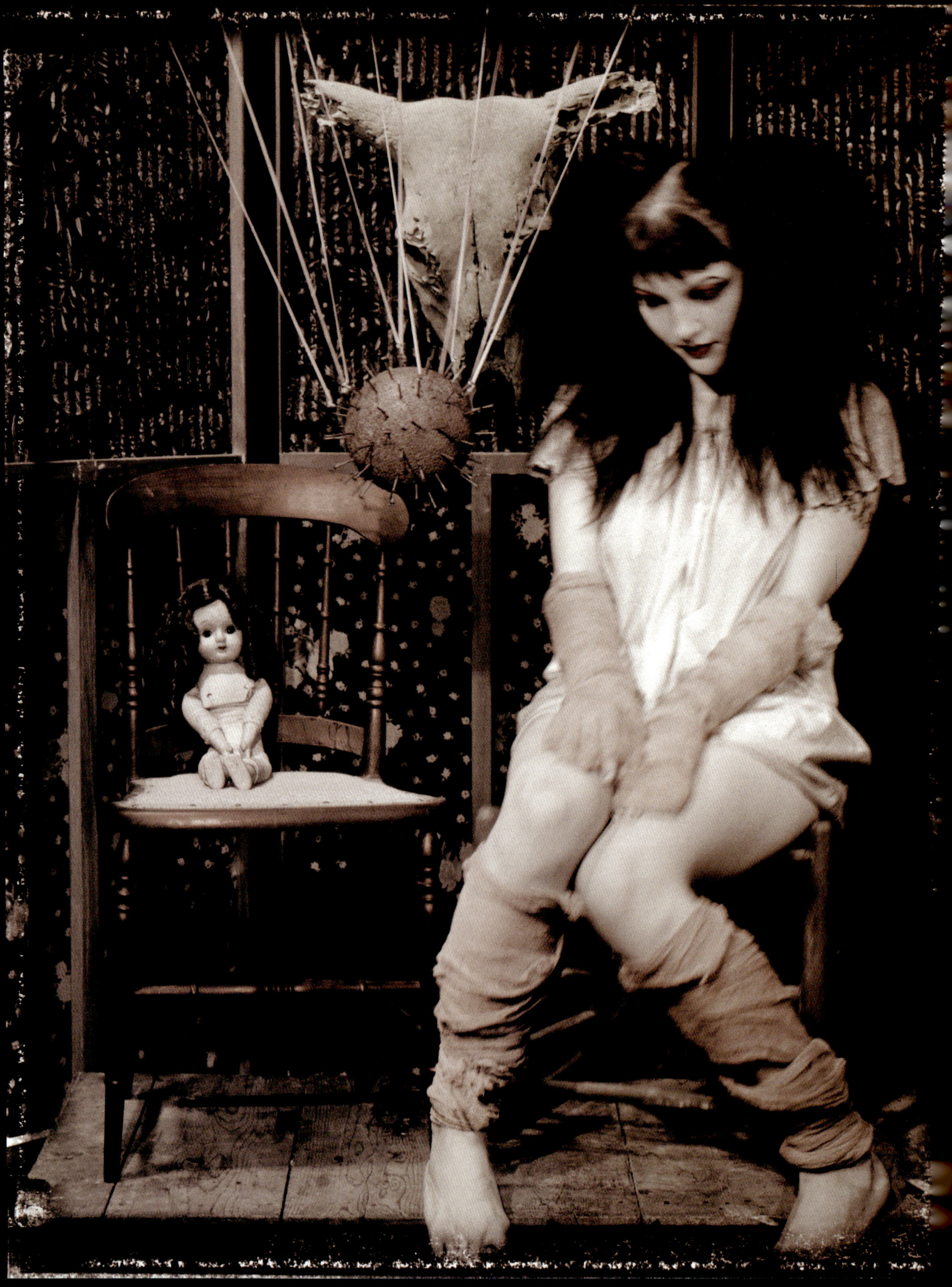

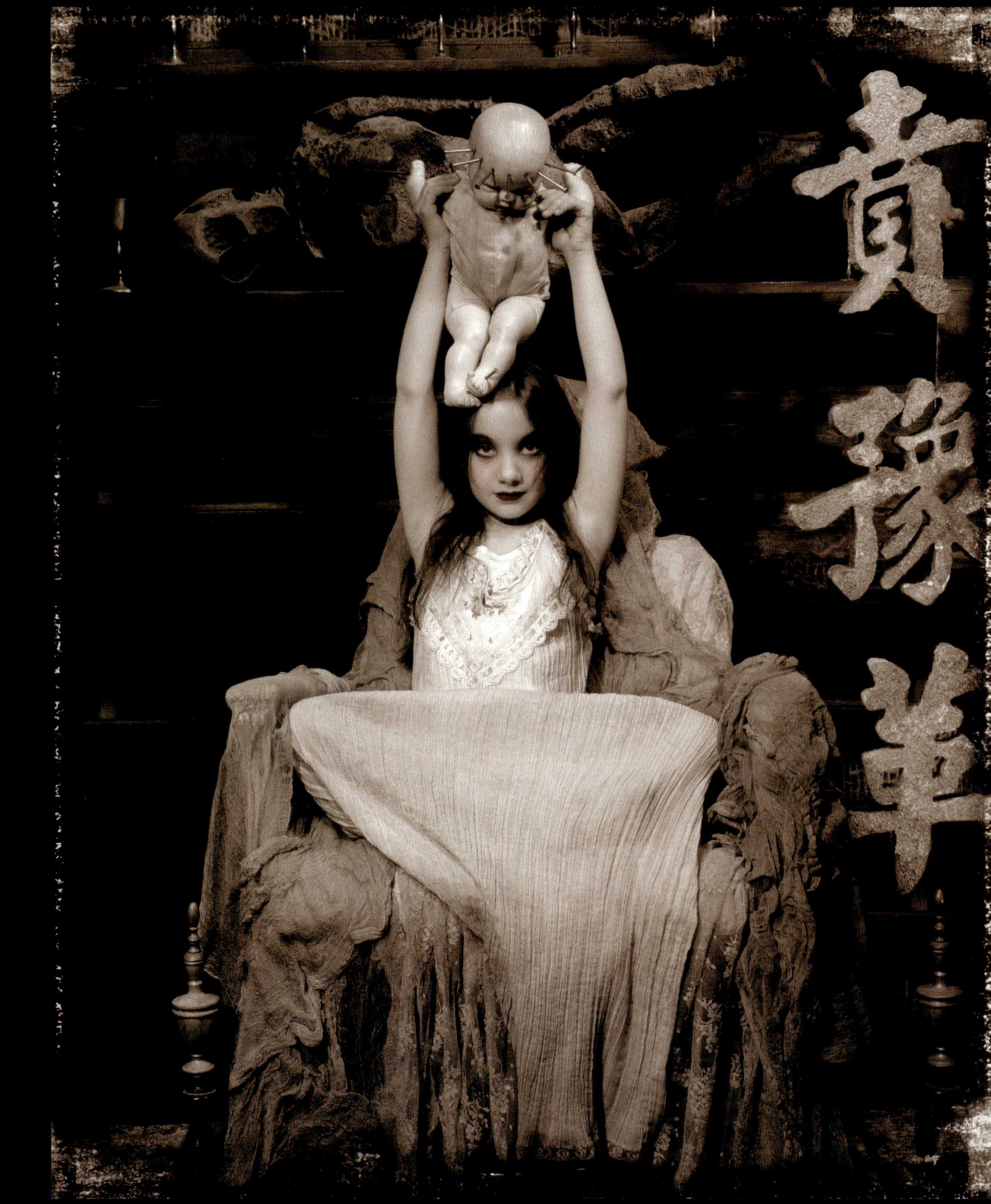

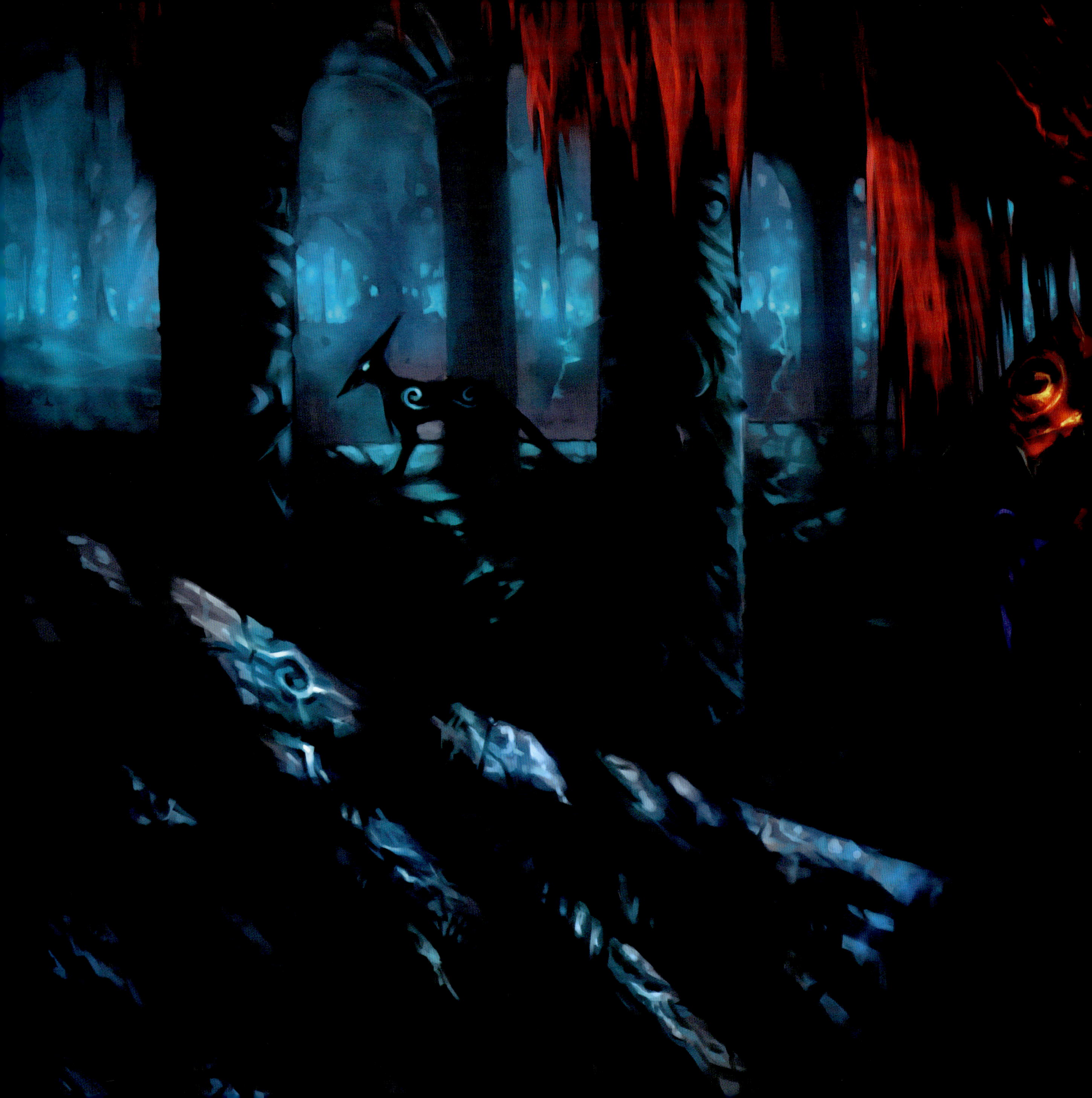

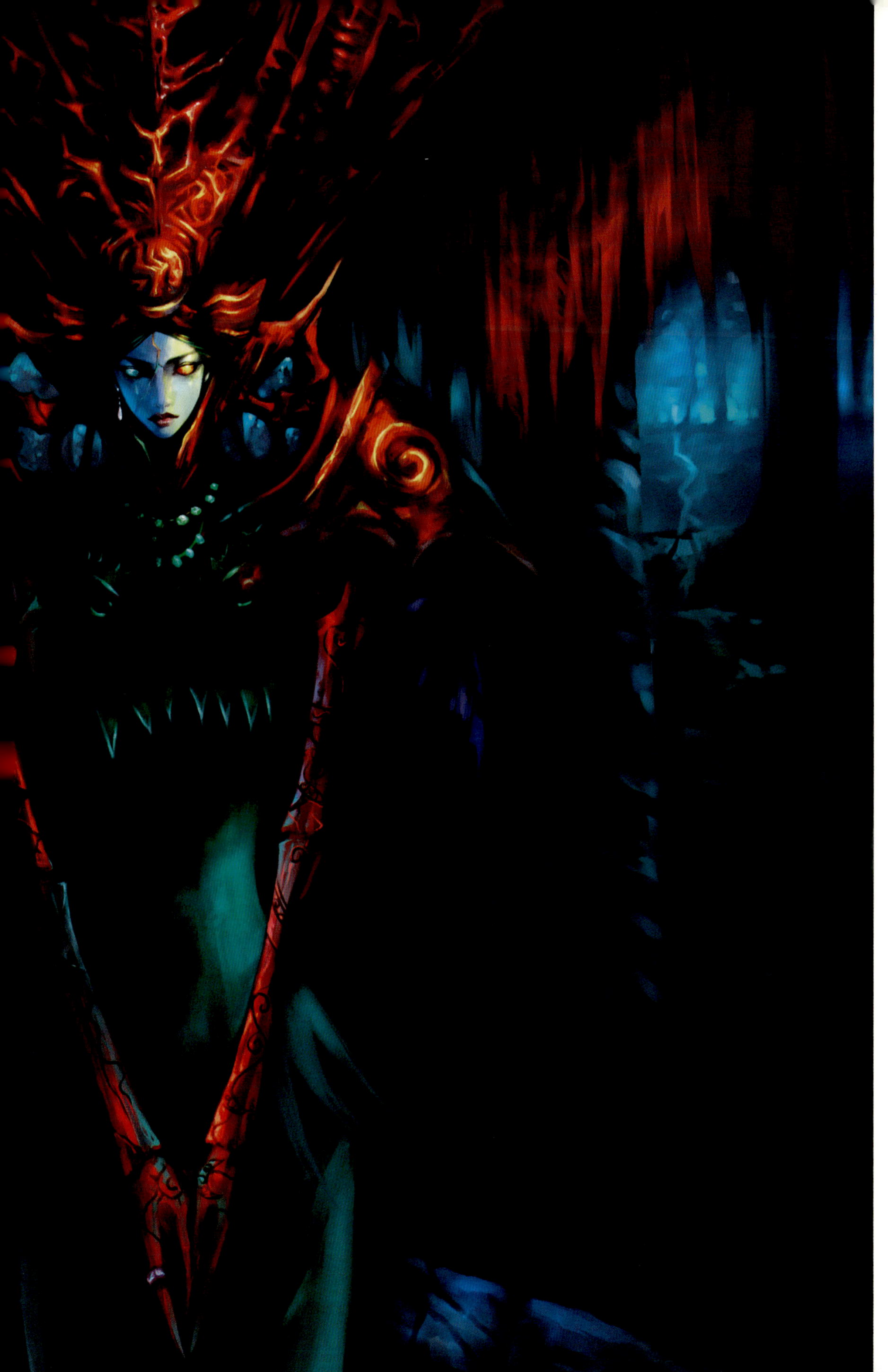

◀ **The Queen of Dreamland**
Xiao-chen Fu
Pencil, digitally painted
www.krishnafu.com

Rich dynamic colors contrast with gloomy lighting to create a dreamlike atmosphere in ***The Queen of Dreamland****, created using pencil and painted in Adobe Photoshop. Fu explains: "I felt the Dreamland is a nice and true place, so I drew this series about it. This one is the second in the series."*

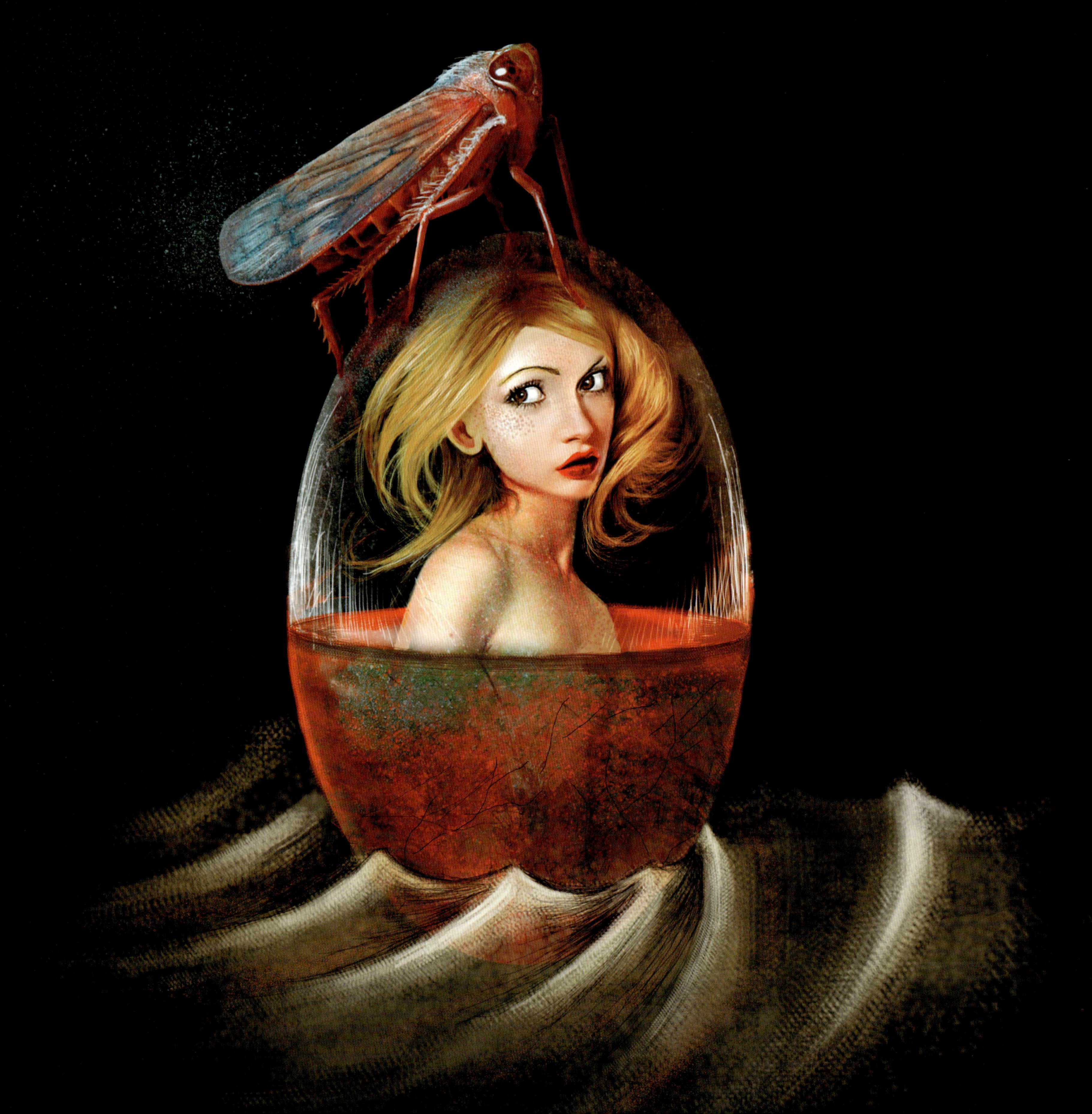

◀ **When Pandora Looked She Saw**
Lisa Falzon
Digital painting
www.lisafalzon.com

Falzon's masterful use of the digital medium has founded a beautiful surreal vision inspired by classical myth. "Again I turn to a myth here. I like to give it my own twist. I've often wondered whether the box Pandora opened could be considered a gateway to another world, rather than a box within our own. I imagined Pandora able to navigate through this other world, full of insects and sin, with perfect impunity if she were to devise some sort of cover and move around as if in a submarine."

▶ **Birch**
Kuang Hong
Digital painting
www.zemotion.net

Hong used Corel Painter to digitally paint this stunning beauty, the cruel thorns and clutching branches offsetting the soft face and features of the girl within. "This was a private commission to paint a portrait of Thora Birch in my own interpretation. There were very few guidelines and limitations, except to keep to my darker style."

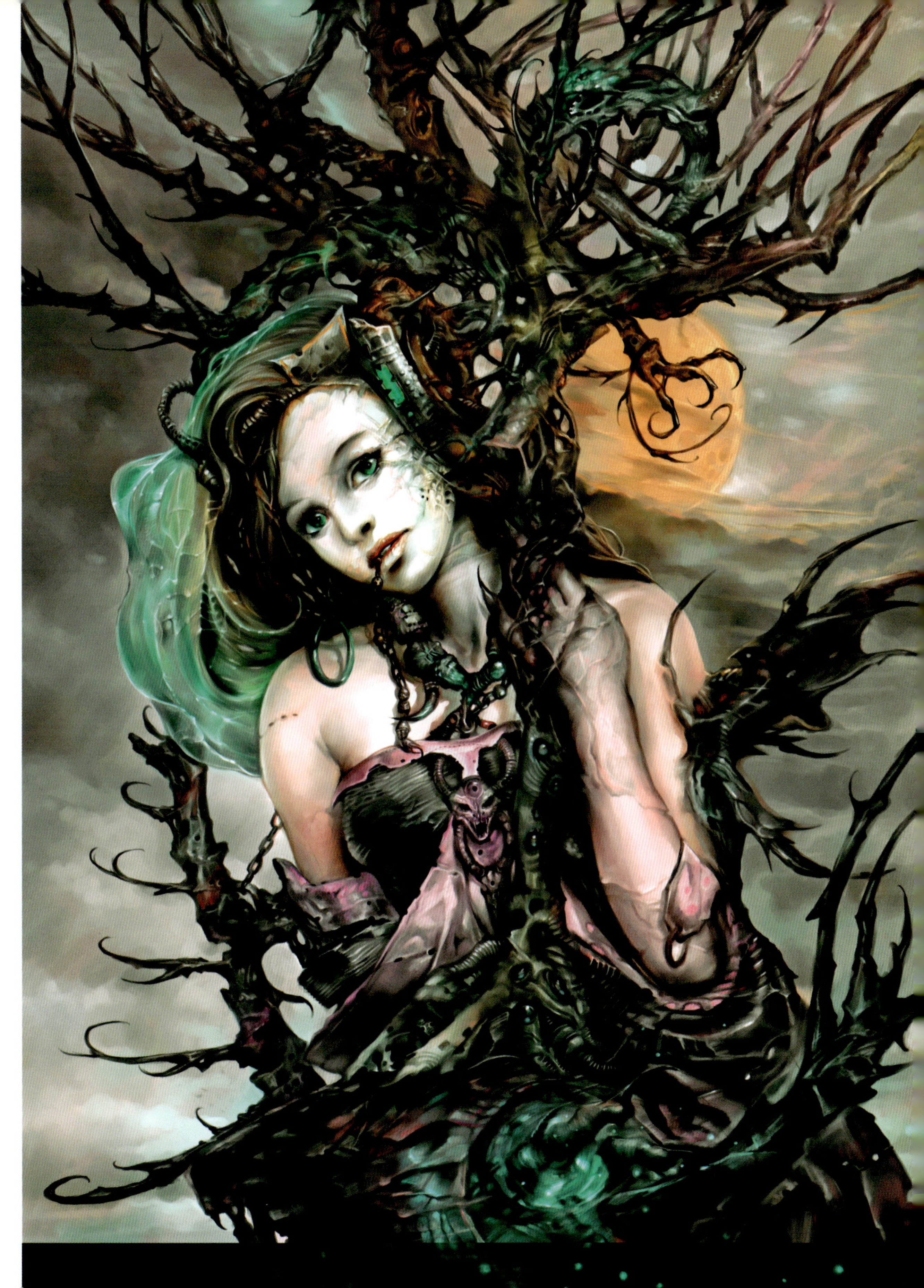

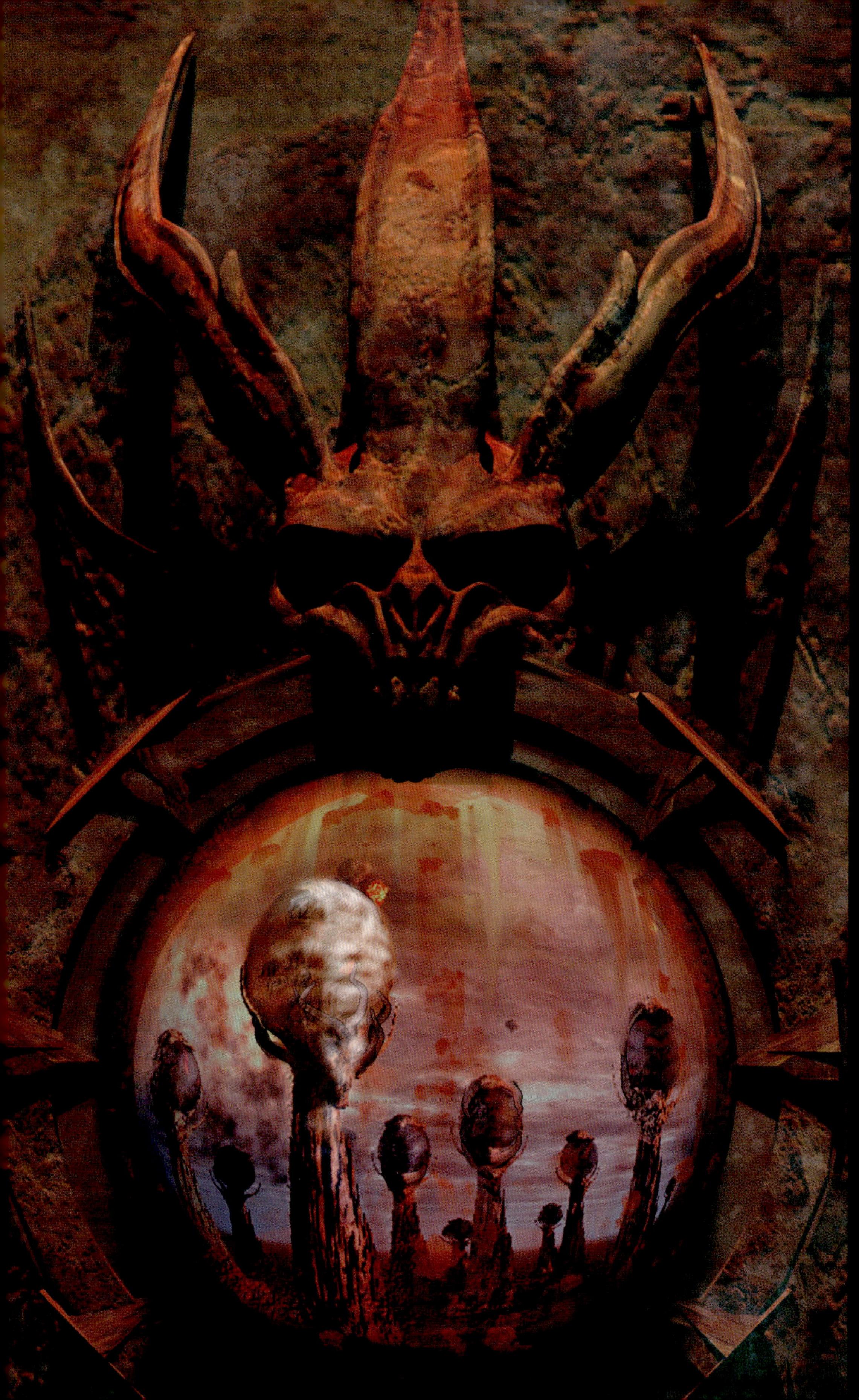

◀ **Lumley Three**
Eric Scala
Digital painting
www.ericscala.com

A sense of depth and dimension was created by Scala using Bryce, Adobe Photoshop, and Corel Painter software. The unusual skull detail and the bizarre landscape have elements of science fiction and horror—highly appropriate as this was a third book cover for one of Brian Lumley's often Lovecraftian novels.

▶ **Purgatory**
Kimberly Myatt
Digital painting
www.beetlebones.net

A beautiful figure, corrupted with underlying terror. "This was a rehash of an old idea I had, to depict purgatory in a way that made sense to me. I painted like a demon, completing this piece in one sitting. My technique was similar to my usual way of painting, however, with this one I painted over the black-and-white foundation on a color layer set to multiply, and another set to overlay. I had a little trouble getting the faces on his tattoo to look how I intended them to so I used the liquify tool to distort them further."

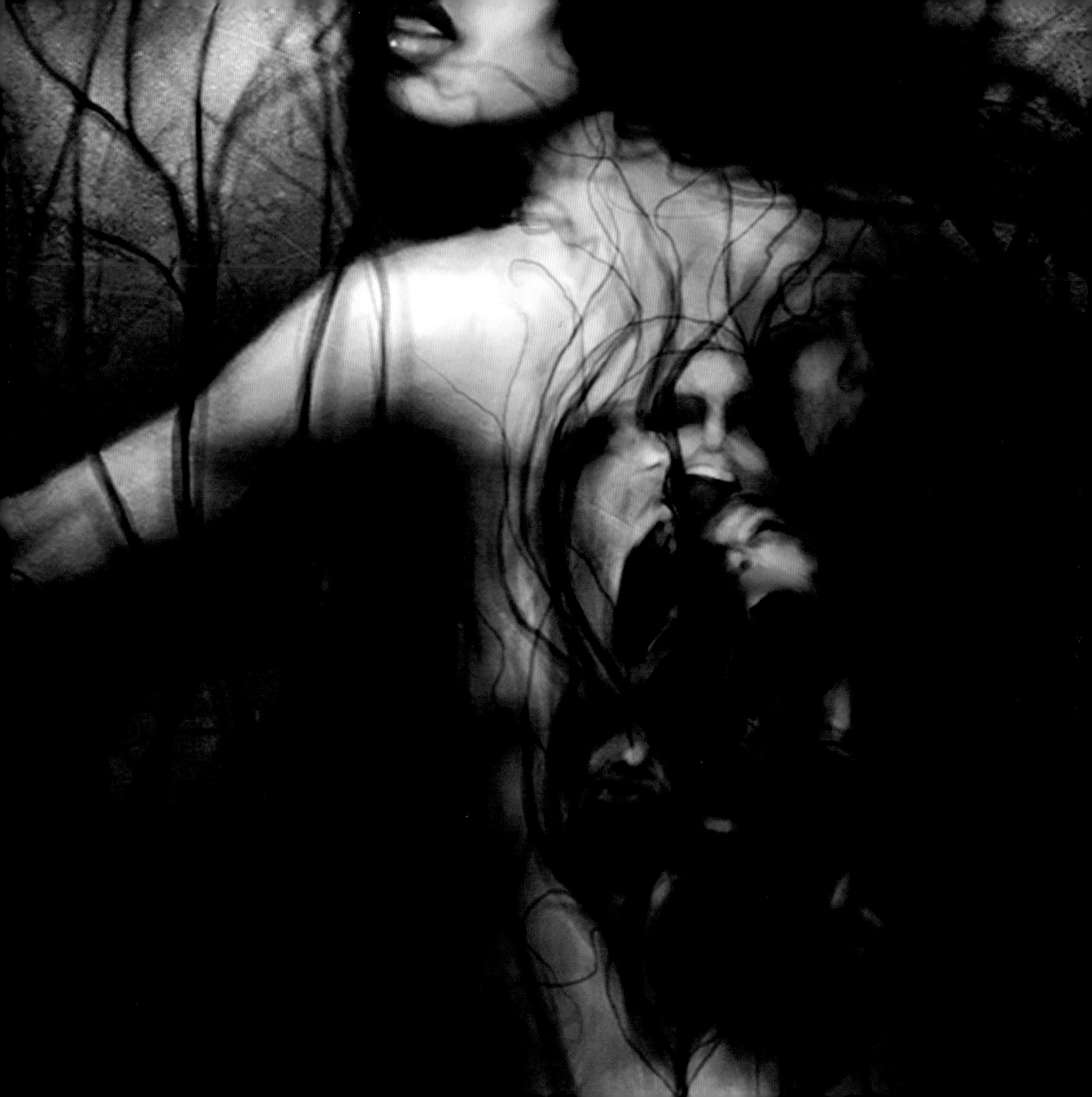

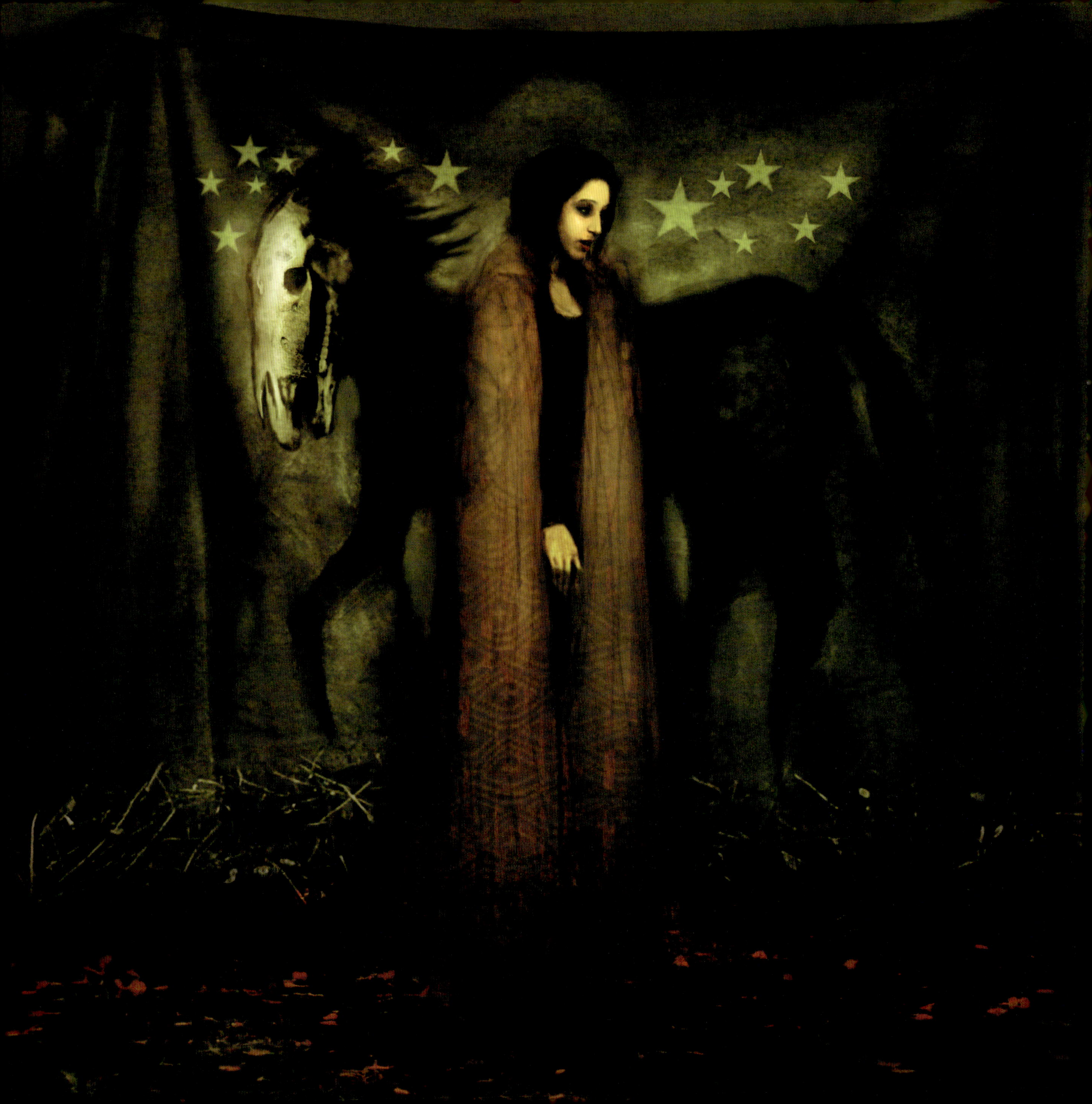

◀ **Nightmare Rider 2000**
Samuel Araya
Photography and digital manipulation
www.samael.epilogue.net

Araya's digital composition of a skeletal horse and a female figure is painted in dark hues. "This was featured on the **Thornography: Harder, Darker, Faster** *CD, by the internationally acclaimed band* **Cradle of Filth**. *It's probably one of my favorite pieces, heavily inspired by Gustav Klimt's paintings. It's a photograph shot in my studio, and heavily overpainted in Adobe Photoshop."*

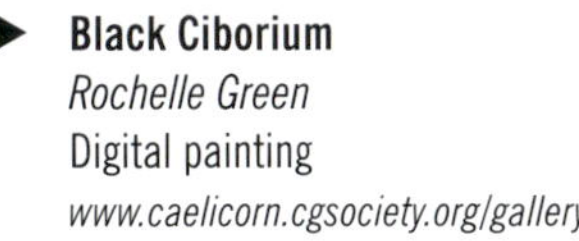

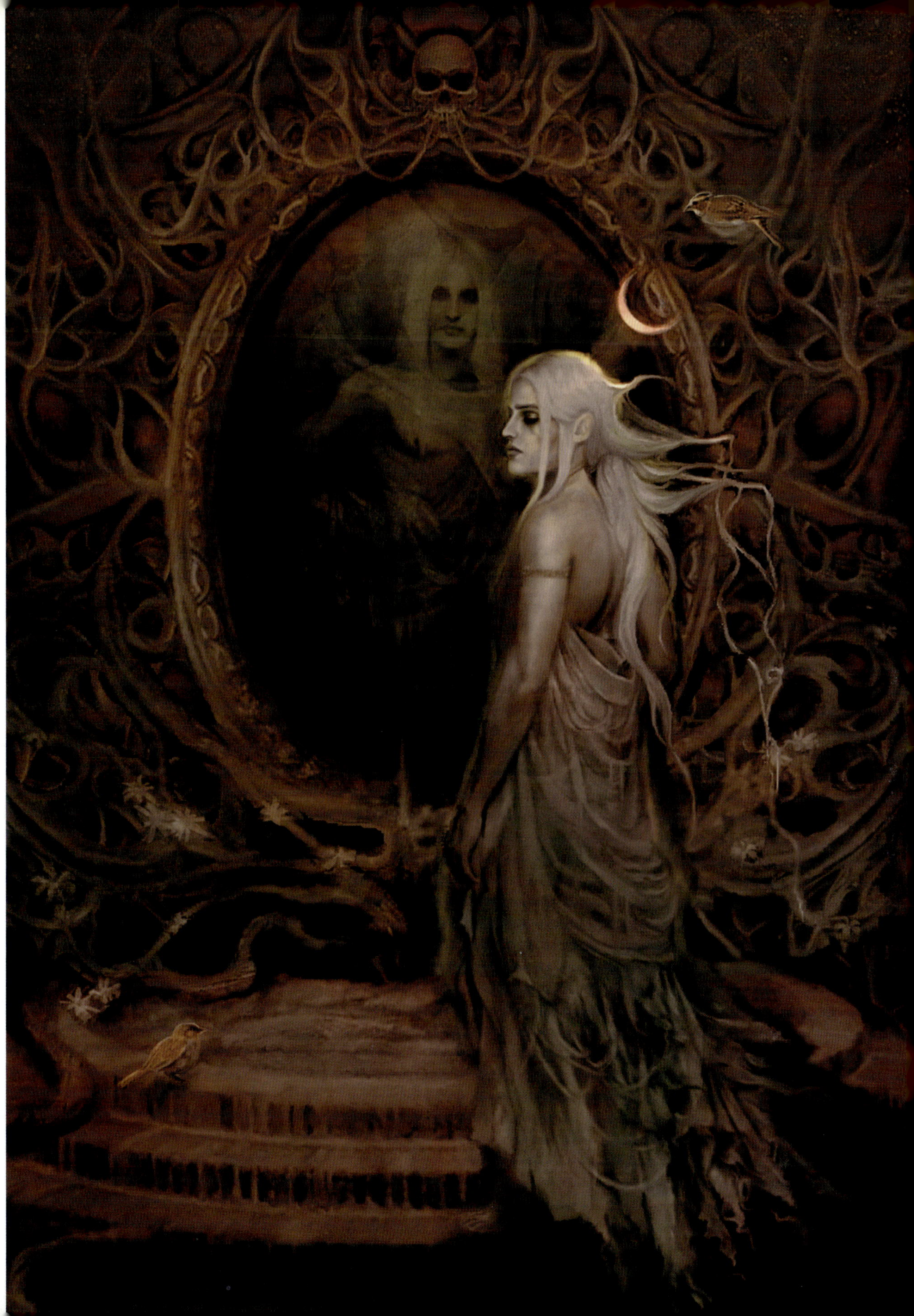

▶ **Black Ciborium**
Rochelle Green
Digital painting
www.caelicorn.cgsociety.org/gallery

Green's delicately painted digital work balances dark elegance with underlying decay. "I have always imagined a Faerie as being a dark and Gothic beauty, synonymous with decay, and a whole strata of light and shadow. I wished to convey some sense of this with a ghostly but youthful main figure, mirrored by an even darker and more shadowy shape. Where there is opulence there is also rot—so I picked a selection of earthy, compost hues."

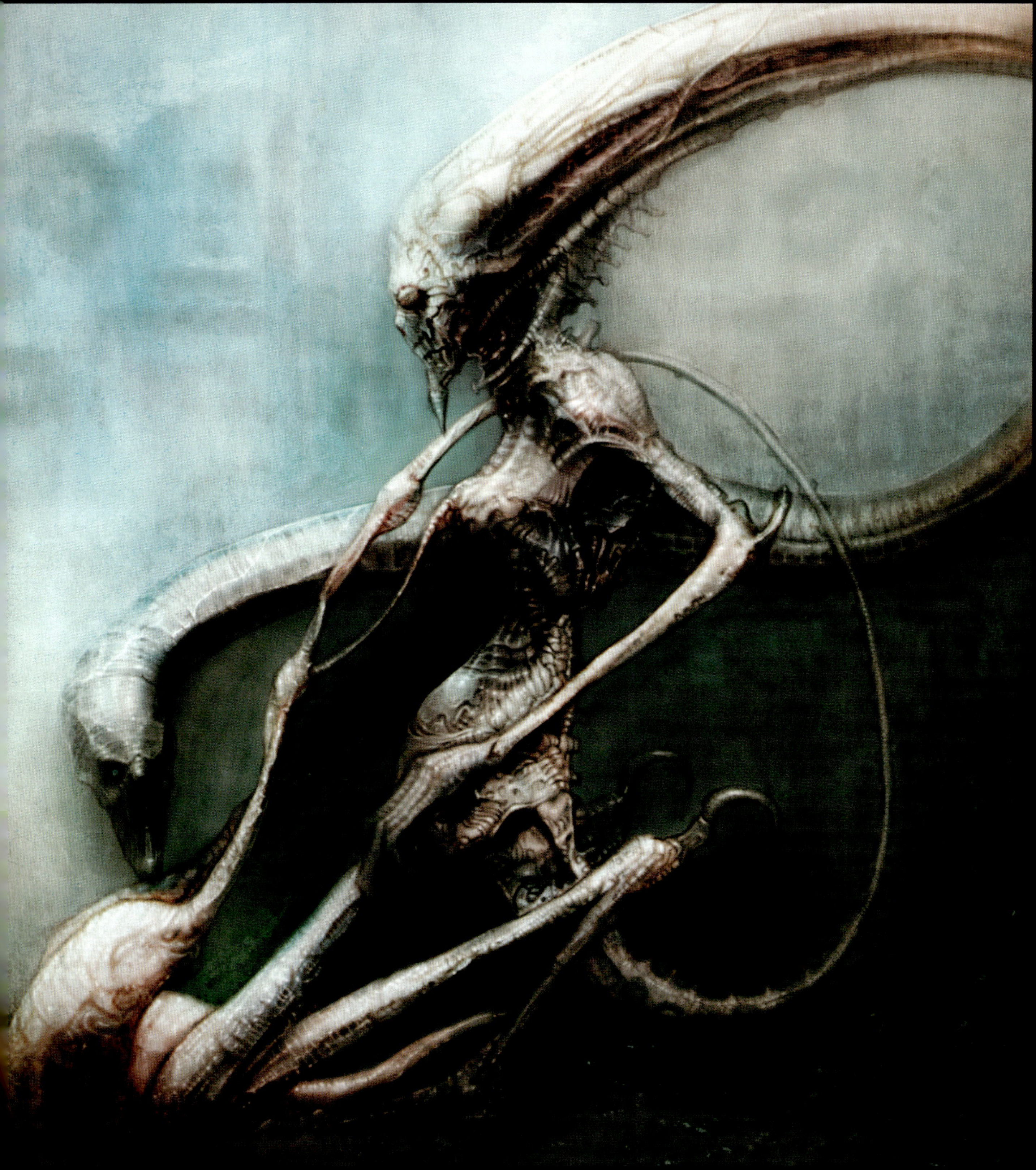

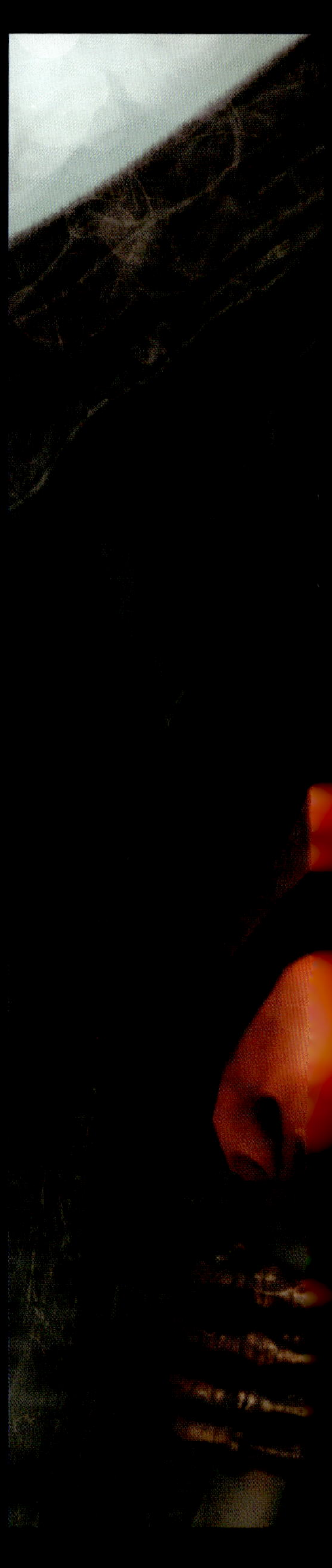

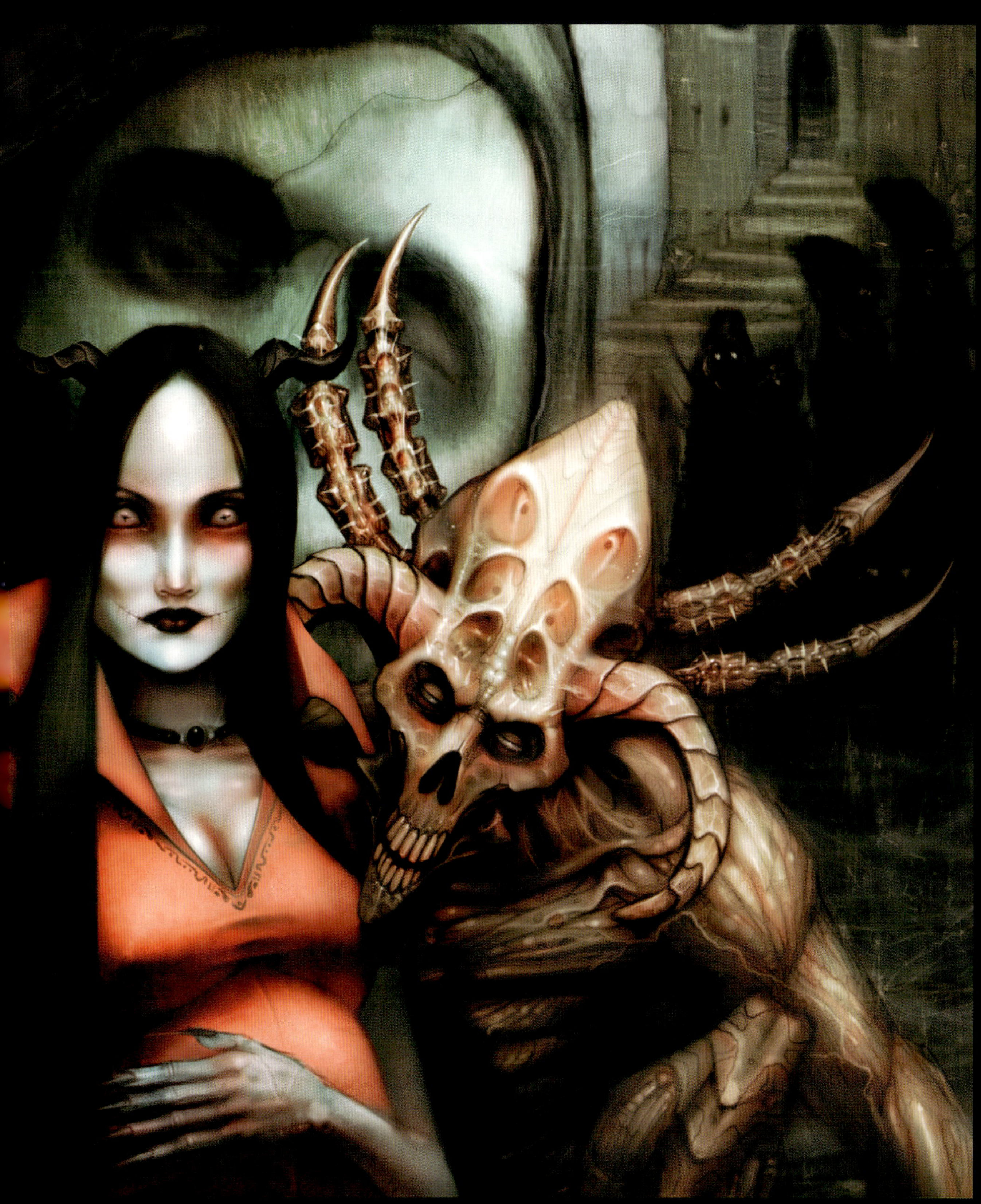

◀◀ **Nourish**
Robert Thomas
Digital painting
www.mindsiphon.com

A cold, yet somewhat organic digital painting from Robert Thomas—very alien with some Gothic, industrial overtones. ***Nourish*** *is a beautiful piece of art. "This piece represents an otherworldly and grotesque family unit. This is one of the first pieces I did where I started incorporating lots of detail into my art."*

◀ **Seed**
Robert Thomas
Digital painting
www.mindsiphon.com

*A wicked digital painting with a dark fantasy theme from Thomas. "****Seed*** *originally started out as a small doodle I sketched on a sticky note. This piece depicts the coming birth of a demon. My goal was for the viewer to make their own interpretation about the piece."*

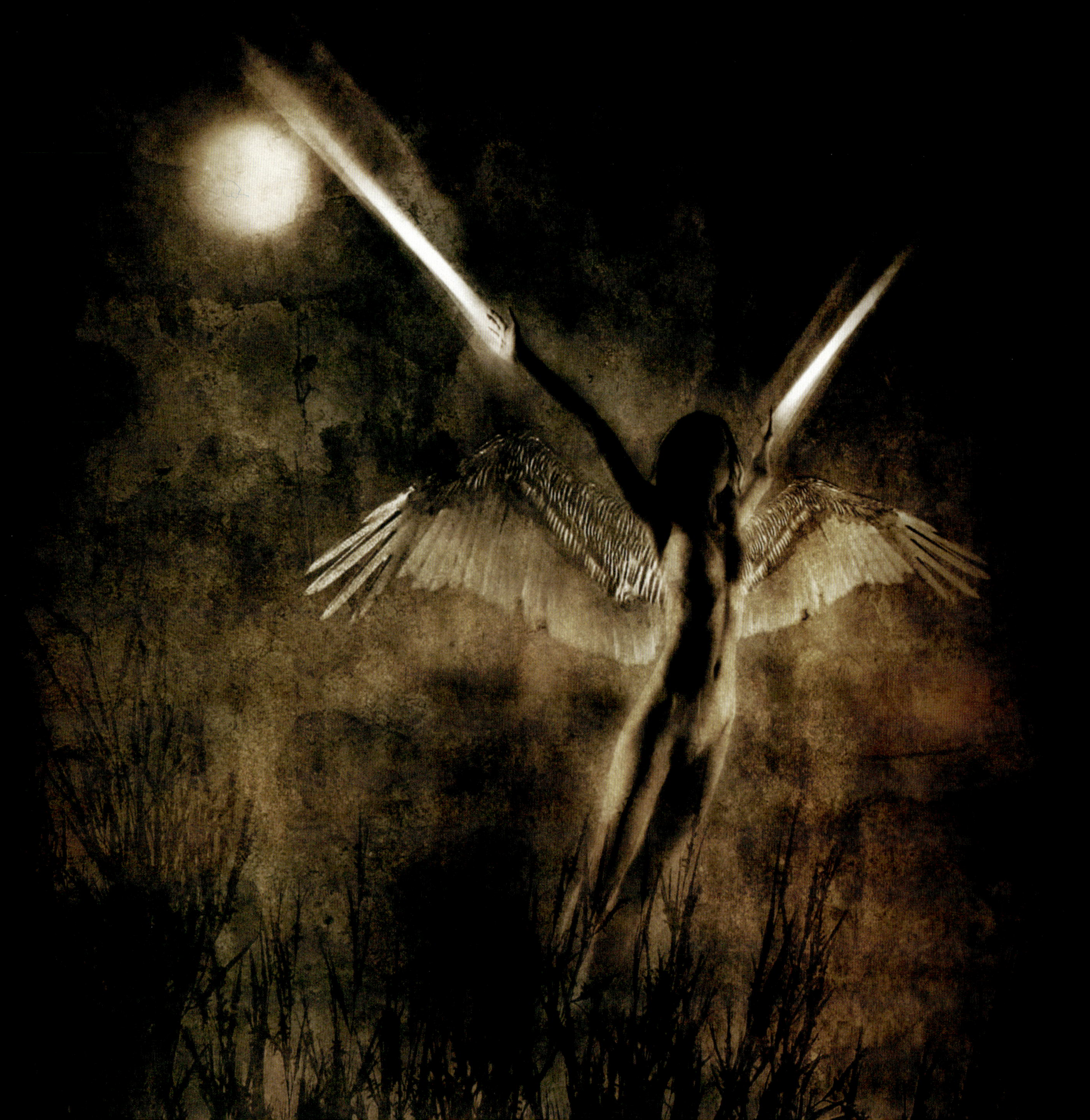

◄ **Break Into Dreams**
Jarno Lahti
Photography and digital manipulation
www.kaamos.com

Artist Jarno Lahti's ethereal work, ***Break Into Dreams,*** *was created in Adobe Photoshop using photography and a Wacom Graphics Tablet.*

"World has crushed me down
At the end I will rise
My spirit cannot die
It's time to break into dreams."

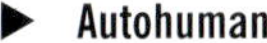

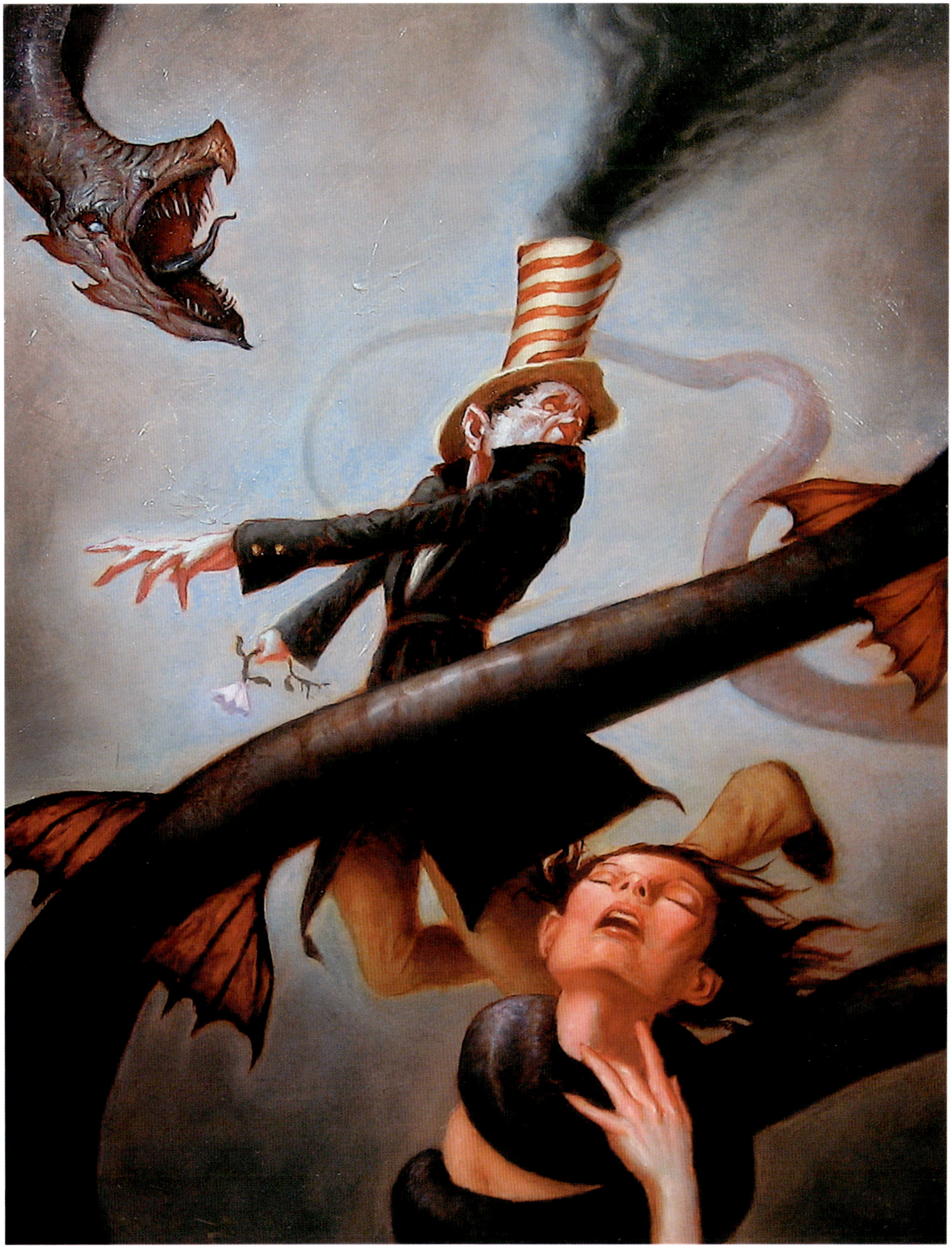

► **Autohuman**
Scott Altmann
Oil on linen, on board
www.scottaltmann.com

*A clearly Gothic oil painting, "****Autohuman****" exudes a circus-like atmosphere. Atlmann explains: "I had been preoccupied with imagery of creepy men with bluish-skin and striped top hats, with smoke flowing out the top. For this piece I painted directly onto linen, without an underpainting. There is a considerable amount of palette knife work in the background. I think the most successful part of the painting is the man's face, which I painted without using a reference."*

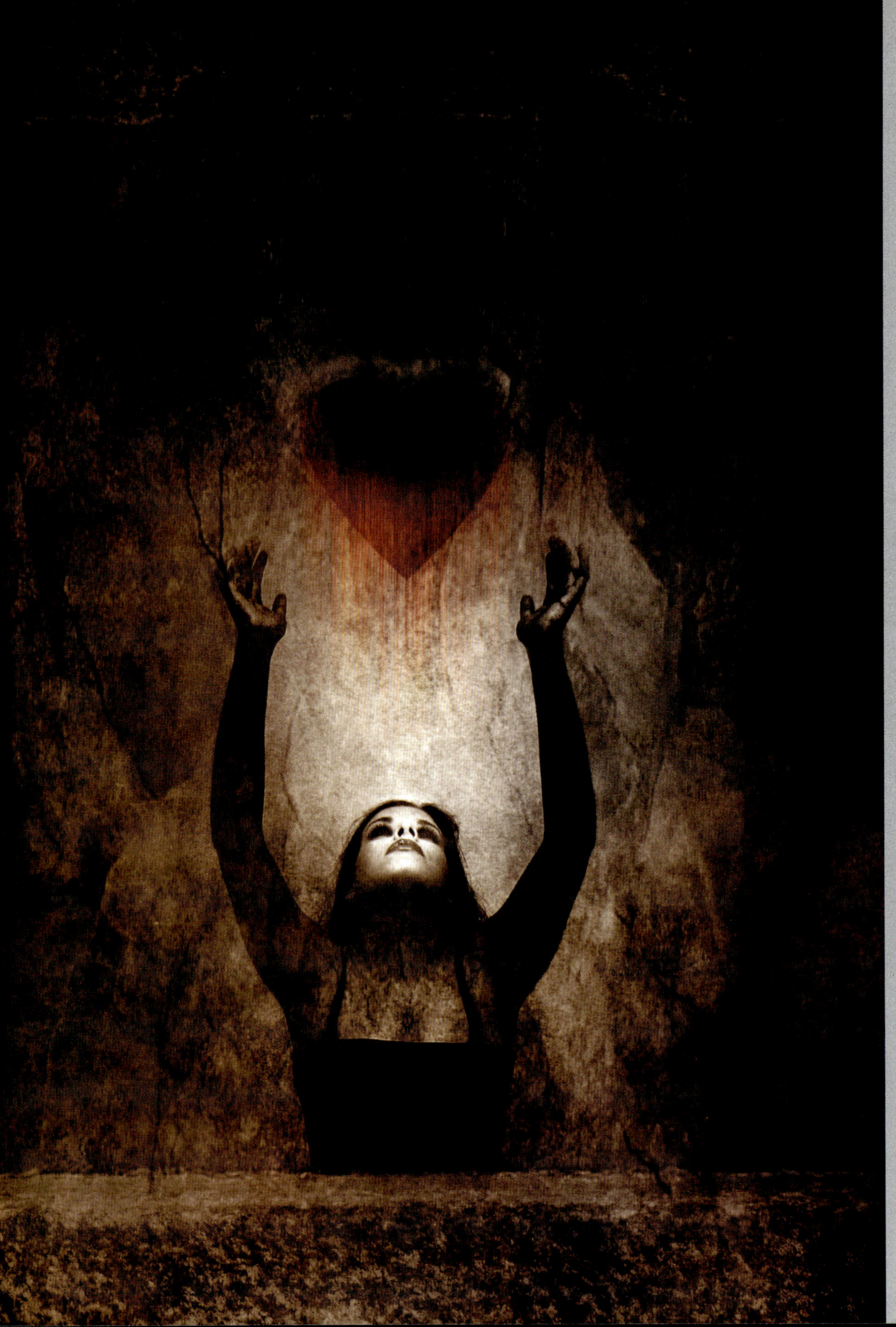

◀ **Hold At All Costs**
Jarno Lahti
Photography and
digital manipulation
www.kaamos.com

Lahti's painting is a haunting image of one who cannot let go of the past. A brooding image, with a dark palette and a blood-red heart, ***Hold At All Costs*** *combines photography and Adobe Photoshop.*

"You were everything
and more to me
That was my tragedy
That was my death
But I don't want to
let you go
Still I try to hold you
at all costs."

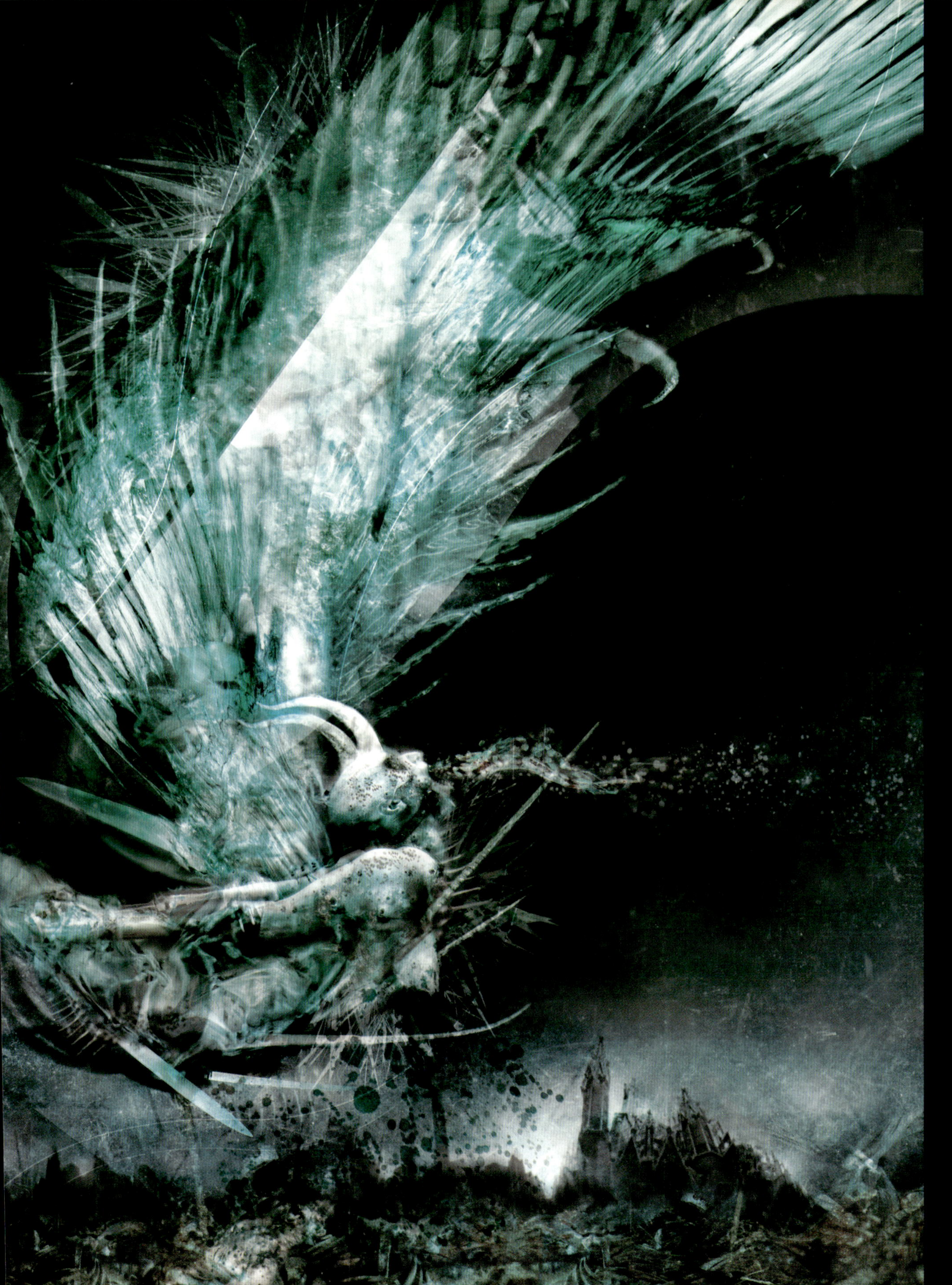

Visitation of the Plague
Ralph Manfreda
Photography and digital manipulation
www.cryptonaut.com

A terrifying vision of plague and disease, swooping over an unsuspecting populace. Manfreda created this piece in Adobe Photoshop by using different materials, such as photographs, drawings, and surfaces, that have been scanned and manipulated. "At the end of time an angel will come to redeem mankind from mental suffering."

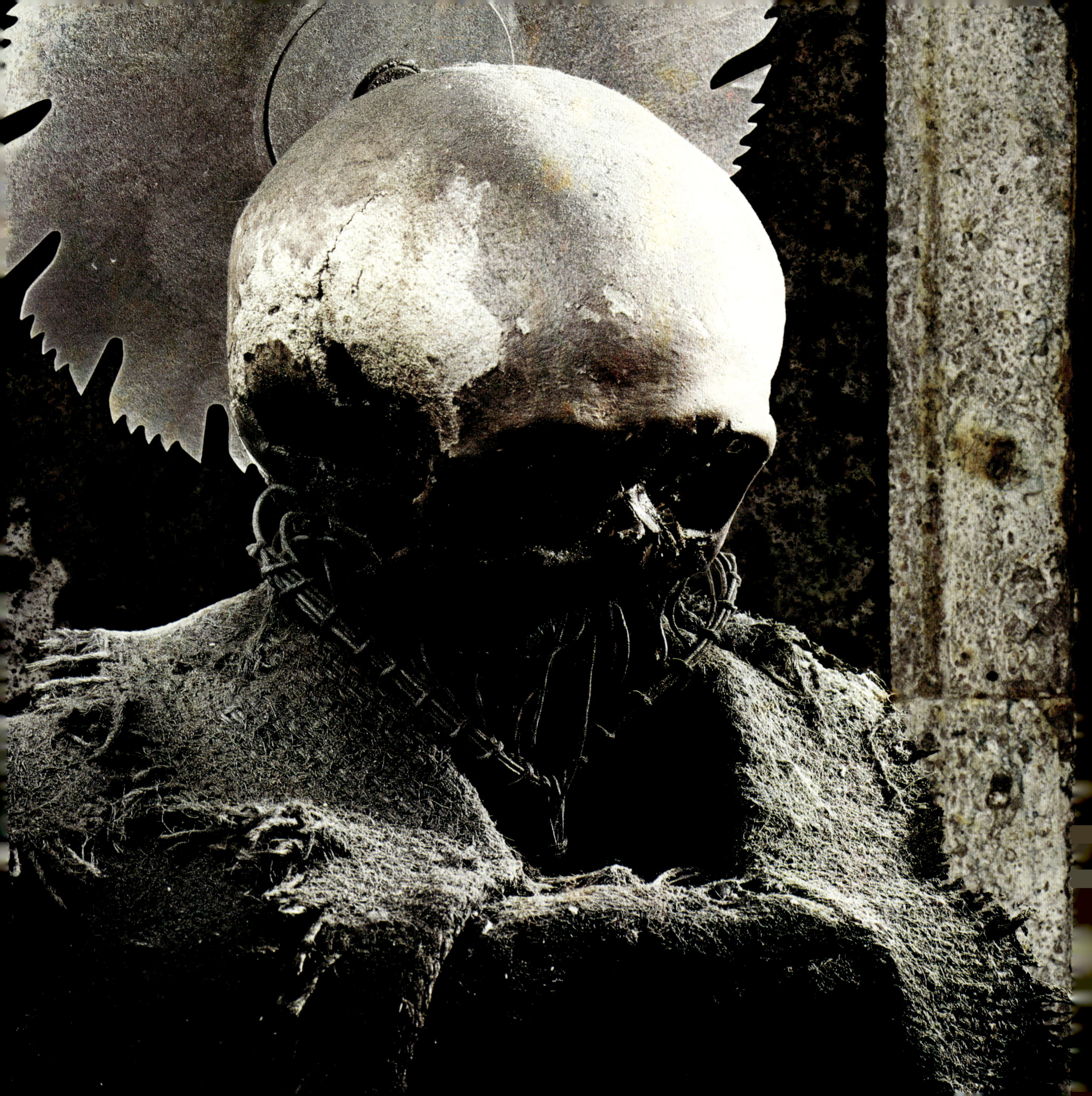

CHAPTER 7
CREEPY CREATIONS

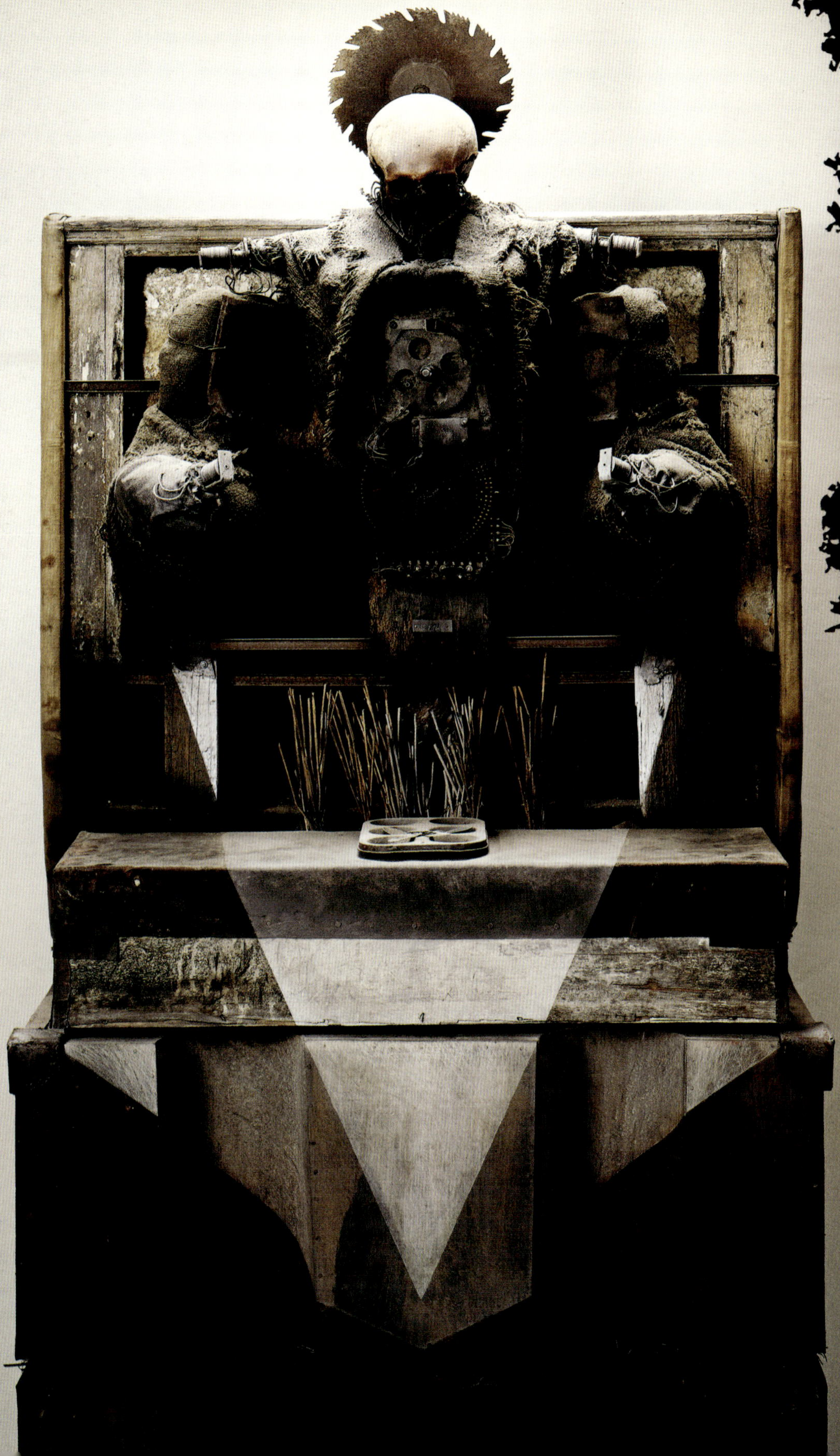

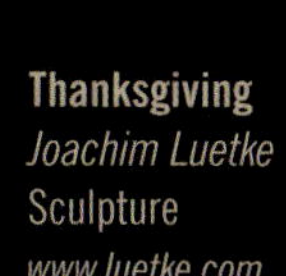

◀ **Thanksgiving**
Joachim Luetke
Sculpture
www.luetke.com

Dark military overtones and feelings of desperation and deat emanate from Luetke's ironicall titled ***Thanksgiving****. His iconic sculpture is assembled from a variety of stark materials with rough and jagged textures.*

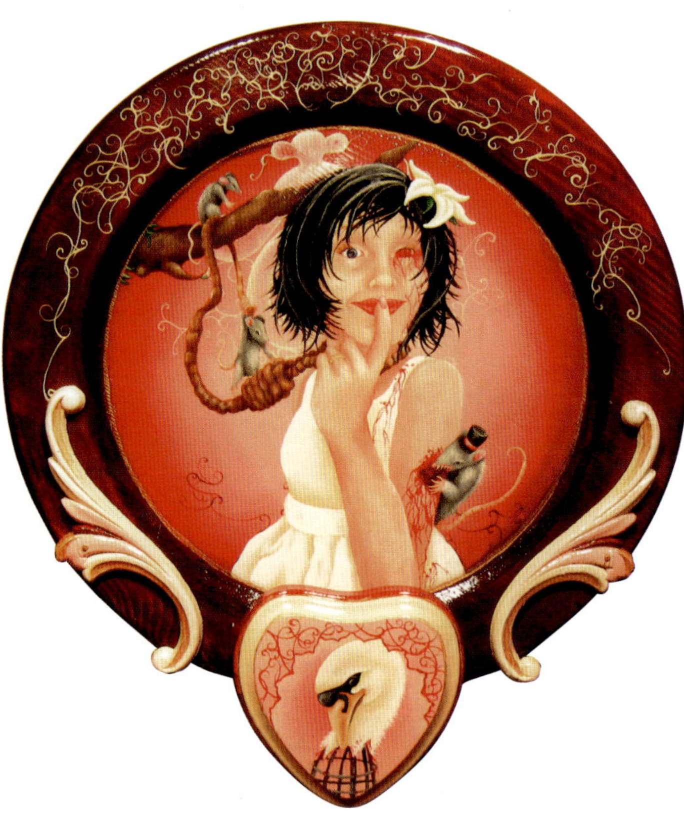

◀ **Do You Know What It's Like To Be Cursed?**
Kristen Ferrell
Acrylic on wood
www.kristenferrell.com

An almost humorous but subtly sinister painting on wood from Kristen Ferrell. "Being a serial monogamist, I'm constantly dedicated (or married) to people. These people are always a handful and after going through handful after handful, I started to wonder what horrible acts I'd committed in a previous life to be rewarded with so much stress. This piece was created using acrylic on assembled wooden plaques with a high-gloss treatment."

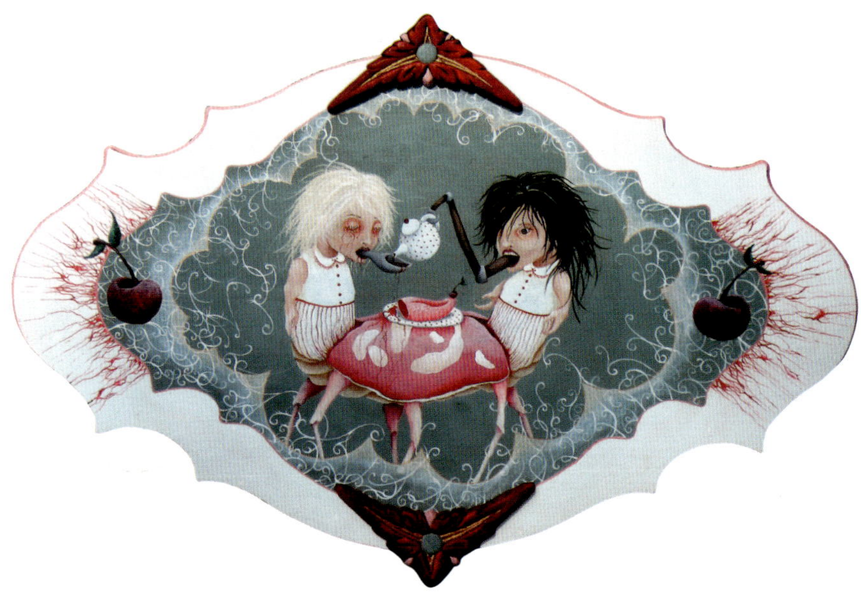

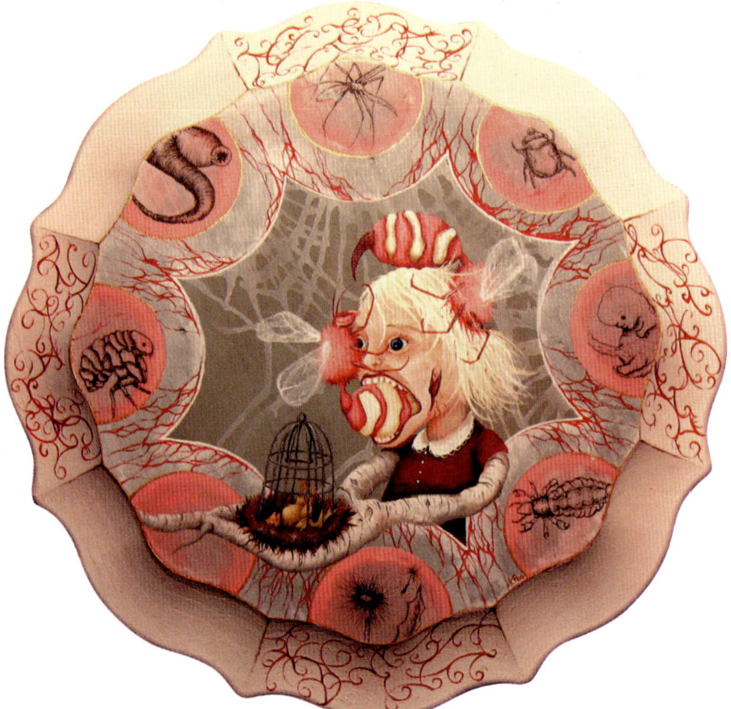

◀ **You Are What You Eat**
Kristen Ferrell
Acrylic, pen, and ink on wood
www.kristenferrell.com

A delicately painted homage to parasites. Looking closely, you will notice a human fetus amongst the various creepy-crawlies, ostensibly feeding from the mother by an umbilical cord. "Parasites attach themselves to a host and will feed on it to the point of destruction. Thoughts such as paranoia, fear, and hate work the same way: they cling to our brain and devour all sanity and structure until all that's left are the scraps that no one wants. This was created using acrylic, pen, and ink on wood with a high-gloss treatment."

▲ **You Don't Miss The Water 'Til The Well Runs Dry**
Kristen Ferrell
Acrylic on wood
www.kristenferrell.com

Another beautiful glossy wood painting from Ferrell, this time featuring a tea party gone terribly wrong. "We all have two sides of our psyche, the positive and the destructive. If the two don't learn to play nicely together, we quickly find ourselves drained."

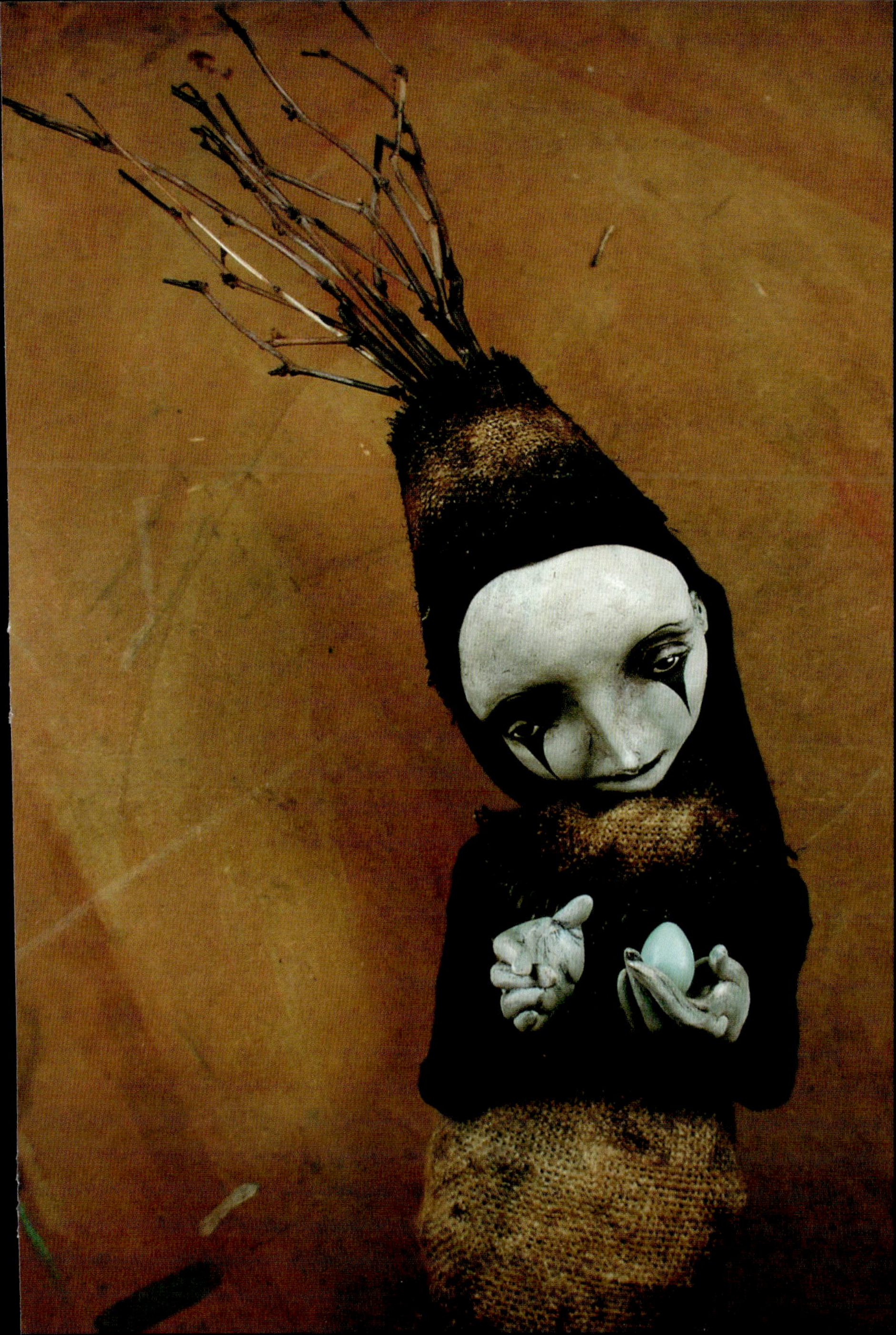

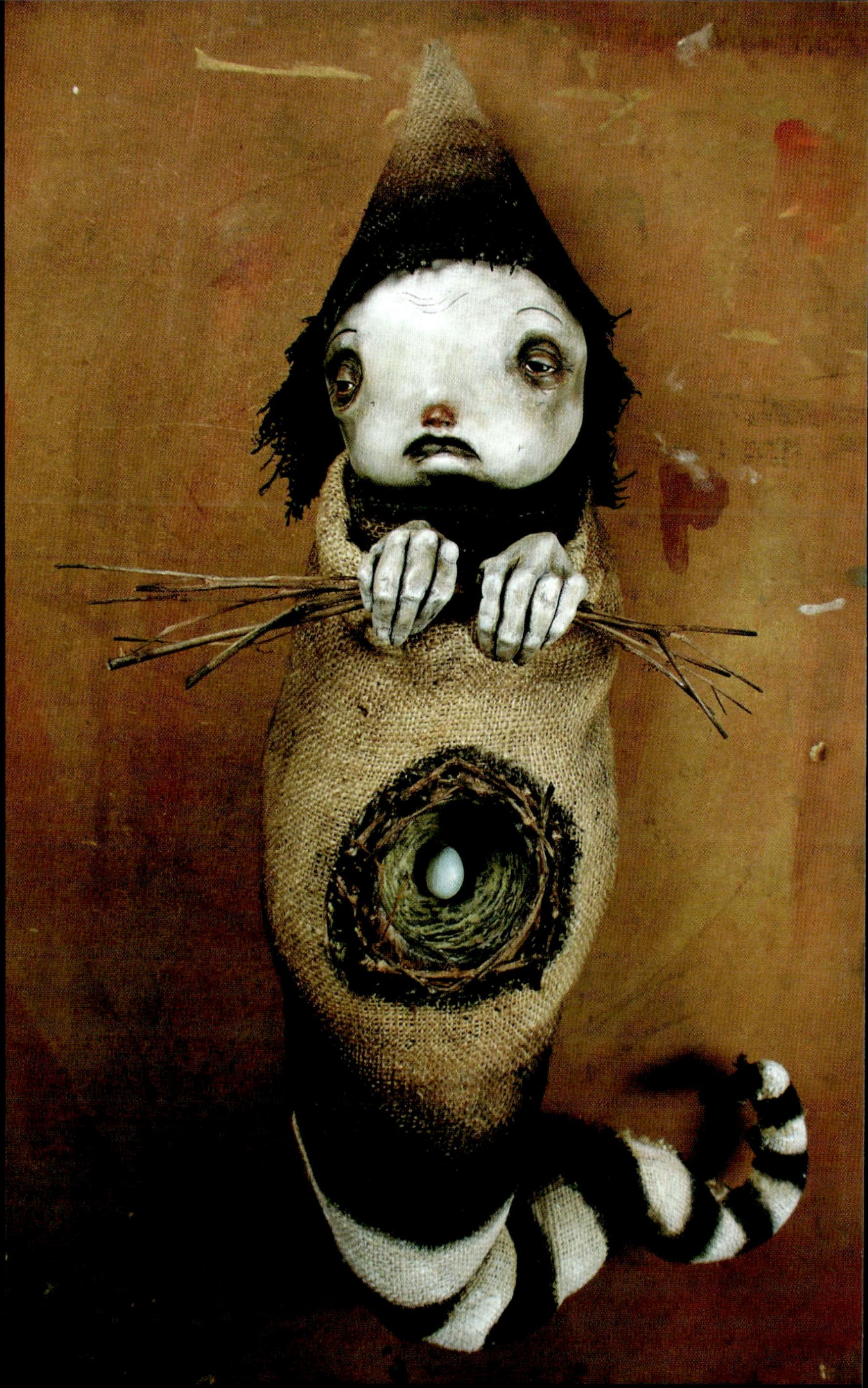

▲ **Doll #7**
Scott Radke
Sculpture
www.scottradke.com

"I used burlap, wire, wood, clay, and twigs from the Cuyahoga River bed for this sculpture. I wanted to incorporate nature in my work. I used acrylic paint to give the burlap a burned look. I suppose the eggs represent a new beginning, but I like the viewer to decide."

▲ **Doll #2**
Scott Radke
Sculpture
www.scottradke.com

A doll from a series of Radke's amazing sculptural works. The face is slightly distorted, but conveys emotion and thought. Radke explains: "I start with a head and let the personality dictate what they will become. I do not think, or plan out my work from the start too much."

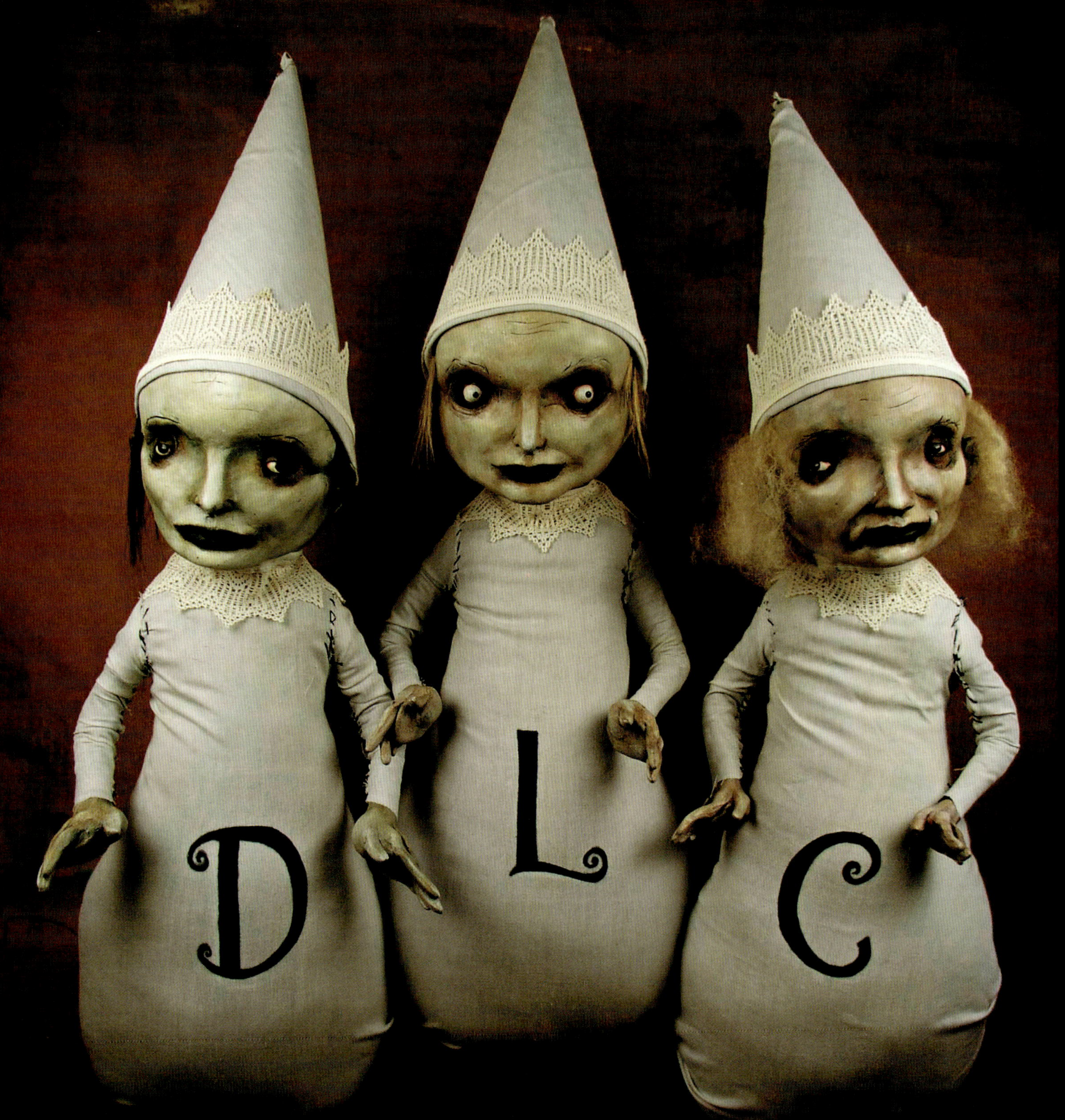
D
L
C

◀ **De La Costa**
Scott Radke
Sculpture
www.scottradke.com

Scott Radke's trio of pointy-capped creations are grimly Gothic, yet quite endearing. "These three figures were a permanent installation for De La Costa, a restaurant in Chicago, Illinois. They are in the likeness of the cook and the two owners, although I only had simple descriptions to go by, no photographs. I used wire, wood, clay, and some old doilies I had for the trim on their hats and necks."

◀ **Steam Insect**
Christopher Conte
Sculpture
www.christopherconte.com

Conte's magnificent **Steam Insect** *is a "found object" sculpture, using seemingly mundane objects to create a wonderful creature. "This piece was inspired by late-nineteenth-century steam engines. It's built from a combination of found medical parts, precision gears, and cast bronze components, using the ancient lost-wax process."*

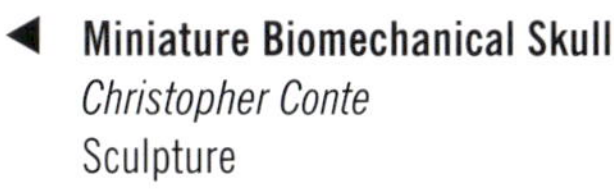

◀ **Miniature Biomechanical Skull**
Christopher Conte
Sculpture
www.christopherconte.com

Artist Christopher Conte fashioned this biomechanical masterpiece using unconventional materials. He explains: "This piece is a combination of antique sewing machine parts, miniature hand-blown glass eyes, along with stainless-steel components. All are attached to a polyurethane skull to complete the sculpture."

▲ **Articulated Singer Insect**
Christopher Conte
Sculpture
www.christopherconte.com

Forgotten sewing machine parts find new life as an insect, courtesy of artist Christopher Conte. "It was built entirely from vintage parts, including antique drawing instruments, and a vintage Singer sewing machine attachment. It's fully articulated at every joint."

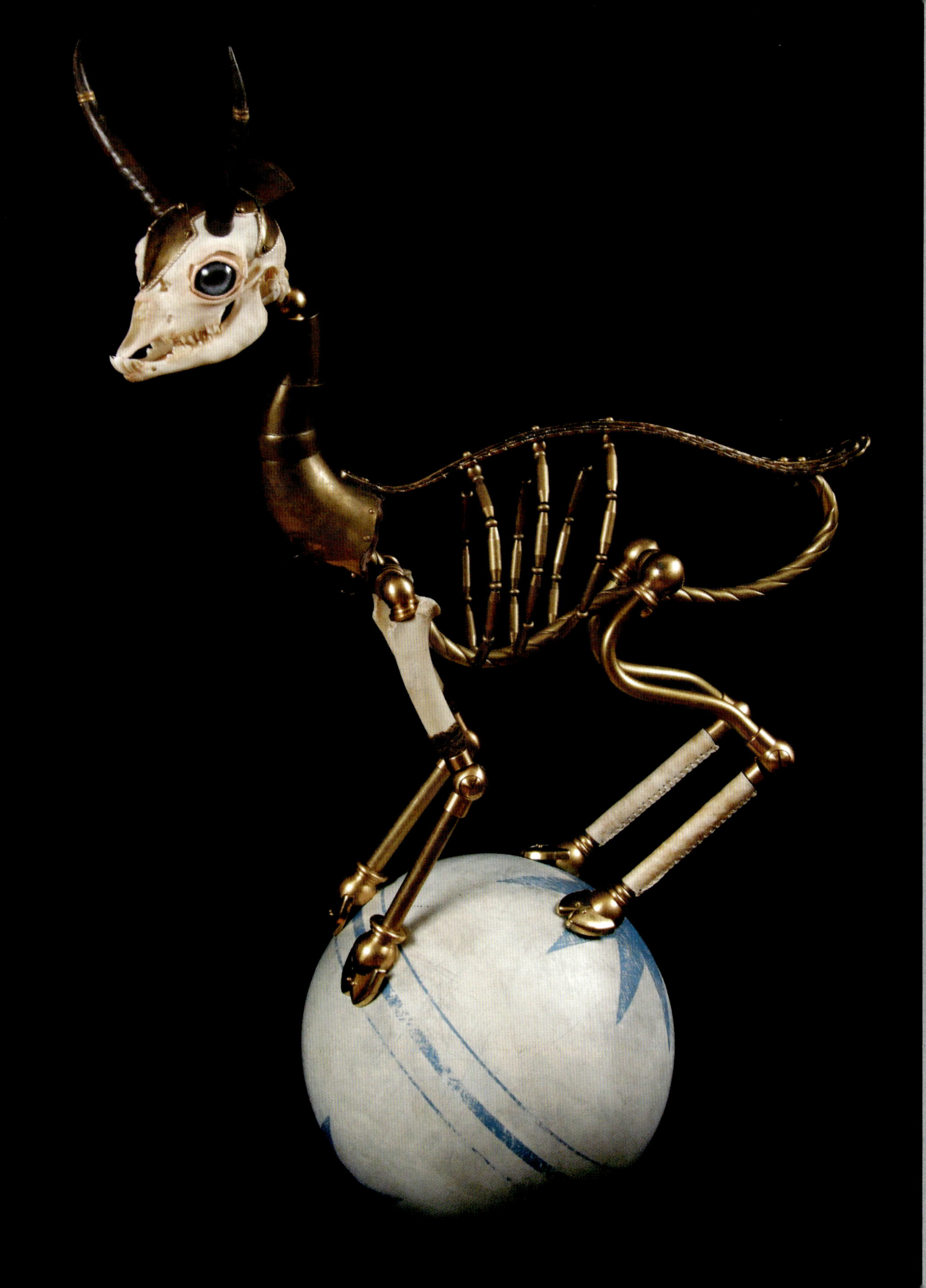

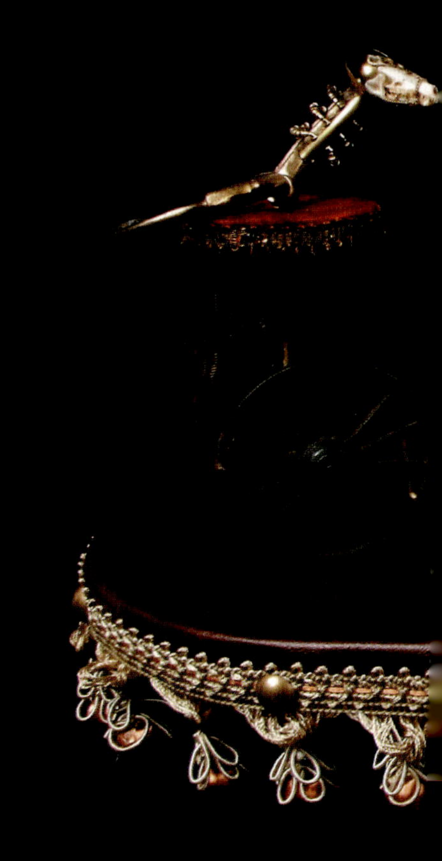

◄ **Marcel**
Jessica Joslin
Sculpture
www.jessicajoslin.com

"Marcel is a creature reminiscent of a 'dik dik,' a small African antelope. This piece draws inspiration from the whimsical, decadent aesthetic of the fin de siècle circus. It is constructed from an assortment of found materials: antique hardware; cut, and reconfigured brass horns; bones; velvet; glass eyes set in eyelids formed from antique gloves; hoofs which were once shoe taps; and lamp finials. All of these combine seamlessly to create an illusion that it might spring to life when no-one is looking. There is a lot of engineering that goes into making them seem natural and effortless, as if they were meant to be."

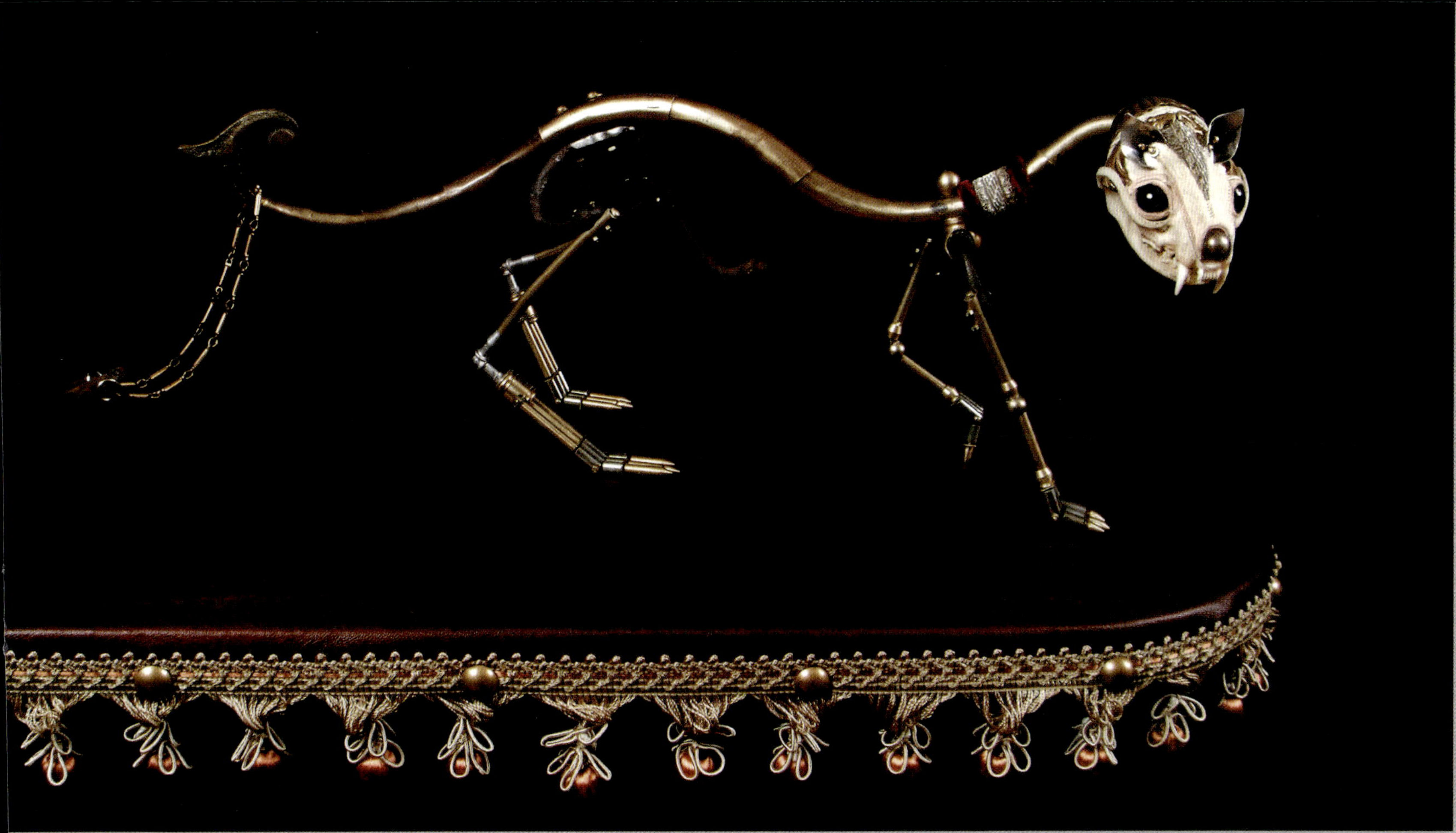

▲ **Lambert & Salvia**
Jessica Joslin
Sculpture
www.jessicajoslin.com

"I am fascinated by osteology, from both an aesthetic, and engineering perspective. Bodies are perfect machines and the structural variety between species is intriguing. The shape of each of my creatures is a distillation of form; both internal and external structures of the animal, reinterpreted through the materials that I find beautiful. They are constructed using a range of techniques, dependent on the material. The parts are assembled without welding, because heating would destroy the patina on the antique metal. I use mechanical fastenings instead. In this piece, a single one of Lambert's feet is comprised of more than 20 separate parts."

► **Marco**
Jessica Joslin
Sculpture
www.jessicajoslin.com

"Marco was inspired by images of the Victorian era circus, and organ grinders' monkeys. For me, there is a wonderful quality about the spectacle of performing animals. They seem at once grotesque and playful. They may be beloved companions, but they did not choose to be so—there is a part of them that stays wild. They are familiar, yet mysterious. I think of my creatures as pets and friends. That is why I name them, rather than 'title' them. At a certain point when building a new piece, they start to reveal their own unique personality. They begin to breathe."

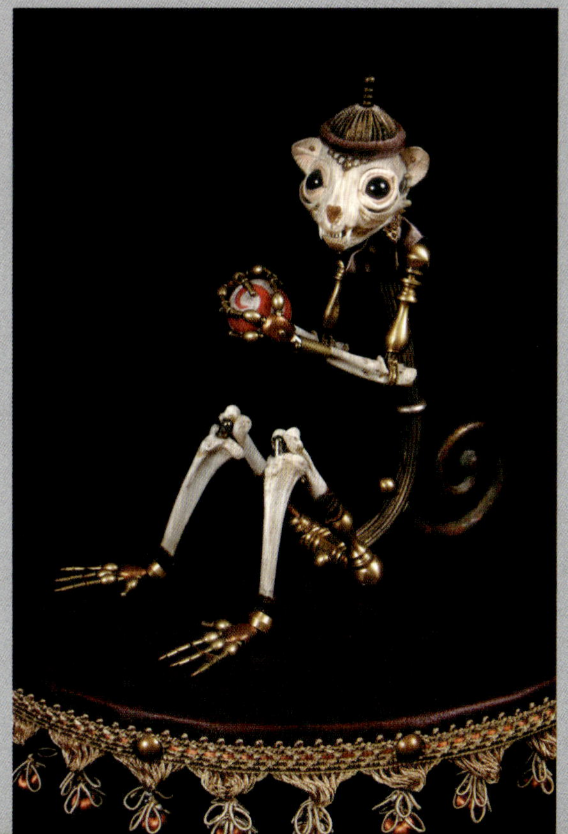

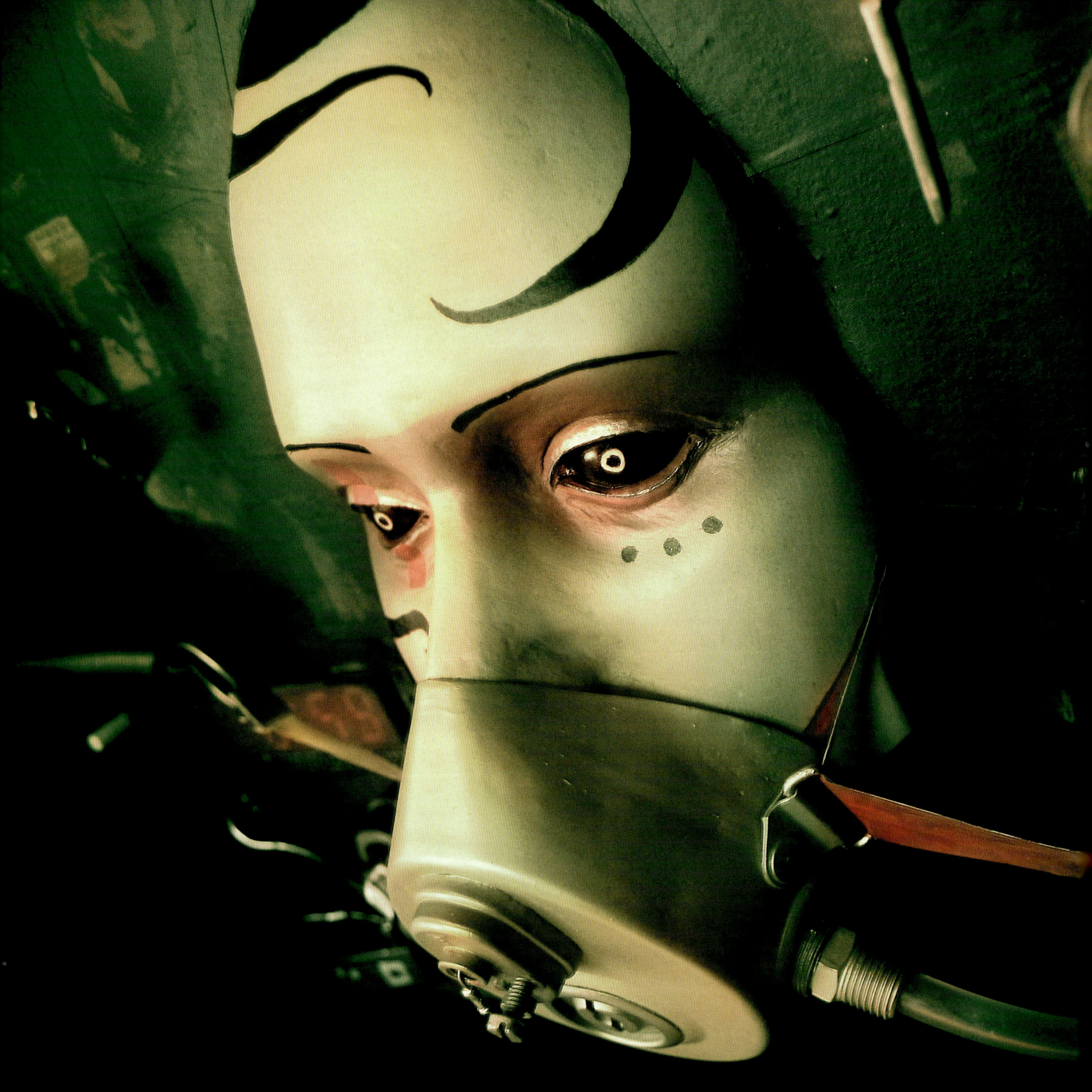

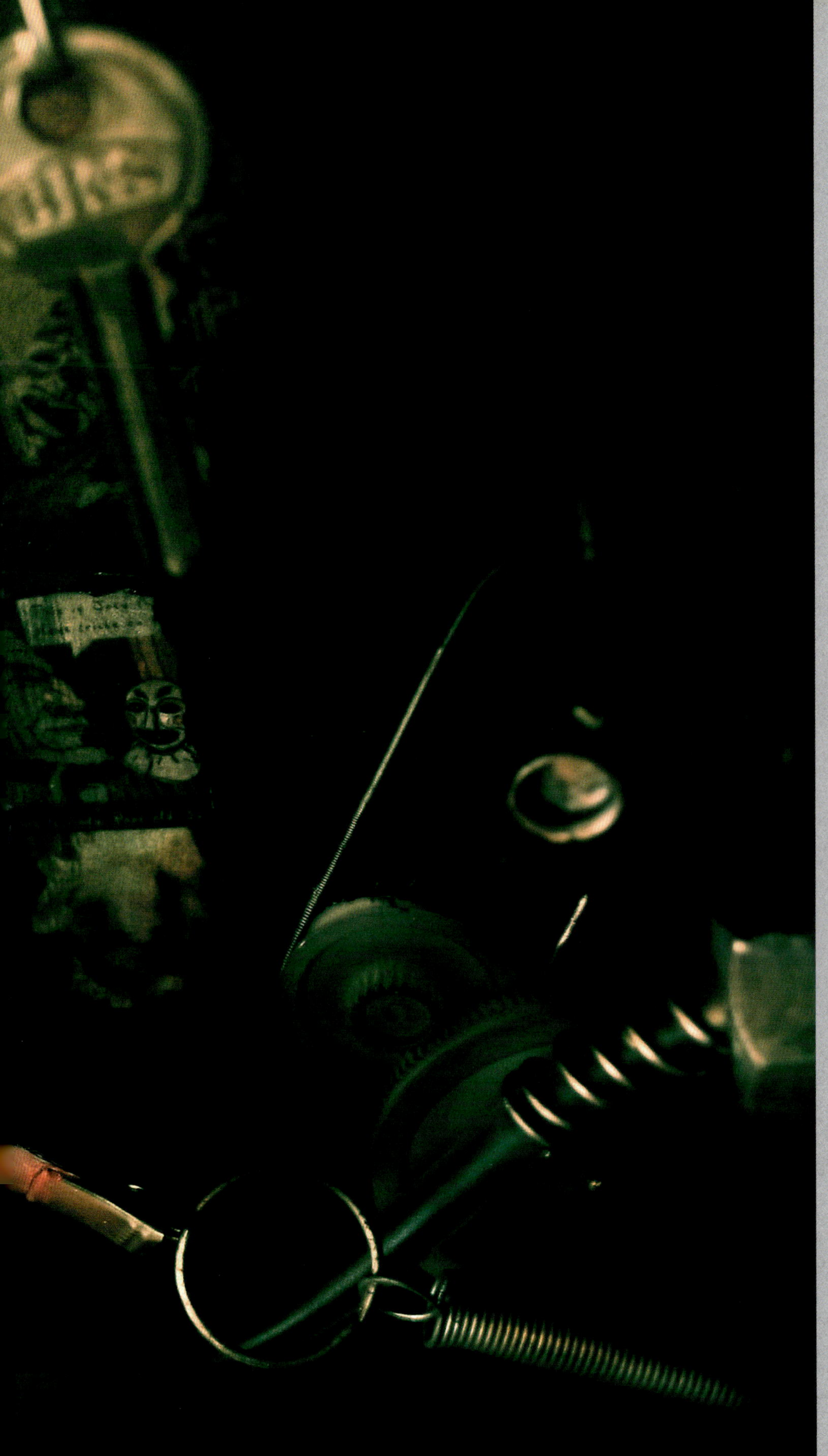

◀ **Say No Good**
Oliver Wetter
Sculpture
www.fantasio.info

Oliver Wetter's mixed media creation is inspired by modern horror. "This one is the first piece in a series consisting of three half-plaster sculptures, the counterpart to the well-known saying: 'Hear no evil, see no evil, speak no evil.' There are variations of this sculpture digitally remastered in printed editions. The main influence and inspiration for the series was the movie ***Saw****. I had the idea to make faces coming out of a wall and tie them into a storyline."*

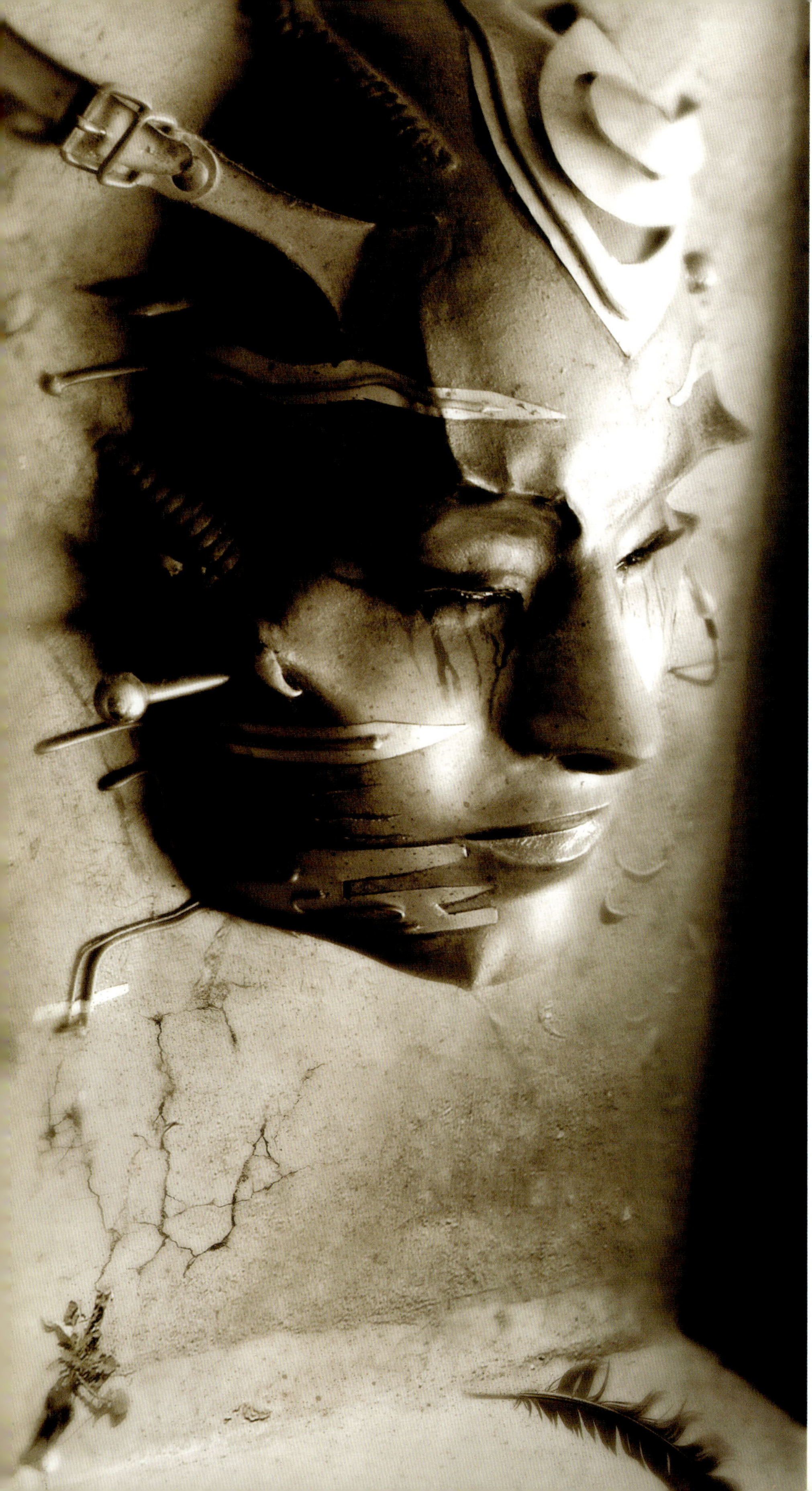

◀ **S-T-I-L-L-L-I-F-E**
Oliver Wetter
Mixed media
www.fantasio.info

"This piece was the first I created using a plaster sculpture and Adobe Photoshop. For the original sculpture I used a plaster mask of a friend which I put on a wooden board and sculpted over. It was painted and then decorated with trash, aluminum, and PVC. The original color was deep violet, painted with an airbrush. It was photographed and placed in Photoshop, where it was mixed with a sepia tone and depth of field blur, and a drop-shadow from an imaginary wall to add depth. The face was inspired by H. R. Giger, but it was important to take a different direction: more plasticity and depth."

▶ **The Swinegoblin**
Thomas Kuebler
Sculpture
www.thomaskuebler.com

"There are odd little footprints down by the shed.
The cat won't come out from under the bed.
All of my children's dolls were beheaded.
All of the clothes in my closet were shredded.
The pantry is littered with half-eaten bread.
The traps were all sprung, but no rats are dead.
Whatever on earth could it possibly be?
This mischievous presence I have yet to see...

Based on folklore of trolls and fairies, this scultpture was made using fibreglass and silicone. I wanted to give life to the noises in the attic from all those tales told to children to get them to behave. I recall, as a child, the ominous flickering shadows cast by a single candle, creating ghastly images on my wall. My mind filled in the details of this dark, leaping vision, and this little wretch was the result."

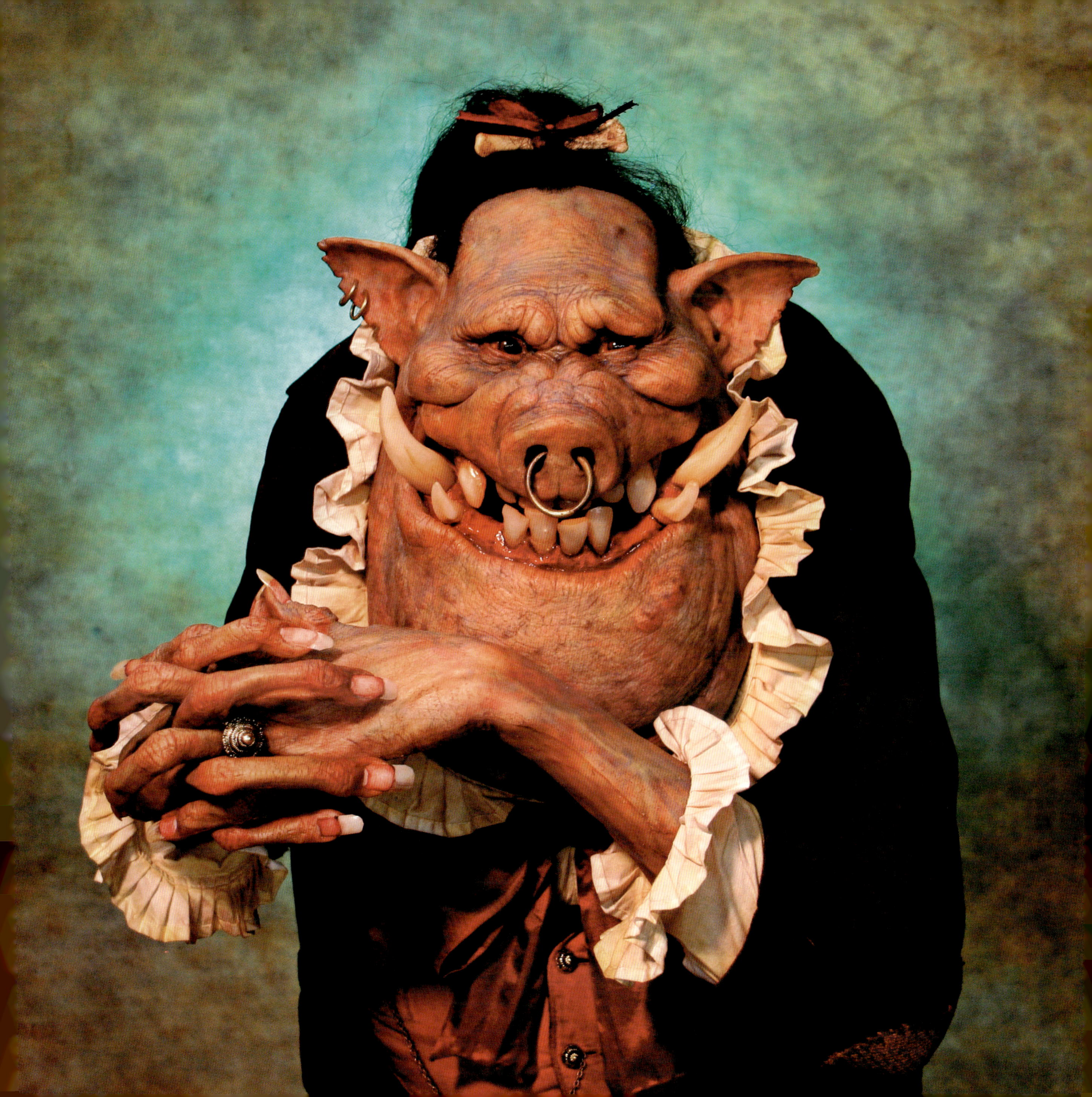

Seizures
Judith Schaechter
Stained glass
www.judithschaechter.com

Schaechter's creation features a twisted figure reminiscent of Wyeth's ***Christina's World****. She seems stricken, perhaps with seizures, and is surrounded by an overwhelming display of delicately painted, winged insects. The piece is created entirely in stained glass. "I use flash glass—a type of handblown glass with two layers of color. I sandblast and engrave the glass, then paint and fire it in a kiln."*

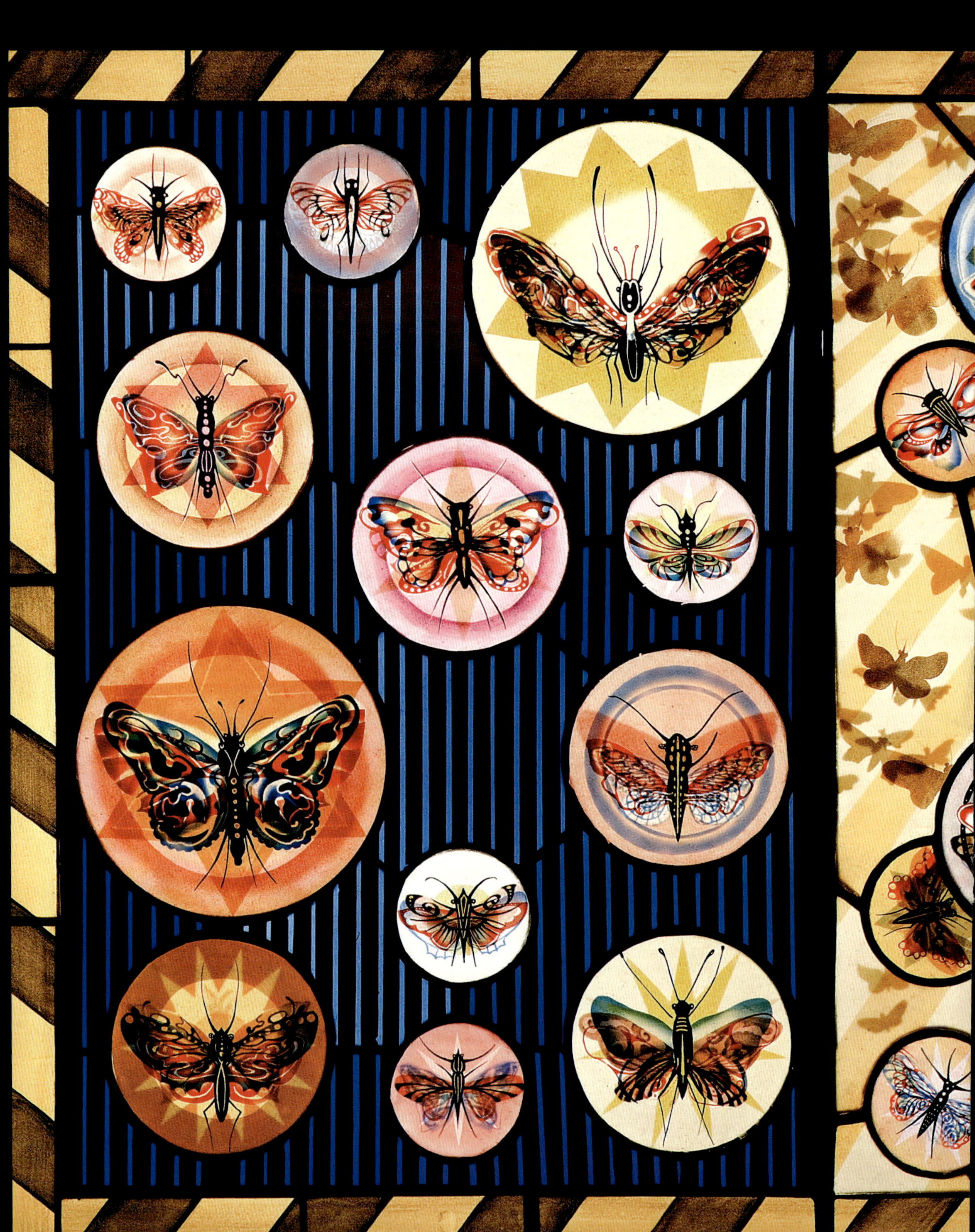

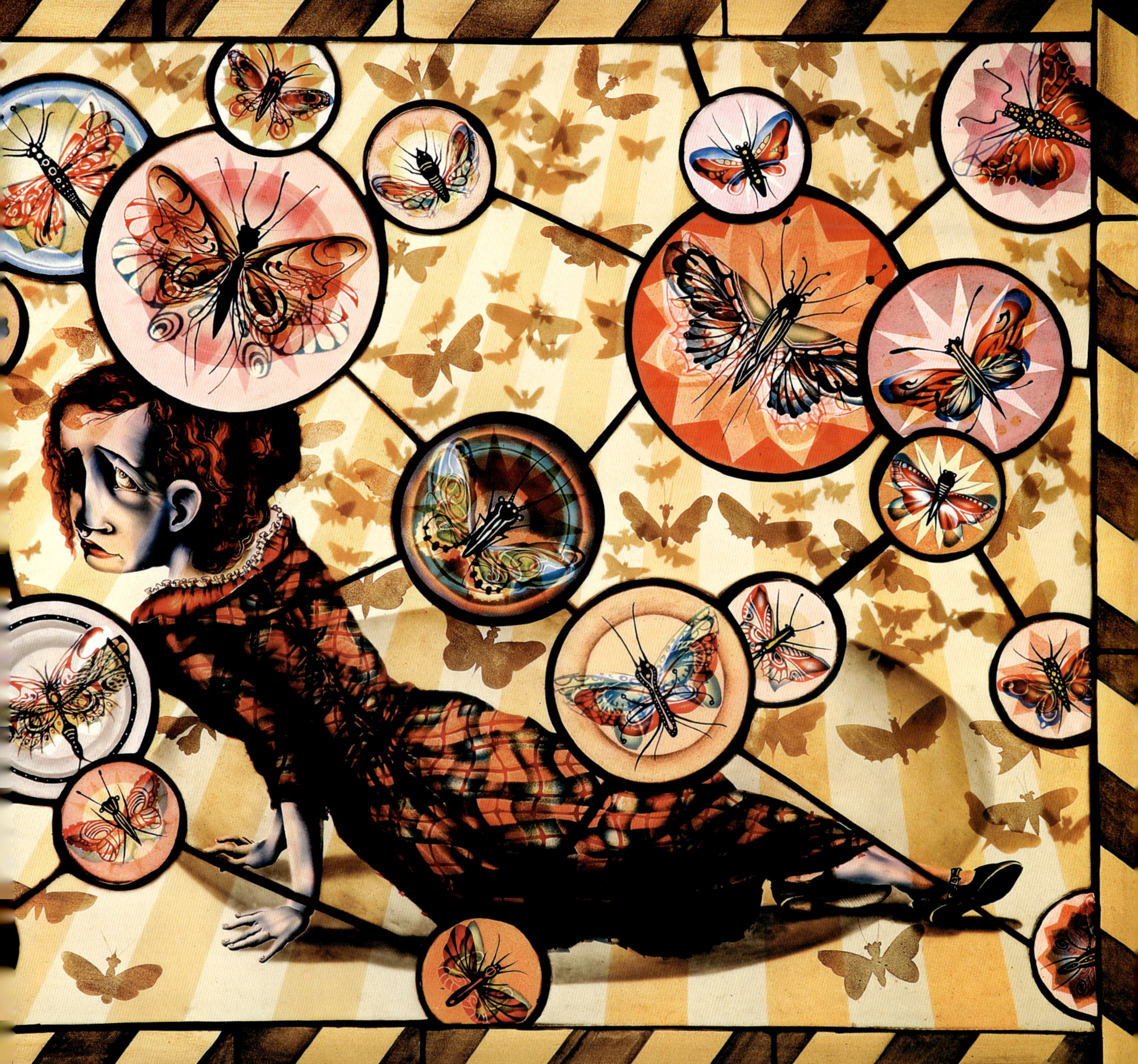

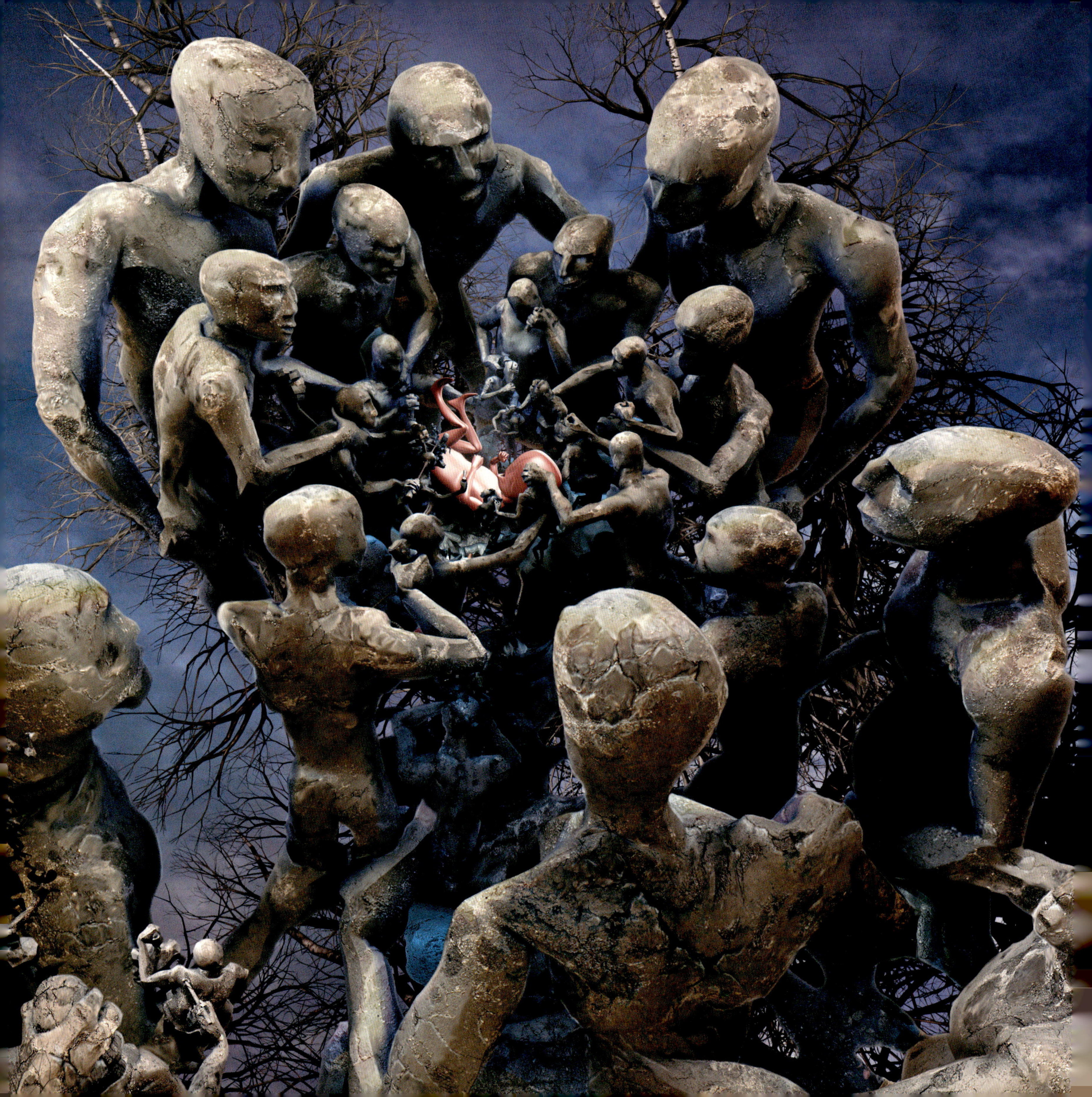

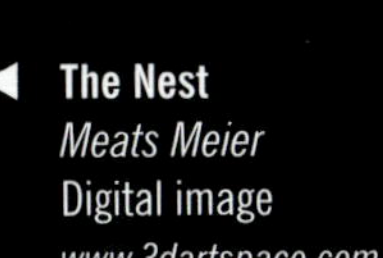

◀ **The Nest**
Meats Meier
Digital image
www.3dartspace.com

Meier's elaborate composition of hard stone beings clustered around a pink human baby is a startling image. His sophisticated use of Maya, Zbrush, and Adobe Photoshop gives this image a rich feeling of depth and texture. "The rock people are nurturing their new baby."

▶ **Project 5**
Catherine Burris
Sculpture
www.catherineburris.com

Catherine's contemporary narrative art manifests in her bizarre three-dimensional assemblages. **Project 5** *is no exception: a re-figured head, looking balefully at the viewer. "My pieces are inspired by a range of influences that hope to convey feelings of the fantastical and the familiar."*

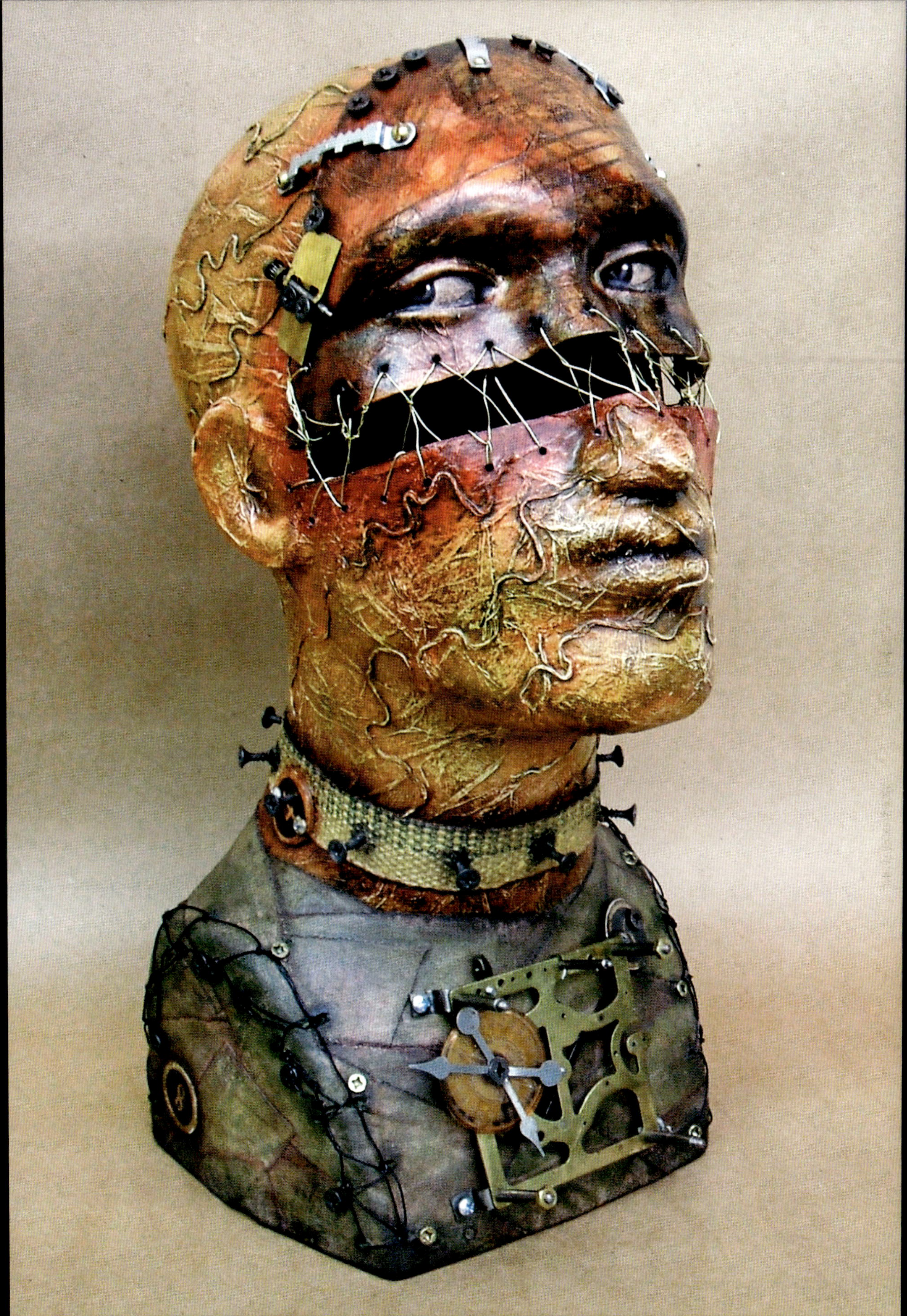

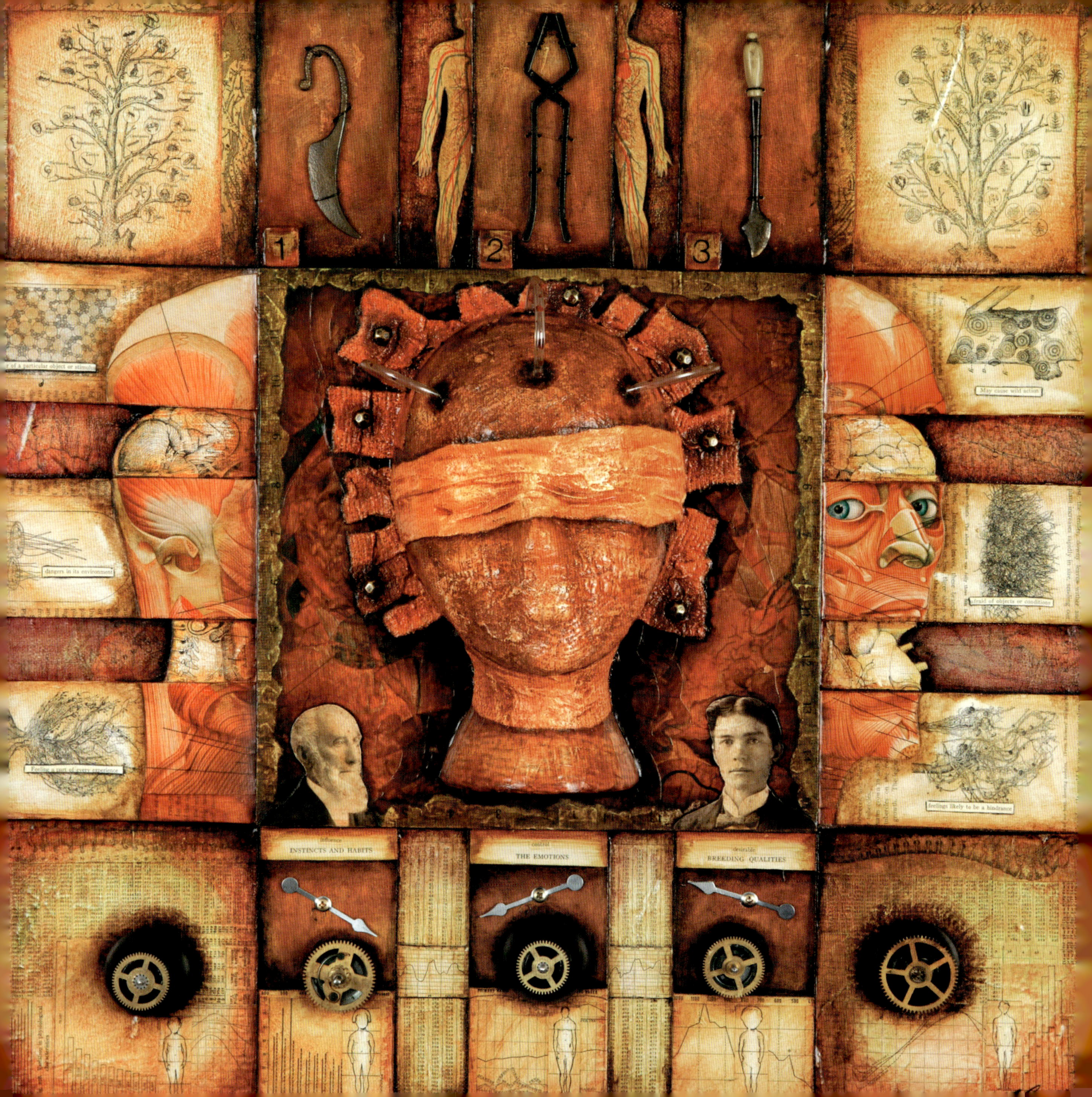
1
2
3
of a particular object or stimulu
May cause wild action
dangers in its environment
afraid of objects or conditions
feelings likely to be a hindrance
INSTINCTS AND HABITS
THE EMOTIONS
BREEDING QUALITIES

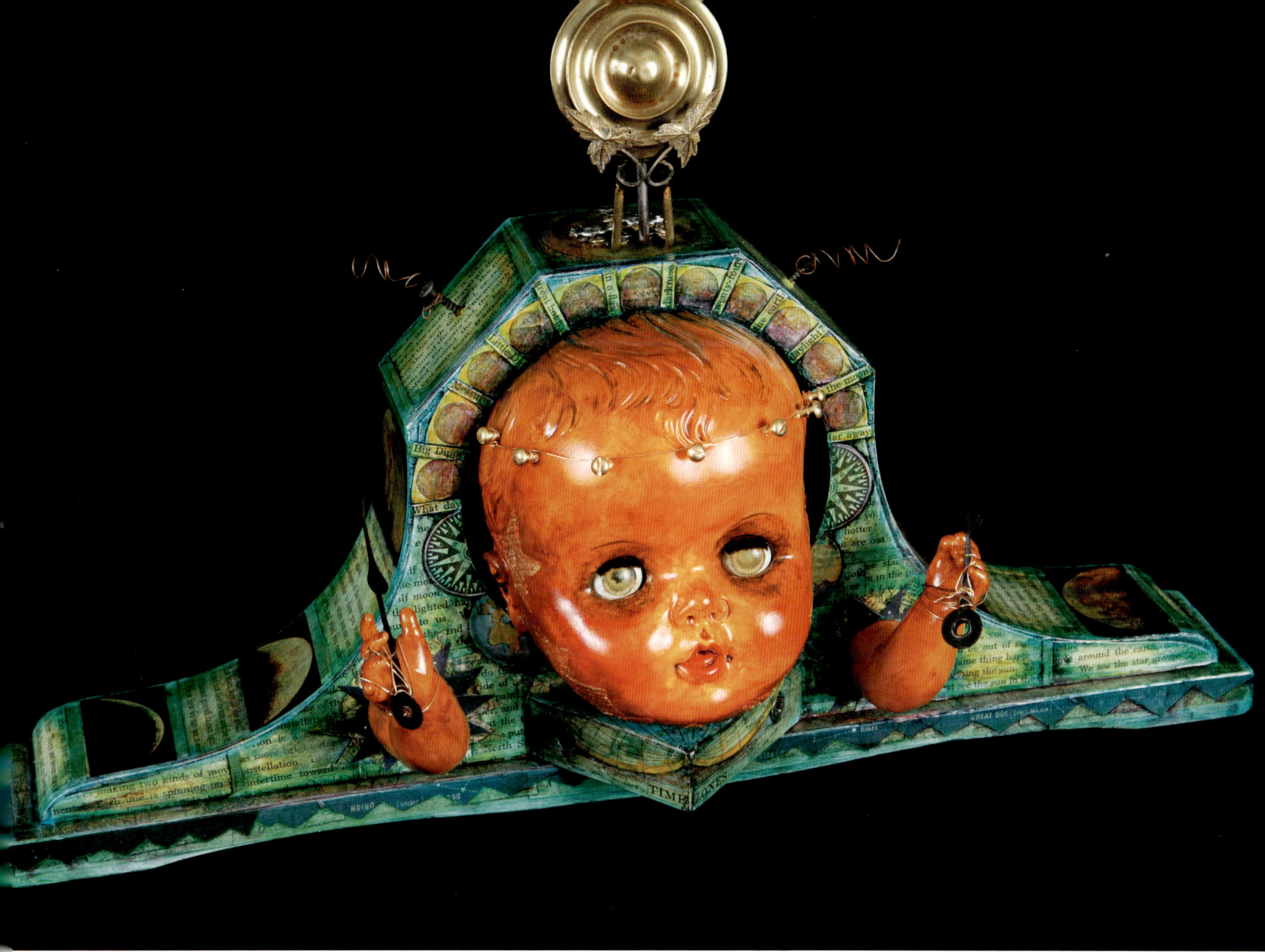

◀ **The Experiment**
Catherine Burris
Mixed media
www.catherineburris.com

A highly intricate piece, Burris's ***Experiment*** *uses medical imagery and antique surgical implements to evoke an uneasy feeling. "In my work I have a passion for patterns, texture, hidden detail, and unexpected imagery. The unrefined, mundane, or forgotten is reborn. My assemblage work gives me freedom to explore and expand upon the unreal and the familiar."*

▲ **Tick Tock Baby Blue**
Catherine Burris
Sculpture
www.catherineburris.com

A not-so-cuddly baby doll stares innocuously from an ancient timepiece. Burris explains: "My art may initially revolve around a particular object, but I never begin with a clear view of what the finished piece will be. Motivated, excited, and amused by the seemingly automatic process of just 'doing' the work, it reveals itself, piece by piece until the picture is complete."

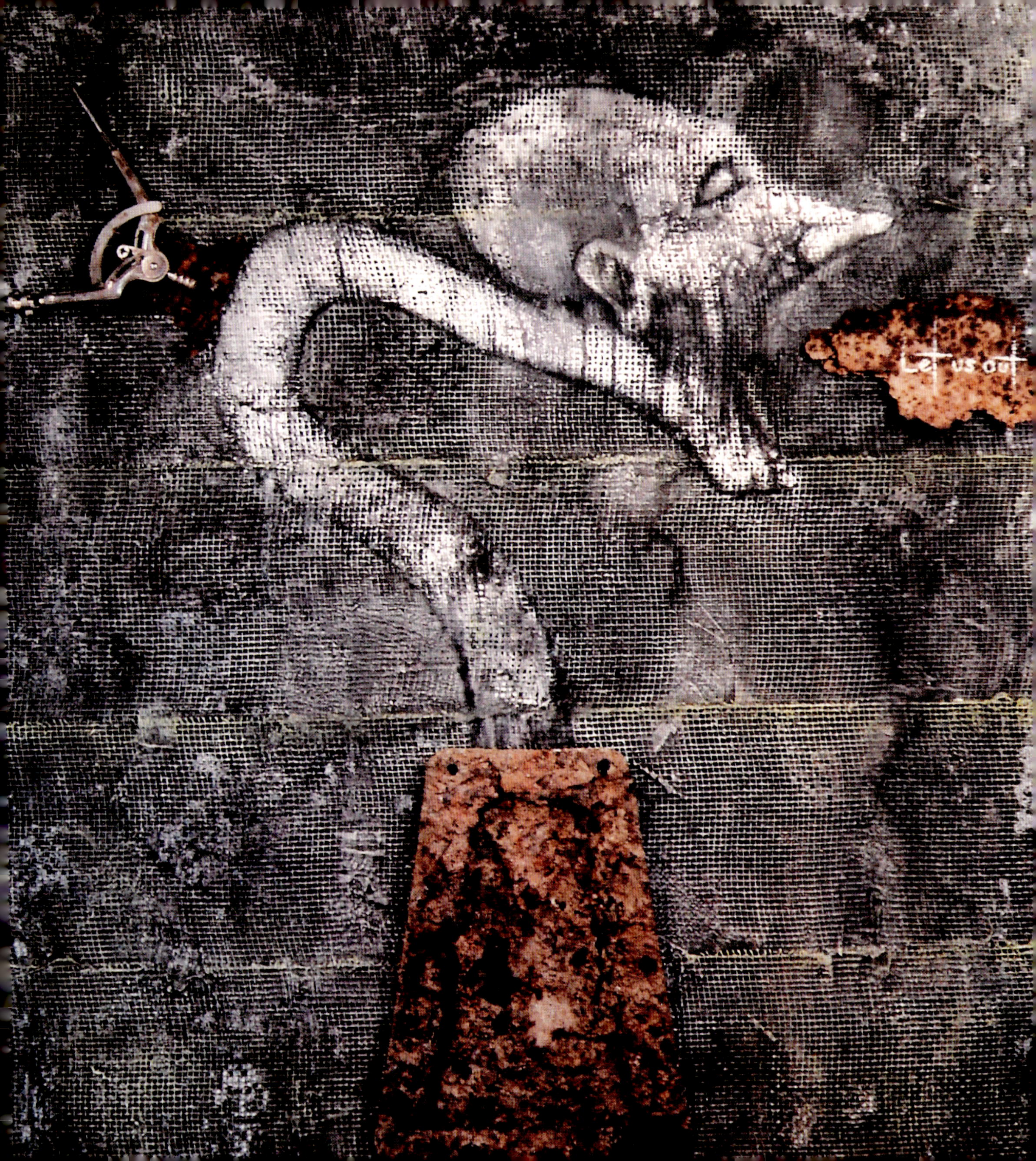
Let us out

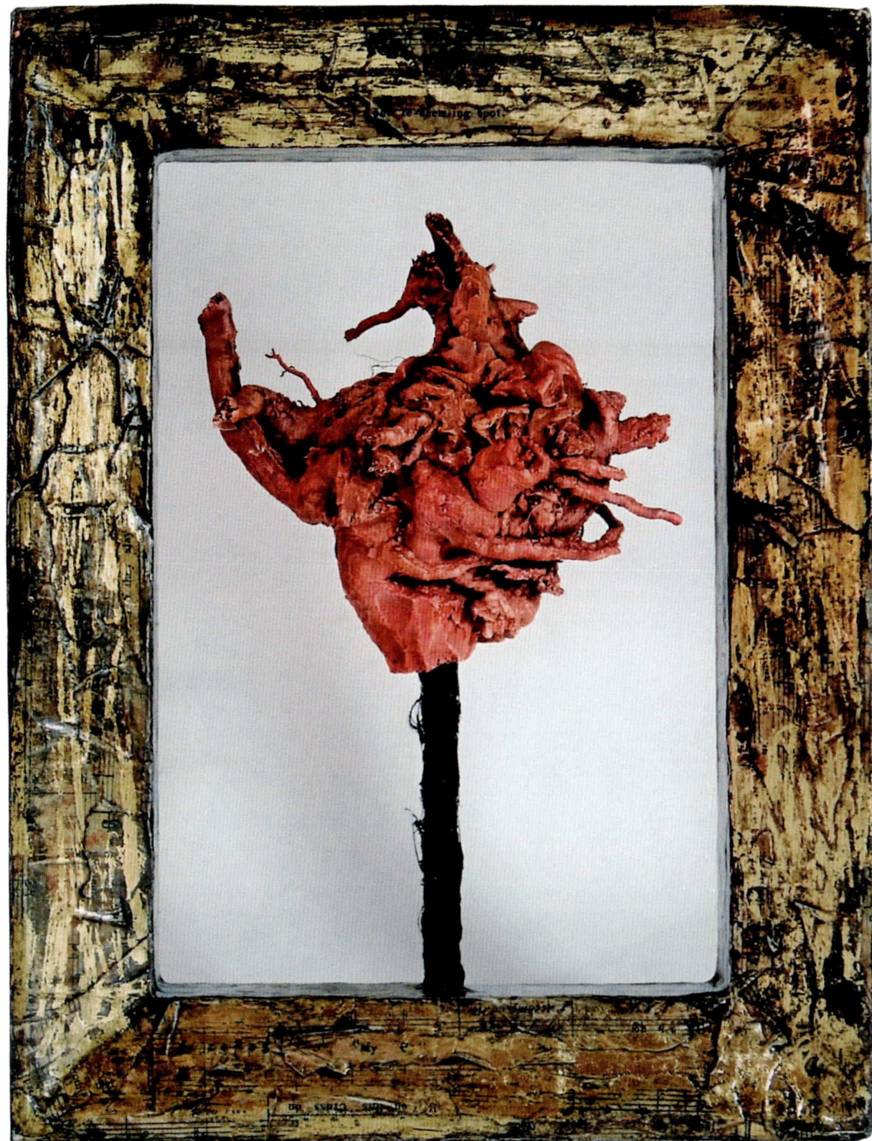

◀ **Pandora**
indio
Mixed media
www.desolatebeauty.com

*"**Pandora** is based on the Greek myth. I depicted the box here with a rusted piece of metal. What flies out of it is one of the evils that escaped. This evil springs out with the aid of its pitiful wing made from a pencil, compass, and door hinge. The rotted metal in the mouth hints at the entity's noxious nature."*

▲ **Passion**
indio
Sculpture
www.desolatebeauty.com

*The impression of a human heart. Indio explains: "I created **Passion** to pay homage to the Nine Inch Nails music video **Closer**. The 'heart' is a knotted plant root that I found on a hiking trail. The wooden frame was sealed with gold leaf and small pieces torn from an antique book of church music."*

▼ **Male 1**
indio
Mixed media
www.desolatebeauty.com

*"When I created the **Male** series I wanted to parody the thoughts men have towards women. **Male 1** uses sculptural elements within a painting: it was born from the destruction of another painting (hence the sewn-up canvas). The piece represents a peek inside the mind of a man. The dolls are reduced to parts and meat, and the two painted figures at the top can only repeat the same set of words into each other's mouth."*

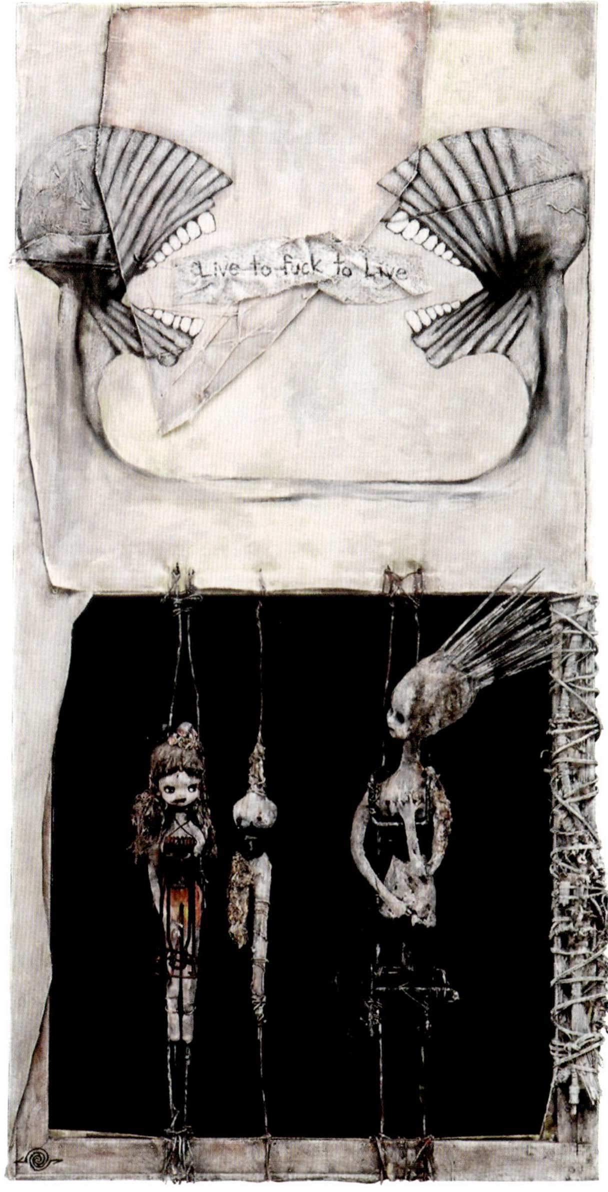

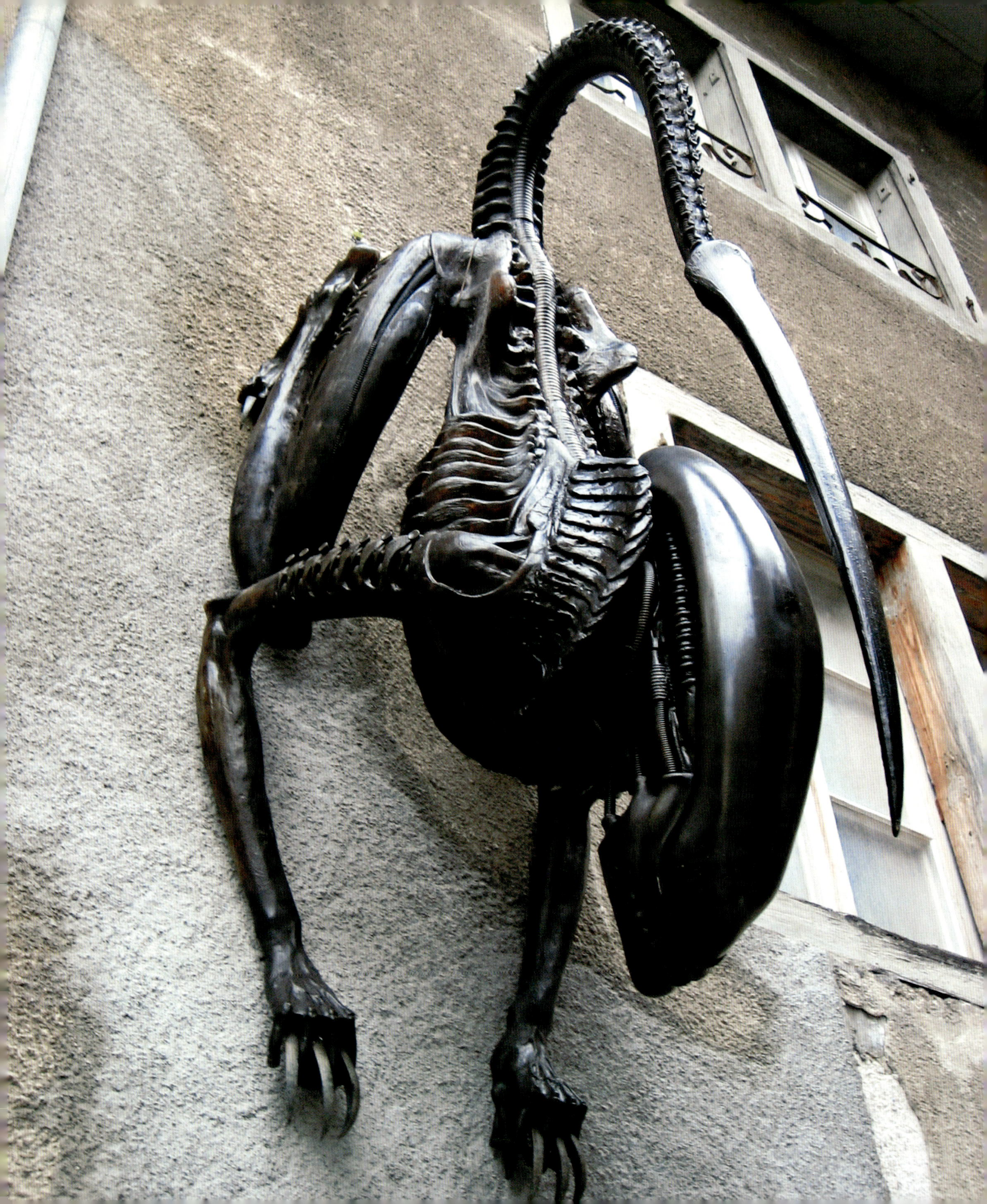

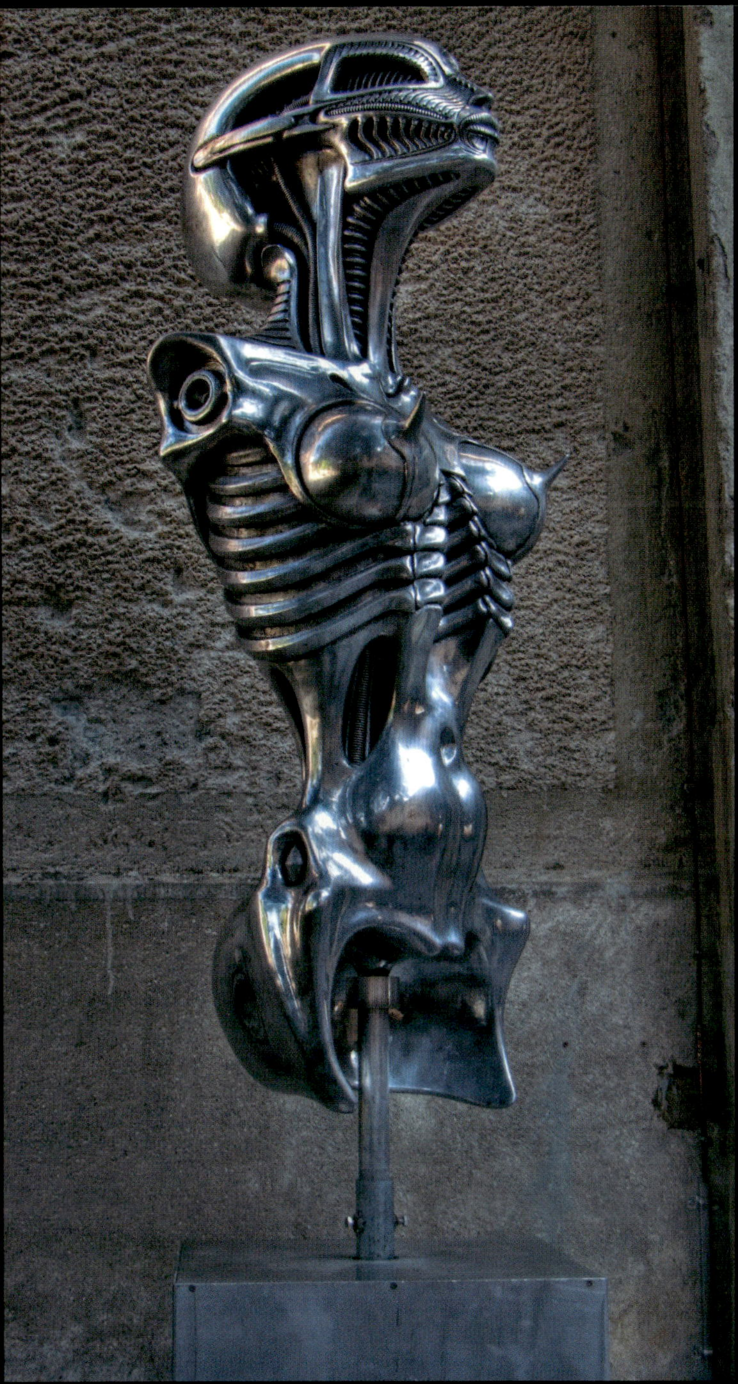

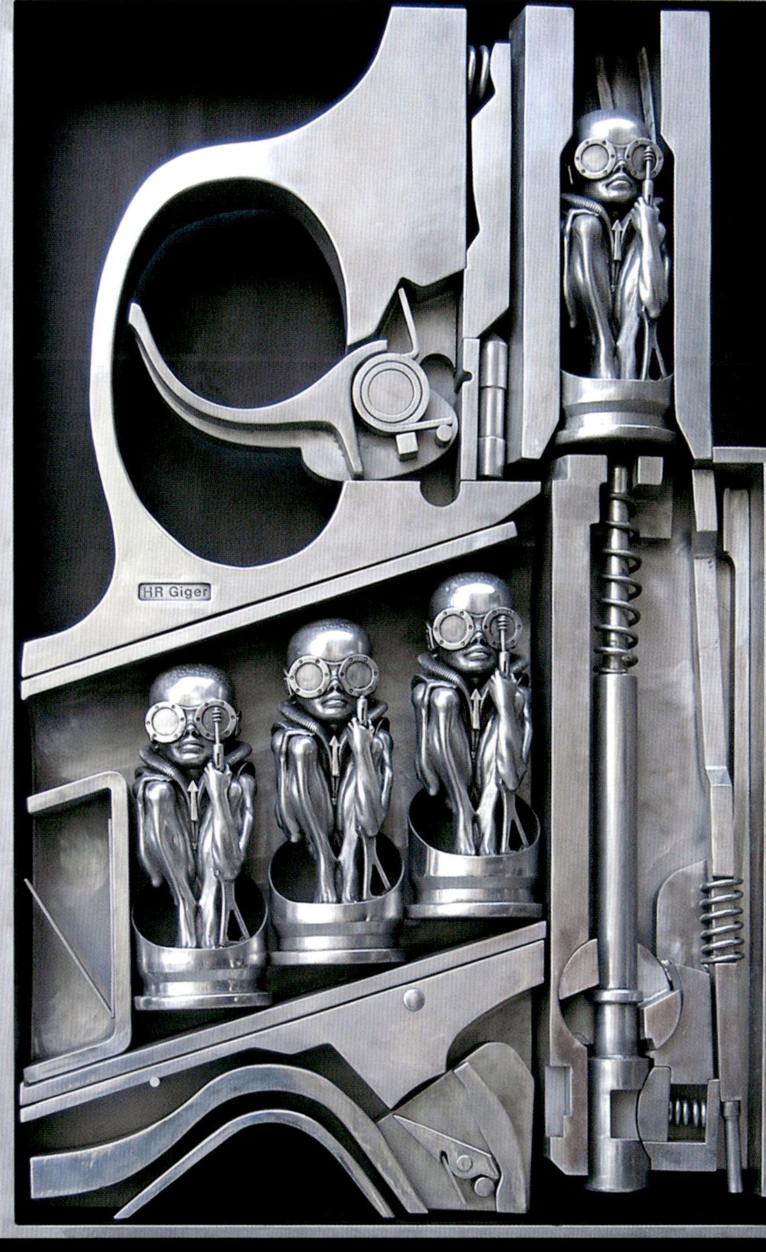

◀ **Necronom**
H.R. Giger
Fiberglass and metal sculpture
www.HRGiger.com

Reminiscent of his Oscar-winning designs for Ridley Scott's classic film, ***Alien****, H.R. Giger's* ***Necronom*** *greets visitors outside the Giger Museum in Gruyères, Switzerland. The museum is a labyrinthine structure with two-meter-thick walls, which displays work from Giger's 40-year career.*

▲ **Biomechanoid**
H.R. Giger
Aluminum sculpture
www.HRGiger.com

H.R. Giger is a true master of biomechanical art. His innovative visions continue to evolve and inspire artists of all generations. His svelte and coldly mechanical creation ***Biomechanoid*** *vividly illustrated the genesis of what Giger sees as the next step in the evolution of mankind: the symbiosis of man and machine.*

▲ **Birthmachine**
H.R. Giger
Aluminum sculpture
www.HRGiger.com

The ***Birthmachine*** *is H.R. Giger's artistic manifestation of his belief that the greatest threat to civilization is the approaching overpopulation of the planet. The sculpture, a cut-away of a loaded Walther pistol, is Giger's three-dimensional recreation of his 1967 pen-and-ink artwork.*

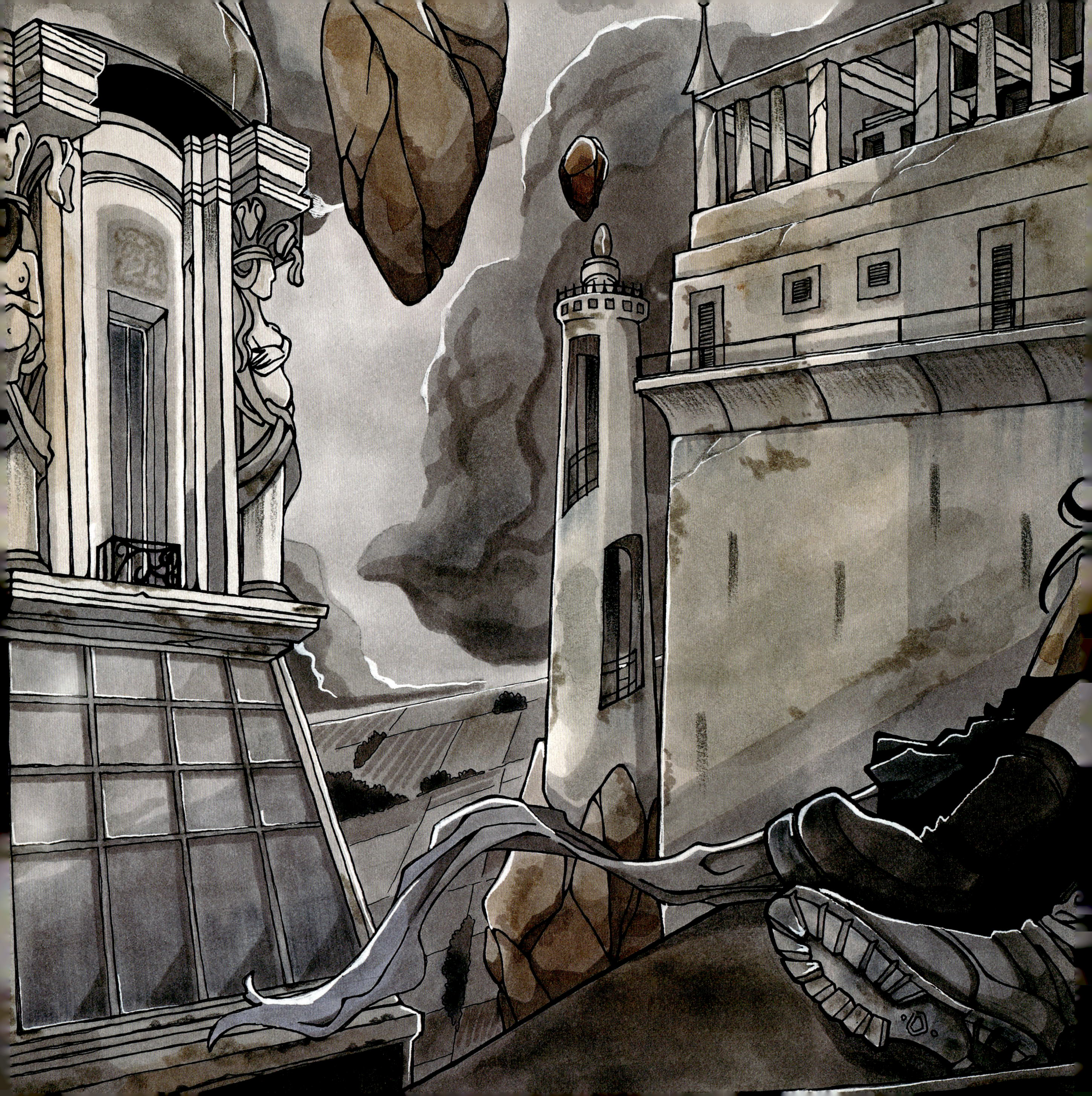

CHAPTER 8

GRIM COMICS

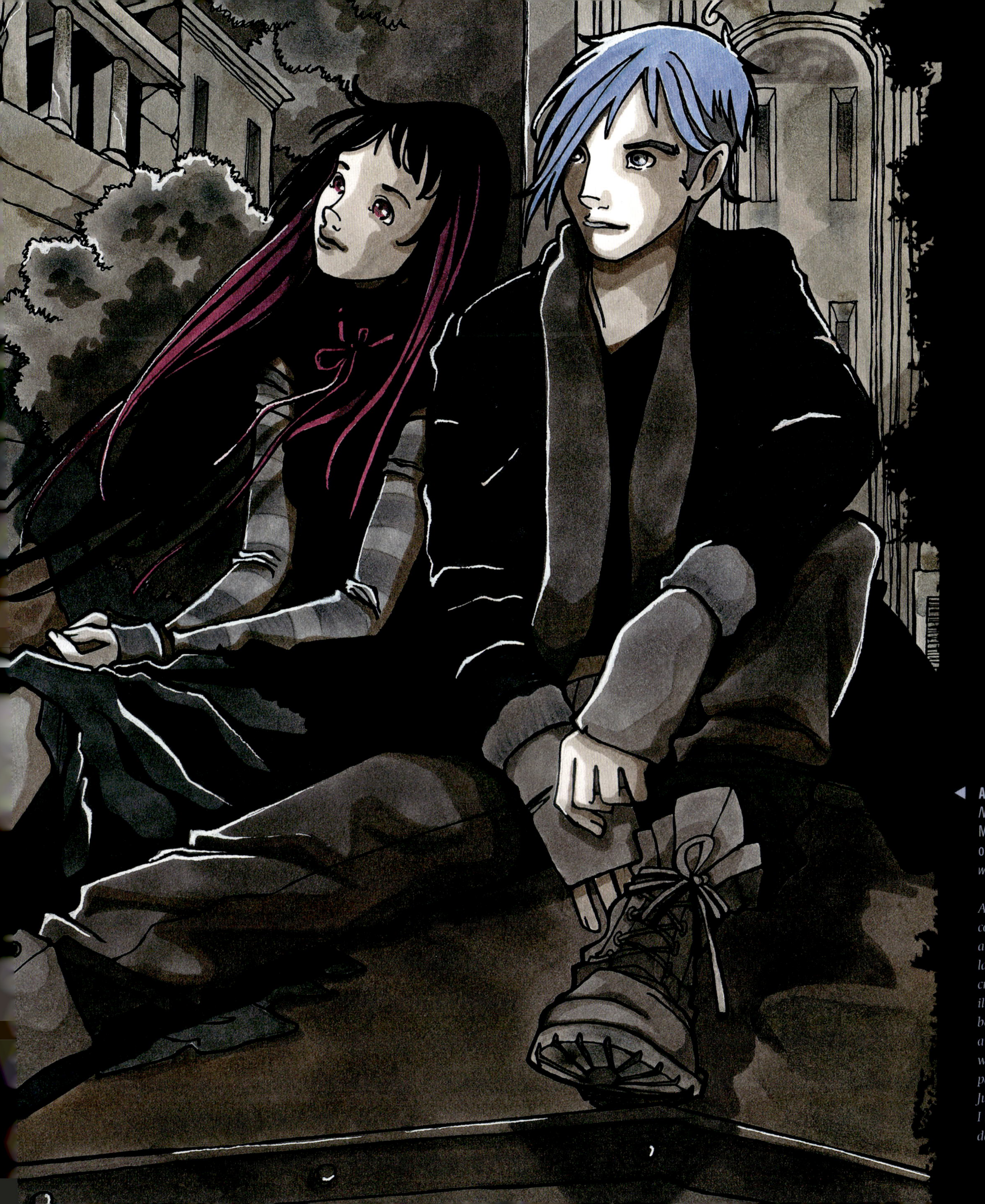

◀ **Autumn Has Come**
Natalia Pierandrei
Markers and watercolors on watercolor paper
www.nati-art.com

A quiet moment with a young couple enjoying the Gothic architecture and unique landscape of Pierandrei's creation. "This is one of several illustrations I drew for a comic book project of mine. It's actual, a dark sci-fi story that I started writing some time ago. The painting features Olimpia and Jude, two of the main characters I like drawing buildings and detailed backgrounds."

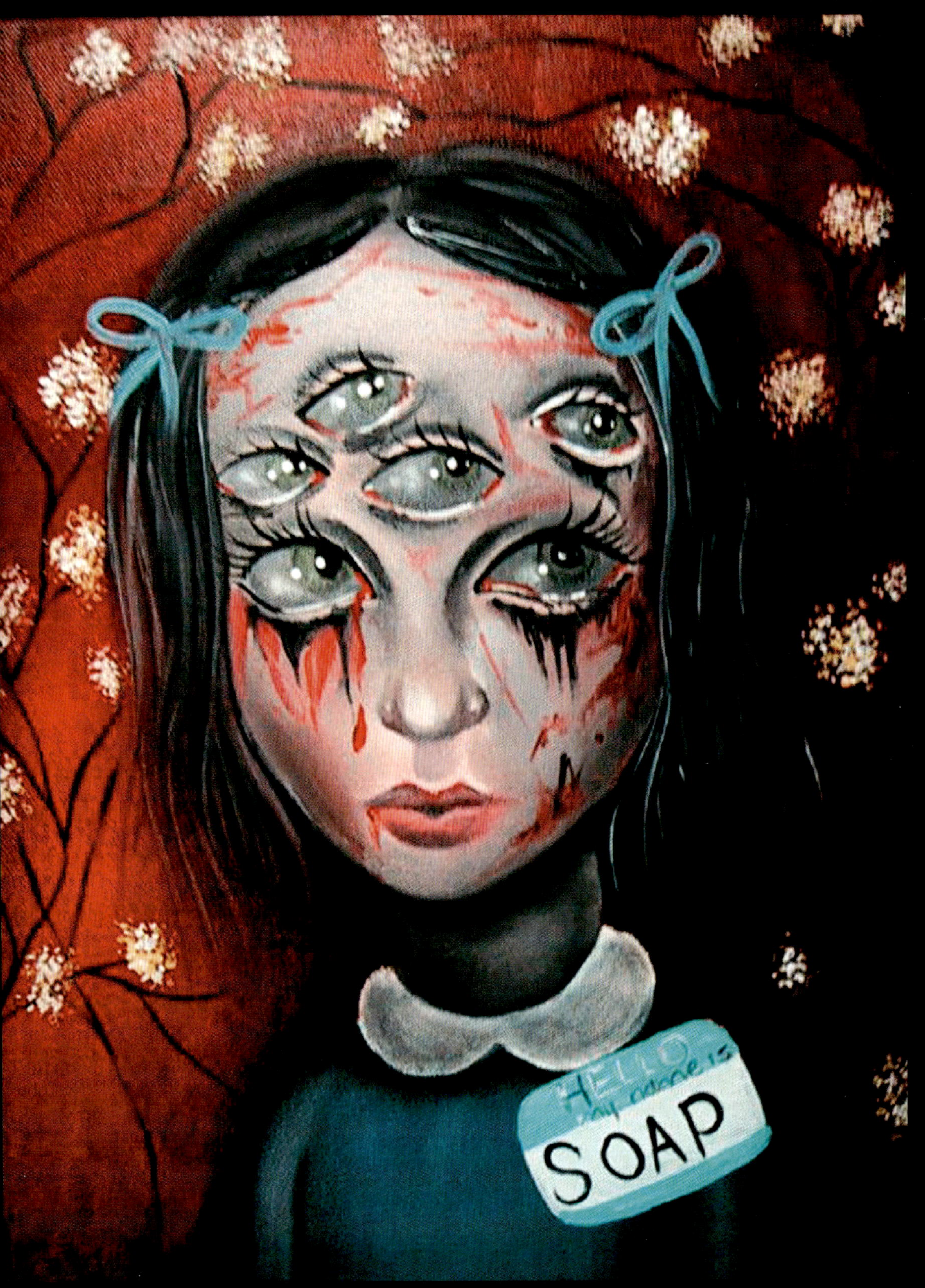

◀ **My Name is Soap**
Abril Andrade
Acrylic on canvas
www.abrilandrade.com

Pop surrealism has Gothic overtones in Andrade's ***My Name is Soap*** *painting. The over-abundance of eyes on the girl's face gives a feeling of paranoia and discomfort, a feeling we have all dealt with at one time or another. Andrade describes her as "a little shy girl with no friends in a new school."*

▶ **Antgirl**
Abril Andrade
Acrylic on canvas
www.abrilandrade.com

Andrade's purposeful distortion of the girl's face evokes a phantasmagorical feeling to ***Antgirl****, "A girl that grows from the grass surrounded by her ant friends."*

▶ **Midnight Walk**
Abril Andrade
Acrylic on canvas
www.abrilandrade.com

Andrade's exaggerated characters often have expressions of hope and innocence, despite their grotesque features. "She's walking a fat cat in the middle of the night."

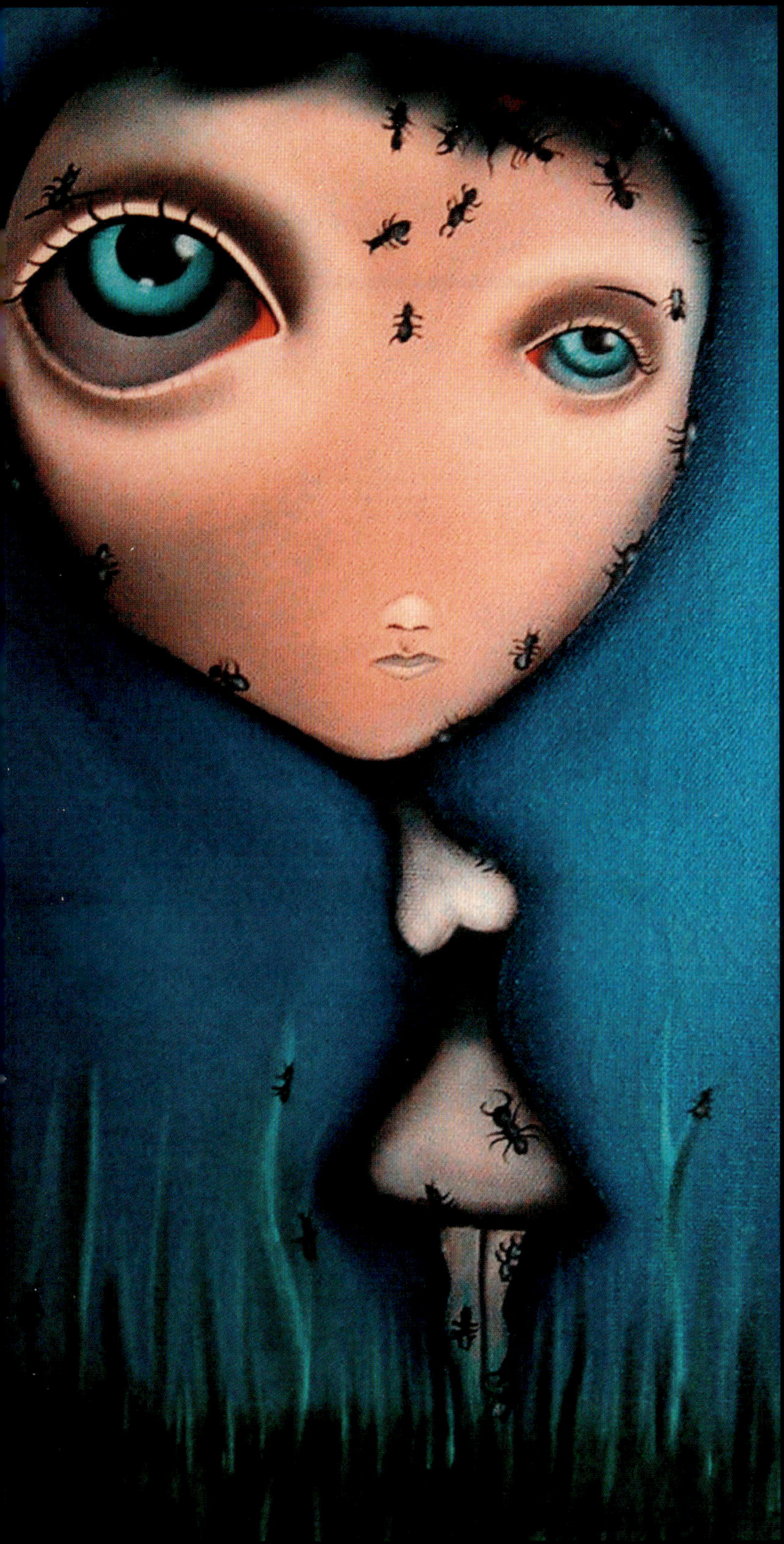

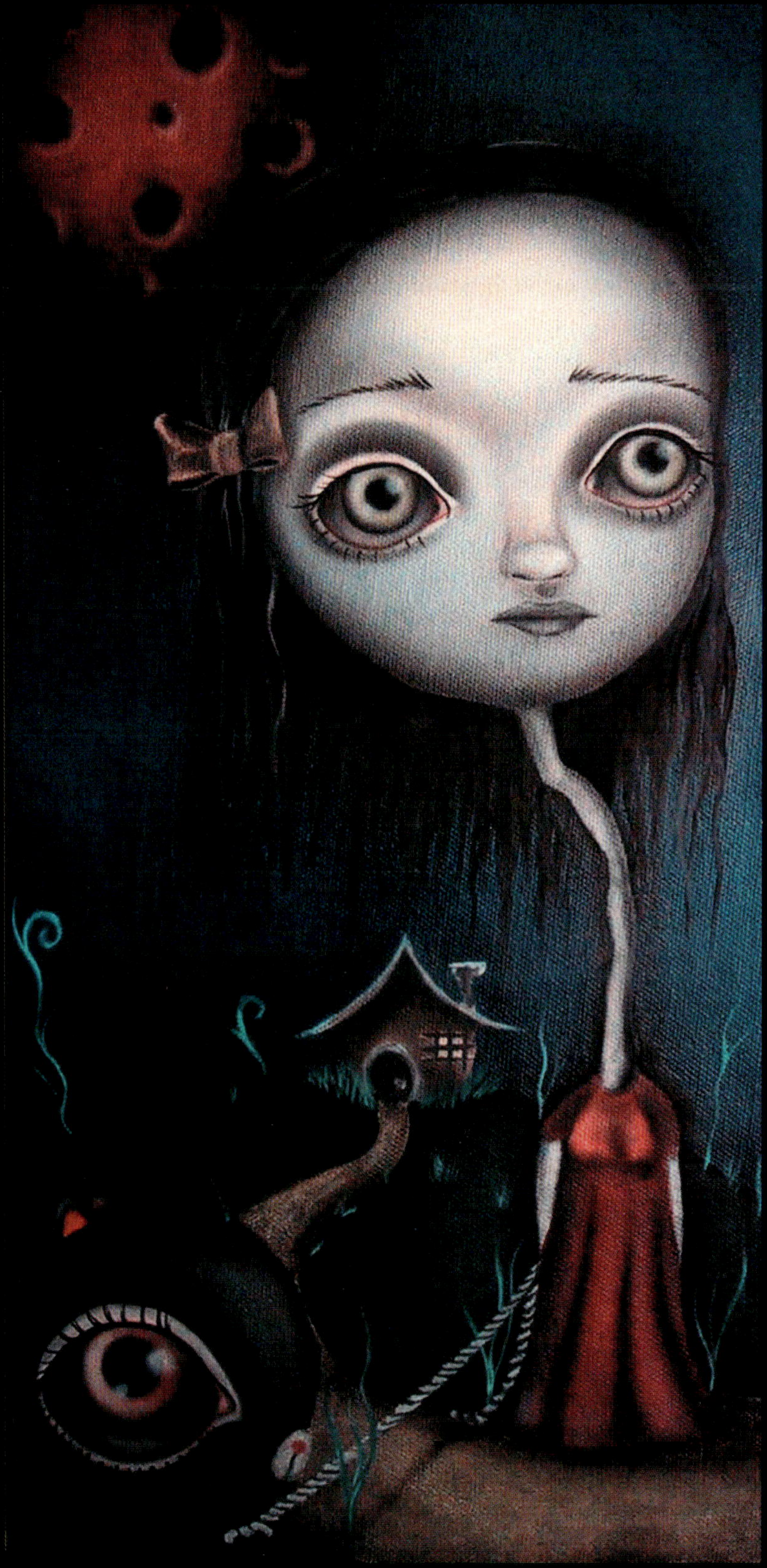

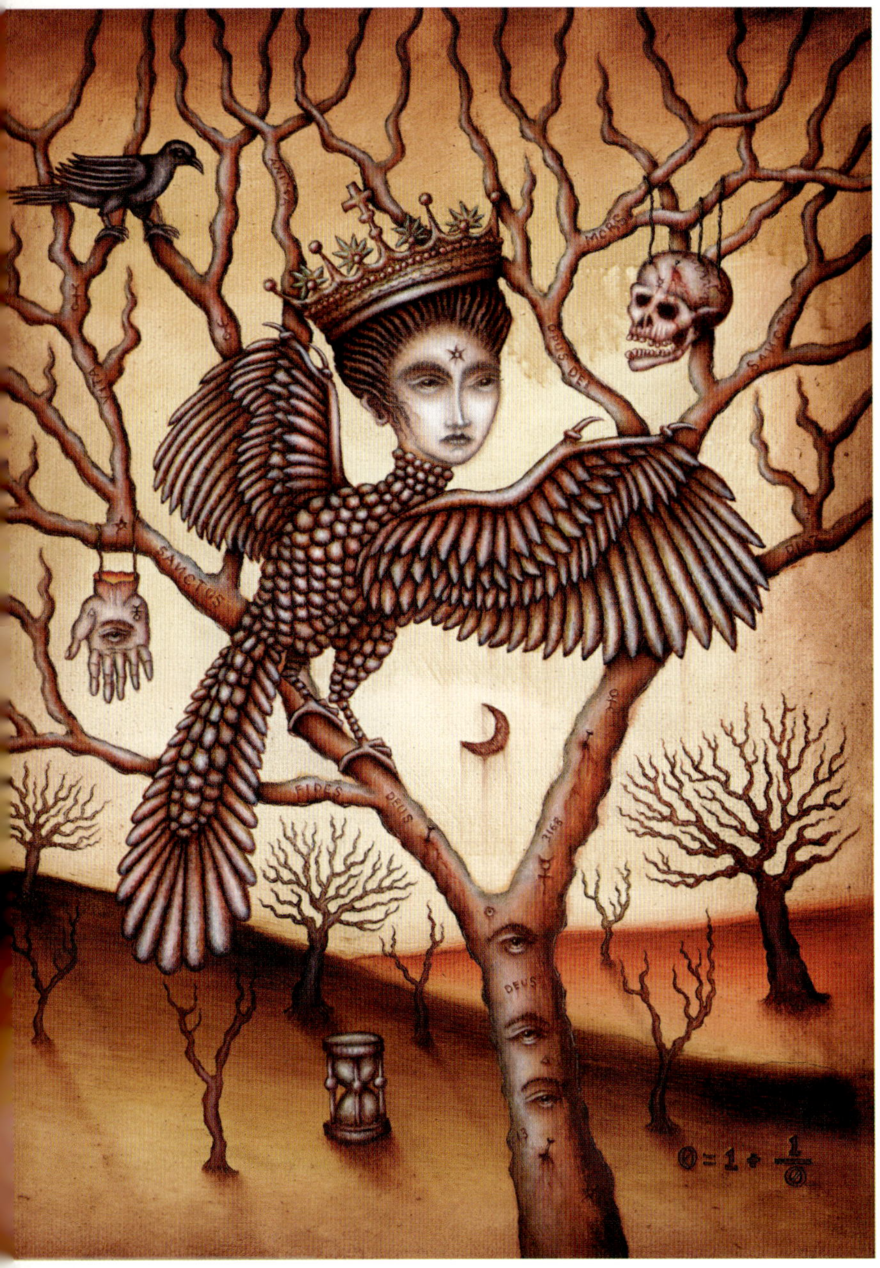

▲ **Mysterium Natura**
Daniel Martin Diaz
Oil on wood
www.danielmartindiaz.com

__Mysterium Natura__ is a mysterious piece indeed. Daniel Martin Diaz has created this image using the traditional method of oil paint on wood, and there is a feeling of history and mysticism behind this work. Occult as well as religious elements can be found in this painting, both as inscriptions on the wood of the tree and surrealistically integrated into the surrounding landscape.

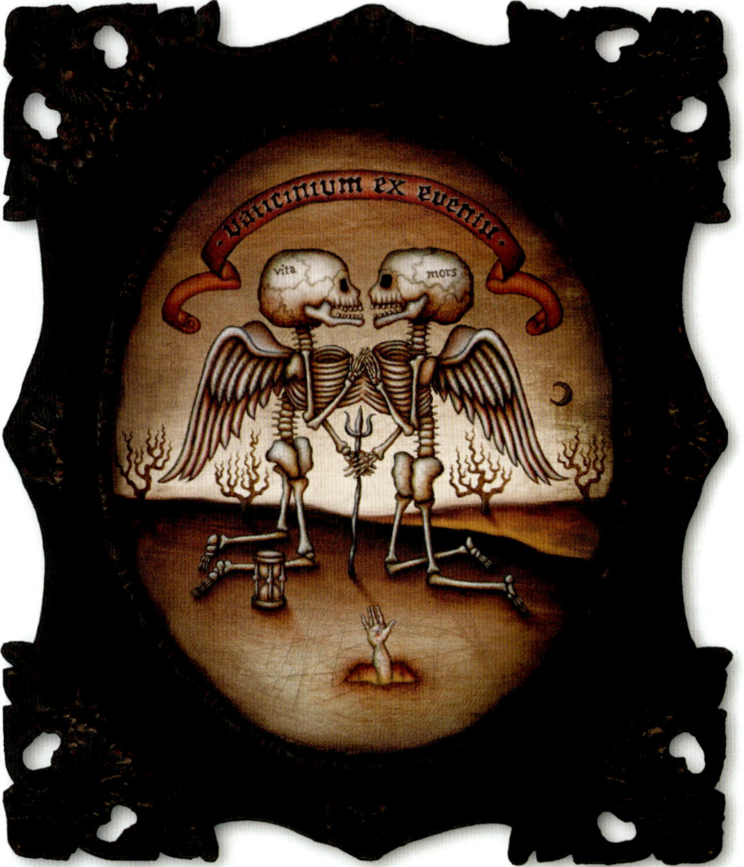

▲ **Aeternus Vita**
Daniel Martin Diaz
Oil on wood
www.danielmartindiaz.com

__Aeternus Vita__, meaning eternal life, is a beautiful oil painting by Daniel Martin Diaz. Two skeletal winged figures touch—their skulls emblazoned with the Latin words Vita and Mors, meaning life and death. The sepia-toned color scheme and desolate landscape give a sinister edge to the piece as well as an aged feel. Religious undertones are implied by the stigmata-inflicted hand in the foreground.

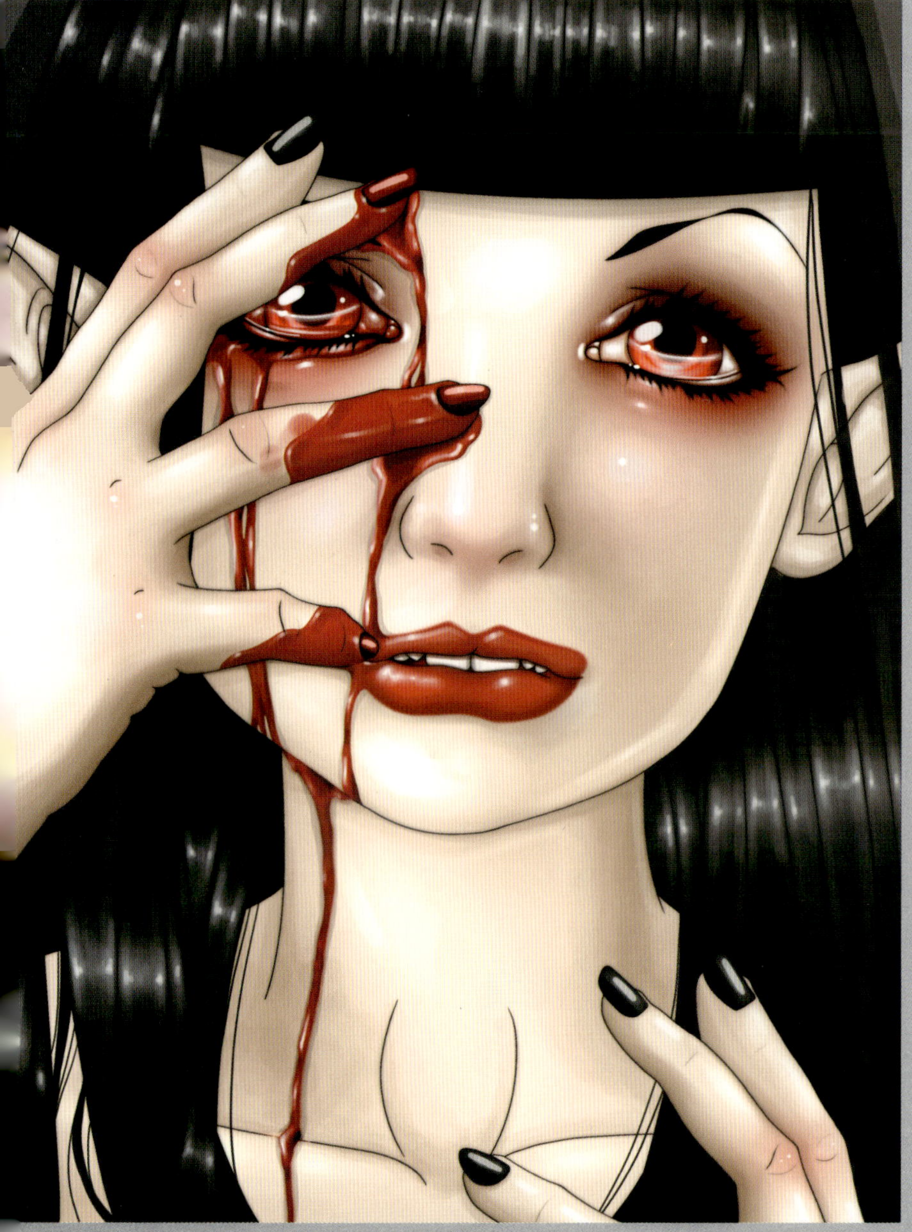

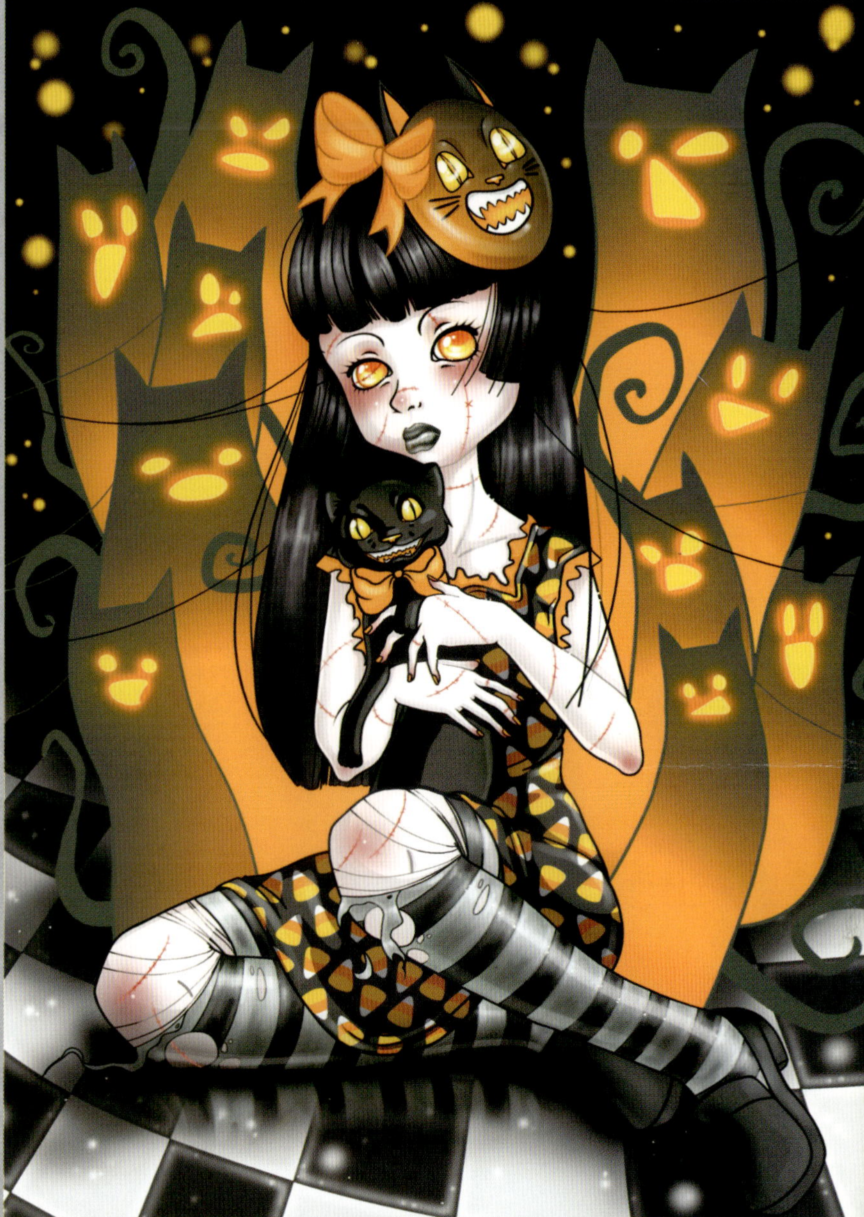

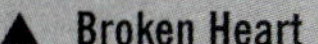

▲ **Broken Heart**
Krisgoat
Digital painting
www.krisgoat.com

An overtly Gothic image of a bloodstained beauty, despair and longing showing in her scarlet eyes. Krisgoat created this digital image using a Wacom Graphics Tablet, painting in Adobe Photoshop from scratch. "This is a realistic portrait of one of my most famous characters: The Dark Valentine girl who has featured in a few of my pieces. She is usually accompanied with a cracked heart-shaped glass leaking blood, representing the broken heart she is constantly suffering from."

▲ **Trick**
Krisgoat
Digital painting
www.krisgoat.com

*A light-hearted but decidedly Goth look at Halloween. With anime stylings and simple, but beautifully rendered lines, Krisgoat incorporates an Asian influence into this piece. Painting in Adobe Photoshop, she explains: "**Trick** was created for Halloween. She has a sweeter sister named Treat. I've added my favorite Halloween elements; glowing jack-o-lantern-like faces, candy corn, a vintage black cat, and an Asian horror film girl."*

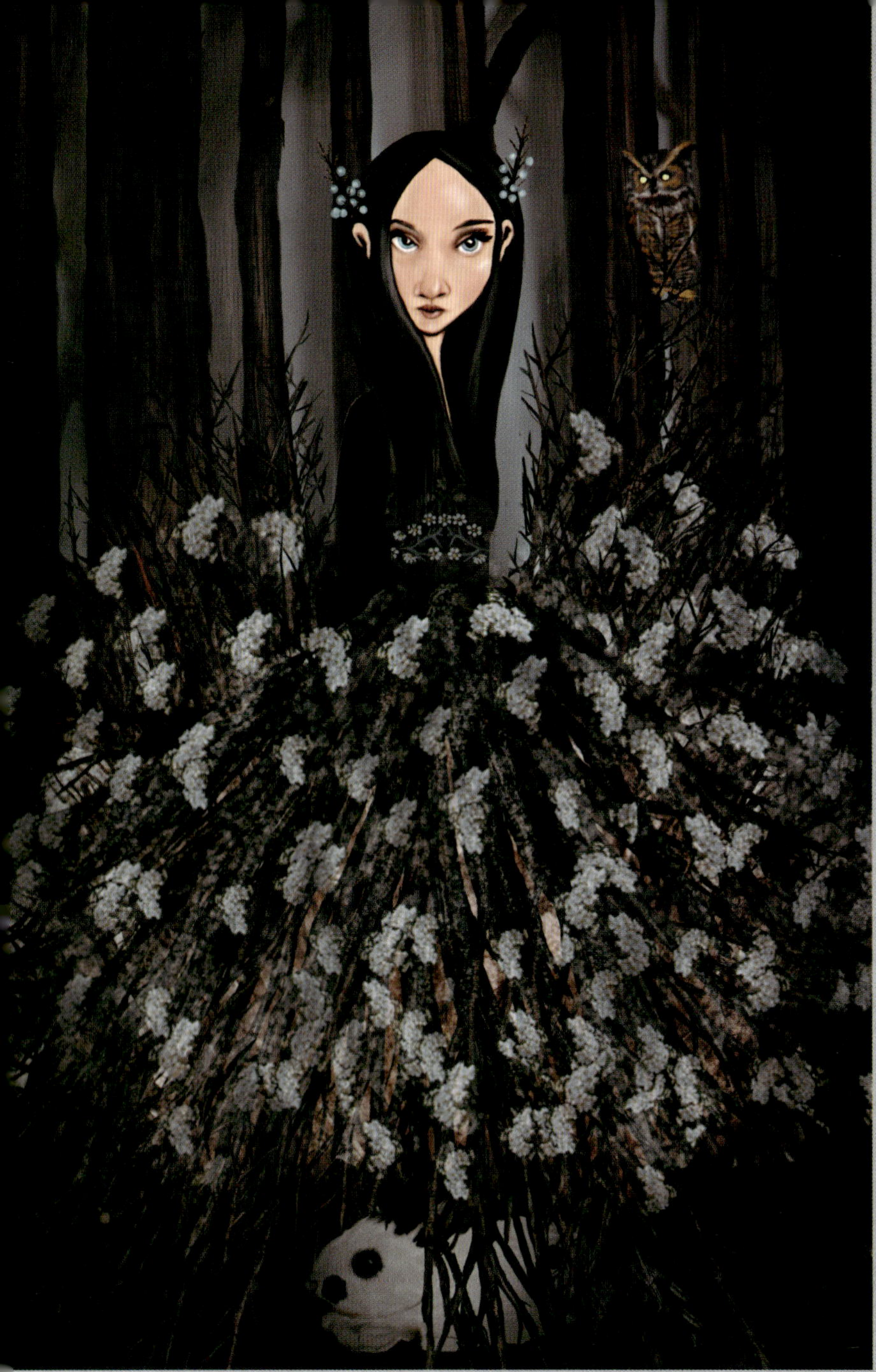

▲ **Blackthorn—Prunus spinosa**
Greta James
Pencil, digitally painted
www.gretajames.com

*James creates her interpretation of the fierce blackthorn plant with this somber sprite, using pencil, Adobe Photoshop, and a Wacom Graphics Tablet. "**Blackthorn** is known as mother of the woods as it reclaims damaged land with its impenetrable thorny thicket, and provides a safe nursery for sapling trees and young animals, until they are strong enough to burst out from under her canopy."*

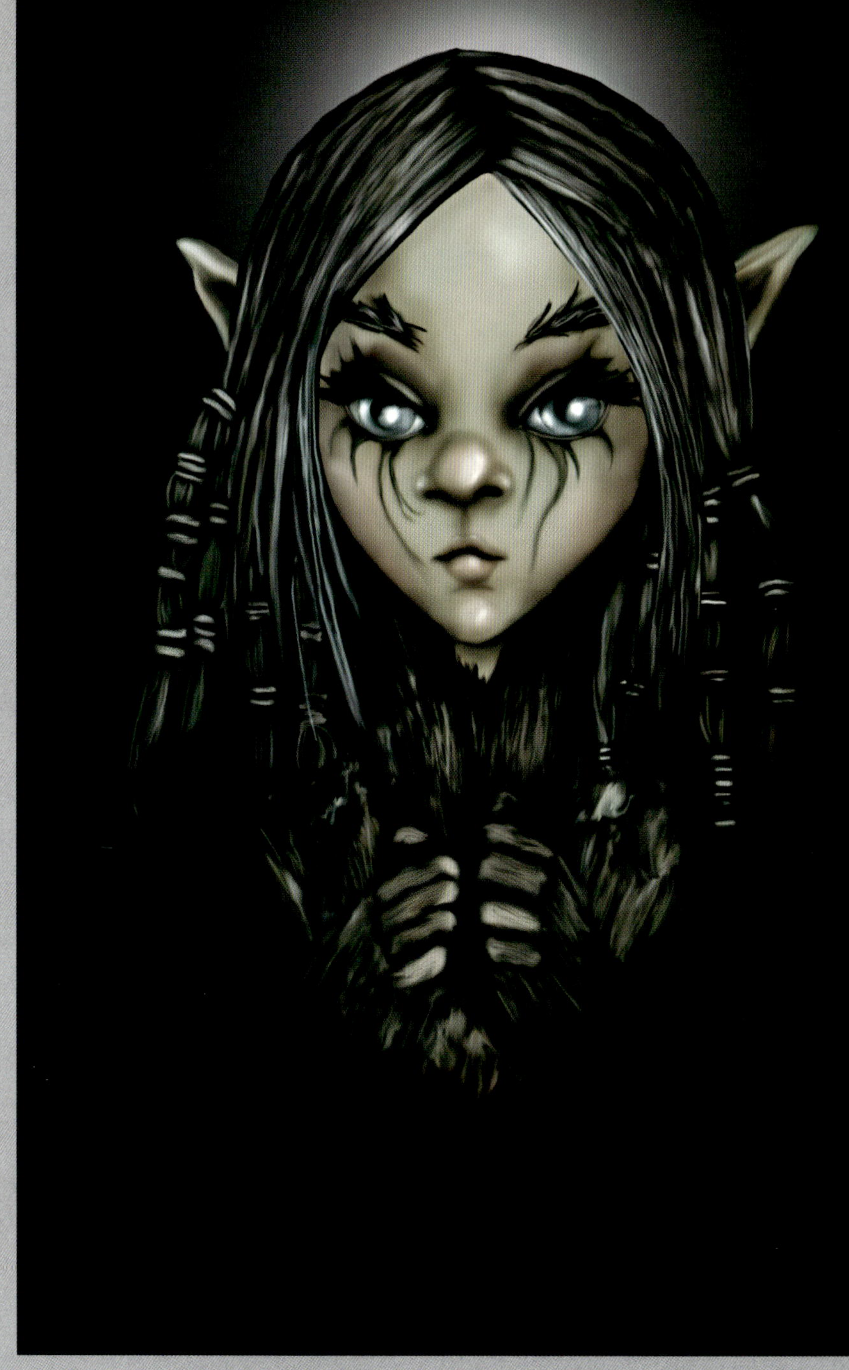

▲ **Little Brown Bat—Myotis lucifugus**
Greta James
Pencil, digitally painted
www.gretajames.com

Long since associated with the Gothic subculture, bats hold a mysterious elegance. James has depicted this nymph-like creature clutching a brown bat, perhaps a shared moment communing with one of nature's misunderstood creatures. "The only true flying mammal, bats transformed themselves from mere rodents creeping upon the earth into magnificent flying creatures."

Trio
Laura Yanmei Law
Digital painting
www.yanmei.net

Law's bewitching trio of blood-sucking beauties are surely up to no good in a local cemetery! "This started out as a portrait of a friend re-imagined as a vampire. While working on the painting I decided she needed a victim so I added another friend. Later I felt that the composition was unbalanced and added a third character based upon myself. Although the painting is dark and slightly violent in nature it was done as pure fun for the people involved. For the painting I used Adobe Photoshop and a Wacom Graphics Tablet."

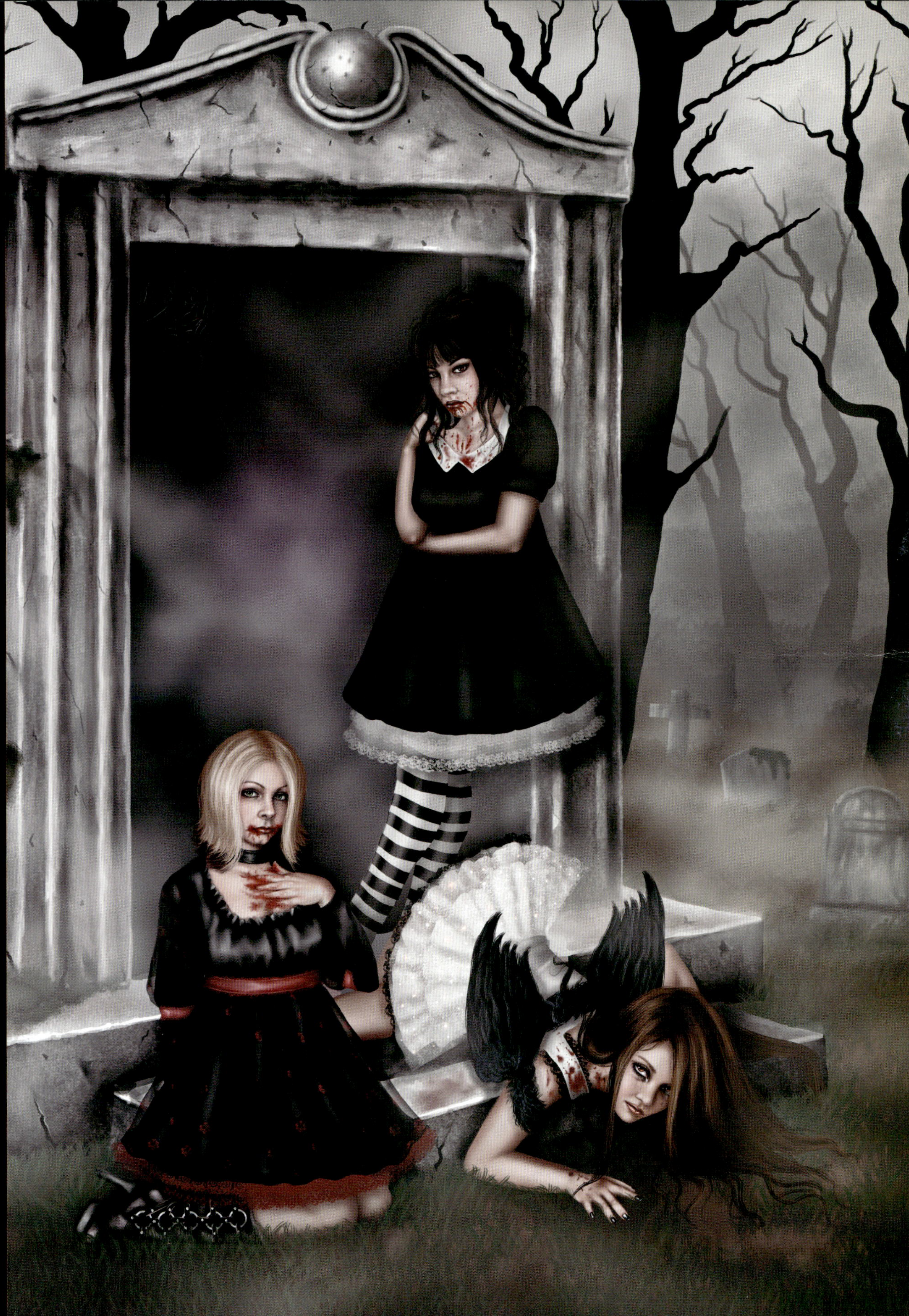

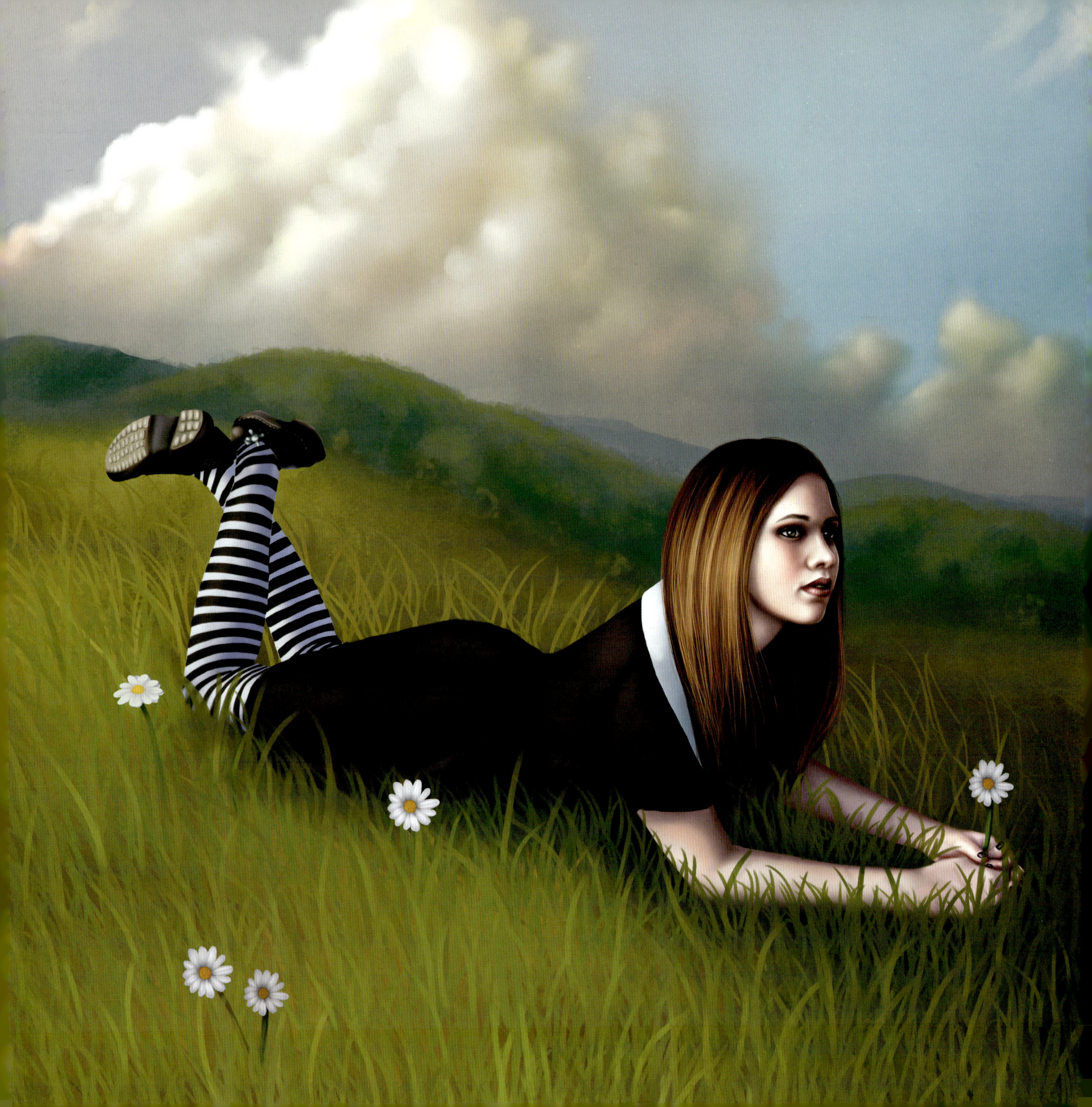

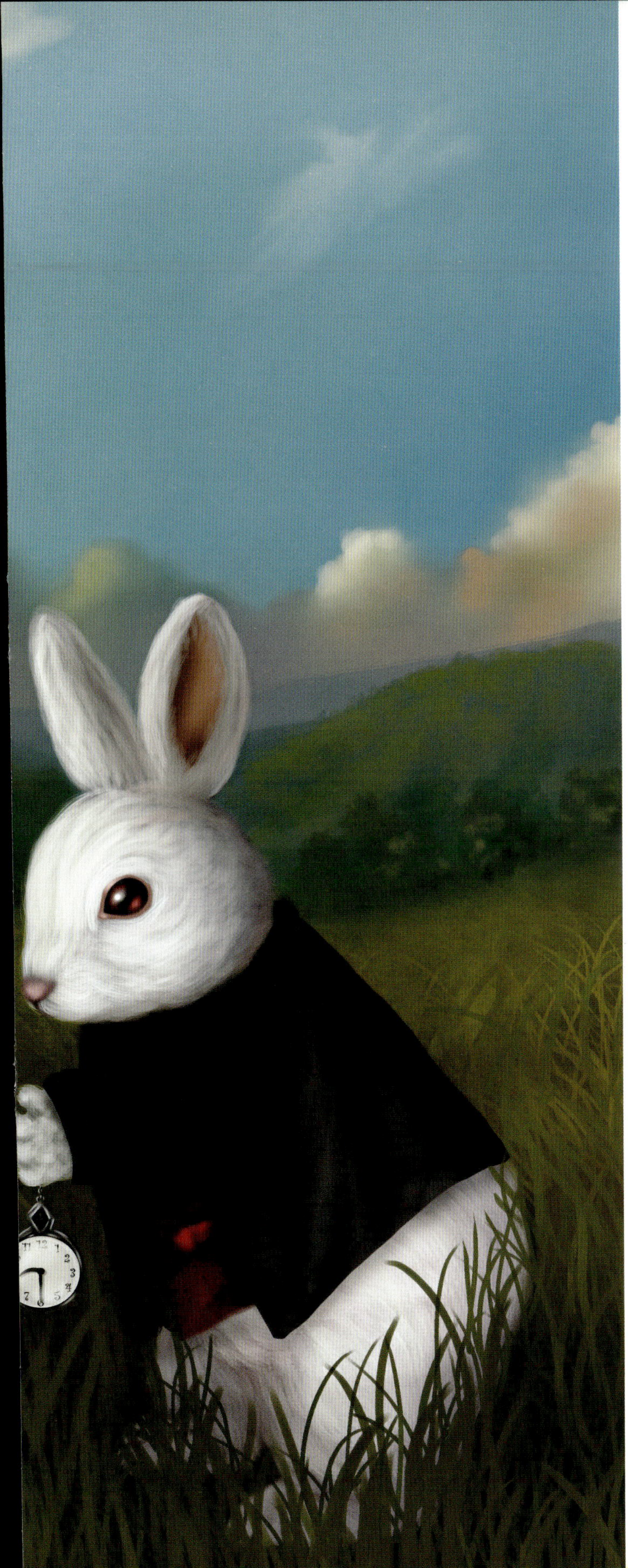

◀ **Alice Meets the White Rabbit**
Laura Yanmei Law
Digital painting
www.yanmei.net

Lewis Carroll has long since been an inspiration in Gothic culture. From his Victorian tales to Walt Disney's charming cartoon, to American McGee's macabre computer game, there has always been an Alice for every generation. Laura gives her rendition of Alice as a young Goth girl, a little sullen but also wistful, meeting the infamous White Rabbit. "As a child I loved ***Alice in Wonderland****. A few summers ago I picked the book up and although I was very familiar with the story, reading it as an adult revealed a darker, stranger dream world than I had imagined in my younger years. It inspired me to do a slightly older version of Alice with a bit of a Gothic twist. For the painting I used Adobe Photoshop and Corel Painter."*

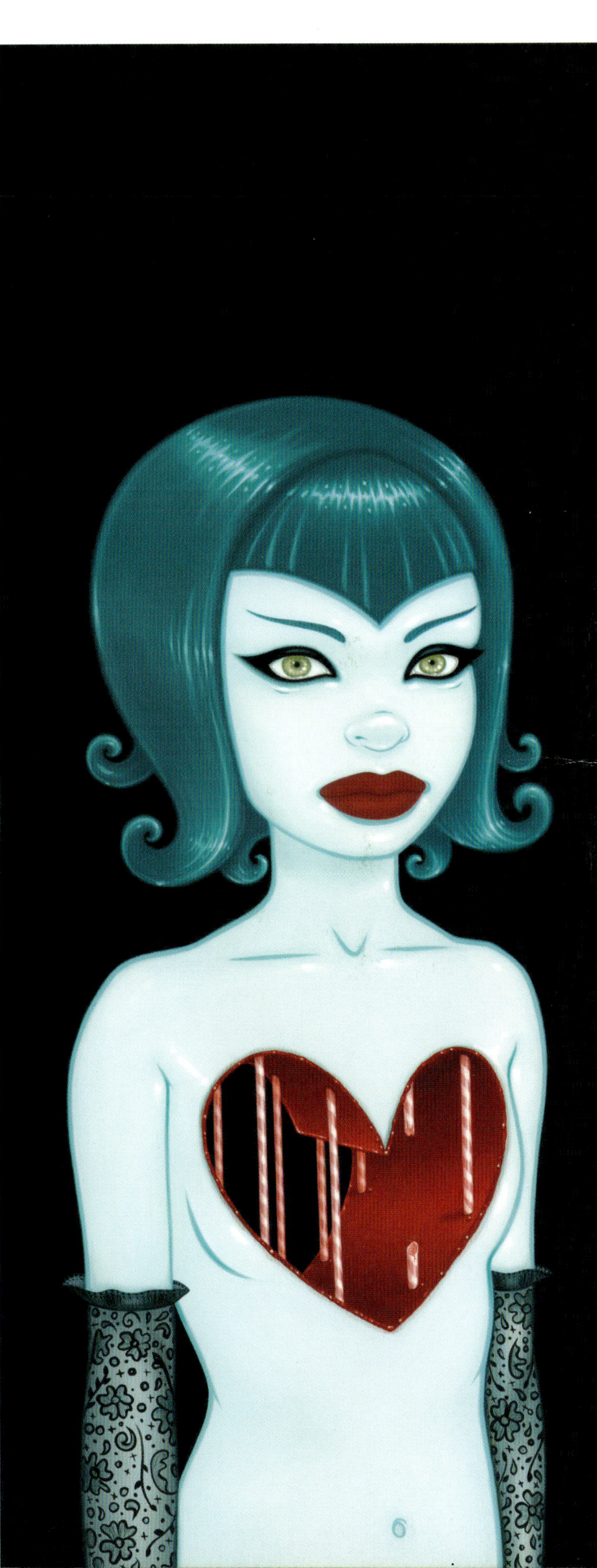

▶ **Sometimes I Want a Hug**
Tara McPherson
Acrylic on birch
www.taramcpherson.com

"The title for this painting came as I was walking home from a bad night out and thought the title aloud. It hit me so hard when I said it out loud that I knew I needed to make a painting called that. I drew this the next day."

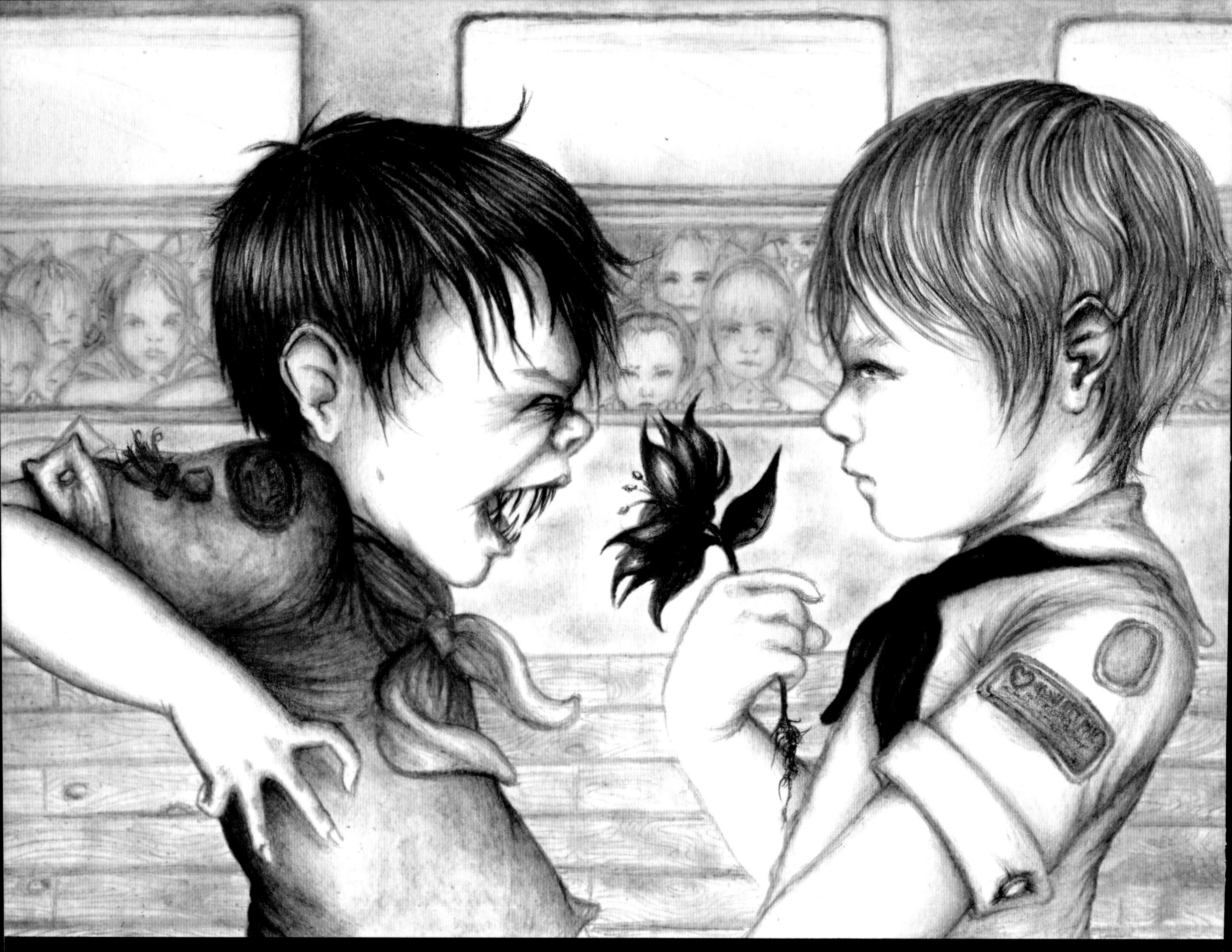

▲ **Of Love He Spoke**
PeeMonster
Graphite on Bristol board
www.peemonster.net

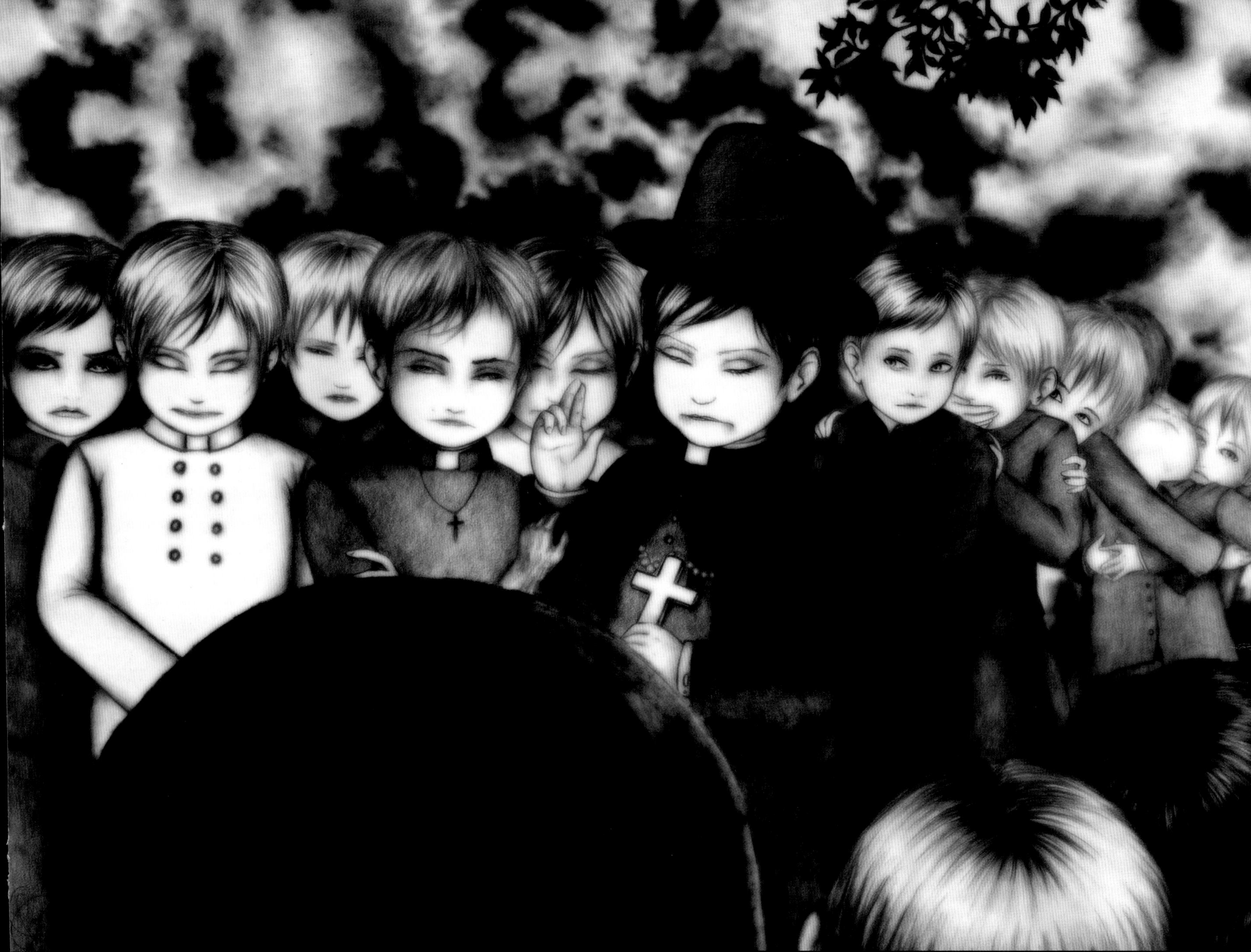

▲ **Primus Mortem**
PeeMonster
Graphite and charcoal on Bristol board
www.peemonster.net

A disturbing scene featuring countless children in a funeral setting, Pee Monster's ***Primus Mortem*** *is drawn beautifully in graphite and charcoal — the high contrast, and almost over-exposed quality giving a dreamlike feel to the piece. "These boys, in a sense, created their own story to share with me, and I actually did not fully understand it until long after the drawing had been completed. They are good boys."*

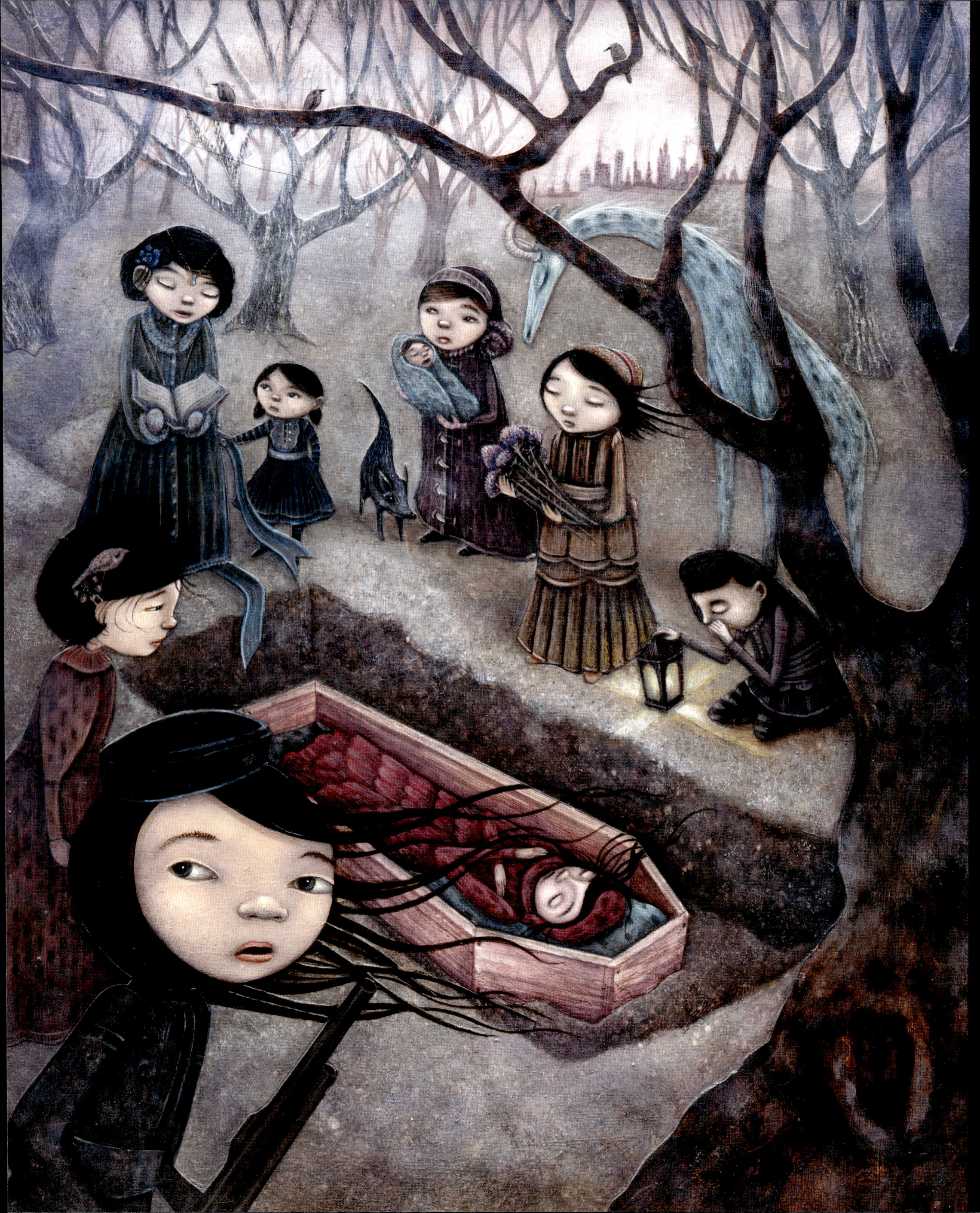

unday Mourning
aime Zollars
crylic and collage
ww.jaimezollars.com

dreamlike funeral scene, ollars's ***Sunday Mourning*** *eatures children and animals n mourning, with a desolate ndustrial skyline in the distant ackground. "This piece featured n the show* ***Melancholia*** *at the opro Nason Gallery, in Santa Monica, California. It depicts bleak future world, where esources are scarce and children re left to solve adult problems. he piece was created using ieces of patterned collage nd acrylic paint."*

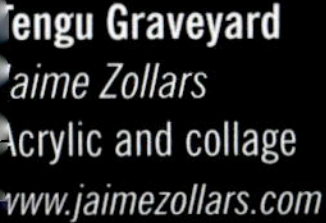

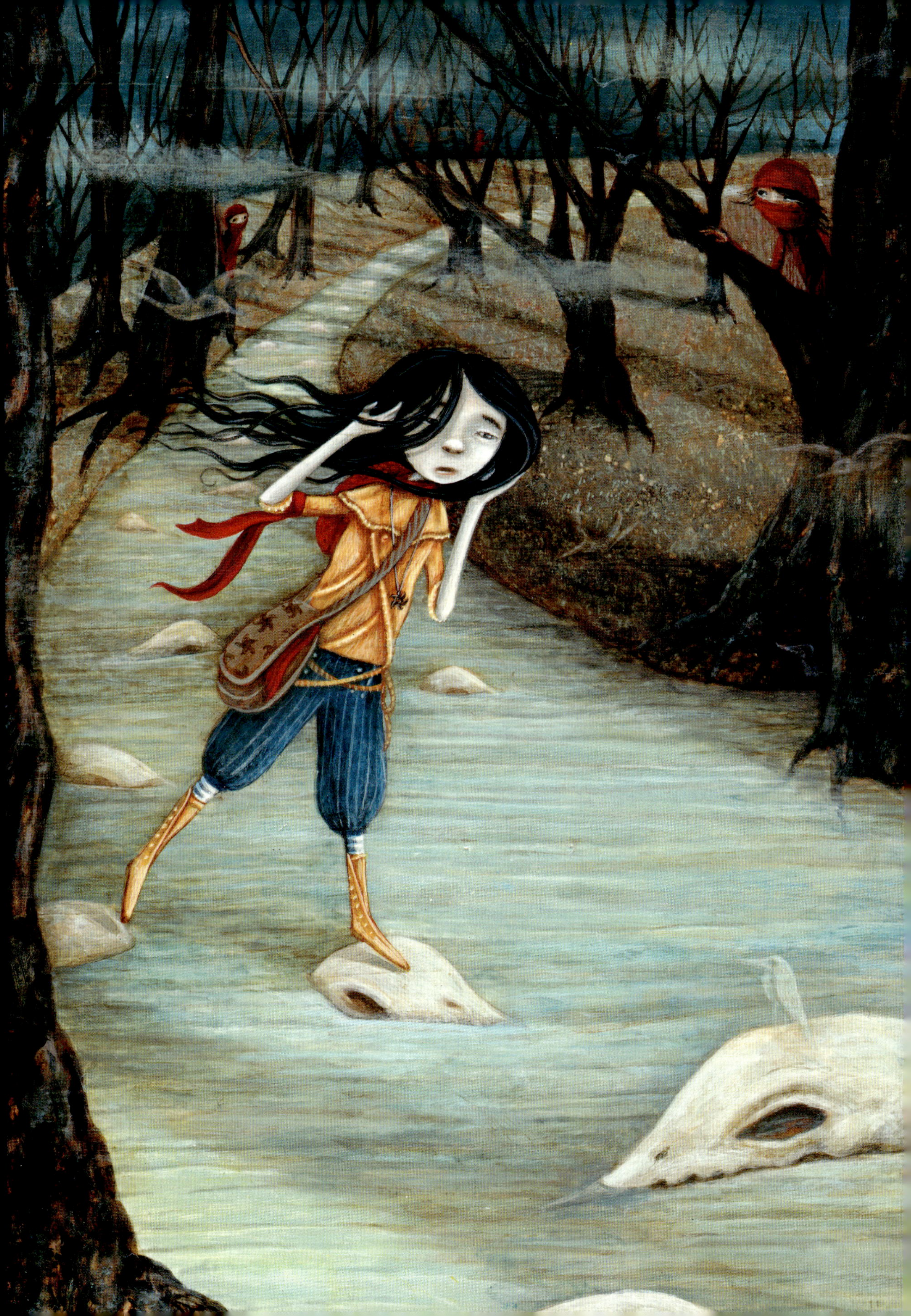

engu Graveyard
aime Zollars
crylic and collage
ww.jaimezollars.com

ollars's delicate illustrative style s perfect for creating beautiful torybook-like paintings. "This iece featured in the ***Ninja Show*** *at Gallery Nucleus in lhambra, California. The mage depicts a young female inja stepping cautiously over he skulls of the Tengu, the ird-like men who are feared y ninjas in Japanese myth."*

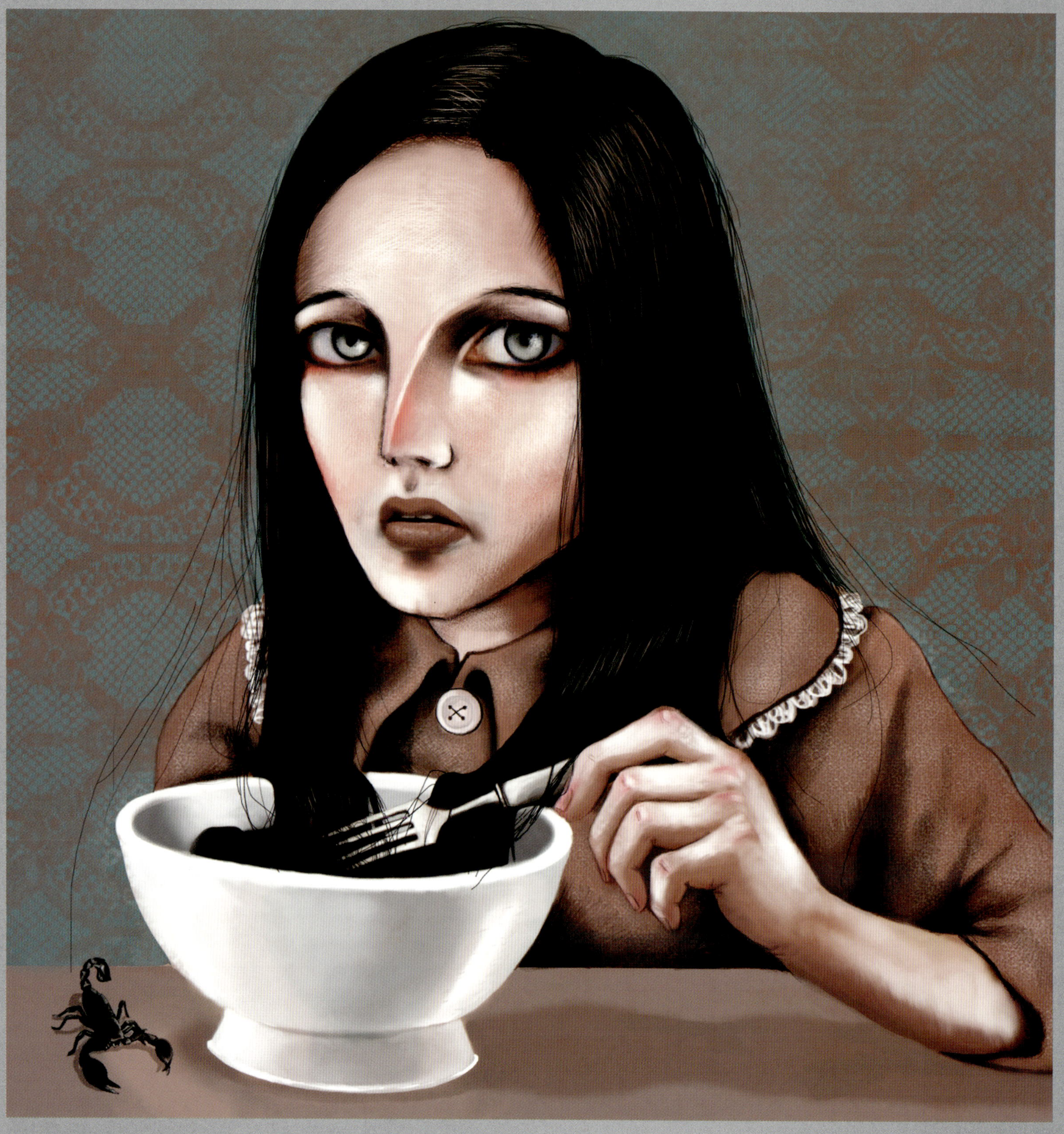

◀ **My Poison Contingency Plan**
Lisa Falzon
Digital painting
www.lisafalzon.com

A seemingly bizarre digital painting from Falzon has a very interesting and unusual idea behind it. She explains: "A bezoar—a stone of calcified hair found in stomachs of goats and, sometimes, humans who suck on their own hair—was thought to be a potent cure for poisons in medieval times. Here I wanted to show a girl eating her own hair so as to create bezoars—a 'Plan B' in case she gets poisoned. I wanted to depict a schemingly paranoid individual."

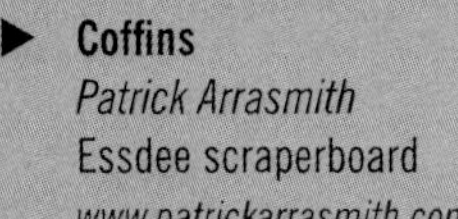

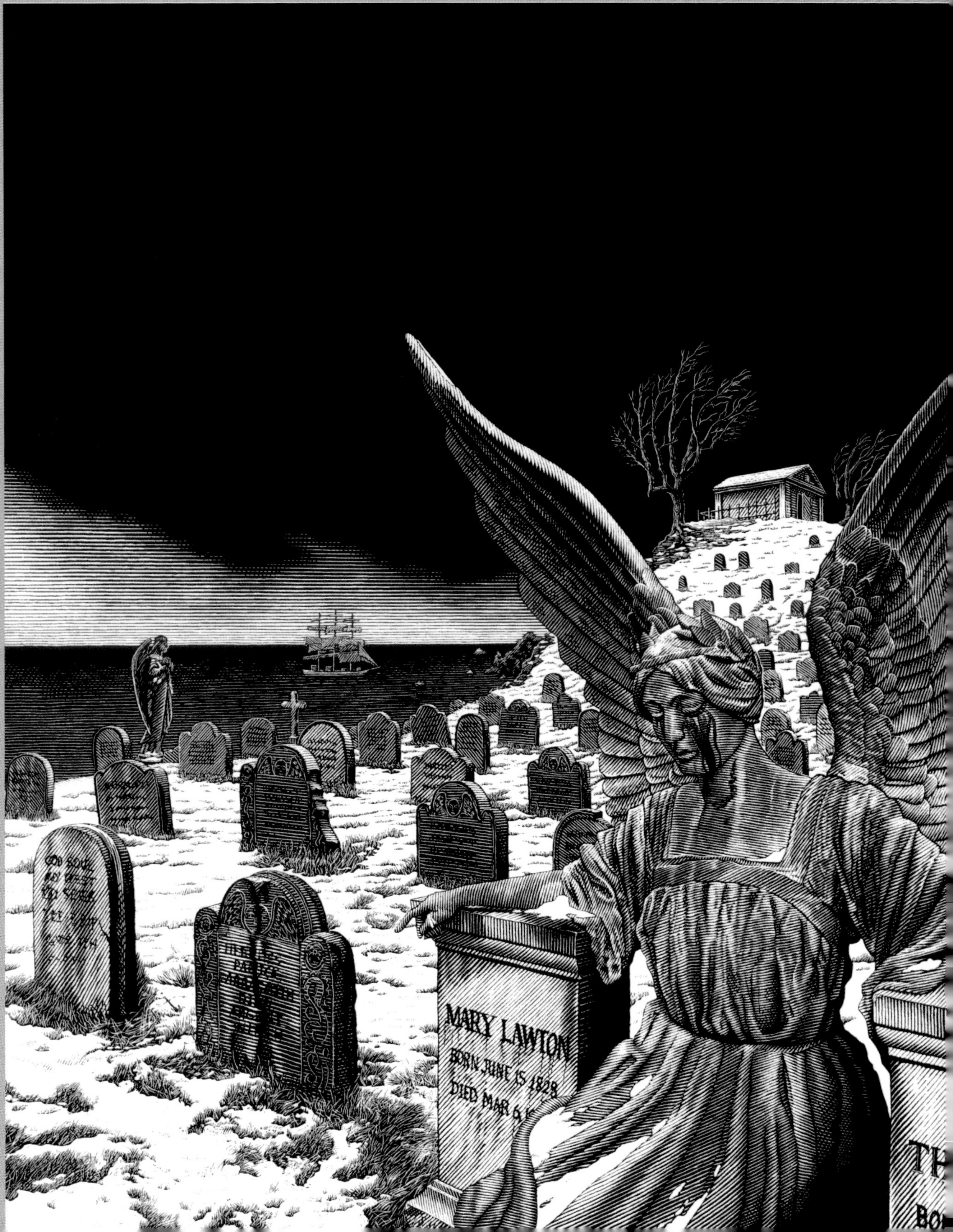

▶ **Coffins**
Patrick Arrasmith
Essdee scraperboard
www.patrickarrasmith.com

A highly detailed, quiet cemetery scene done in scraperboard by Patrick Arrasmith. "This is an illustration for a book cover by Rodman Philbrick. The angel in the foreground comes from an actual cemetery in Newport, Rhode Island. I had shot photographs of the statue years before and the imagery fitted perfectly with the narrative of the book."

JOHN U. ABRAHAMSON
www.johnua.com
jua@johnua.com
Pernecare Deus *p50*
Vates *p56*
Dies Irae *p57*

SCOTT ALTMANN
www.scottaltmann.com
about@scottaltmann.com
Autohuman *p149*

CHRISTIAN ALZMANN
www.christianalzmann.com
calzmann@sbcglobal.net
Stationed *p94*
Maintenance *p95*
Extremity *p97*

MYKE AMEND
www.mykeamend.com
myke@mykeamend.com
Hope (The Light At The End) *p48*
The Wait *p53*
Exterminating Angel *p119*

RACHEL ANDERSON
www.silverstars.us
silverstars1@gmail.com
Queen of Hearts *p81*

ABRIL ANDRADE
www.abrilandrade.com
abrilandrade@yahoo.com
My Name Is Soap *p176*
Antgirl *p177*
Midnight Walk *p177*

SAMUEL ARAYA
www.samael.epilogue.net
paintagram@gmail.com
Rapacious *p58*
Dread The Fallen *p78*
Nightmare Rider 2000 *p144*

PATRICK ARRASMITH
www.patrickarrasmith.com
patrickarrasmith@
earthlink.net
BlurBurn *p51*
Apsara *p61*
Coffins *p189*

CARRIE ANN BAADE
www.carrieannbaade.com
carrieannbaade@
carrieannbaade.com
The Severance of Creeping
Charlotte *p128*
The Ecstasy of Madam
Dolorosa *p129*

BETHALYNNE BAJEMA
www.bajema.com
bajema519@yahoo.com
Lux *p68*
Sepia Stain *p68*

JASMINE BECKET-GRIFFITH
www.strangeling.com
jasminetoad@aol.com
Shallow Grave *p8*
Bleak Mourning *p10*

DAVID BOWERS
www.dmbowers.com
davidmbowers@comcast.net
The Price of Honey *p67*

MATT BRADBURY
mattbradbury.epilogue.net
mattbradbury2000@yahoo.com
Blood Drinker *p34*
Tomb of The Night Terrors *p115*

PAT BRENNAN
www.moonmomma.co.uk
pat_brennan@ntlworld.com
Limelight *p72*
Indecision *p73*

BROM
www.bromart.com
Angel *p6*
The Plucker *p114*

CATHERINE BURRIS
www.catherineburris.com
moonwood@sbcglobal.net
Project 5 *p167*
The Experiment *p168*
Tick Tock Baby Blue *p169*

PATRICK BYERS
www.101industries.ca
patrick_byers@hotmail.com
X-Ray Angel *p92*

CANIGLIA
www.caniglia-art.com
caniglia@caniglia-art.com
Her Future Has Already
Begun *p74*

LAUREN K. CANNON
www.navate.com
lkcannon@comcast.net
The Gate of Slaughter *p23*
Mhiet'e *p27*

EDEN CELESTE
www.edenceleste.com
eden@edenceleste.com
Lupis *p43*

KARI CHRISTENSEN
www.karichristensen.com
info@karichristensen.com
Cyberfaery *p93*

DORIAN CLEAVENGER
www.dorianart.com
corbly@city-net.com
The Chambermaid *p21*

CHRISTOPHER CONTE
www.christopherconte.com
deathcom4@aol.com
Miniature Biomechanical
Skull *p157*
Steam Insect *p157*
Articulated Singer Insect *p157*

KEVIN CROSSLEY
www.kevcrossley.com
bombjak69@hotmail.com
Ascension Study *p54*

DANIEL MARTIN DIAZ
www.danielmartindiaz.com
dmd@danielmartindiaz.com
Mysterium Natura *p176*
Aeternus Vita *p176*

LISA FALZON
www.lisafalzon.com
info@lisafalzon.com
The Misery of Proserpine *p26*
When Pandora Looked
She Saw *p140*
My Poison Contingency
Plan *p188*

KRISTEN FERRELL
www.kristenferrell.com
kristenferrell.clothing@
gmail.com
Do You Know What It's Like
To Be Cursed? *p154*
You Don't Miss The Water 'Til
The Well Runs Dry *p154*
You Are What You Eat *p154*

GUS FINK
www.gusfink.com
gusfink@hotmail.com
Dunce *p102*
Stick Girl *p103*
Children of Yesterday *p120*
Mock Wedding *p121*

LINDA JOYCE FRANKS
www.nimbvs.com
ljfranks@nimbvs.com
Angelique *p22*
The Ruins of Ecclesia *p117*

XIAO-CHEN FU
www.krishnafu.com
krishna860@hotmail.com
Go to Avalon *p40*
Nightmare *p122*
The Queen of Dreamland p138

H.R. GIGER
www.hrgigermuseum.com
www.hrgiger.com
www.hrgigeragent.com
les@baranyartists.com
Necronom *p172*
Biomechanoid *p173*
Birthmachine *p173*

ANNE YVONNE GILBERT
www.yvonnegilbert.com
gilbertandnanos@rogers.com
Dracula *p66*
Bride of Frankenstein *p113*

DAVID GOUGH
www.davidgoughart.com
david@davidgoughart.com
Nightspirit *p130*

ROCHELLE GREEN
caelicorn.cgsociety.org/gallery
caelicorn@gmail.com
Black Ciborium *p145*

RYOHEI HASE
www.ryoheihase.com
ryohei_hase@yahoo.co.jp
Not Knowing Why She Can't
See And Can't Breathe *p12*
Inferiority Complex *p79*
Melancholy *p125*

KUANG HONG
www.zemotion.net
noah@zemotion.net
Bride of Lucifer *p39*
My World *p98*
Birch *p141*

SHANNON HOURIGAN
www.shannonhourigan.com
shannon@shannonhourigan.
com
Wolf *p31*
Cry *p33*
Speak *p37*
Portrait *p80*

TINA IMEL
www.tinaimel.com
info@tinaimel.com
Youth is Wasted On
the Young *p38*
Swan Maidens of Charenton *p82*
Love at 5am *p83*

INDIO
www.desolatebeauty.com
indio@desolatebeauty.com
Pandora *p170*
Passion *p171*
Male 1 *p171*

ANTTI ISOSOMPPI
www.isosomppi.com
anatheme@gmail.com
For I Have Sinned *p124*

DESIRÉE ISPHORDING
www.desireeisphording.com
disphording@gmail.com
Deer Woman *p70*
Rafinesque Awaiting Sleep *p71*
The White Doe of Nara *p131*

GRETA JAMES
www.gretajames.com
greta@gretajames.com
Blackthorn—Prunus
spinosa *p180*
Little Brown Bat—Myotis
lucifugus *p180*

JESSICA JOSLIN
www.jessicajoslin.com
jessica@jessicajoslin.com
Marcel *p158*
Lambert & Salvia *p159*
Marco *p159*

JASON JUTA
www.jasonjuta.com
jason@jasonjuta.com
Black Widow *p32*

STEVEN KENNY
www.stevenkenny.com
stevenkenny@earthlink.net
Semaphore *p25*

ULRIKE KLEINERT
www.dreamaddiction.de
adorna@gmx.net
Meraphis *p52*

KYRI KONIOTIS
kyri.epilogue.net
k_koniotis@hotmail.co.uk
Sacrifice *p44*
Descent Into Darkness *p108*

KRISGOAT
www.krisgoat.com
krisgoat@krisgoat.com
Broken Heart *p179*
Trick *p179*

THOMAS KUEBLER
www.thomaskuebler.com
tskuebler@earthlink.net
The Swinegoblin *p163*

CAMILLE KUO
www.camilkuo.com
camilkuo@hotmail.com
Master and Mistress *p76*
Mistress *p76*
Tear Down Heaven *p107*

JARNO LAHTI
www.kaamos.com
kaamos@kaamos.com
Break Into Dreams *p148*
Hold At All Costs *p150*

TOM LAVELLE
www.portalrun.epilogue.net
tlfantasyart@aol.com
Black Roses and Bite Marks *p62*

LAURA YANMEI LAW
www.yanmei.net
laura@yanmei.net
Trio *p181*
Alice Meets the White Rabbit *p182*

LAURIE LIPTON
www.laurielipton.com
Lady Death *p69*
Family Reunion *p112*

LOLA
www.lolastrangeart.com
lola@lolastrangeart.com
Where Owl Perched Pockets
Hold All the Souvenirs p132
"Was That Too Loud?"
She Whispered *p134*
Luminous Edge of
Beginnings *p135*

JOACHIM LUETKE
www.luetke.com
Image Eye-Luetke Prod. Vienna
The Veteran *p84*
Divine Heresy *p88*
Kreator *p90*
Thanksgiving *p152*

RALPH MANFREDA
www.cryptonaut.com
ralph.manfreda@chello.at
Visitation of the Plague *p151*

MARTIN MCKENNA
www.martinmckenna.net
martin@martinmckenna.net
Talisman of Death *p49*

TARA MCPHERSON
www.taramcpherson.com
tara@taramcpherson.com
Sometimes I Want a Hug *p183*

MEATS MEIER
www.3dartspace.com
meats@sketchovision.com
Primitive City *p86*
The Apple *p87*
Four Horsemen *p96*
The Nest *p166*

ERLEND MØRK
www.erlendmork.com
Our Faces As Our Days *p55*
Birthmark *p100*
House of Discord *p110*
Narrentraum *p111*

KIMBERLY MYATT
www.beetlebones.net/pale
palemajesty@gmail.com
Unholy Feast *p20*
In The Gaze of Angels *p43*
Watcher *p106*
Purgatory *p143*

HOANG NGUYEN
www.liquidbrush.com
hoang@liquidbrush.com
Eternal Sorrow *p14*
Memories *p15*
Mathilda *p99*

LESLIE ANN O'DELL
www.shyble.com
shyble@hotmail.com
Evol *p19*
3 *p30*
Twofold *p64*
Fall *p65*

VINCE PACKARD AKA "CANNIBOL"
www.cannibol.com
cannibol@hotmail.com
Flower Girl *p4*

MICHAEL PARK
www.myspace.com/michaelpark
michaelparkart@gmail.com
The Bride *p118*

GEORGE PATSOURAS
www.mkrevolution.net
slickgreekgeo@hotmail.com
Anguish *p47*
Save Us *p109*

EGIL PAULSEN
www.egilpaulsen.com
egil.paulsen@gmail.com
Masquerade *p17*
Lost Circle *p18*

PEEMONSTER
www.peemonster.net
luvbutyns@yahoo.com
Of Love He Spoke *p184*
Primus Mortem *p185*

NATALIA PIERANDREI
www.nati-art.com
natalia_pierandrei@alice.it
Autumn Has Come *p174*

SCOTT RADKE
www.scottradke.com
scott@scottradke.com
Dolls #2 *p155*
Doll #7 *p155*
De La Costa *p156*

CHRIS RAHN
www.rahnart.com
chris@rahnart.com
Blue Tattoo *p46*

MICHAEL RYAN
www.michaelryanart.com
email@michaelryanart.com
Seated Woman *p36*

JOHN SANTERINEROSS
www.santerineross.com
john@santerineross.com
Beauty of Silence *p28*
Porcelain Child *p29*
Fruit of the Secret God *p136*
Prisoner of Our Childhood *p137*

ERIC SCALA
www.ericscala.com
ericscala@yahoo.com
Pandora *p75*
Lumley Three *p142*

JUDITH SCHAECHTER
www.judithschaechter.com
judith@judithschaechter.com
Seizures *p164*

CHARLI SIEBERT
www.unimaginative.org
charli@unimaginative.org
Something Inside *p102*
Blinding *p103*

ANNE STOKES
www.annestokes.com
email@annestokes.com
Vampire *p35*
Lord of Time *p42*
Gothic Siren *p60*
Aracnoid *p91*

DAVID STOUPAKIS
www.davidstoupakis.com
david@davidstoupakis.com
Red Ribbon *p77*
The Day the Frogs Rain
Down *p126*
The Messenger *p127*

ROBERT THOMAS
www.mindsiphon.com
mindsiphon11@yahoo.com
Nourish *p146*
Seed *p147*

OLIVER WETTER
www.fantasio.info
fantasiox@gmx.de
Say No Good *p160*
S-T-I-L-L-L-I-F-E *p162*

BENITA WINCKLER
www.eeanee.com
benita@eeanee.com
Lucrezia Navarre *p16*
Jadefox *p63*

CHET ZAR
www.chetzar.com
chet@chetzar.com
Sister *p116*

GRACJANA ZIELINSKA
www.vinegaria.com
Sometimes They Leave
Fingerprints *p24*

JAMIE ZOLLARS
www.jamiezollars.com
jamie@jamiezollars.com
Red Bird Battalion *p2*
Sunday Mourning *p186*
Tengu Graveyard *p187*

Acknowledgments

This book has been an amazing voyage for me, both as an artist myself and more importantly as an aficionado of all Gothic art. It has been a true pleasure absorbing myself in, literally, thousands of exquisite and intriguing images from hundreds of artists around the world. I would hesitate to even refer to it as "work," as poring over countless visions of dark beauty with a glass of wine in my hand rather falls more into the "leisure" category for me. It has been a fabulous excuse to delve into the darker sides of the internet, to rummage hungrily through exotic books, magazines, and other imagery—searching for what helps best represent contemporary Gothic art.

First, I would like to thank my husband Matty, for putting up with me during this project—and all of my projects actually. I would also like to thank my sisters, Amber and Kachina, who have taught me the nature of collaboration and cooperation!

Thirdly, I would like to thank the good folks at Ilex Press for approaching me with this book project, as it has been a joy.

And most importantly, I would like to thank the phenomenal artists who submitted work for this book. It is my deepest regret that we weren't able to include each and every one of you. But alas, 1,200-page, full-color art books just aren't in the stars sometimes, and are hard on the wrists! There are many more who belong in this book and to them, and to those who did make the cut, thank you for making the world a beautiful place with your hard work and your visions.

I'd also like to thank David Gough, just for the heck of it…

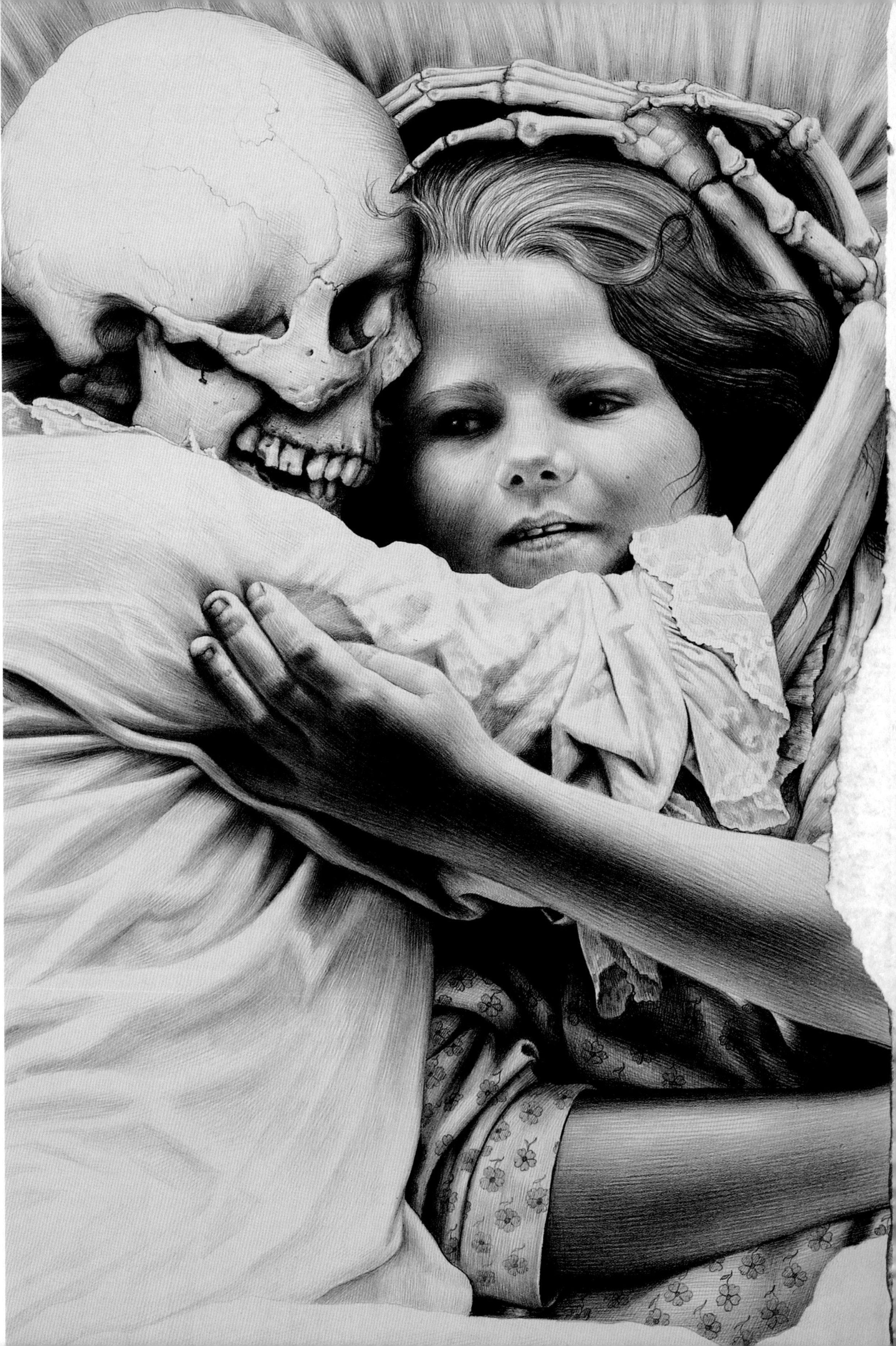

▶ **Death and the Maiden**
Laurie Lipton
Pencil on paper
www.laurielipton.com